Palgrave Studies in the Enlightenment, Romanticism and the Cultures of Print

Palgrave Studies in the Enlightenment, Romanticism and the Cultures of Print will feature work that does not fit comfortably within established boundaries—whether between periods or between disciplines. Uniquely, it will combine efforts to engage the power and materiality of print with explorations of gender, race, and class. By attending as well to intersections of literature with the visual arts, medicine, law, and science, the series will enable a large-scale rethinking of the origins of modernity.

Titles include:

For full list of titles, see: www.palgrave.com/series/palgrave-studies-in-the-enlightenment,-romanticism-and-the-cultures-of-print/PERCP

Adriana Craciun • Simon Schaffer
Editors

The Material Cultures of Enlightenment Arts and Sciences

palgrave
macmillan

Editors
Adriana Craciun
University of California
Presidential Chair
University of California, Riverside
Riverside, USA

Simon Schaffer
Professor of History and
Philosophy of Science
University of Cambridge
Cambridge, UK

Palgrave Studies in the Enlightenment, Romanticism and the Cultures of Print
ISBN 978-1-137-44579-7   ISBN 978-1-137-44379-3   (eBook)
DOI 10.1057/978-1-137-44379-3

Library of Congress Control Number: 2016943653

Cover image © Courtesy of the Captain Cook Memorial Museum, Whitby

Printed on acid-free paper

This Palgrave Macmillan imprint is published by Springer Nature
The registered company is Macmillan Publishers Ltd. London

Acknowledgements

The editors wish to thank the following for their financial and intellectual support of this project and its associated collaborations: Cambridge University's Centre for Research in Arts, Social Sciences and Humanities and the University's School of Humanities and Social Sciences; the University of California Multicampus Research Group on 'The Material Cultures of Knowledge, 1600–1830'; the University of California Humanities Research Institute; the University of California, Riverside Chancellor's Research Initiative; and the Huntington Library. We are grateful to Katy Barrett and Sophie Waring for initiation and direction of 'Things that Matter'; to Simon Goldhill for his energetic encouragement; to Anne Mellor and Cliff Siskin for their support of this volume at Palgrave; and to Ben Doyle and Tom René for their editorial assistance and patience.

CONTENTS

Contributors

Samuel J.M.M. Alberti: National Museums Scotland, Edinburgh, UK

Josefine Baark: Visual Studies Department, Lingnan University, Hong Kong

Alexi Baker: Centre for Research in Arts, Humanities and Social Sciences, University of Cambridge, UK

Katy Barrett: National Maritime Museum, Royal Museums Greenwich, London, UK

Jennifer Basford: St George's, University of London, London, UK

Mary M. Brooks: Department of Archaeology, Durham University, Durham, UK

Luisa Calè: Department of English and Humanities, Birkbeck University of London, London, UK

Adriana Craciun: Department of English, University of California, Riverside, Riverside, CA, USA

Faramerz Dabhoiwala: Faculty of History, University of Oxford, Oxford, UK

James Davey: National Maritime Museum, Royal Museums Greenwich, London, UK

Richard Dunn: Royal Museums Greenwich, London, UK

Jonathan Eacott: Department of History, University of California, Riverside, Riverside, CA, USA

Catherine Eagleton: Asian and African Collections, British Library, London, UK

Anne Gerritsen: Department of History, University of Warwick, Coventry, UK

Tara Hamling: Department of History, University of Birmingham, Birmingham, UK

Philippa Hubbard: Institute of Advanced Study, University of Warwick, Coventry, UK

Charles Jarvis: Department of Plant Sciences, Natural History Museum, London, UK

Jonathan Lamb: Department of English, Vanderbilt University, Nashville, TN, USA

Billie Lythberg: Mira Szaszy Research Centre, University of Auckland, Auckland, New Zealand

John McAleer: Department of History, University of Southampton, Southampton, UK

Leanna McLaughlin: Department of History, University of California, Riverside, Riverside, CA, USA

Amy Miller: National Maritime Museum, Royal Museums Greenwich, London, UK

Jane Munro: Keeper of Department of Paintings, Drawings and Prints, Fitzwilliam Museum Cambridge, Cambridge, UK

Maia Nuku: Associate Curator for Oceanic Art, Metropolitan Museum of Art, New York, NY, USA

Amiria Salmond: Anthropology Department, University of Auckland, Auckland, New Zealand

Simon Schaffer: Department of History and Philosophy of Science, University of Cambridge, Cambridge, UK

Patricia Seed: Department of History, University of California, Irvine, Irvine, CA, USA

Kim Sloan: Department of Prints and Drawings, British Museum, London, UK

Mary Terrall: Department of History, University of California, Los Angeles, CA, USA

Sophie Waring: Modern Collections Curator, Museum of the History of Science, Oxford, UK

Hannah Williams: School of History, Queen Mary University of London, London, UK

Alexander Wragge-Morley: Department of History, University College London, London, UK

LIST OF FIGURES

CHAPTER 1

Introduction

Adriana Craciun and Simon Schaffer

These Creatures were as large as Partridges, I took out their Stings, found them an Inch and a half long, and as sharp as Needles. I carefully preserved them all, and having since shewn them with some other Curiosities in several parts of Europe; upon my Return to England I gave three of them to Gresham College, and kept the fourth for my self. (Jonathan Swift, *Travels into Several Remote Nations of the World by Lemuel Gulliver*, book 2, 1726)[1]

The largest room, or rather the largest apartment, would not be too great a space to contain collections of every kind of Nature's different productions. What an immense and wondrous assemblage! How indeed to make a correct idea for one-self of the spectacle offered to us by all the types of animals, vegetables, and minerals, if they were assembled in one and the same place, and seen, so to speak, at a glance? This display, varied to infinity by the smallest steps, cannot be conveyed through any description, save by the very objects of which it is composed (Denis

---

[1] Jonathan Swift, *Travels into Several Remote Parts of the World by Lemuel Gulliver*, 2 vols. (London: Benjamin Motte, 1726), vol. 1, 65–66.

A. Craciun (✉)
Department of English, University of California, Riverside, Riverside, CA, USA
e-mail: adriana.craciun@ucr.edu

S. Schaffer
Department of History and Philosophy of Science, University of Cambridge, Cambridge, UK
e-mail: sjs16@cam.ac.uk

© The Author(s) 2016
A. Craciun, S. Schaffer (eds.), *The Material Cultures of Enlightenment Arts and Sciences*, Palgrave Studies in the Enlightenment, Romanticism and the Cultures of Print, DOI 10.1057/978-1-137-44379-3_1

Diderot, 'Cabinet d'histoire naturelle', *Encyclopédie, ou dictionnaire raisonné des sciences, des arts et des métiers*, vol. 2, 1752).[2]

Here is a list of things: a penny coin shipped from Birmingham to west Africa, a hand-engraved sextant destined for a voyage to China, an ulcerated oesophagus removed from a London woman, an English book made of Polynesian barkcloth, a French artist's colour box, a bundle of bound papers carrying seditious verses from the Glorious Revolution, an embroidery concealing a bird skull, a ceramic cup discarded in a Chinese kiln, and centuries-old *Banksia* seeds entombed in a Pacific shipwreck. *Things* may be the wrong term here. We might as well speak of objects, artifacts, waste, commodities, specimens, ephemera, relics, artworks, instruments, souvenirs. Each of these terms is bound up with specific economic models, of making, seizure, collection, appropriation, storage and exchange. Such characteristic economies all possess their own remarkable histories.[3] Thus, even naming turns out to be a difficult and slippery task, sometimes brutally anachronistic or inaccurate. In the Enlightenment's exemplary printed assemblage, the alphabetic array and brightly lit tabulations of the *Encyclopédie*, the orderly disposition and proper nomenclature of things and tasks were taken to be crucial for a project to catalogue and master the processes of labour and the world of newfangled goods.[4] The very activity of classification—an enterprise so characteristic of Enlightenment arts and sciences, in natural history and chemistry, in markets and workshops—could barely be pursued or even understood unless seen as entirely entwined with the production, distribution and movements of the mass of commodities and artifacts that freshly populated eighteenth-century worlds.[5]

Taxonomy and terminology mattered, especially in the histories of the occupants of this commodity system. Enlightened inventiveness, commonly identified with the enterprises of ambitious manufacture and global traffic, was much devoted to the production of new things as well as of novel

---

[2] Denis Diderot, 'Cabinet d'histoire naturelle', in *Encyclopédie ou Dictionnaire Raisonné des Sciences, des Arts et des Métiers*, 17 vols. (Paris: Briasson, 1751–1765), vol. 2, 489.

[3] Susan Stewart, *On Longing: Narratives of the Miniature, the Gigantic, the Souvenir, the Collection* (Durham: Duke University Press, 1993), 151.

[4] Cynthia J. Koepp, 'The Alphabetical Order: Work in Diderot's *Encyclopédie*', in Steven Laurence Kaplan and Cynthia J. Koepp (eds.), *Work in France: Representations, Meaning, Organization and Practice* (Ithaca: Cornell University Press, 1986), 229–257; Antoine Picon, 'Gestes Ouvriers, Opérations et Processus Techniques: La Vision du Travail des Encyclopédistes', *Recherches sur Diderot et l'Encyclopédie* 13 (1992), 131–147.

[5] William Reddy, 'Structure of a Cultural Crisis: Thinking about Cloth before and after the French Revolution', in Arjun Appadurai (ed.), *The Social Life of Things: Commodities in Cultural Perspective* (Cambridge: Cambridge University Press, 1986), 261–284; John Brewer and Roy Porter (eds.), *Consumption and the World of Goods* (London: Routledge, 1993); Michael Kwass, 'Ordering the World of Goods: Consumer Revolution and the Classification of Objects in Eighteenth-Century France', *Representations* 82 (2003), 87–116, on 88; Ursula Klein and Wolfgang Lefèvre, *Materials in Eighteenth-Century Science* (Cambridge, MA: MIT Press, 2007), 63–79.

processes.[6] Eighteenth-century metropoles were peculiarly fascinated and disturbed by this kind of innovation in the inhabitants of the world of goods. Part of the trouble, and the appeal, was the puzzle of mutability. None of the things in our list was so robust that it preserved just the same sense in all the milieux where it happened to find itself, yet none was quite malleable enough simply to borrow its character entirely from its surroundings. As Nicholas Thomas has argued, artefacts cannot be defined solely by their makers' intent: they are all the things they become. Roger Chartier has comparably urged that in studies of eighteenth century material cultures, consumption must not be seen as passive, but rather as part and parcel of worlds in which goods were appropriated anew, redirected and redefined, and often bound up with conflict and resistance.[7] The careers of such things were often a challenge to received notions of the good order of creation, precisely because of their protean quality and the sheer difficulty of fixing their character.

Some people hoped it might be possible to get things to define themselves, if only they could become sufficiently eloquent. Within the fraught workings of long-range commodity trade in particular, this became a principal aim of the name systems that Europeans invented in the eighteenth century. Thus, in 1763 the pre-eminent Swedish naturalist Carl Linnaeus lectured that by associating naming with diagnosis of properties, his labels would allow every-one 'to distinguish any plant whatsoever at first glance, even if it came from farthest India, since the plant itself informs them about its name, its taste, its smell, its properties, powers and uses, yes, points them with a finger, as it were, to all that is known about it, for the good of mankind'.[8] While later scholars have been somewhat less sure than Linnaeus that such things can reliably speak their character, it has become a major concern in studies of Enlightenment culture to use the eloquent testimonies of that epoch's material worlds to make new sense of its life and labour. According to what has been called a kind of 'methodological fetishism', it has been argued that it is precisely when objects misbehave or err, when they resist or escape the apparently directive powers of their makers and users, that they are then registered as things with their own agency and character.[9]

Conceptual tools drawn from variants of the new materialism at work across the humanities and social sciences can be brought to bear on the eclectic range of materials assembled in this collection. *The Material Cultures of Enlightenment*

---

[6] Maxine Berg, 'From Imitation to Invention: Creating Commodities in Eighteenth-Century Britain', *Economic History Review* 55 (2002), 1–30, on 1.

[7] Nicholas Thomas, *Entangled Objects: Exchange, Material Culture and Colonialism in the Pacific* (Cambridge, MA: Harvard University Press, 1991), 4; Roger Chartier, *Cultural History: Between Practices and Representation* (Ithaca: Cornell University Press, 1989), 41.

[8] Lisbet Koerner, *Linnaeus: Nature and Nation* (Cambridge, MA: Harvard University Press, 1999), 45.

[9] Arjun Appadurai, 'Introduction: Commodities and the Politics of Value', in Appadurai (ed.), *The Social Life of Things: Commodities in Cultural Perspective* (Cambridge: Cambridge University Press, 1986), 5; Bill Brown, 'Thing Theory', *Critical Inquiry* 28 (2001), 1–22, on 6–7.

Arts and Sciences explores the generative potential of materiality in rethinking the Enlightenment, and more broadly eighteenth-century studies. Attention to materiality in general, and material culture specifically, is a welcome corrective, or complement, to the traditions of intellectual and textual history that dominate Enlightenment and eighteenth-century historiography. If the task of the human sciences is to make the familiar unfamiliar and the unfamiliar familiar, our book pursues this defamiliarizing project with a focus on the transculturated material culture shared by humanistic inquiry. To this end, the work assembles a host of well-known and more humble or obscure objects in the fashion of a rather loosely ordered cabinet. There may, indeed, be a specific aspect of eighteenth-century commerce and aesthetics in play in the arrangement of this collection. Playful vocabulary and disposition are scarcely avoidable, and in some ways desirable, in dealing with such Enlightenment goods as appear here: terminologies of grammar and semantics became entangled with the idioms of market and commodity culture. As James Bunn has noted, for example, *import* had the sense both of commodity acquisition and of the conveyance of meaning. Eighteenth-century critics sometimes condemned the apparent accumulation of individual objects of curiosity and value, imports looted or purchased with no special care for their original import. 'I have got twenty things of China that are of no use in the world', exclaims a London lady of distinction to Oliver Goldsmith's astonished and disgusted Mandarin visitor in his *Citizen of the World* (1760). 'Look at those jars, they are of the right pea-green,' she continues, 'these are the furniture!' It was a fashionably enlightened commonplace, much in question in the contributions to this book, that arguments about possession and use were bound up with the places where such goods were made, or stored, or displayed, or manipulated.[10]

Debates about luxury and commerce, about threats to the good order of domestic life and the moral conduct of a society of orders, can be re-examined and better analysed by tracing such objects' pathways. Commenting on an early eighteenth-century painted cloth now hung in a Gloucestershire manor house, Tara Hamling explains how traditional art history has neglected the material form of such apparently domesticated decorative crafts. Similarly, Alexi Baker's exhibit of an early eighteenth-century telescope shows how conventional histories of scientific instruments have mistakenly and patronisingly neglected the vital role played by retailers and 'toymen' in such trades. In her remarks on a 1790 Staffordshire earthenware plate decorated with an image of a pair of compasses, Katy Barrett points out that warnings against the evils of consumption were widely consumed as marketable commodities. There was thus a fundamental relation between judgements of the morality of goods and of the appropriate ways in which they should be acquired, stored and displayed. The relation was

---

[10] Oliver Goldsmith, *The Citizen of the World, or Letters from a Chinese Philosopher to His Friends in the East*, 2 vols. (London: J. Newbery, 1762), vol. 1, 49; James H. Bunn, 'The Aesthetics of British Mercantilism', *New Literary History* 11 (1980), 303–321, on 304 ('import'), 313 (Goldsmith).

marked in contemporary language. For example, one sense of *case*, referring to a state of affairs or a persuasive argument, which in the later eighteenth century came to refer to a matter of detection and inquiry (Latin *casus*), somewhat strangely converged in English with the other sense of case (Latin *capsa*), a secure containment, a place for storage and accumulation. This is a book of cases, in both senses.

In some respects, cases are arrayed here according to principles of eighteenth-century disposition: a well-entrenched distinction between naturalia and artificialia, a connoisseur's privilege granted to objects understood as exotic, a separate gathering of paper materials handwritten, engraved or printed. Yet recognizing that readers do not read in linear fashion, these assemblages group longer essays with a series of shorter exhibits, inviting readers to explore the many possibilities evoked in longer case studies by considering a series of alternative objects of attention. As Adriana Craciun's and Mary Terrall's essays show, seeds recovered from a shipwreck or insects dissected in a Parisian cabinet speak to the value of natural curiosities in Enlightenment sciences. However, they also 'put on view a record of work and pleasure, inventions and techniques, sociability and exchange' reaching far outside metropolitan scientific circles.[11] Several of the exhibits bring out the multi-dimensionality and ambiguity of objects' construction. Just as Mary Delany's *Flora Delanica*, cut-paper collages of plants described here by Kim Sloan, often included original leaves or flowers, so the late seventeenth-century embroidery on show in Mary Brooks's exhibit incorporated birds' beaks, perhaps finches or linnets. Such needlework could be considered as a novel form of a natural history cabinet, or an affective memorialization of beloved animal companions, or a genteel form of feminine material culture with rich connections to networks of science.

The brief glimpse caught of these extraordinary hybrid objects opens up new directions for longer analyses and recombinations. More conventional themes of Enlightenment public culture, such as the investment in publicity and celebrity on display in Faramerz Dabhoiwala's exhibit of a 1765 portrait of the courtesan Kitty Fisher, or the colonial circulation of currency linked with the 1790s Soho-made coin described by Catherine Eagleton, can be queried and reorganized by close attention to objects' pathways. Fisher's portrait is artfully balanced between composure and manipulation of its audiences; the coin moved between Birmingham, Sierra Leone and the polite cabinets of fashionable London. 'Tracking the story of this rather ordinary-looking penny links together several topics that are often considered separately when looking at the late eighteenth century', Eagleton explains.[12] The assemblages proposed here are designed to encourage such fluid readings, playing with scale of attention and analysis, through which in future work exhibits may become essays and vice versa.

[11] Mary Terrall, 'Handling Objects in Natural History Collections', this volume.
[12] Catherine Eagleton, 'Sarah Sophia Banks, Adam Afzelius and a Coin from Sierra Leone', this volume.

An aim of this collection is to make the case both for objects' surprising mobility and for their 'implacability', a term that Jonathan Lamb's essay here adopts from Theodor Adorno's discussion of the new powers of objects in an age of aggressive technology. Adorno damned the ways in which engagement with such things had been reduced to mere functionality: 'what does it mean for the subject that there are no more casement windows to open?' However, along with other contributors, Lamb explores many ways in which eighteenth-century systems of property and production found these mundane things remarkably animated, live actors in new and complex social worlds.[13] The capacity to render images of the human body as manipulable and movable objects reinforced the ambiguous relation between animation and commodity. This is evident both in Jane Munro's exhibit of a French artist's mannequin and in Josefine Baark's essay on the astonishing mechanical models of Chinese shops, houses and their occupants shipped to the Danish court in the mid-eighteenth century. These mechanisms inevitably raised questions of things' eloquence. In enlightened worlds, such things sometimes spoke volumes in the golden age of it-narratives, whether of coins and jewels, or of pens and pins, while at other times they all remained stubbornly silent. Not only were things' voices mutable, so was their relation with society. As Barbara Benedict has put it, apparently animate and purposeful objects were 'the new immigrants' to eighteenth-century markets and homes, often of alien origin, ubiquitous and somewhat threatening, frequently questioning the precise identity of persons and of their stories.[14]

As readers will discover, the things and tales in this collection therefore enjoy plural connections to one another and are not self-identical. Sophie Waring shows how a nautical almanac may function as a calculated instrument of nautical science in one time and place, and as useless waste paper later. Similarly, Kim Sloan demonstrates how a meticulously fabricated paper-cut collage appears as a three-dimensional botanical specimen in a herbarium at one moment, and presented differently it becomes a meticulously crafted work of art circulating among elite women. An ulcerated oesophagus may begin as a fragment of a person, but over centuries of preservation in the Hunterian Museum its social and physical life can morph to tell new stories about disease and human bodies, removed from the lifespan of its human origins. As Samuel Alberti shows, this fragment of a named subject has in its long life become a composite object, and like many of the things in our collection, 'is then not only conceptually hybrid (person/thing,

---

[13] Theodore Adorno, *Minima Moralia: Reflections on a Damaged Life* (London: New Left Books, 1974), 40; Jonathan Lamb, 'Persons and Things', this volume.

[14] Jonathan Lamb, *The Things Things Say* (Princeton: Princeton University Press, 2011), 201–229; Mark Blackwell, 'The It-Narrative and Eighteenth-Century Thing Theory', in Blackwell (ed.), *The Secret Life of Things: Animals, Objects and It-Narratives in Eighteenth-Century England* (Cranbury: Associated University Presses, 2007), 9–18; Barbara Benedict, 'Encounters with the Object: Advertisements, Time and Literary Discourse in the Early Eighteenth Century Thing-Poem', *Eighteenth-Century Studies* 40 (2007), 193–207, on 194.

subject/object), but also physically hybrid'.[15] By not affixing the varied things and hybrid objects of our collective imaginations into monological taxonomies—medical specimens, scientific instruments, printed books—we want to keep alive the transformational potential that the essays in this volume rediscover.

The kinds of transformation evinced by these things were certainly not defined merely by a simple change of address, as it were. They also changed their state. This mattered especially in the enterprises of natural history and experimental philosophy, in gardens and laboratories, workshops and store-rooms. The problems of objects' recalcitrant shiftiness became acute there: it was embarrassingly evident that they were uninterested in inquirers' aims. So experimenters and naturalists designed special set-ups where materials could better and more directly respond to examination: objects could, so it has been argued, then at last be made to *object* to inquiries about their nature and properties.[16] Anne Gerritsen's exhibit, a damaged and discarded Jingdezhen coffee cup made for the European market, shows just how much material deformation can teach about the global systems of exploitation and commerce in play in the eighteenth-century world. In the practical dialogues of eighteenth-century sciences, such substances were explicitly understood as capable of mutation, displaying desirable or distressing alteration, melting or rotting, capable of fracture or deformation. Concerns with materials' transience and disintegration worked across apparently fixed cultural divides. Maia Nuku's essay on Tahitian *to'o* describes the horror with which missionaries in the Pacific responded to 'the fragile ephemerality of god images that incorporated organic materials and feathers "soon rotten"'.[17] Sanctity, and commercial value, seemed bound up with things' capacity to survive. As Hal Cook has pointed out, novel storage systems were explicitly designed somehow to halt the processes of change, to stop time so as to secure the worth of a commodity form. The pharmacy jar on show in Jennifer Basford's exhibit here is a typical example of the linkage established between conservation and the attempt to establish commercial repute and status. Cases, jars, boxes and bottles became increasingly vital components of the preservation techniques and inventory investments of the world of goods.[18]

There were equivalent interests in the Enlightenment's publishing trade, which so often sought somehow to catalogue and thus preserve worlds of knowledge and commerce reckoned dangerously transient and vulnerable to the passage of time or the threat of *l'infâme*. Domestic labour concentrated especially on the essential task of preservation against loss. So, too, did the

[15] Samuel Alberti, 'A Pathological Pot', this volume.

[16] Bruno Latour, 'When Things Strike Back', *British Journal of Sociology* 51 (2000), 107–123, on 116.

[17] Maia Nuku, 'Unwrapping Gods: Illuminating Encounters with Gods, Comets and Missionaries', this volume.

[18] Harold J. Cook, 'Time's Bodies: Crafting the Preparation and Preservation of Naturalia', in Pamela H. Smith and Paula Findlen (eds.), *Merchants and Marvels: Commerce, Science and Art in Early Modern Europe* (London: Routledge, 2002), 223–247, on 225–229.

work of pharmacists and assayers in the Enlightenment's kitchens, distilleries, mines and forges. They laboured hard both to maintain substances' qualities and to transform them so as to generate more valuable, allegedly purer or more essential forms. 'Salts, metals and semi-metals are far from being produced by nature in a state of perfection, or in that degree of purity which they are commonly supposed to have when they are first treated of in Books of Chymistry', declared the authoritative French chemist Pierre-Joseph Macquer in 1751. He therefore detailed the way in which pharmacists and assayers worked to make such substances. Since the key materials of eighteenth-century chemistry, for example, were not at all found in nature, but rather in the outputs of innovative workshops, artisans' activities challenged many of the established distinctions between natural and artificial goods. These were crucial distinctions, often called into question by the eighteenth-century materials on show here. As Richard Dunn explains in an essay and associated exhibit, in the instrument trades there were fraught relations between the status of an individual maker, such as the masters John Bird and Jesse Ramsden, and the mechanization of engraving and experiment. These kinds of productive work offered yet another principal source of objects' impressive malleability of status and property.[19]

Such objects were migrants in the most literal sense too. The social lives of things made possible and were sustained by the global and postcolonial frameworks through which the eighteenth-century 'world of moving objects' and the Enlightenment appear in scholarship today.[20] It is made evident in this collection how the iconography and materiality of global systems of war, navigation and trade were relentlessly made present to metropolitan consumers. In maritime Britain, the status of naval power was entirely wrapped up with the many ways in which mariners and vessels were turned into objects of consumption and display. James Davey's exhibit of an image of a warship launch at Deptford, just like the portrait of the polar explorer James Clark Ross described by Amy Miller, formed part of these enterprises of moral propaganda. Eighteenth-century materials show how close were links between such campaigns and the systems of circulation and accumulation established worldwide. Jonathan Eacott's essay on luxury goods and tropical consumption in British colonies explores the many ways in which moral arguments about the status of exotic commodities, and the rival claims of indigenous and imperial systems of material life, were developed in these intensely global systems. The notion of an 'empire of goods', typically used by historians to make sense of the material culture of the Atlantic colonial world, could be extended with modifications at least as aptly to the networks that linked the Asia-Pacific region with its European markets.[21] The region was

[19] Pierre-Joseph Macquer, *Elements of the Theory and Practice of Chymistry*, 2 vols. (London: Nourse and Millar, 1758), vol. 1, 205; Klein and Lefèvre, *Materials in Eighteenth-Century Science*, 72–74.

[20] J.G.A. Pocock, *Virtue, Commerce, and History* (Cambridge: Cambridge University Press, 1985), 109.

[21] T.H. Breen, *The Marketplace of Revolution: How Consumer Politics Shaped American Independence* (Oxford: Oxford University Press, 2004).

made present to European consumers through the workings of many linked markets and systems of appropriation. Patricia Seed describes the crucial Pacific map made by the great French cartographer Guillaume Delisle and extensively adapted later in the eighteenth century, while Billie Lythberg's exhibit puts on show the remarkably widely promoted and exotically imaginative wallpapers that French designers produced of the inhabitants of the Pacific islands.

The hybrid objects featured in this book's collection bear witness to exotic genealogies of modern knowledge, often generated far from the European metropoles and their centres of classification and calculation, through diverse human and non-human agencies and encounters. Articles such as automata and coffee cups, commodities ranging from sugar to barkcloth, significantly populate the exhibits gathered here. John McAleer describes a punchbowl made in China around 1785 specifically to meet the demand of Thames shipbuilders, while Charles Jarvis traces a valuable plant between the Chinese coast, the networks of the East India Company, metropolitan botany and colonial economy in the American plantations. As Maxine Berg has argued, luxury imports from Asia changed European economies through systems of imitation and import substitution. It is noteworthy that Enlightenment Europe did not in the main seek to import Asian techniques, but rather Asian goods, and then sought ways of making similar commodities. 'Domestic manufacturers emulate the foreign in their improvements, and work up every home commodity to the utmost perfection of which it is susceptible', David Hume explained in 1752. 'Their own steel and iron, in such laborious hands, become equal to the gold and rubies of the Indies.'[22] The relation between the claims of Enlightenment, global trade networks and the status of materials like iron and steel was thus very close. This was not necessarily because of accelerated flows of practical knowledge between manufacturers and artisans, but, rather, because of important connections between the ornamental, enlightened and philosophical associations of such substances as refined steel, especially in trades such as clockmaking and surgery.[23]

No doubt this had major effects, too, on systems of practical knowledge and of publicity in print. It-narratives accompanied hosts of advertisements for lost goods and those brought to market. Colin Jones points out how through such worlds of paper in the French urban markets the commerce in words and things became 'a laboratory for experiments in individual subjectivity'.[24] Novel and mobile objects were surrounded by innovative kinds of description, and

[22] Maxine Berg, 'In Pursuit of Luxury: Global History and British Consumer Goods in the Eighteenth Century', *Past and Present* 182 (2004), 85–142, on 90–91, 109–12, 130; David Hume, *Essays and Treatises on Several Subjects*, 4 vols., 2nd ed. (Edinburgh: Kincaid and Donaldson, 1753), 15.

[23] Chris Evans and Alun Withey, 'An Enlightenment in Steel? Innovation in the Steel Trades of Eighteenth-Century Britain', *Technology and Culture* 53 (2012), 2–29.

[24] Colin Jones, 'The Great Chain of Buying: Medical Advertisement, the Bourgeois Public Sphere and the Origins of the French Revolution', *American Historical Review* 101 (1996), 13–40, on 26.

thus of genres of information and of news. Charts and journals, catalogues and images all proliferated around the market system and the long-range social links across the globe. Philippa Hubbard's exhibit of a 1749 trade card reminds us of the central importance of sophisticated paper advertising, and the role of female entrepreneurs in such a system. The collections on show in this book are designed to draw readers' attention to the relational properties of these enlivened things, highlighting their mobility, transindividuality and intermediality. The discussion by Billie Lythberg, Maia Nuku and Amiria Salmond of an apparently ephemeral label once attached to a Maori cloak brought to Britain on James Cook's first voyage reveals much of the complex relations set up by such marks and traces. Texts thus appear here as inscribed things among other kinds of objects. Likewise, authors and artists are not the privileged creators of intellectual or aesthetic property, but agents in a broader understanding of the history of inscription, marking, collecting and engraving. The geographies travelled by these textual things can span oceans of time and space, as shown in Billie Lythberg's exhibit of Polynesian barkcloth books made in England. Their social lives also reveal a radical dynamism inherent in material texts, but often eclipsed by our fixation with preservation, collection and identification. Thus, tales of textual survival also testify to their profound ephemerality, as in the extra-illustrated books unbound in Luisa Calè's essay, or the ephemera of paperslip poetry designed to disappear in Leanna McLaughlin's work, or the contentious medical knowledge embodied in the aesthetic properties of an anatomical atlas, as Alexander Wragge-Morley shows.

In this eighteenth-century world of moving objects and plural Enlightenments, knowledge was typically pursued across a terrain shared by the arts and sciences.[25] This shared terrain persisted in diverse popular institutions until the early nineteenth century, often in the name of enterprises of material production and economic reorganization.[26] Our case is that the material culture of this shared knowledge of the arts and sciences is uniquely valuable for a proper understanding of the genealogy of our disciplines, their blindspots and privileged categories.

This collection emerges from the cross-disciplinary collaboration of two research groups over the course of two years: Cambridge University's 'Things that Matter' series in its Centre for Research in Arts, Social Sciences and Humanities, and the University of California Multicampus Research Group on 'The Material Cultures of Knowledge, 1600–1830'. All but one of the essays, and many more of the exhibits, included here emerged out of two workshops held jointly in 2012: the first at the Huntington Library and the second

---

[25] On the 'false unity' of 'the Enlightenment' and 'the Enlightenment Project', see J.G.A. Pocock, 'Enthusiasm: The Antiself of Enlightenment,' *Huntington Library Quarterly* 60 (1997), 7–28 and his *Barbarism and Religion Vol. I: The Enlightenments of Edward Gibbon* (Cambridge: Cambridge University Press, 1999); Sankar Muthu, *Enlightenment Against Empire* (Princeton: Princeton University Press, 2003), 259–266.

[26] Jon Klancher, *Transfiguring the Arts and Sciences: Knowledge and Cultural Institutions in the Romantic Age* (Cambridge: Cambridge University Press, 2013), 38–44.

at Cambridge University. They reflect a cross-fertilization of ideas across our two groups and academic cultures. Together with the exhibits drawn from Cambridge's highly successful 'Things that Matter' series, the essays contribute an object-focused approach to the new materialism visible across studies of the global eighteenth century, the Enlightenment and histories of disciplinarity. Our groups have independently pursued possibilities for interdisciplinarity that material objects hold across the humanities, and we joined together in a series of collaborative workshops that combined the expertise of historians of science, literature, material texts, Enlightenment and art, as well as curators of leading museums and libraries. In organizing this collection it has seemed important that it thus not codify disciplinary rigidity, but rather illuminate the exotic indisciplines at work in the arts and sciences. By avoiding the reinscription of the anachronistic divisions of knowledge of our twenty-first-century academies, it becomes possible to discern the predisciplinary 'disorder of things' at work throughout the eighteenth century and so evident in the collection assembled here.[27]

---

[27] Luisa Calè and Adriana Craciun, 'The Disorder of Things', *Eighteenth-Century Studies* 45 (2011), 1–13.

PART I

Natural Curiosities

CHAPTER 2

Handling Objects in Natural History Collections

Mary Terrall

Kaspar Utz, the eccentric aesthete and hero of Bruce Chatwin's novel *Utz*, formed his taste for eighteenth-century decorative arts in the Dresden museums in the 1920s, and went on to build his own vast collection of Meissen porcelain. After the war, having ceded his land and castle to the new communist state, he hung on to his precious porcelain, and even managed to add to the collection, improbably stored in his shabby apartment in Stalinist Prague. Utz's sensibility was anything but socialist:

> "An object in a museum case," he wrote, "must suffer the de-natured existence of an animal in the zoo. In any museum the object dies—of suffocation and the public gaze—whereas private ownership confers on the owner the right and the need to touch. As a young child will reach out to handle the thing it names, so the passionate collector, his eye in harmony with his hand, restores to the object the life-giving touch of its maker. The collector's enemy is the museum curator. Ideally, museums should be looted every fifty years, and their collections returned to circulation."[1]

Such circulation, of course, made Utz's collection possible—some of his cherished figurines had very likely been looted from one place or another before being sold on the international market. Chatwin's novel reminds us of the fraught and consequential sets of meanings, including emotional attachments,

---

[1] Bruce Chatwin, *Utz* (New York: Viking Penguin, 1988), 20.

M. Terrall (✉)
Department of History, University of California,
Los Angeles, CA, USA
e-mail: terrall@history.ucla.edu

© The Author(s) 2016
A. Craciun, S. Schaffer (eds.), *The Material Cultures of Enlightenment Arts and Sciences*, Palgrave Studies in the Enlightenment, Romanticism and the Cultures of Print, DOI 10.1057/978-1-137-44379-3_2

embedded in collections, whether of naturalia or works of art.[2] If they are living collections, like that of Utz, the contents do not simply sit in their designated places, as items are touched, examined, moved around, broken, loaned, or given away. By focusing on the "harmony of eye and hand"—the handling and manipulation of collected objects, especially for scientific purposes—I explore the significance of tangibility and three-dimensionality, widening the scope beyond the related notions of visibility, looking, seeing, and aesthetically pleasing display that inform much of the literature on collections.[3]

If Utz had lived in eighteenth-century Paris, he would very likely have cultivated a much more diverse collection. Even people who specialized in porcelain, say, or engravings, or shells, or anatomical preparations, would also display at least some notable items of completely different kinds, and often collected across many categories. Certain items—like crocodiles and whale bones hanging from the ceiling—were ubiquitous. By the 1730s, exotic shells from all corners of the world filled specially designed tables and cases in the cabinets of aristocrats (including many women), doctors, merchants, apothecaries, lawyers, writers, and priests. Very few of these cabinets were restricted to shells, just as very few connoisseurs confined their acquisitive impulses to pictures or antiquities alone.

Recent scholarship has delved into the diverse purposes, methods, meanings, and values associated with collecting, challenging the linear evolution from Renaissance curiosity and eclecticism to Enlightenment rationality, from *Wunderkammer* to ordered sequences and grids.[4] Daniela Bleichmar, for example, has shown how art and science informed each other in many eighteenth-century collections, focusing on the development of a particular notion of taste, and the role of aesthetics in collections of naturalia.[5] A central figure in her story is Antoine Dézallier d'Argenville (an avid collector himself), whose book on shells depicted valuable specimens from aristocratic collections. D'Argenville aspired to be a kind of taste maker, teaching his readers

---

[2] Chatwin, whose first career was as an expert for the British auction house Sotheby's, modeled his fictional character Utz on a Czech collector he met in Prague in the 1960s. The porcelain obsession of both collectors, fictional and historical, echoes the acquisitive desires of their eighteenth-century predecessors. For the layered meanings attached to collections across time and generations, see also Edmund de Waal, *The Hare with Amber Eyes: A Family's Century of Art and Loss* (New York: Farrar, Straus, Giroux, 2010).

[3] The literature on collections in the early modern period has become too large to inventory comprehensively. In addition to works cited later, see Krzysztof Pomian, *Collectors and Curiosities: Paris and Venice, 1500–1800*, trans. Elizabeth Wiles-Portier (Cambridge: Polity Press, 1990).

[4] On shell collections, see Bettina Dietz, "Mobile Objects: The Space of Shells in Eighteenth-Century France," *British Journal for the History of Science* 39 (2006): 363–382; E.C. Spary, "Scientific Symmetries," *History of Science* 42 (2004), 1–46. On minerals, Jonathan Simon, "Taste, Order, and Aesthetics in Eighteenth-Century Mineral Collections," in *From Public to Private: Natural Collections and Museums*, ed. Marco Beretta (Sagamore Beach, MA: Science History Publications, 2005), 97–112.

[5] Daniela Bleichmar, "Learning to Look: Visual Expertise Across Art and Science in Eighteenth-Century France," *Eighteenth-Century Studies* 46 (2012), 85–111.

how to appreciate visual displays, and how to arrange their own collections.[6] His book became an essential reference for shell collectors and the merchants who supplied them, and also for naturalists working on marine animals.[7] If the connoisseur had to learn to look, visitors to collections of naturalia—many of whom were or aspired to be collectors themselves—also had to learn to handle and examine specimens. People were looking at things, to be sure, but also picking them up, talking about them, reading their labels, putting them under magnifying lenses, comparing them to other specimens. The men and women in these rooms ranged from academicians to casual visitors of all social ranks, from travelers on their Grand Tours to students or apprentices. Some of them were regulars, working intently on particular objects or classes of objects, going back and forth to the library, in and out of the house. Proprietors, with their assistants and advisers, lived with their collections, continually acquiring new material, and incorporating their specimens into a whole range of research programs. They sliced things open, subjected them to chemical tests, measured, heated, and tasted them, and carried them across town to display to colleagues. Showing visitors around meant handling objects too, as did arranging, trading, cataloguing, and so on. Rooms filled with arrays of specimens were sites of sociability and of various kinds of work. The objects themselves were continually evolving, shifting locations, decaying, moving from one collection to another, and even from one type of collection to another.[8]

The more we study eighteenth-century collections and collectors, the more apparent it becomes that there was no typical collector, or collection. Nor, as Bettina Dietz argues, did hard-and-fast lines distinguish "scientific" from "amateur" collectors in this period.[9] Much of what we have to infer obliquely from surviving sources (auction catalogues, scientific papers, atlases, natural history books, inventories after death, letters) would have been well known to contemporaries: collections were changing constantly, objects moved in and out of different collections, the practices around collecting cut across social and intellectual lines. And the objects in collections often became resources for scientific work.

---

[6] D'Argenville wrote an essay on how to arrange a natural history collection, first published in *Mercure de France* (1727), reprinted in Antoine Dézallier d'Argenville, *Histoire naturelle éclaircie dans deux de ses parties principales, la lithologie et la conchyliologie* (Paris,1742), 192–7. The book went through three editions, each with slightly different components.

[7] Daniel Margocsy, *Commercial Visions: Science, Trade and Visual Culture in the Dutch Golden Age* (Chicago: University of Chicago Press, 2014), 64.

[8] A similar point about the mutability of collections is made by E.C. Spary, "Pierre Pomet's Parisian Cabinet: Revisiting the Invisible and the Visible in Early Modern Collections," in *From Public to Private: Natural Collections and Museums*, ed. Marco Beretta (Sagamore Beach, MA: Science History Publications, 2005), on 78. "We might ... represent the early modern cabinet as a constant flux, with specimens shifting to accommodate new acquisitions or to compensate for old ones, a choreography of hands moving to bring together, describe, examine, preserve, mount, and of eyes moving between and among specimens and texts."

[9] Dietz, "Mobile Objects," 365.

In this essay, I will be using a few objects and a few collectors, plucked from their places in the spectrum of natural history collecting in eighteenth-century France, and examining them from all angles, to investigate the scientific uses and meanings of cabinets of naturalia. How did the objects in collections enter into research agendas? Or, put differently, how were these objects handled? Taxonomy was only a small part of the knowledge made by manipulating the specimens in collections. They became the raw material for a variety of experimental and observational work, often pursued in the same space where objects were mounted, arranged, preserved, and displayed.[10] Once we recognize the ways in which these resources functioned, we will start to notice the situation of natural history cabinets relative to other spaces: laboratories, libraries, shops, gardens, pens where living animals were kept, quarries where fossils were dug out, seashores, fields, and forests. And that will bring us back to the people living with and working in these collections.

CLAUDE-JOSEPH GEOFFROY

The topography of Paris was studded with collections of all sorts, and continually traversed in all directions by collectors, their interlocutors, suppliers, and assistants, and by the objects of their attention. One notable landmark was the home of Claude-Joseph Geoffroy (1685–1752), scion of a wealthy apothecary family and younger brother of Etienne-François (famous for his table of chemical affinities). Both brothers were assiduous members of the Academy of Sciences, where they frequently presented their research on chemical or botanical matters. At their father's death, with Etienne-François established as a physician and professor at the Collège Royal, Claude-Joseph took over the lucrative business of ministering to the pharmaceutical needs of the rich and famous, including the highest ranks of the nobility. He inherited part of his father's sizeable library and art collection, along with the valuable drugs cabinet (*droguier*).[11] The shelves and boxes of the drugs cabinet stored items of animal, vegetable, and mineral origin: snakes in bottles, medicinal minerals and earths, bezoars (concretions taken from animal stomachs), precious and semi-precious stones, seeds, barks, roots, dried plants, and distilled plant oils and essences.

Geoffroy's wealth increased steadily, thanks to a series of canny financial and real estate deals, and he indulged his penchant for collecting to expand his natural history cabinet far beyond the materials necessary to his thriving trade. The

---

[10] On the museum as a place for experiment and conversation in the Renaissance, see Paula Findlen, *Possessing Nature: Museums, Collecting, and Scientific Culture in Early Modern Italy* (Berkeley: University of California Press, 1994), esp. Chap. 6.

[11] On the apothecary business, social position, and growing wealth of three generations of the Geoffroy family, see David Sturdy, *Science and Social Status: The Members of the Académie des Sciences, 1666–1750* (Woodbridge, UK: Boydell Press, 1995), 324–42. At Claude-Joseph's death in 1752, the contents of the pharmacy, including the *droguier*, were valued at 21,000 *livres*. Sturdy, 326.

Geoffroy establishment (the pharmacy, plus the collections and library, and residential quarters for family and staff, sometimes including apprentices) occupied two adjacent houses on rue Bourgtibourg in the parish of Saint Paul in Paris. The shop and the drugs cabinet filled ground-floor rooms entered from a courtyard where carriages deposited customers and visitors.[12] In his guide to Paris collections in the early 1740s, Dézallier d'Argenville mentioned Geoffroy's 1,800 crystal jars of preserved specimens, displayed in armoires above ranks of drawers containing fossils, figured stones, and other dry specimens. "This *droguier*," d'Argenville noted, "arranged on shelves, occupies two sides of the room, with preserved snakes in glass tubes set into the columns of the furniture. The third side is the library of natural history and medicine. The ceiling is decorated with several crocodiles, scaly lizards, snakes and other reptiles."[13] The term *droguier*, at least in principle, indicated a narrower scope than the more capacious "cabinet"—a word used for the collection as well as the room, and sometimes the furniture, in which it was kept. Pharmaceutical stock shaded into the contents of the display in the drugs cabinet, which encompassed rare and costly items in addition to materia medica of animal, vegetable, and mineral origin. Although the shop counter was no doubt distinct from the elaborate furniture displaying rare specimens and extended series of objects, not to mention the laboratories further back in the house, these spaces and the activities going on in them were constantly connected.[14] Upstairs from the shop and the *droguier*, Geoffroy's collection continued, with cases and armoires of shells, insects, fossils, corals, gems, and other stones, and injected anatomical specimens. Further rooms exhibited artworks, including antiquities, silver, porcelain (Chinese, Japanese, and Saxon), paintings, and engravings.[15]

Geoffroy's cabinet was a fixture on the Parisian collecting scene for decades, familiar to travelers, connoisseurs of art and shells, naturalists, merchants, pharmacists, and academicians; some of these were undoubtedly his customers as well. The association of the drugs portion of the collection with the apothecary business did not detract from the value of the whole collection or the individual specimens within it, many of which were comparable to things collected by the well-heeled clients who bought his remedies. While it was admired and perhaps envied by visitors, the collection also supplied materials for Geoffroy's academic

[12] Sturdy, *Science and Social Status*, 337–8.

[13] D'Argenville, *Histoire naturelle éclaircie*, 208. The merchant Gersaint also mentioned Geoffroy's collection in his list, noticing especially the minerals, fossils, metals, and shells: Edme Gersaint, *Catalogue raisonné de coquilles, insectes, plantes marines, et autres curiosités naturelles* (Paris, 1736), 31.

[14] On the meaning and contents of a *droguier*, see Spary, "Pierre Pomet's Parisian Cabinet."

[15] The art collection was started by his father, Mathieu-François, but vastly expanded by Claude-Joseph. Sturdy, *Science and Social Status*, 327. Some of the porcelain would not have been out of place in Utz's collection in Prague: C.-J. Geoffroy owned a mantel clock decorated with flowers and figures of Saxon porcelain; two candlesticks in the same style; and "two seated figures, also of Saxon porcelain, representing a sailor and a lacemaker." *Catalogue raisonné des minéraux, coquilles, et autres curiosités naturelles contenues dans le cabinet de feu M. Geoffroy de l'Académie royale des sciences* (Paris, 1753), 92.

researches, performed in the same laboratory where he and his apprentices did pharmaceutical distillations and fermentations. His many contributions to the Academy of Sciences include experiments and analyses of aromatic plant oils from the Indies, cakes of sal ammoniac from Egypt, boric acid (used medically as a sedative), therapeutic salts, antimony, and so on. Sometimes laboratory operations were on display too: in a paper on igniting essential plant oils, he reported to the academy on spectacular experiments he had performed in his laboratory for the edification of "distinguished personages [*personnes de consi-dération*]," probably his customers and fellow collectors.[16]

The most extensive sequence in Geoffroy's *droguier*, singled out for particular mention by d'Argenville, were the bezoar stones.[17] These objects, concretions taken from a variety of animal stomachs and other organs, had long been staples of the apothecary's trade, and because of their monetary value and their variety they were eminently collectible as well. Since the medieval period, bezoars had been used in European medicine as poison antidotes and as components of many other remedies.[18] Valuable enough to be counterfeited, and often mounted in precious metals, they recalled the curiosity cabinets of previous generations, when they had carried magical or emblematic associations. The first bezoars brought to Europe came from Persian mountain goats; by the seventeenth century, merchants added stones from South American goats to their inventories. By the eighteenth century, the term was used for stones from all sorts of animals, as well as the artificial ones known as Goa stones. Some of the stones on Geoffroy's shelves had elaborate filigree settings in gold or silver gilt or enamel; some were unique oddities, like the rhinoceros bezoar with an uneven surface resembling the human brain, or an elephant bezoar weighing two and a half pounds.[19] Most doctors no longer considered bezoars to be

[16] C.-J. Geoffroy, "Différens moyens d'enflammer, non-seulement les huiles essentielles, mais même les baumes naturels, par les esprits acides," *Mémoires de l'Académie royale des sciences* (Paris, 1726), 95–105; the presentation was also reported in the *Mercure de France*, June 1726, 1371–3.

[17] D'Argenville, *Histoire naturelle éclaircie*, 207. He also mentioned the series of sigillated earths, another class of objects with medical and magical associations; these do not appear in the auction catalogue of Geoffroy's collection, so they must have been sold separately, perhaps with the *droguier*.

[18] Bezoars were adopted in Europe from Arabic medicine; they were also used in China. In addition to its classic use as an antidote, bezoar was used in remedies for vertigo, epilepsy, palpitations of the heart, jaundice, colic, and "so many other illnesses that it will be no doubt quite accurate to say that it is a kind of panacea, or a universal remedy..." The stones continued to be valuable commodities, although this article noted that many doctors no longer prescribed the use of bezoar. "Bezoard," in Jacques Savary des Bruslons and Philemon-Louis Savary, *Dictionnaire universel de commerce, d'histoire naturelle, et des arts et métiers*, 3 vols. (Geneva, 1742), 1:435–38, quotation on 436.

[19] These are mentioned in the catalogue of Pedro Davila's collection, with a note that they had been bought at the Geoffroy sale. *Catalogue systématique et raisonné des curiosités de la nature et de l'art, qui composent le cabinet de M. Davila*, 2 vols. (Paris: Briasson, 1767), 1:501–2. Rhinoceros stones were also collected by Hans Sloane; see Sloane, "A Letter from Sir Hans Sloane ... containing accounts of the pretended serpent-stone ... and the Rhinoceros Bezoar, Together with the

panaceas or all-purpose antidotes, as they had been in earlier periods, but they still appeared in compilations of materia medica and recipe books, and they remained essential elements of any *droguier*.[20]

Early in his academic career Geoffroy experimented with some of his bezoars. He was interested in how they were formed, why they occurred in so many different shapes, and how to recognize artificially produced stones. Since merchants and travelers could hardly be counted on for accurate information about origins, "on these sorts of matters, a good examination is sometimes worth more than many stories."[21] He did not interrogate their medicinal virtues—he was not testing them as drugs so much as investigating their structure and composition. "Properly speaking, the bezoar is a stony substance taken from any animal, composed of several layers or envelopes, like onions, and which has some power to resist poison," he wrote.[22] At this time, he had not yet accumulated the whole remarkable series later flagged by d'Argenville. Geoffroy's laboratory study of the stones, written up for the academy, thus related directly to his collecting practice, since he needed to assess the value and authenticity of stones before buying them, as well as to his apothecary business. When he explained how to distinguish true from counterfeit stones, he was implicitly certifying the wares in his compounding shop as genuine.

In his laboratory, Geoffroy examined dozens of bezoars of various shapes and origins, slicing, heating and burning, tasting and smelling them. Cut in half, they revealed concentric layers of different thickness and sometimes of different color. They broke apart along the boundaries of the layers when struck or heated. When he bit into the stones, they would crack along the boundaries of the layers, "and stick to the teeth like a mildly glutinous matter that slightly tints the saliva." When he burned them, they ignited easily: "They seem to contain volatile salts and oil. The residue resembles the *Caput mortuum* left in the retort after distilling animal matter."[23] After describing the range of textures and colors of the outer surface and the various layers, he soaked them in water and spirits and wine to see if they would dissolve. (They did not) As he sliced open more and more stones, he found all sorts of substances at their centers: straw, hair, pebbles, wood, talc, and various seeds, some resembling cherry pits and coffee beans. This led him to explore how the object at the core determined the final shape of the bezoar. In some he could see how a seed or bean had swelled with moisture in the animal's stomach, then served as a mold for the "bezoardic matter"—the animal's secretions—before shrinking back and drying, leaving a hollow at the center. Finally, he summarized the various

---

Figure of a Rhinoceros with a Double Horn," *Philosophical Transactions* 46 (1749–1750), 118–125.

[20] See, e.g. L.D. Arnault de Nobleville and François Salerne, *Suite de la matière medicale de M. Geoffroy*, 7 vols. (Paris, 1757), 4: 319–24, for uses of different kinds of bezoars.

[21] C.-J. Geoffroy, "Observations sur le bezoard, et sur les autres matières qui en approchent," *Mémoires de l'Académie royale des sciences* (Paris, 1710), 235–242, on 235.

[22] Ibid., 236.

[23] Ibid., 237.

features of true bezoars that could be determined simply by sight or touch, in order to avoid destructive tests on valuable stones. And he noted that for medical use, the apothecary had to take care when grinding a piece of bezoar into powder not to break into the foreign matter at the center.[24]

As his collection grew, Geoffroy continued to study his bezoars, and to acquire new ones. In a second paper in 1712, he reported on stones from European and New World beavers, found in the pouches known as "castoreum" and used widely in medicine. He opened many of these pouches to look for stones, comparing specimens from Canada, Danzig, and the Rhone valley, including some harvested by an apothecary near Avignon and sent as a gift. Then he turned to his botanist colleagues at the Jardin du roi for help with identifying plant materials that might account for the characteristic shapes of some bezoars. Acacia seeds, recently sent from Senegal to the botanical garden, turned out to be similar in shape to some of his bezoars. Opening the acacia seed pods—common in northern and western Africa but rare in Paris— he found them astringent and gummy. When soaked in water, they swelled up and tinted the water with the same reddish tint produced by bezoar stone infused in water. From the distinctive shape and chemical properties of the seeds, Geoffroy inferred the natural process of bezoar formation in animals, where the astringent seeds would cause animal secretions to congeal around them. He conjectured further that counterfeiters could use the same seeds to form the artificial stones that apothecaries tried to avoid.[25] The acacia seed pods themselves took their place in Geoffroy's cabinet, alongside other exotic plant products like betel leaves, quinine seeds, and nutmeg fruits.[26]

Geoffroy's examination of all these bezoars made him suspicious of the claims of a well-known pharmacopeia, the *Histoire des drogues* of the seventeenth-century Parisian apothecary Pierre Pomet, which has been studied by Emma Spary.[27] Pomet described the hairy outer envelope of a bezoar in his own collection as a great curiosity, and represented this specimen in the plate illustrating his article (see Fig. 2.1). Geoffroy knew that Pomet's cabinet, or some of it, was still kept at the botanical garden, where he was able to identify the hairy bezoar in question, cut in half by Pomet to show its layers. On careful inspection, Geoffroy found, with the help of the botanists Sebastien Vaillant and Bernard de Jussieu, both demonstrators at the royal garden, that the purported outer coat of Pomet's bezoar was not integral to the stone at all, but "an exotic fruit into which Pomet, or some charlatan who deceived him, had very adroitly inserted a bezoar stone." Vaillant then found some fruits of

---

[24] Ibid., 240–1.

[25] C.-J. Geoffroy, "Suite des observations sur les bezoards," *Mémoires de l'Académie royale des sciences* (Paris, 1712), 199–208, acacia seeds on 200–1.

[26] *Catalogue raisonné des minéraux, coquilles, et autres curiosités naturelles contenues dans le cabinet de feu M. Geoffroy de l'Académie royale des sciences* (Paris, 1753), 36.

[27] Spary, "Pierre Pomet's Parisian Cabinet." Pomet's *Histoire des drogues* was first published in 1694, with a second edition in 1695; several others followed, including translations in German and English, but these came out well after Geoffroy's papers on bezoars.

Fig. 2.1   Persian mountain goat, with Pomet's bezoar stone in cross-section, showing concentric layers and hairy outer sheath (Pierre Pomet, *Compleat History of Drugs*, 2nd ed. (London, 1725, Bk. 2, 10. Courtesy of History and Special Collections, Louise M. Darling Biomedical Library, UCLA)

the very species, a type of palm native to Egypt, in the garden, and "had no trouble making bezoars in sheaths [*tuniques*], exactly like the bezoar so prized by Pomet." Geoffroy made some more himself: "and it is not useless for the perfection of natural history that such frauds should be carefully exposed."[28]

Just as Geoffroy moved easily from the counter in the pharmacy, to the shelves of the *droguier*, to the laboratory and his natural history cabinet, and then across town to the academy and the botanical garden, the bezoar stones themselves were not confined to the pharmacopeia. They were commodities, curiosities, art objects (mounted in precious metals), and material for experiment. By the eighteenth century, the heyday of the bezoar stone as a repository of near-magical power as all-purpose antitoxin and panacea had certainly passed. A remarkable "curiosity," like the hairy stone that Pomet treasured, was subject to debunking in the laboratory or the garden. Yet the stones had hardly disappeared. Geoffroy accumulated specimens originating from every possible animal, including humans; merchants still imported them, sometimes selling them for substantial sums, and they continued to appear in prescriptions.

---

[28] Geoffroy, "Suite des observations," 202.

Geoffroy died in 1752, leaving a vast estate, including three houses, stocks, shares, and other financial instruments, the pharmacy business, an extensive library, and the collections, including all branches of natural history, anatomical specimens, porcelain, silver, and gems. He left the business and the cabinets to his son Claude-François, himself an apothecary and a collector, recently elected to the Academy; the will charged Bernard de Jussieu with making sure the collection stayed intact.[29] In spite of these testamentary precautions, the untimely death of the younger Geoffroy just one year later resulted in the dispersal of everything at auction in 1754.[30] In addition to the shells, which were at the height of their value at the time, one of the most noteworthy elements of the collection was the set of bezoars, "undoubtedly the most beautiful series one could see [anywhere]."[31] The auction catalogue cited Geoffroy's academic papers on the origins of bezoars: "All bezoars have a pit, or some hard matter at their center, which served as the basis of their formation. The material that produces the stone accumulates by layers around this core, as one can see in several bezoars in the series, which have been sliced open for the purpose."[32] The catalogue listed bezoars mounted in precious settings in mixed lots with stones from rhinos, porcupines, monkeys, pigs, and goats.[33] By the time of the sale, the bezoars had been separated from the *droguier*, sold as part of the pharmacy business. The enormous variety and the geographical reach of their origins earned them a place in the heterogeneous collection of naturalia and artworks.

At auction, the whole series of bezoar specimens passed into the hands of the wealthy fine art connoisseur Pedro Davila, himself a naturalist and a pillar of the collecting community in Paris in the 1750s.[34] Davila continued to add to Geoffroy's bezoars with specimens sent by his contacts in South America, before selling off his own collection in 1767. The sale catalogue of Davila's collection makes particular mention of the stones from the beaver's pouch, discussed by Geoffroy, other stones cut in half to show the concentric layers,

---

[29] This arrangement is mentioned in Grandjean de Fouchy, "Eloge de M. Geoffroy," HAS 1752, 163. On the will and inventory of the estate, see Sturdy, *Science and Social Status*, 334–9.

[30] Grandjean de Fouchy, "Eloge de M. Geoffroy," *Histoire de l'Académie royale des sciences* 1752, 153–164. See also "Avertissement," in *Catalogue raisonné des minéraux* .... (Paris, 1753). According to the catalogue, the large *droguier* had been sold previously, as part of the apothecary business (v).

[31] *Catalogue raisonné ... M. Geoffroy*, 79. Repeated in J.-B.-L. Romé de Lisle, *Catalogue systématique et raisonné des curiosités de la nature et de l'art, qui composent le cabinet de M. Davila*, 3 vols. (Paris: Briasson, 1767), 1: 505.

[32] *Catalogue raisonné ... M. Geoffroy*, 79.

[33] Ibid., 79–81. On porcupine bezoars, and especially two eighteenth-century specimens in the collection of the Royal Pharmaceutical Society Museum, see Christopher J. Duffin, "Porcupine Stones," *Pharmaceutical Historian* 43 (2013): 13–22.

[34] Davila claimed to have bought Geoffroy's whole set of bezoars. Romé de Lisle, *Catalogue systématique et raisonné ... M. Davila*, 1:505. On Davila, a native of Guayaquil, and his collection, see Juan Pimentel, "Across Nations and Ages: The Creole Collector and the Many Lives of the Megatherium," in *The Brokered World: Go-Betweens and Global Intelligence, 1770–1820*, ed. Simon Schaffer, et al. (Sagamore Beach, MA: Science History Publications, 2009), 321–54.

porcupine and monkey bezoars, several specimens from India mounted in gold and enamel, and Goa stones.

Jean-Etienne Guettard

The story of Geoffroy's bezoars shows how objects moved through collections, in and out of the laboratory and the pharmacy, from merchant ship to cabinet, from cabinet to Academy meeting room and botanical garden, into print, and eventually perhaps to the auction house. Along the way, they were used for a variety of purposes. For another angle on the manipulation of objects in and around scientific collections, I turn to Jean-Etienne Guettard (1715–86), a naturalist of the generation after Geoffroy. Guettard came from a modest background, trained in Paris as a botanist and a doctor, and divided his professional life between working for wealthy collectors and pursuing his own scientific work in botany, mineralogy, and related areas of natural history. Over a long career, he observed, described, and collected minerals (including fossils) in extensive travels across Europe, contributing to an ambitious mineralogical atlas.[35]

While studying medicine in the 1740s, Guettard lived in the household of René-Antoine de Réaumur, a powerful figure in the Paris Academy of Sciences and proprietor of one of the largest natural history collections in Paris at the time.[36] Réaumur's collection reflected and nourished his scientific work, including research on methods and apparatus for preserving and displaying specimens (see Fig. 2.2).[37] The collection grew continually for decades, through the influx of objects arriving from distant correspondents as well as those collected locally. As a curatorial assistant to this enterprise, and as a collector and observer in his own right, Guettard's work was essential to the life of Réaumur's collection. In turn, Réaumur's patronage paved the way for the young man's appointment to the academy in 1743. Although the full range of tasks he performed for Réaumur cannot be documented in detail, enough clues survive to give us some insight into the kinds of work involved in building and maintaining a natural history collection, and the research uses to which it might be put.

Where Geoffroy acquired many of his specimens from merchants, Réaumur did not patronize shops or auctions, relying on excursions to the countryside and the generosity of his friends and correspondents to fill his boxes and jars.

---

[35] For an overview of Guettard's life, work, and character, see Condorcet, "Eloge de M. Guettard," in *Histoire de l'Académie royale des sciences* (Paris, 1786), 47–62.

[36] On Réaumur's household as the training ground for young naturalists and future academicians, see Mary Terrall, "Masculine Knowledge, the Public Good, and the Scientific Household of Réaumur," *Osiris* 30 (2015), 182–201. On the collection, Terrall, *Catching Nature in the Act: Réaumur and the Practice of Natural History in the Eighteenth Century* (University of Chicago Press, 2014), Chap. 6.

[37] R.A. F. de Réaumur, "Moyens d'empêcher l'évaporation des liquides spiritueuses, dans lesquelles on veut conserver des productions de la nature de différens genres," *Mémoires de l'Académie royale des sciences* 1746, 483–538.

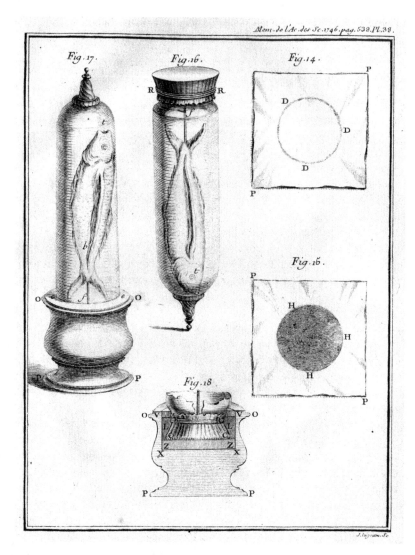

Fig. 2.2 Techniques and materials for preventing evaporation in sealed specimen jars, with mounted and preserved fish as finished display (R.-A. F. de Réaumur, "Moyens d'empêcher l'évaporation des liquides spiritueuses, dans lesquelles on veut conserver des productions de la nature de différens genres," *Mémoires de l'Académie royale des sciences* (Paris, 1746), plate 38.)

At any given time, several people were working for him on the research under way in and around the house; any of these assistants, artists, or servants would bring in specimens whenever opportunity arose. Excursions might be organized to collect caterpillars, say, or sea anemones, or freshwater hydra, or birds' nests, and any time Réaumur made a journey to the provinces or a trip across town, he picked things up along the way. Spider egg cases, chrysalises, birds' eggs, fossil shells, butterflies—anything that crossed his path might find its way to the laboratory or the collection or the academy's meeting room.

Guettard was often outdoors in the spring and summer months. At Réaumur's behest, he traveled to the Atlantic coast several times to gather and sketch and experiment on sea creatures of all kinds, shipping some of them back to Paris, where they ended up on the shelves of the cabinet.[38] "The season of herborizing and gathering insects has arrived, and for several months Mr. Guettard ... has done nothing but traverse the countryside in our vicinity," his patron wrote to a correspondent interested in seeing a particular fossil. "When he is sedentary again I will have him find [the fossil] for you in my collection."[39] In the so-called dead season, when collectors came indoors, Guettard worked on organizing and cataloguing the collection, showing visitors around and doing analyses in the laboratory.[40] He sent specimens out on loan, and unpacked shipments coming in. Some of the items he catalogued, like the large sequences of birds' eggs and nests, showed up later in his contributions to the Academy of Sciences.[41]

After leaving Réaumur's household, Guettard shifted his attention increasingly to mineralogy, and especially the geography of mineral distribution. On his excursions throughout France, he started his own collection of rocks and fossils. In 1748, these attracted the attention and admiration of Louis, Duke of Orléans, who invited Guettard to move, along with his mineral collection, up to the Abbey of Sainte-Geneviève, where the duke maintained a well-stocked chemical laboratory and a rapidly growing natural history collection. The two men shared a commitment to Jansenist theology as well as to natural history, and Guettard stayed with the duke as curator of his collections until the latter's death in 1752. The specimens the naturalist brought with him became the foundation of a rich geological cabinet, which grew rapidly through Guettard's efforts and the duke's far-reaching connections.[42]

Although neither fashionable nor wealthy, Guettard became intimately familiar with the natural history cabinets of the capital's elite, through his connections first to Réaumur and then to the Duke of Orléans. At his death, the duke left his valuable collection of naturalia to Guettard, but the latter

[38] On Guettard's experiments on the regeneration of sea stars, see Terrall, *Catching Nature*, 124–5. Some of his rough sketches survive in Guettard to Réaumur, 12 July 1745, Archives de l'Académie des Sciences (Paris), dossier Guettard.

[39] Réaumur to Louis Bourguet, 29 July 1741, Bibliothèque publique et universitaire, Neufchâtel, Ms. 1278.

[40] Guettard's draft inventory of Réaumur's collection in Bibliothèque centrale du Muséum d'histoire naturelle (Paris), Ms. 1929 (iii).

[41] J.E. Guettard, "Mémoire sur les nids des oiseaux," *Nouvelle collection de mémoires sur différentes parties intéressantes des sciences et arts*, 3 vols. (Paris: Lamy, 1786), 1: 324–418. This paper was read to the academy in the 1760s, but not printed in the journal.

[42] On the invitation to join the duke at the Abbey of Sainte-Geneviève, see Guettard, "La collection des corps marins fossiles ...," (autograph ms.), Bibliothèque centrale du Muséum d'histoire naturelle (Paris), Ms. 323, f. 89. Condorcet mentions their shared religious views, "Eloge de M. Guettard," 57.

ceded it to his patron's son Louis-Philippe, the new duke, in exchange for a stipend and lodgings in the Palais Royal. Guettard continued as curator of the collection, with the freedom to leave Paris on long geological expeditions from time to time.[43] He peppered his many academic papers with descriptions of and reflections on the rocks, crystals, fossils, and mineral specimens sent to the duke's collection, witnessed in his own travels, or collected in the field.[44] With the financial support of his patrons and the academy, he accumulated not only specimens but a large archive of drawings and engravings of many of these objects. Towards the end of his life, he remarked ruefully that he had accumulated more images than he knew what to do with: "I never stopped having drawings and engravings made of the many items of natural history that came into my hands."[45]

Much of Guettard's mineralogical work was dedicated to the geography of rocks, rock formations, mines and minerals, and fossils.[46] Large-scale patterns of deposits, represented on mineral maps by chemical symbols and "bands" of similar rocks, were juxtaposed with close examination of individual specimens, including the rare and unusual objects that collectors valued. Wherever he traveled, he combined field observations with visits to collections. Here I will pick out just a few of the things he came across, objects that mediated relations between collectors, and between local meanings and academic science. Tracking specimens leads us to the people who lived with them, and the significance they were given in different contexts.

In 1760 Guettard traveled through eastern France and Alsace, continuing up the Rhine valley through Germany and Austria, and then east to Warsaw.[47] Mapping and inventorying rock formations and soil types in quarries, riverbeds, mines, and cliff faces, he sought out collectors and their cabinets wherever he could, from provincial manor houses to the emperor's collection in Vienna. One of his first stops was the château at Agey, near Dijon, the home of Mme Fuligny-Damas, countess of Rochechouart. The widowed countess had transformed her estate into a monument to contemporary natural history and natural philosophy. Enticing Guettard to add the château to his itinerary, she alerted him to the unique features, as well as the extent, of her collections: "No one before me, to my knowledge, has exploited the quarries of her region to form a useful collection, pleasing to the eye, and presenting the treasures of the

---

[43] Condorcet, "Eloge de M. Guettard," 57.

[44] See, for example, Guettard, "Mémoire sur plusieurs morceaux d'histoire naturelle, tirés du cabinet de S.A.S. M. le duc d'Orléans," *Mémoires de l'Académie royale des sciences* 1753, 369–400.

[45] Guettard, *Nouvelle collection de mémoires*, 1786, vol. 3, 413.

[46] Condorcet called this style of mineralogy "*geographie naturelle*" by analogy to *histoire naturelle*. Condorcet, "Eloge de M. Guettard," 53.

[47] Map of the route to and from Poland, with notations of characteristic rock formations in Guettard, "Observations minéralogiques faites en France et en Allemagne: Seconde partie," *Mémoires de l'Académie royale des sciences* 1763, following p. 228.

provinces, with which I have paved the mineral cabinet."[48] The countess welcomed Guettard enthusiastically, giving him the run of her collections, and he worked there intently for some days. Reporting back to one of his Parisian correspondents, the wealthy collector Madame du Boisjourdain, Guettard called Agey the "most interesting [*curieux*] and the most instructive" of the cabinets he visited en route to Warsaw. He particularly mentioned the stone floor tiled with polished octagons that showed off the striking variations in the region's marble, much of it filled with a profusion of marine fossils. Many more stones, mineral ores, and fossils filled the shelves and drawers in the room, and he went on to note madrepores, crystals, sands and soils, and a shell collection "that would not be out of place in Paris."[49]

In the cabinet so thoughtfully arranged for both work and pleasure, Guettard encountered more variety, and more remarkable individual specimens, than he could possibly have found in a few days in the field. The marble floor, laid out for visual effect, gave him an inventory of local marbles, since the countess had recorded the provenance of each piece of stone. From his detailed description of each type, it becomes clear that Guettard spent a good deal of time on hands and knees, examining the marble with his lens, and making notes on the characteristic fossils in each tile. Eventually, when he got back to Paris, he reported to the academy on some of the highlights of his tour, including the countess's prized floor.[50] Cataloging the Burgundian marbles, he disregarded the location of the 54 different kinds in the elegant patterned floor and grouped them instead according to the types of fossil they contained: "belemnite marble," "oolitic marble," "starry marble," and the like. The polished marble floor was a rarity, meant to be admired; it also, as the countess recognized, fitted nicely into Guettard's project to map rock formations and fossil deposits. For the naturalist, it presented a series of related specimens, valuable for its completeness as well as for its singularity and its beauty, much like the series of bezoars in Geoffroy's collection—and also like a "beautiful" set of Burgundian fossils the countess sent as a gift to the duke's cabinet, where Guettard could study them at his leisure.[51]

Most such sequences incorporated items that collectors delighted in handling and comparing. Guettard made a point of having a drawing made of one such object in Agey, a petrified sea star he picked out as the most striking single item in the countess's impressive fossil collection. This object had to be handled to be appreciated. The fossil had been embedded in a piece of limestone; the stone had fortuitously broken open "in such a way that the star stands out in

[48] Rochechouart to Guettard, 8 September 1759, Bibliothèque municipale de Clermont-Ferrand, Ms. 339, f. 74–5.

[49] "Extrait d'une lettre écrite par M. Guettard à Mad. du Boisjourdain au sujet du cabinet de Madame la comtesse de Rochechouart," 4 July 1760 (from Warsaw). Rochechouart papers, Bibliothèque municipale de Bourg-en-Bresse, Ms. E. 409.

[50] Guettard, "Observations minéralogiques faites en France et en Allemagne: Première partie," *Mémoires de l'Académie royale des sciences* 1763, 144.

[51] Ibid., 143.

relief on one piece and its impression is hollowed out in the other." The form of the animal was perfectly preserved in stone. On the three-dimensional relief, "one can easily distinguish the scaly parts, which have turned into a white calcite [*spath*], with a yellowish tinge on the surface; and the mouth, which these animals have in the center of their body, is very distinct, as are the little points or feet around the borders of the five large rays [of the star]."[52]

The Countess of Rochechouart's sea star, described to the Paris Academy and represented in an engraved plate, stood in for the many unusual specimens Guettard examined in his travels (see Fig. 2.3). The picture does not fully capture the peculiarities described in the text; only by manipulating it could the two halves be fitted together, and only close inspection would reveal the texture and color variations on the surface. The other singular object depicted on the same plate, a petrified pine cone, was owned by a different collector, one M. Moll in Vienna. This kind of petrified plant material, much of it found locally in Vienna and the surrounding region, was one of Moll's specialties. He showed his visitor an impressive variety of different kinds of "petrified or agatified" wood, sliced thinly and polished, under a microscope, where the distinctive internal structure was clearly visible and identifiable.[53] The pine cone, complete in every detail and slightly compressed on one side, had turned into metallic pyrite rather than agate, something Guettard had not previously seen. In the plate, he juxtaposed these two fossil highlights from his journey, from different collections, thus bringing the objects to his colleagues in Paris, and to envious collectors who might read the journal.

Guettard spent his life as a naturalist—whether working with plants, marine animals, fossils, or rocks—moving between collections and field, examining, transporting, discussing, describing, and organizing objects. His papers single out specific things like the pine cone or the sea star as rarities, but then put them in relation to other objects, as they might have been arranged in an ideal cabinet formed from all the collections Guettard knew. His oeuvre—by no means systematic, but voluminous—could be seen as a virtual collection drawing on all the others, including the ones Guettard himself supervised. This synthesis, although never completely comprehensive, was only made possible by the dispersed community of people of all social ranks who made their specimens available to Guettard to be examined by whatever means necessary, and then described, drawn, and engraved. These collectors included wealthy ladies (Mme de Bandeville, Mme de Courtagnon, Mme de Boisjourdain), aristocrats (the two dukes Guettard worked for, the Countess of Rochechouart), fellow naturalists (Moll, Réaumur), and many others, including provincial apothecaries and physicians, many of them named in print along with their specimens.

[52] Ibid., 143–44; he described the same fossil to Mme du Boisjourdain as one of the most remarkable pieces in the Agey cabinet.

[53] For the pine cone, see Guettard, "Observations minéralogiques: seconde partie," 220–221. The drawing was made by Moll's son and given to Guettard during his visit, with Moll's detailed description of it.

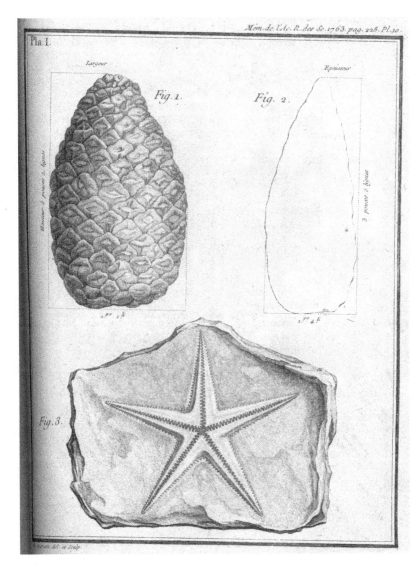

Fig. 2.3 Petrified pine cone, with measurements, and fossil sea star (J.-E. Guettard, "Observations minéralogiques faites en France et en Allemagne," Mémoires de l'Académie royale des sciences (Paris, 1753), plate 10.)

Guettard often started with objects close at hand in the duke's rich collection, and brought in related items as appropriate. A study of sponges, for instance, drew on materials from at least five different Paris collections. In Fig. 2.4, we see specimens from Mme de Bandeville's collection: the cylindrical "*trage*" arranged in a loop to show its unusual length, and two others where the sponge grew on a hard piece of coral or other accretion. The peculiar hybrid look of

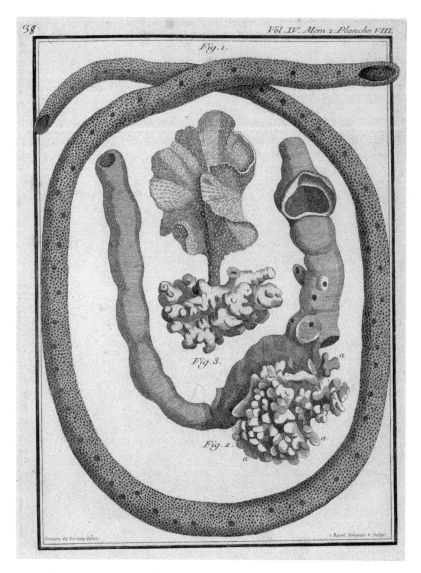

Fig. 2.4 Sponges from the collection of Mme de Bandeville J.-E. Guettard, Nouvelle collection de mémoires sur différentes parties intéressantes des sciences et arts, 3 vols. (Paris, 1786), vol. 1, Mem. 2, Plate 8. Permission to publish granted by University of Strasbourg, Service Commun de la Documentation (France)

the specimen labeled "Fig. 2.2" in this plate initially made Guettard suspect it had been doctored by an unscrupulous merchant, but "having examined it with care, and even with a magnifying lens, it was apparent that art had played no part in its shape."[54]

[54] Guettard, *Nouvelle collection de mémoires*, 3 vols. (Paris, 1786), 1: 146.

Through these few examples we have seen the way in which natural history collections, whatever the motivations and interests and predilections of their owners, were linked in a variety of ways, through time and across space. Individual objects provide clues to these dynamic connections, as do the movements and actions of the people who handled them. When Chatwin's fictional porcelain collector referred to giving life to his figurines with his touch, he was evoking the intense engagement of the senses with these objects of desire. The collections I have looked at here took on a sort of life as well, under the eyes and hands of naturalists and connoisseurs. Many of these eighteenth-century naturalists had the same kind of intimate familiarity with their specimens as Utz had with his porcelain pieces. For collectors like Geoffroy and Guettard, this provided a foundation for their scientific work, and for the complex social and patronage relations that made the culture of collecting thrive.

CHAPTER 3

Curious Work

Mary M. Brooks

Affluent girls and women in seventeenth-century England produced an exuberant, uniquely English embroidery called 'curious work' to distinguish it from the 'plain work' learnt by those who earned their living through the needle. Such embroidery was a gendered practice, a performative process that was a moral act suitable for the obedient daughter of the socially ambitious and the Christian woman. The social value created by making was as important as the made thing, challenging our assumptions about the importance of the surviving things.

Evidence of a feminized material culture, these embroideries depict biblical and classical narratives, allegorical figures or pastoral scenes with realistic or fantastical flora and fauna. The designs often draw on European print traditions such as Gerard de Jode's *Thesaurus Sacrarum Historiarum Veteris Testamenti* (Antwerp, 1585) and seem to have been transferred from print to textile by professional, probably male, pattern drawers, although the embroideries themselves fall outside formal art historical canons. Many survive as flat panels. Others were mounted professionally as boxes or mirror frames. Texture and colour were clearly important. These embroideries may be worked in smooth silk or glittering metal threads with three-dimensional motifs, enhanced by sequins, pearls, corals and garnets. The use of hair and iridescent feathers further links the natural and the made. There can be a compressed grandeur and tension in the sculptural figures clad in swirling garments, but there are also contradictory elements of homegeneity and variance. The use of source prints for the figures, flora and fauna means that motifs are frequently repeated, but in different com-

M.M. Brooks (✉)
Department of Archaeology, Durham University, Durham, UK
e-mail: mary.brooks@durham.ac.uk

© The Author(s) 2016
A. Craciun, S. Schaffer (eds.), *The Material Cultures of Enlightenment Arts and Sciences*, Palgrave Studies in the Enlightenment, Romanticism and the Cultures of Print, DOI 10.1057/978-1-137-44379-3_3

Fig. 3.1 WA.OA414 Anonymous, English—Embroidered picture: *The Sacrifice of Isaac*, dated 1673, © Ashmolean Museum, University of Oxford

binations. Variation comes from the highly individual stitched interpretations where contemporaries perceived 'fancy'—originality and individuality—to lie.

Peter Mundy's 1634 description of the Tradescant's collection of natural curiosities of 'beasts, fowle, fishes, serpents, wormes … pretious stones … a little garden with divers outlandish herbes and flowers …'[1] could be describing one of these embroideries. Viewing the embroideries from the perspective of cabinets of curiosities removes them from comparison (inevitably as failures) with pictorial traditions. Although less systematic or encyclopedic, they share a common interest in exotic materials from around the world and in interlinking the natural and the made. From this perspective, their contemporary name, 'curious works', takes on a new resonance.

Radiography provides a different way of 'seeing' things. The Biblical story of the sacrifice of Isaac was a frequently embroidered story, conveying the virtues of obedience to parental authority and of faith in divine love. The Ashmolean Museum's version of *The Sacrifice of Isaac* has some highly dimensional elements (Fig. 3.1). Examining the radiographs of the sculptural birds revealed a so far unique feature: their beaks are actual birds' beaks, probably

[1] P. Mundy, *The Travels of Peter Mundy in Europe and Asia, 1608–1667* (London: Hakluyt Society, 1919), III (1), p. 3.

from either finches or linnets. Where did these beaks come from? Were they from the kitchen? Gervase Markham's *Hunger's Prevention* (1621) describes how to catch and prepare wild birds for the table and numerous recipes gave instructions on their cooking.[2] Or did the embroiderer memorialize her pet birds in her work? Nature and artifice are closely linked here, raising further questions about how to read the meanings in both the making and the made of 'curious work'.

Acknowledgements Mark Norman, Head of Conservation, The Ashmolean Museum, Oxford, for radiography and Dr Sonia O'Connor, University of Bradford, for radiographic interpretation.

---

[2] G. Markham, *Hunger's Prevention or the Whole Art of Fowling* ... (London: A[ugustine] Math[ewes] for Anne Helme and Thomas Langley, 1621) and, for example, recipes in *The Whole Duty of a Woman* (London: J. Gwillim, 1696).

CHAPTER 4

The Lives of Mrs Delany's Paper Plants

Kim Sloan

In October 1772, Mary Delany wrote to her niece that she had invented a new way of imitating flowers. Sitting in her bedroom at Bulstrode, she had noticed the similarity between a geranium and a piece of bright scarlet paper she had on her table. She cut the shapes of the flower out of the paper and used green paper for the leaves and stalk, creating a picture of the geranium; when the Duchess of Portland entered the room she mistook the paper petals for real ones, exclaiming: 'What are you doing with the geranium?'[1] This apocryphal story serves as a naissance for the lives of Mrs Delany's paper plants, so celebrated in her lifetime that they merited a place in Erasmus Darwin's *The Loves of the Flowers*, part of his epic poem *The Botanic Garden* (1789–91)[2]:

> So now DELANY forms her mimic bowers,
> Her paper foliage, and her silken flowers;
> Her virgin train the tender scissars ply,
> Vein the green leaf, the purple petal dye:

Although the picture of a geranium (BM 1897,0505.529*) was inscribed by Mrs Delany as her first sample, another collage, of green tea (Fig. 4.1), is actually

---

[1] Related in Mark Laird and Alicia Weisberg-Roberts (eds.), *Mrs Delany & Her Circle* (New Haven and London, 2009), p. 225, citing passage from Llanover, Lady Augusta Waddington Hall (ed.), *The Autobiography and Correspondence of Mary Granville, Mrs Delany* (London, 1861–2; 6 vols in 2 series), ser. II, vol. 2: 215; see also Ruth Hayden, *Mrs Delany and Her Flower Collages*, 2nd ed. (London: British Museum, 1992).

[2] Cited in 'Introduction', Laird & Weisberg-Roberts, *Mrs Delany*, 2009, p. 13.

K. Sloan (✉)
Department of Prints and Drawings, British Museum, London, UK
e-mail: ksloan@britishmuseum.org

© The Author(s) 2016
A. Craciun, S. Schaffer (eds.), *The Material Cultures of Enlightenment Arts and Sciences*, Palgrave Studies in the Enlightenment, Romanticism and the Cultures of Print, DOI 10.1057/978-1-137-44379-3_4

Fig. 4.1   Mary Delany, *Thea Viridis (Polyandria Monogynia)*, from an album (Vol. IX, 55); Green Tea. 1771. Collage of coloured papers, with bodycolour and watercolour, on black ink background. 322 × 211 mm (1897,0505.856). The *Flora Delanica* were nearly 1000 cut-paper collages of plants created by Mary Delany (1700–88) between 1771 and 1782, presented in ten albums to the British Museum by her descendant Lady Llanover in 1897 (register numbers 1897,0505.1 to 974)

inscribed on the verso with an earlier date, '10 Novr. 1771'. Made of hundreds of tiny pieces of cut paper, the flowers in Mrs Delany's *hortus siccus*, as she herself termed the collection, are more tactile than the watercolour on paper that they resemble from a distance; it is only when one handles them that their real make-up becomes apparent. Often incorporating an actual leaf or flower, pressed and dried as in a real herbarium, Mrs Delany glued the coloured pieces of paper and plant onto black ink backgrounds, appended their Linnaean and common names on a label and affixed her monogram 'MD' cut in red paper to a corner; she inscribed the date, place of execution, name of the donor of the plant and its number in her sequence in pen and ink on the verso. At some point a grey paper border was added to most of them, to enable them to be handled and turned over without damaging the original sheet. They were carefully organized alphabetically into ten albums, loosely inserted between pages with tissue, each volume provided with a list. Like a herbarium, they lived on bookshelves and were viewed by turning the pages of the albums. In the 1980s, a selection was mounted in the typical cream mounts of the British Museum's Prints and Drawings (P&D) Department for an exhibition.

   Pilgrimages are made to the P&D Study Room by those wishing to view 'the Mrs Delanys' in person, to appreciate the intricacy of the technique and accuracy of the recreation of the original plants. These visitors only see the paper collages in the cream mounts, unaware of the grey borders, the versos or the albums. Others see them through glass frames or in cases in exhibitions, but most people view them reproduced in books, where invariably the image is cropped to the edge of the black sheet alone, and where the delicate three-dimensional quality of the original is flattened to printer's ink and the colour a vague approximation of the original—far removed in time and space from the original plant, the act of cutting paper, or that of turning the pages of an album.

CHAPTER 5

A Pathological Pot

Samuel J.M.M. Alberti

To most of us, this is a strange-looking lump of bleached matter, recognizably organic, suspended in an unfamiliar receptacle. But to any pathologist, anatomist or surgeon of a certain age, this object is unmistakably a fluid-preserved morbid specimen: a *pathological pot*. At the core of this thing is the fragment of a human being. It was once a person.

Like many other exhibits in this volume, it has only survived since its eighteenth-century origins because it has been frozen in time in a museum collection. Museums are full of things-that-were-once-alive: taxidermy, herbaria, even fossils. This pot belongs to a sub-category, human remains, that was afforded particular significance. These were to be found in cabinets of curiosity, and later in specialized natural history, anatomy and Egyptology collections. It is likely that this fragment was once part of 'Mrs. P—', a London patient of the Scottish physician Maxwell Garthshore.[1] She succumbed to this carcinoma of the oesophagus in 1783 at the age of 52, and Garthshore asked the surgeon–anatomist John Hunter to subject her corpse to a post-mortem examination.

Hunter removed the lower portion of Mrs P's trachea and, noting the severe ulceration, he preserved her oesophagus with alcohol in a glass jar within his

---

[1] M. Garthshore, 'A Case of Difficult Deglutition Occasioned by an Ulcer in the Oesophagus, with an Account of the Appearances on Dissection', *Medical Communications* 1 (1784), 242–55; L.W. Proger, *Descriptive Catalogue of the Pathological Series in the Hunterian Museum of the Royal College of Surgeons of England*, 2 vols. (Edinburgh: Livingstone, 1966–72); S.J.M.M. Alberti, *Morbid Curiosities: Medical Museums in Nineteenth-Century Britain* (Oxford: Oxford University Press, 2011); S.D.J. Chaplin, 'John Hunter and the "Museum Oeconomy"', 1750–1800 (Ph.D. thesis, King's College London, 2009).

S.J.M.M. Alberti (✉)
National Museums Scotland, Edinburgh, UK
e-mail: s.alberti@nms.ac.uk

© The Author(s) 2016
A. Craciun, S. Schaffer (eds.), *The Material Cultures of Enlightenment Arts and Sciences*, Palgrave Studies in the Enlightenment, Romanticism and the Cultures of Print, DOI 10.1057/978-1-137-44379-3_5

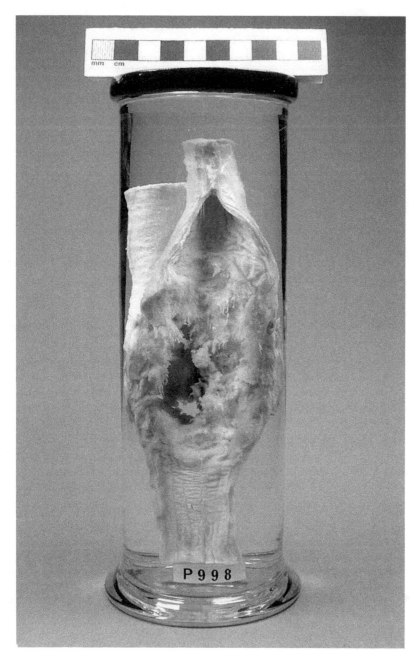

Fig. 5.1   Object RCSHC/P 998: ulcerated oesophagus of 'Mrs P' preserved in alcohol
in a glass jar. Hunterian Museum at the Royal College of Surgeons

14,000-strong collection in his home in central London. There it remained, beyond Hunter's death a decade later, until his collection was opened at the core of the Royal College of Surgeons' Museum on Lincoln's Inn Fields, where it remains to this day. At the turn of the millennium the object was catalogued as RCSHC/P 998: Royal College of Surgeons Hunterian Collection/pathological specimen 998.

Slowing down time, the aim of museum preservation, requires ongoing work. The original pitch cover has been replaced with a glass lid and the fluid has been changed many times. This object is then not only conceptually hybrid (person/thing, subject/object), but also physically hybrid. This specimen is now as much preservative as it is tissue, its glass jar a characteristic part of the overall composite. There is actually little left that was Mrs P and this specimen is barely recognizable as part of a body. It is also rather small: the jar is 230 mm by 80 mm, and the great majority of specimens in medical collections are even smaller. It is portable (if delicate), and can be handled, lifted, studied and moved around.

Over the course of its after-life, 'she' became 'it', representative not of *her* story, but rather of gullet cancer. Hunter materialized her illness, generating a physical thing to represent an intangible disease concept. No longer a singular person, her throat epitomized the disease. Parts of the body of one (former) person like this gullet were displayed alongside similar parts from other bodies. In Hunter's collection this object is one of tens of thousands of fragments of illness: from the era of the *Encyclopédie*, it became one page in a three-dimensional encyclopedia of disease.

CHAPTER 6

The Seeds of Disaster:
Relics of La Pérouse

Adriana Craciun

After more than 200 years of searches for the shipwrecks of the legendary La Pérouse expedition, in 2011 it seemed that survivors had been located at last. In 1785, Jean François de Galaup, Comte de La Pérouse, sailed with an army of naturalists, artists, gardeners, and astronomers on a scientific circumnavigation to rival that of the three voyages by James Cook. La Pérouse, his ships the *Boussole* and *Astrolabe*, and all the crew disappeared into the uncharted Pacific three years later. The subject of ongoing searches and intense speculation, La Pérouse's shipwreck was first located in the 1820s on the reef of Vanikoro in the Solomon Islands. Since then, hundreds of objects recovered from the wreck have been returned to France. In 2003 the Association Solomon repatriated to France skeletal remains believed to be a crewmember's, which in June 2011 were reinterred beneath a monument to "L'inconnu du Vanikoro" in the grounds of the château de Brest.

However, the Unknown of Vanikoro was overshadowed by a recovered passenger with hopes of an unprecedented restoration: *Banksia*. *Banksia* is the genus of an Australian tree named for Joseph Banks, the president of the Royal Society and naturalist companion of Cook on his first Pacific voyage. The *Banksia* seeds in question were collected by La Pérouse's naturalists in Botany Bay, the expedition's last known stop before disappearing. The seeds were salvaged in 1986 by La Pérouse relic hunters, and archived in the museum of Nouméa in French New Caledonia. In December 2010, six *Banksia* seeds completed their voyage back to Brest, 222 years after they set sail.

La Pérouse's *Banksia* seeds were the subject of a unique experiment in the Conservatoire botanique national de Brest in 2012. Working with the biotech

A. Craciun (✉)
Department of English, University of California, Riverside, CA, USA
e-mail: adrianac@ucr.edu

© The Author(s) 2016
A. Craciun, S. Schaffer (eds.), *The Material Cultures of Enlightenment Arts and Sciences*, Palgrave Studies in the Enlightenment, Romanticism and the Cultures of Print, DOI 10.1057/978-1-137-44379-3_6

company Vegenov Bretagne Biotechnologies Végétales and with a grant from the Australian government, the Conservatoire attempted to regenerate six *Banksia* seeds recovered from the *Boussole*. This experiment was designed effectively to locate (botanical) survivors of France's most famous shipwreck, allowing the expedition to complete its circumnavigation.

THE ENGLISH LA PÉROUSE

I became interested in the ongoing searches for La Pérouse in my research on the power of past Arctic disasters (as opposed to new discoveries) to draw future European voyagers across three centuries. I had completed research on the best-known British Arctic disaster, that of John Franklin in 1845, who had himself in the past retraced earlier Arctic disasters, and whose disappearance had drawn dozens of international rescue and salvage efforts, from 1850 to 2014.[1] Shipwreck and disaster, in the Arctic and elsewhere, have a long history of popular appeal, in all manner of visual, literary, and dramatic forms. What was new, and unstudied, in the case of the Franklin disaster and its long international legacy was the central importance of the material relics of the disaster, not only to the official searchers, but to a wide range of public debates over Franklin's significance for British (and now Canadian) national identity, history, and heritage.

From 1848 onwards British and US searchers collected thousands of objects from dozens of Franklin disaster sites across the Canadian Arctic: buttons, scraps of clothing, tin cans, scientific instruments, broken tools, illegible books, a handful of dubious bones, objects that were immediately referred to as the "Franklin relics." These objects were exhibited for decades in prestigious government institutions like the British Museum, the United Services Institution in London's Whitehall, and Sir Christopher Wren's magnificent Painted Chapel in Greenwich, where some of Franklin's relics shared the same central room as Admiral Lord Nelson's coat from the battle of Trafalgar. In 2014 the Canadian government, after six years of intensive searching, located one of the Franklin ships, making international headlines and launching an intensely nationalistic debate about the nature of Canadian Arctic identity and heritage.

Today, Franklin often appears as a singular figure in the international history of disaster, enjoying an unmatched devotion that continues to fund national efforts to search for, collect, and now preserve more relics and remains. Yet in the nineteenth century, while Franklin's relics shared the same displays as those of England's greatest naval heroes, Nelson and Cook, it was La Pérouse who was considered Franklin's closest companion in disaster. Franklin's allies looked to the example of La Pérouse's ardent international searchers, his relic displays, his grieving widow, and the carefully crafted "mystery" surrounding him as models for their own efforts. Franklin was the English La Pérouse.

---

[1] A. Craciun, 'The Franklin Mystery', *Literary Review of Canada* (May 2012), 3–5.

Working on the changing exhibitions and representations of the "Franklin relics," I became interested in how this connection between La Pérouse and Franklin, two "singular" national heroes whose disappearances remained a "mystery" for so long, was made possible by the wealth of material relics that were recovered, exhibited, and represented from both disasters. In short, I was interested in how the nineteenth-century age of the public museum made possible the open-ended recuperation, the circling of the "great tombless death" described by Michel de Certeau,[2] of both La Pérouse and Franklin.

The "Franklin relics" and their display differed in important respects from those of La Pérouse, which I will briefly mention before moving on to La Pérouse himself. First, the objects recovered from the Arctic were usually small personal items and fragments preserved in ice; there were few large pieces of iron or timber (until 2014). Consequently, the London displays were in small cases, allowing affective, intimate responses from spectators, and resembling on one level Victorian grief culture and its cult of personal mementos. Second, the Franklin objects posed a series of conundrums: they often had legible inscriptions, such as heraldic crests or commercial brand names, and these inscriptions were readily visible in visual representations like the *Illustrated London News*'s engravings and the more lavish lithographs produced by professional artists.[3] However, only one legible document has ever been recovered from the wreckage to this day, the one-page "Victory Point" record noting Franklin's death and the abandonment of the ships. The overwhelming abundance of material objects, and their visible associations with trade, frustrated Victorians who struggled to assemble these piles of broken, ordinary, commercial objects from the present, in meaningful ways that evoked religious, scientific, and patriotic value. Third, many of the Franklin objects collected and exhibited in London had been reauthored by Inuit, a fact noted by Franklin searchers but one that complicated their efforts at classification in revealing ways (along the continuum of alien/native, craft/science, metropolitan/peripheral, civilized/savage) that have yet to be incorporated into our current discussions of the interrelations of nineteenth-century museum culture, anthropology, and exploration.

Most of these distinctive features of the Franklin searches and relics are not present in the case of La Pérouse, but placing the cult of Franklin in relationship to that of La Pérouse, instead of relating both to Cook in the eighteenth century, can help us see how a public fascination with disaster relics helped shape a distinctly nineteenth-century cult of the explorer.[4] The Franklin relics are unique in their widely disseminated images and impact on subsequent

---

[2] M. de Certeau, 'Writing the Sea', *Heterologies: Discourse on the Other*, trans. Brian Massumi (Minneapolis: Minnesota University Press, 1986), 142.

[3] A. Craciun, 'The Franklin Relics in the Arctic Archive', *Victorian Literature and Culture* 42.1 (2014), 1–30.

[4] On the importance of relics for explorer figures, see F. Driver, *Geography Militant: Cultures of Exploration and Empire* (Oxford: Blackwell, 2001). On the break between this and earlier mechanisms for distinguishing agents of exploration, see A. Craciun, 'What is an Explorer?', *Eighteenth-Century Studies* 45.1 (2011), 29–51.

exploration history, but they share with La Pérouse's relics a nineteenth-century configuration as monuments to contested national ideals that also reveal the overshadowing of discovery by disaster.

SEARCHING FOR LA PÉROUSE: CIRCLING THE VOID

The Brest Conservatoire's attempt to complete the mission of La Pérouse's lost ships with a cycle of accumulation at such a great temporal distance is unique. *Banksia*'s regeneration represents an imaginative attempt at a unique kind of closure, and a validation of Bruno Latour's description of "science in action" as the ability "to act at a distance on unfamiliar events, places and people." As an extension of the long-range scientific networks of which La Pérouse was a prime example, the collaboration between the Conservatoire, the biotech company Vegenov, the French and Australian governments, and the Museum of Nouméa (New Caledonia) extends Enlightenment imperial science's ability to act at a distance in both space and time.

In *Science in Action*, Latour famously used the La Pérouse expedition as his paradigmatic example of how centers of calculation initiate cycles of accumulation of "immutable mobiles" transferred over vast distances in space. Acting at a distance on "events, objects, and people," writes Latour, requires that science render these unfamiliar things mobile, stable, and combinable, so that "they can be accumulated, aggregated, or shuffled like a pack of cards."[5] Here, Latour followed quite closely La Pérouse's own idealized vision of what his voyage would accomplish, as La Pérouse described the efforts of his naturalist the Chevalier de Lamanon:

> his desire to see everything, to combine everything, to describe everything had no bounds other than those imposed by nature herself; clouds, air, soil, stones, minerals, all these were brought into his naturalist's vast programme.[6]

The sole survivor of the La Pérouse expedition, Barthélemy de Lesseps, had disembarked in Kamchatka with copies of the expedition's journals, charts, and

---

[5] B. Latour, *Science in Action* (Cambridge: Harvard University Press, 1987) 223. Since the publication of *Science in Action*, numerous critiques have been published of Latour's overemphasis on the immutability characterizing his "mobiles" and "centres of calculation." An excellent response in this regard is Michael Bravo's essay on the La Pérouse incident that Latour uses as his paradigmatic example of the written document as the immutable mobile (the map drawn in the sand at Sakhalin and then transformed into written data by the French), detailing how Latour's account minimizes oral and ethnographic encounter (Bravo, 'Ethnographic Navigation and the Geographical Gift', in C. Withers and D. Livingstone (eds.), *Geography and Enlightenment* (Chicago: Chicago University Press, 1999), 199–235). In *Do Glaciers Listen? Local Knowledge, Colonial Encounters and Social Imagination* (Vancouver: University of British Columbia Press, 2005), Julie Cruikshank also examines the relationship of La Perouse's writings to oral indigenous accounts.

[6] La Pérouse, Preface, *The Journal of Jean-François de Galaup de la Pérouse 1785–1788*, trans. and ed. John Dunmore, 2 vols. (London: Hakluyt Society, 1994–1995), vol. 1, 4.

observations up to that point; for over a year he trekked across Siberia to return these combinable, immutable forms of knowledge to Paris, arriving as if from the dead and demonstrating in Latour's account the significance of the material and mundane networks of science in producing knowledge as "abstraction" and "theory."

Yet the singularity of La Pérouse's example is due not just to the miraculous reappearance of de Lesseps and his immutable mobiles, but also to the multiple cycles of accumulation repeated throughout the nineteenth and twentieth centuries by relic hunters. These relic hunting expeditions retraced La Pérouse's voyage and remained a part of French cultural memory for 200 years, amplifying and reinscribing his initial scientific circuit as one also encompassing heterogeneous interests like *ancien régime* nostalgia, expatriate pilgrimage, and disaster tourism. In short, it is curious that Le Pérouse served as Latour's paradigmatic example of Enlightenment science at a distance, when the real source of his uniqueness was the unprecedented nineteenth-century transformation of his eighteenth-century disaster into the occasion for an ongoing cycle of recuperations.

French searches in the revolutionary era, by Bruni d'Entrecasteaux and Jacques de la Billardière, had failed to locate La Pérouse's wreck.[7] However, in 1826 an East India Company (EIC) agent and sandalwood trader, Peter Dillon, came across a silver French sword guard and spoon in the possession of a Tikopia islander who had obtained it from a remote island in the Solomon Islands, Vanikoro. Dillon believed it to be from La Pérouse's ship and persuaded the EIC to fund a search expedition with him in command. Like Franklin's searchers 25 years later, Dillon relied on indigenous oral accounts and collectors for his discoveries, buying hundreds of objects from Vanikoro, Tikopia, and nearby islands and establishing the approximate location of the wrecks. Dillon returned triumphantly not only with numerous objects from the lost ships, including a ship's bell, but with oral accounts of the final days of the La Pérouse survivors. These included rumors that many of the French had died in violent struggle with Vanikoro islanders after the wreck, and that some had escaped and sailed away in a small boat. Dillon did not suggest that the La Pérouse survivors were cannibalized by Vanikoro islanders, but his *Narrative* began with a controversial account of his own close escape in Fiji, where he described in graphic detail witnessing a supposed "cannibal feast" of which he nearly became a part.[8]

---

[7] Mathew Flinders had also tried to locate La Perouse's ships in August 1803, on his voyage around Australia (*A Voyage to Terra Australis,* 2 vols. (London: 1814), vol. 2, 172).

[8] Dillon's description of the cannibal feast is a seminal account in nineteenth-century European visions of South Pacific cannibalism; see G. Obeyesekere, 'Narratives of the Self: Chevalier Peter Dillon's Fijian Cannibal Adventures', in B. Creed and J. Hoorn (eds.), *Body Trade: Captivity, Cannibalism and Colonialism in the Pacific* (London: Routledge), 69–111). The most thorough biography of Dillon remains James Davidson's *Peter Dillon of Vanikoro: Chevalier of the South Seas* (Oxford: Oxford University Press, 1975).

On his long voyage from Vanikoro to Paris, Dillon displayed La Pérouse objects publicly aboard his ship the *Research* and in institutional settings like those of the Asiatic Society and the East India Company. His discoveries were reported widely in the colonial and metropolitan press (described sometimes as objects, articles, vestiges, and most often as "relics"), although not visually reproduced. According to the *Sydney Gazette*, his initial display of the relics in Sydney was "daily thronged with visitors who are laudably anxious to witness and examine those remains of the wreck."[9] A lengthy account of Dillon's search and discovery, including a long inventory and evaluation of the objects he recovered, was published in *The Asiatic Journal* on his return to Calcutta, where he exhibited the relics at the Asiatic Society and Government House at the invitation of the Governor General.[10] In London, Dillon displayed the La Pérouse objects in the East India Company Baggage Warehouse, where the French Ambassador examined them before Dillon brought them on to Paris.[11] In Paris, he met Charles X, who awarded him an annuity and the Order of Chevalier, and Dillon visited the objects at the Admiralty with de Lesseps, the sole survivor, who also affirmed their provenance.[12]

The most detailed source for information about the collection sites and circumstances for all the objects Dillon located was his own two-volume *Narrative and Successful Result of a Voyage in the South Seas ... to Ascertain the Actual Fate of La Pérouse's Expedition* (1829). Dillon was careful to document the authenticity and provenance of every object (with third-party verification from the French agent aboard his ship), due to a controversy surrounding his initial find of the sword hilt, the authenticity of which had been disputed. The search and recovery of Franklin relics would follow closely this pattern established in La Pérouse's case, with the key difference that in the 1850s the periodical and daily presses were much more visually oriented thanks to the emergence of the *Illustrated London News*, the *Magasin pittoresque,* and the numerous "printed museums."[13] The Franklin relics would proliferate chiefly in visual representations, while the collection of La Pérouse relics remained primarily accessible in the actual exhibitions, exhibition reviews, and the textual accounts of Dillon and Jules Dumont D'Urville.

Like the Franklin searchers to come, Dillon remained perplexed by the absence of textual records and verbal inscriptions among the recovered objects themselves:

[9] Quote from January 1828 *Sydney Gazette*, included in 'Vestiges of La Pérouse', in *The Asiatic Journal and Monthly Miscellany* 26 (July–December 1828), 381.

[10] 'La Pérouse', *The Asiatic Journal and Monthly Miscellany* 26 (1828), 443–52. See also the Asiatic Society's assessment of the relics in that same vol., 715–6; see also 'Captain Dillon's Voyage', *Oriental Herald* 19 (October–December 1828), 145–53.

[11] P. Dillon, letter to the editor, *Morning Chronicle* (20 January 1829), 3.

[12] P. Dillon *Narrative and Successful Result of a Voyage in the South Seas*, 2 vols. (London: Hurst, Chance, & Co., 1829) 2: 397–9.

[13] C. Georgel, 'The Museum as Metaphor in Nineteenth-Century France', in D. Sherman and I. Rogoff (eds.), *Museum Culture* (Minneapolis: University of Minnesota Press, 1994), 113–22.

It cannot for a moment be supposed that such enlightenment men as the Count de la Pérouse and his officers would remain on this island several months without leaving some accounts of their misfortunes, either engraved on the rocks, stones, trees, or buried in the earth, with instructions to guide future navigators where to find it.[14]

It is hard to conceive of a shipwreck without a Robinsonade, as Dillon repeats while buying piles of wreck iron from islanders but finding no inscriptions: "during so long and lonesome a seclusion from the civilized world," the survivors must have inscribed a written record, he argues, "when their only pleasure would have been derived from erecting such memorials of the disaster which separated them from society, and consigned them to a savage land."[15] The missing textual records held such power over the imagination that they were at last discovered in 1870—by Captain Nemo aboard the *Nautilus*, no less. Sealed in a tin box like botanical specimens, the precious manuscripts still showed annotations in the handwriting of Louis XVI, their metonymic function relative to the *ancien régime* intact in Jules Verne's novel.

A French government search led by Dumont D'Urville arrived in the Solomon Islands just after Dillon's discovery was made public; disappointed that an "unknown Englishman" had discovered "the theater of the catastrophe,"[16] Dumont D'Urville collected many more substantial objects, including ships' guns. He had built a monument to La Pérouse on Vanikoro, one that also served a function as a surveying landmark and that would be destroyed and rebuilt repeatedly (Fig. 6.1). Like Dillon, Dumont D'Urville did not devote visual attention to representing the actual relics, with the exception of two small engravings inserted in his text, and a sketch of the underwater debris field awkwardly inserted out of geographical sequence in the atlas.[17] Regarding the subsequent overshadowing of his discoveries by those of the French searchers who followed his trail, Dillon wrote that Dumont D'Urville "must have found it almost as easy to find relics of the Wrecks at the Island, as it would be to collect bullets and bones on the field of Waterloo six months after the battle was fought."[18] Dillon correctly introduced the ugly association of disaster tourism with such recovery efforts, as the lasting popular appeal of both La Pérouse and Franklin owes a great deal to this phenomenon.[19]

[14] Dillon, *Narrative*, 2: 200.

[15] Ibid., 186.

[16] Victor-Emmanuel Charles, *Nouvelles Annales des Voyages* 13 (Paris: Librairie de Gils Fils, 1829) described Dumont D'Urville arriving on the "théâtre de la catastrophe" (127).

[17] For the small illustrations, see Dumont D'Urville's *Voyage de La Corvette L'Astrolabe. Histoire du voyage*, vol. 5 of 5 (Paris: J Tastu, 1833), 184–5 (subsequently *Voyage*). Sainson's debris field sketch ("Gisement des débris de Lapérouse") is in the *Atlas* to the *Histoire de la voyage*, vol. 1, part 3, pl. 240 bis. Peter Dillon, letter to editor, *The Morning Chronicle* (21 January 1829).

[18] Peter Dillon, letter to editor, *The Morning Chronicle* (21 January 1829).

[19] On thanatourism and Waterloo see A.V. Seaton, 'War and Thanatourism: Waterloo 1815–1914', *Annals of Tourism Research* 26.1 (1999), 130–58; S. Semmel, 'Reading the Tangible Past: British Tourism, Collecting, and Memory after Waterloo', *Representations* 69 (2000), 9–37.

Fig. 6.1 "Inauguration du monument, elevé par *l'Astrolabe* à Lapérouse à Vanikoro" (Lithograph based on drawing by Sainson, in Dumont D'Urville, *Voyage de La Corvette L'Astrolabe*)

Of course, the La Pérouse relics, like the Franklin relics, also enjoyed pride of place in national museums, and continue to do so. The Musée de la Marine in Paris began as the Musée Dauphin, established by Charles X in the Louvre in 1827 and coinciding with Dillon's return with the La Pérouse relics; it was opened to the public as the Musée de la Marine in 1837.[20] In its first room, surrounded by artifacts from Oceania, stood a massive funerary obelisk, to which was attached a monstrous concretion of the La Pérouse debris (Fig. 6.2).[21] In its formal symmetry and monumental height, incorporating only scientific, maritime, and military objects, the imposing "Pyramide de la Pérouse," as it was known, did not invite the intimate attention and affective response that the Franklin relics did, in their small display cases and seemingly informal groupings of personal and scientific objects together. The Pyramide stayed within funerary obelisk convention and contained only one verbal inscription (on the ship's bell, "Bazin ma fait," confirming its provenance), so that its relics were

[20] The La Pérouse collection played a central role in the new museum (as did the 1827 French role in the decisive battle of Navarin in Greece), but the new 1827 Musée incorporated earlier royal maritime collections dating back centuries; see A. Chatelle, *Le Musée de la Marine* (Paris: Editions de L'Institut Maritime et Colonial, 1943).

[21] 'Museé de la Marine', *Le Magasin pittoresque* 6 (1838), 272. The pyramide remained in the musée as late as 1931; see G.A. King, 'First Fleet Relics', *Sydney Morning Herald* (24 January 1931), 9.

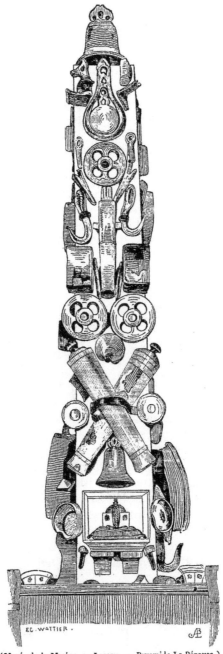

(Musée de la Marine, au Louvre. — Pyramide La Pérouse.)

Fig. 6.2   Pyramide la Pérouse (*Le Magasin pittoresque* 6(1838) 272)

readable iconographically, but not as a catalogue of lost and found commodities, as in the heterogeneous Franklin relics. When the largest cache of Franklin relics was displayed at the prestigious United Services Institution in their small cases in 1859, one exhibition reviewer lamented the absence of the kind of large objects found in Paris's Musée de la Marine:

> It must long remain a matter of astonishment and humiliation to an Englishman that, with all the vaunted and undoubted supremacy of Britain as a naval power, we have no such brilliant assemblage of objects of interest to naval men, as are to be found in the Marine Museum of Paris.[22]

The vast majority of the hundreds of La Pérouse objects recovered by Dillon and Dumont D'Urville were iron; because of the tropical climate, underwater site, and indigenous interest in collecting and trading in iron specifically, the objects preserved are of a significantly different nature, with a different difficulty in relation to the "museum effect," than the tiny scraps of fabric, paper, wood, thread, needles, buttons, and china exhumed from the frozen ground in the Franklin sites.

As with the Franklin relics, it was largely indigenous collecting, use, and reauthorship that made these objects accessible to European searchers. Virtually every La Pérouse object returned by Dillon was collected by islanders and brought to him for exchange, and the same is true of most of the Franklin relics collected in the 1850s–1880s. Inuit reauthorship of Franklin relics is readily visible today and was commented on by Victorians, although this aspect of European recuperation of their disastrous voyages has received little scholarly attention.[23] In archeology, anthropology, and ethnohistory there exists work on the lasting impact of wreck iron, for example, in changing the patterns of indigenous trade, mobility, and technology, in Oceania and in the Arctic, but this work has only begun to be taken up by historians of exploration and of exhibitions in Europe. At least 25 percent of Dillon's La Pérouse objects had been altered by islanders, and the objects' dispersal among several Santa Cruz islands hundreds of kilometers apart illustrates substantial indigenous interest in and exchange of this debris as ornamental and utilitarian exotic objects.[24]

In fact, we can trace the movement of La Pérouse relics from Vanikoro's wreck sites, long before they were collected by Dumont D'Urville and Dillon,

---

[22] 'The Royal United Services Institution', *The Leisure Hour* 435 (April 1860), 260. La Pérouse was invoked as precedent in the 5 June 1856 Memorial sent to Prime Minister Palmerston by a group of Arctic explorers urging further Franklin searches (F. McClintock, *Voyage of the 'Fox' in the Arctic Seas* (London: John Murray, 1859), 363–4).

[23] A. Craciun, 'Franklin Relics'.

[24] G. Clark, 'Indigenous Transfer of La Pérouse artefacts in the southeast Solomon Islands', *Australian Archeology* 57 (2003), 107. On the traditional songs in Tikopia that may reflect on encounters with La Pérouse, see R. Firth, *Tikopia Songs* (Cambridge: Cambridge University Press, 1990), 261–4.

to the efforts of one islander, a Tikopian chief named Thamaca (Matakai II, Ariki Taumako). According to Dillon,

> all things procured by me … [had] been carried thither by one of [Tikopia's] chiefs, named Thamaca, a great sailor and fighting man, having made during his lifetime ten voyages to [Vanikoro], from whence, in one of his excursions, he brought two of the natives to his own island.[25]

Like La Pérouse, Matakai was also lost at sea on a long-distance voyage; an example of the "hidden histories of exploration"[26] increasingly coming to the fore in scholarship, the voyages of the "great sailor and fighting man" Matakai clearly intrigued Dillon. Native collecting, reauthorship, and use of exotic French artifacts transformed these objects, if we recall Nicholas Thomas's reminder that objects "are not what they were made to be but what they have become."[27] The subsequent introduction of these now exoticized objects, transformed by disaster, distance, and indigenous agency, into French national museum spaces attests to the transcultural dimensions of their unique historicity.

Following the discovery of the wrecks, French commemorations of the La Pérouse disaster spanned the wholly conventional or functional, like the Pyramide de La Pérouse and the memorial erected on Vanikoro by Dumont D'Urville, and the extraordinary, in the case of two cenotaphs designed but never built by French architects: Vien's "Cenotaph in honor of the explorers who perished in the voyage of M. de La Pérouse," which won the *prix d'emulation* in the 1788 French Academy of Architecture competition,[28] and Henri La Brouste's "Commemorative Monument to the La Pérouse Shipwreck." What is distinctive about Vien's 1788 and La Brouste's 1830 cenotaphs for La Pérouse is their amplification of what Richard Etlin describes as a "space of absence," a tradition that Etlin argues is not fixed to a chronological period or teleology, but persisted from its Enlightenment origins through the twentieth century.[29] Designed to be located in Oceania, rejecting the classical vocabulary of their peers, and instead incorporating the boulders and mountains (and wreckage, in La Brouste's) of their imagined sites, the La Pérouse cenotaphs minimalized the individual heroic explorer, instead amplifying his absence and the power of the spaces in which he disappeared.

---

[25] Dillon, *Narrative*, 2, 128.

[26] F. Driver and L. Jones, *Hidden Histories of Exploration* (London: Royal Holloway, University of London, in association with the RGS-IBG, 2010).

[27] N. Thomas, *Entangled Objects: Exchange, Material Culture and Colonialism in the Pacific* (Cambridge, MA.: Harvard University Press, 1991), 4.

[28] Reproduced as pl. 64 in H. Rosenau, 'Engravings of the *Grands Prix* of the French Academy of Architecture', *Architectural History* 3 (1960) 15–180, on 99.

[29] R. Etlin, *Symbolic Space: French Enlightenment Architecture and Its Legacy* (Chicago: Chicago University Press, 1996) 189.

La Brouste's cenotaph is particularly significant in the way in which he incorporated the objects and ship fragments recently returned from Vanikoro, which according to architectural historians developed a new iconographic vocabulary that eschewed the academic practice of relegating objects to a decorative function.[30] Vien's and La Brouste's cenotaphs were never built, but they suggest alternative possibilities of how a "tombless death" of a mass disaster like that of La Pérouse or Franklin might have been memorialized, as a radical challenge to the Christian hagiography and individual hero worship that predominated, certainly in British displays and monuments devoted to explorers throughout the nineteenth century.[31] Vien and La Brouste had both used the occasion of this singular disaster and its absent subjects to attempt to say something new, unlike the designer of the monstrous Pyramide de La Pérouse that was actually built and displayed. The monuments erected to La Pérouse, beginning with Dumont D'Urville in Vanikoro, were interchangeable with similar colonial monuments to Cook and other European voyagers that mushroomed all around their global routes, often erected by expatriate groups eager to signpost their connections to metropolitan powers and to "elicit a devotional attitude toward history"[32] in the service of empire.

THE RESTORATION OF LA PÉROUSE

As La Pérouse's disappearance in 1788 nearly coincided with the disappearance of the *ancien régime*, rescue efforts were overtaken by revolutionary events in Paris, which moved more quickly than the Pacific-bound ships. One search expedition by Aristide Dupetit-Thouars was funded by the Legislative Assembly and private backers, and left in August 1792; by the time they reached South America, one-third of the crew had died of disease and France had become a republic at war, its ships no longer welcome abroad. Imprisoned and impoverished, Dupetit-Thouars was the first of many La Pérouse searchers to be overtaken by revolutionary events.

The National Assembly had funded an earlier and larger official expedition to locate La Pérouse, led by Entrecasteaux aboard the *Recherche* and *Espérance* in 1791. He fared even worse than Dupetit-Thouars: struck by disease, Entrecasteaux and his second-in-command both died early in the voyage, leaving behind two ships fissured by the same ideological and class divisions that were tearing France apart.[33] By the time the search ships reached the Dutch colony of Surabaya in October 1793, Louis XVI had been executed, and

[30] M. Bressani and M. Grignon, 'Henry Labrouste and the Lure of the Real', *Art History* 28.5 (2005), 712–51, on 717.

[31] See B. Tomlinson, 'The explorers of the North-West Passage: Claims and Commemoration,' *Church Monuments* 22 (2007), 111–32.

[32] M. Adams and N. Thomas, *Cook's Sites: Revisiting History* (Dunedin: University of Otego Press, 1999), 107.

[33] H. Richard, *Le Voyage d'Entrecasteaux* (Paris: Comité des travaux historiques et scientifiques, 1986); F. Bellec, *Les Esprits de Vanikoro* (Paris: Gallimard, 2005).

France was a republic at war with the Dutch. The expedition deteriorated as the royalist and republican sensibilities of the officers and scientists, respectively, led to increasing discord, while the crew struggled to stay alive with few resources and confiscated ships. And even Dumont D'Urville, who departed on his search in 1826 under the instructions of Charles X, returned after the July Revolution of 1830, finding himself out of favor with the new regime because of his ties with the old one.

A hostage to the fortune of a bewildering series of revolutionary regimes, wars, fiscal crises, and the search expeditions cursed to replay their conflicts, La Pérouse remained safely wrecked in the Pacific. As one of the popular La Pérouse dramas at the time put it, La Pérouse "was neglected by the volcanic concussions of the French revolution."[34] Even his official writings, saved by the sole survivor of the disaster, de Lesseps, were ideologically volatile and not immediately published. After de Lesseps' epic trek across Siberia carrying La Pérouse's "immutable mobiles," the writings were considered controversial (and expensive to publish) in successive republican circles because of the royalist investment in court science that they represented.

Finally published in 1797 in an edition by Milet-Mureau as La Pérouse's *Voyage autour du monde*, the writings were censored by republicans (frequent references to Louis XVI and to aristocratic forms of government, for example, were altered). The publication was intended to reflect the commitment of successive revolutionary governments to science and the arts despite the crises they weathered: according to the editor, the expensive four-volume octavo edition and the beautiful quarto atlas of maps and natural history illustrations attested to its value as an *"ouvrage national."*[35]

Disappearing on the eve of the Revolution of 1789, La Pérouse reappeared safely on the other side, his relics literalizing the shipwreck of time that such artifacts could represent in an era steeped in antiquarianism. Restoring La Pérouse was accomplished in concert with the larger project of restoring the Bourbon monarchy: it allowed the French to recuperate this crowning accomplishment of Louis XVI's reign seemingly untainted by the catastrophe or causes of revolution. By traveling such a great distance in space, the La Pérouse expedition seemed to escape historical time, as experienced by the French metropolitans searching for him. As survivors of the *ancien régime* on a distant Pacific outpost, La Pérouse's relics afforded a unique occasion to imagine the erasure of revolutionary history itself.

La Pérouse's personal identification with Louis XVI had been cemented in the 1817 painting by Nicolas-André Monsiau, *Louis XVI donnant des instructions à La Pérouse*, commissioned by Louis XVIII and in 1834 included in the

---

[34] *The Life of La Pérouse, the celebrated and unfortunate French navigator*, 3rd ed. (Somers Town: A. Neil, 1801), 43.

[35] L.A. Milet-Mureau, Préface, in La Pérouse, *Voyage de La Pérouse autour du monde* (Paris: de l'Imprimerie de la République, 1797), vol. 1, ix, xvii.

galleries at Versailles, the museum established by Louis-Philippe.[36] Monsiau's painting exemplifies one strand of French Restoration historical artistic practice, which according to Beth Wright eschewed narrating moments of catastrophic action, and instead focused on commemorating character.[37] *Louis XVI donnant des instructions à La Pérouse* remains the most famous image associated with the voyager, binding the fates of explorer and king through their shared kinship with these artifacts and spaces of Enlightenment court science visible in the painting (the Pacific map and globe in Louis XVI's Versailles, where the king indulged a well-known interest in science). The centrality of La Pérouse's relics exhibited in France's first maritime museum also exemplifies the importance of reclaiming prerevolutionary relics to the emergence of nineteenth-century historicism, part of Restoration French painting's commitment "to reclaim the concrete relics of the past, [and] reclaim the French patrimony."[38]

La Pérouse's relics were recuperated as a monument to the *ancien régime* preserved outside historical time; but in order to make this possible, his restorers, Dillon and Dumont D'Urville, had voyaged to Pacific islands radically transformed since La Pérouse's day. Louis Antoine de Bougainville, Cook, and La Pérouse had visited these islands before the missionaries, traders, and colonial officials who followed them had put in motion the systematic and destructive changes that by the 1820s had radically transformed eastern Oceanic societies in particular. Early nineteenth-century explorers like Dumont D'Urville, writes Nicholas Thomas, "encountered a converted Polynesia, a place reordered in various ways by mission influence" that began in the 1790s.[39] Thomas describes how in the first two decades of the nineteenth century the growing presence of sandalwood traders (like Dillon), bêche-de-mer traders, and the establishment of missions soon after, transformed unevenly but sometimes profoundly Pacific societies and European knowledge of them. Dumont D'Urville praised many of these changes in the pejorative argument of his most famous text, the essay "Sur les îles du grand océan," included in his published account of his search for La Pérouse; in that essay he famously developed the influential, racialized distinction between Polynesia and Melanesia, as well as the ethnogeographical category of Océanie/Oceania.[40] In fact, an infamous 1787 violent encounter in Samoa on La Pérouse's voyage had helped transform the European vision of Polynesians in particular, from the eighteenth-century "conventions of soft primitivism" to the violent savagery depicted by nineteenth-century colonial

---

[36] Association Salomon, *Le mystère La Pérouse ou le rêve inachevé d'un roi* (Paris: Editions de Conti, 2008), 172.

[37] B. Wright, *Painting and History During the French Restoration* (Cambridge: Cambridge University Press, 1996).

[38] Ibid., 58.

[39] N. Thomas, *Islanders: The Pacific in the Age of Empire* (New Haven: Yale University Press, 2010), 148.

[40] On that essay's origins and impact, see N. Thomas, *In Oceania* (London: Thames & Hudson Ltd., 2012).

and missionary agents.[41] Featuring prominently in the writings from the early part of the voyage in La Pérouse's *Voyage autour du monde*, and in popular dramatizations and discussions, the Samoa massacre fueled European speculations that the La Pérouse disaster had been initiated by native people, perhaps cannibals, and inspired related calls for Christianization.

Despite his harrowing experience with cannibalism in Fiji, and his conclusion that many of La Pérouse's men had been killed by Vanikoro islanders, Dillon remained critical of the missionary transformation of the islands he visited, and insisted that the Vanikorans in particular are "tractable, generous, and grateful," and "not naturally fierce and bloody."[42] On his return via New Zealand, describing a number of encounters with callous missionaries and generous "heathens," he wrote, "I am persuaded that every genuine Christian will heartily rejoice with me at the failure of the mission in these regions."[43] He continued, "[L]et theorists advance what absurd propositions they may, arts and civilization must precede, and not follow the establishment of christianity."[44] Dillon thus followed in the tracks of La Pérouse and especially of Cook, literally and philosophically, concerned as they were with "improvement" and enlightenment along largely secular lines of arts and sciences (part of the myth of anticonquest that they all embodied), and with the deleterious effects of many aspects of European contact.

Returning from the Pacific with their La Pérouse debris, both Dillon and Dumont D'Urville stopped in the island of St. Helena, as was common practice. Both men made pilgrimages to France's newest and most remote tourist site, the grave of Napoleon, who was buried in 1821 in an enclosed garden surrounded by transplanted willows. The exiled monarch's grave seemed to Dumont D'Urville and Dillon a "bleak and dismal" site,[45] while the lithograph based on the drawing of Louis de Sainson included in Dumont D'Urville's *Voyage*, "Tombeau de Napoléon," highlighted instead the picturesque pleasures that visitors of all political and national affiliations could enjoy at this remote tomb of the "nouveau Prométhée" (indeed, Dumont D'Urville noted that it was not due to necessity but due to desire to visit the remains of Napoleon that they landed).[46]

Dillon described collecting a willow branch as a memento from Napoleon's tomb, a practice so popular with St. Helena tourists that by 1859 one visitor noted that one of the original Napoleon willows "has been so stripped by

---

[41] B. Smith, *European Vision and the South Pacific* (New Haven: Yale University Press, 1989), 104. On the La Pérouse Samoan episode, see J. Linnekin, 'Ignoble Savages and Other European Visions', *Journal of Pacific History* 26 (1991) 3–26.

[42] Dillon, *Narrative* 2: 163, 264–5.

[43] Ibid., 331.

[44] Ibid., 335.

[45] Ibid., 388.

[46] Dumont D'Urville, *Voyage*, 560. Dumont D'Urville's naturalist made two "pilgrimages" to Napoleon's house and grave (*Voyage, 676*).

travellers that nothing but the trunk is left."[47] In fact, Napoleon's famous willows had to be replaced several times over, as they were under constant assault by tourists, with numerous gardens across the globe to this day boasting willows from transplanted cuttings; one Victorian commentator reckoned that Napoleon's willow "memorials have multiplied beyond all calculation."[48]

St. Helena numbers among the 1,600 botanical outposts forming the European global network of imperial science at the turn of the nineteenth century, its gardens of transplanted mulberry praised by visitors like Dumont D'Urville for improving a "barren" rock. Yet as the original burial place of Napoleon, St. Helena is also located in a different colonial geography, not of imperial science but of imperial nostalgia. These remote *lieux de mémoire* of La Pérouse and Napoleon, revisited by the same ships following La Pérouse, allowed visitors from the nineteenth century onwards to visit these respective outposts of *ancien régime* and revolutionary history safely preserved from historical change. By the nineteenth century, the transits of savants and the tours of the leisure classes converged, the latter playing an increasingly important role in the cycles of accumulation that have returned La Pérouse's *Banksia* to France in the twenty-first century. At once scientific specimens, disaster relics, and tourist souvenirs, the errant eighteenth-century *Banksia* seeds inhabit mutually constitutive networks of knowledge. These networks were forged in the nineteenth century and renegotiated in a postcolonial twenty-first century, as the seeds' return was made possible by the collaboration of the National Museum newly established in Nouméa, New Caledonia, in the early days after the Nouméa Accord granted New Caledonia increased independence.

THE SEEDS OF DISASTER: *BANKSIA*

The collection of debris, their exhibition as relics, the large-scale investment in producing textual and visual records, and the monumental commemoration of La Pérouse's voyage in France and in the Pacific are not unique to La Pérouse's case, but are part of the well-known cultures of exploration that flourished in the era of Cook and the aftermath of his death, and became increasingly professionalized and codified in the nineteenth century. What is unique in the case of La Pérouse, I argue, is not the singularity of the human catastrophe, but the foundational example of his disaster as reimagined through the nineteenth-century twinned fates of La Pérouse and Franklin, as the objects of continuing rescue fantasies. The productive absence of La Pérouse is most visible and most remarkable in the current attempts to revive the *Banksia* seeds he collected.

Aboard the *Endeavour* on the first Cook voyage, Daniel Solander and Joseph Banks had collected four species of *Banksia* (Proteaceae) from Botany Bay (the species would later be named after Banks by Linnaeus Jr.). The four *Banksia*

---

[47] B. Taylor, 'A Day at St Helena', *The Atlantic Souvenir* (NY, 1859) 83. The original willows died frequently and were replanted to keep up with the tourist assault; see J. Fennell, 'Napoleon's Tomb and Its Willows', *The Mirror of Literature* 28 (1836) 362–6.

[48] 'Relics and Memorials', *The Ladies' Cabinet* (October 1855), 197–200, on 200.

species (*dentata, ericifolia, integrifolia, serrata*) were among the thousands of plants that they collected; the original specimens are located in the Natural History Museum in London. Banksias were also included among the illustrations for Banks's massive *Florilegium* project as engravings based on Sydney Parkinson's watercolors. Banks employed "an extraordinary array of experts"[49] including 5 artists and 18 engravers to produce 743 engravings over 13 years, but his *Florilegium*, like La Pérouse's voyage, remained unfinished for 200 years. The *Florilegium* was finally completed by the British Museum Natural History in 1990 as an 18-volume edition, using the original copperplates.[50]

Botanical research, collection, and propagation were among the chief scientific priorities of La Pérouse's expedition, and each of his ships carried its own botanist and botanical artist among the other specialized naturalists and artists. This global bioprospecting has been the subject of substantial scholarship, detailing the significant extent to which European commercial and colonial expansion was accomplished through the mass transplantation of non-human animals and plants like coffee, indigo, tea, mulberry, and sugarcane. So full of plant and animal passengers was Cook's third expedition, for example, that Cook joked to Banks that "nothing is wanting but a few females of our own species to make the Resolution a complete ark."[51] Within this "exchangeable" globalized nature, a ship sent to retrace the tracks of Cook's voyages became a veritable "floating forest."[52]

La Pérouse's instructions detailed how they were to follow Cook's traces specifically to monitor the success of the plants and animals that Cook had transplanted. Banksias were among the new plants and animals that Cook's first voyage brought to the attention of European scientific networks and popular audiences eager to see novelties returned from the antipodes. While he was to follow Cook's landfalls closely, La Pérouse was given twofold botanical instructions: to distribute across the Pacific native French plants, and to collect from across the Pacific plants and seeds that may be naturalized in French gardens:

> The navigators cannot be too attentive ... to making copious and diversified collection of the seeds of exotic plants and trees, ... which, naturalising themselves in our soil, may hereafter adorn our plantations, or augment the number of our artificial meadows by their productions.[53]

[49] S. Schaffer, 'Visions of Empire: Afterword', in D.P. Miller and P. Hanns (eds.), *Visions of Empire: Voyages, Botany, and Representations of Nature* (Cambridge: Cambridge University Press, 1996), 335–352, on 344.

[50] J. Banks, *Banks' Florilegium: A Publication in Thirty-Four Parts of Seven Hundred and Thirty-Eight Copperplate Engravings of Plants Collected on Captain James Cook's First Voyage Round the World in H.M.S. Endeavour, 1768–1771* (London: Alecto Historical Editions in association with the British Museum (Natural History), 1980–1990), vol. 13 contains the four *Banksia* plates.

[51] Cook to Banks, 26 November 1776 (qtd. in J.C. Beaglehole, *The Life of Captain James Cook* (Palo Alto: Stanford University Press, 1974), 511).

[52] A. Bewell, 'Traveling Natures', *Nineteenth-Century Contexts* 29.2–3 (2007), 89–110, on 105.

[53] Instructions on Botany in La Pérouse, *A Voyage Round the World, Performed in the Years 1785, 1786, 1787, and 1788*, 3. vols., 3rd ed. (London: Lackington, Allen, and Co., 1807), 1:211; the

These "artificial meadows" (*prairies artificielles*), plantations, and botanic gardens numbered more than 1,600 globally by the end of the eighteenth century, according to Londa Schiebinger, and functioned as "experimental stations for agriculture and way stations for plant acclimatization for domestic and global trade, rare medicaments, and cash crops."[54]

On board these floating laboratories and floating forests, botany was one of the new field sciences, along with geology, geography, astronomy, and even mathematics. As Mary Terrall and others have argued, Enlightenment narratives of scientific discovery elevated men of science to heroic status through the rigors of physical suffering and danger inherent in field work.[55] In the preface to his journal, La Pérouse himself singled out his botanists as daring men of action in this emerging tradition:

> Mr. De la Martinière has enriched botanical science with a wealth of new plants; those who read the description of a newly discovered plant often admire only the scholarship of the person who has classified it: they hardly spare a thought for the great hardships, the risks even, incurred by the one who filched it, so to speak, from nature, who climbed mountains which were almost inaccessible and whose sanctuary was violated through his enthusiasm alone.[56]

The heroic labors of scientific discovery as idealized by La Pérouse were incorporated sympathetically within the heroic value of later nineteenth-century searches for his relics, as would also be the case with Franklin, making both men martyrs to science. The collection and attempted regeneration of La Pérouse's *Banksia* in the Brest Conservatoire represent the most ambitious example of celebrating scientific modernity through this particular Enlightenment vision, effectively a celebration of a disciplinary myth of origin. Yet simultaneously it marks a superannuated, unacknowledged return, not to the eighteenth-century modernity of Cook and La Pérouse, but to nineteenth-century nostalgia and belatedness.

The Brest Conservatoire was the first botanic garden in the world devoted to the preservation of endangered plants and is an important site for the conservation of biodiversity. As an official *conservatoire national* it also has a mandate to help promote the biodiversity of French overseas territories, such as Pacific islands like New Caledonia. For example, the Brest Conservatoire was instrumental in reviving *Ruizia cordata* on the isle of Réunion near Madagascar, which had only two remaining plants in the wild in 1998, by propagating 2,000 new plants by hand-pollination and relocating them to Réunion.[57] However,

---

French ed. reads: 'dont les productions, en se naturalisant dans notre climat, peuvent servir à orner un jour nos plantations, ou à multiplier nos prairies artificielles' (*Voyage de La Pérouse* vol. 1, 172).

[54] L. Schiebinger, *Plants and Empire* (Cambridge, MA: Harvard University Press, 2007) 11.

[55] M. Terrall, 'Heroic Narratives of Quest and Discovery', *Configurations* 6.2 (1998) 223–242.

[56] La Pérouse, Preface to *Journal of Jean-François de Galaup de La Pérouse,* trans. and ed. John Dunmore, 2 vols. (London: Hakluyt Society, 1994–1995), 1:4.

[57] C. Hankamer and M. Maunders, 'The Role of Botanic Gardens in Conservation of Europe's Overseas Territories', *Botanic Gardens Conservation News* 3.1 (1998).

the *Banksia ericifolia* collected by La Pérouse in the Sydney area, later archived in the Nouméa museum in New Caledonia, is not threatened or endangered; on the contrary, it is invasive.

The *Banksia* collected aboard *Endeavour* are shrub-like trees that can grow to 90 feet high, and are capable of regenerating after fire through their lignotubers. They are long-lived plants (potentially 100 years, depending on species), meaning that few plant generations would occur between 1787 and 2012, minimizing the evolutionary changes that biologists could potentially detect when comparing the regenerated *Banksia* to modern specimens. This is in marked contrast to the high-profile successful reanimation in February 2012 of a Siberian plant, *Silene stenophylla*, from a seed that had lain dormant in permafrost for over 30,000 years, which exhibited subtly different traits compared to those of modern specimens.

Rather than serving the current prioritization of biodiversity, the *Banksia* regeneration project seems a temporal extension of the Enlightenment science-at-a-distance paradigm that guided La Pérouse's original voyage. His voyage, like those of Cook, William Bligh, George Vancouver, La Billardière, and d'Entrecasteaux, actually served to render more uniform biota along European trade and exploration routes, an example of "man-made uniformity" that Schiebinger has noted in the Caribbean, where transplanted plants were occasionally mistaken for indigenous ones by eighteenth-century taxonomers.[58]

Banksia had already traveled to Kew with Cook, to Tahiti with Bligh aboard his "floating forest," HMS *Providence*, to Paris with La Billardière, and to the Cape with Dumont D'Urville.[59] In 2011 *Banksia* traveled to Brest, with the hope of being cultivated there in the Jardin des Explorateurs and at Paris's Jardin des Plantes. Yet what would *Banksia*'s voyage to Brest accomplish? After all, *Banksia* is already considered highly invasive in South Africa and Hawai'i.[60] In Australia, *Banksia* is the iconic plant of the Australian bush; its seed cones were the botanical villains, symbolizing aboriginals ("Banksia Men"), in a series of racist children's books popular throughout the twentieth century.[61]

[58] Schiebinger, *Plants and Empire*, 227.

[59] J.-J. de la Billardière collected and illustrated *Banksia nivea* and *Banksia repens* in Australia aboard D'Entrecasteaux's expedition (*Voyage in Search of La Pérouse*, 2 vols. (London: Stockdale, 1800), vol. 1, 465–7). His natural history collections were confiscated in Java by the Dutch and sent to England through the efforts of Joseph Banks (La Billardière vol. 1, 343). The bread fruit plants he collected were cultivated in Java and sent to gardens in Ile de France (Mauritius), Cayenne, and Paris (vol. 1, 344). On later nineteenth-century transplantation of large numbers of Australian flora to South Africa, see B. Bennett, 'Naturalising Australian Trees in South Africa: Climate, Exotics and Experimentation', *Journal of Southern African Studies* 37 (2011) 265–80; N. Rigby, 'The Politics and Pragmatics of Seaborne Plant Transportation 1769–1805', Margarette Lincoln (ed.), *Science and Exploration in the Pacific* (London: Boydell Press and NMM, 1998), 81–100.

[60] G. Seddon, *The Old Country: Australian Landscapes, Plants and People* (Cambridge: Cambridge University Press, 2005); Honig et al., 'The Invasive Potential of Australian Banksias in South African Fynbos', *Australian Journal of Ecology* 17 (1992) 305–12.

[61] M. Gibbs, *Tales of Snugglepot and Cuddlepie* (Sydney: Angus & Robertson, 1918) was the first volume in this series of children's tales. I am grateful to Simon Schaffer for alerting me to Gibbs's "Banksia Men."

Locating botanical survivors, and making possible at long last the completion of La Pérouse's "voyage round the world," represent the rededication of twenty-first-century resources to Enlightenment goals, but as memorialized through nineteenth-century nostalgia. The French government's official support of the Association Solomon's private La Pérouse search in 2008 demonstrates that La Pérouse's legacy remains significant for French national identity, and its national conservatory's dedication to completing his voyage reanimates the inseparable scientific and national priorities of that legacy at an unprecedented remove.

CONCLUSION

In July 2012, the Brest Conservatoire announced that La Pérouse's *Banksia* seeds did not germinate. La Pérouse had sailed in the name of imperial science and the *Banksia* experiment had been a symbolic performance, shoring up this national vision on a truly global stage. Yet ultimately the seeds are more interesting as evidence of Andy Martin's provocative reversal, "the fatal impact of the Pacific on Europe."[62] After all, it was plants like *Banksia* that drew expeditions like La Pérouse's out into "the unknown" and to their deaths.

France's most extravagantly equipped *ancien régime* floating laboratories were sacrificed just as extravagantly for the purpose of bringing home six seeds. In the end, these will be among the most costly seeds in history— taken from an invasive Sydney plant, but bought with the lives of many people, trailing a history of colonial violence across the Pacific. Had the *Banksia* regenerated, the imperial narrative that they were recruited to serve would have appeared even more empty and destructive than it now does. Future spectators encountering these transplanted Pacific visitors in French gardens could have marveled at the power of metropolitan scientific networks, in the age of Enlightenment and in our own. Or, perhaps they may have wondered at the human, cultural, and environmental wastefulness on which this vision of imperial science relies. When the Tahitian Ahutoru, who had voyaged to France with Bougainville, saw transplanted paperbark trees in the Jardin des Plantes he wept openly, an ambivalent response that La Pérouse's *Banksia* would have left open to the future.

Ironically, the Brest attempt to regenerate La Pérouse's *Banksia* destroyed the seeds and in that respect represents yet another transformation of these curious objects. Some of the smallest and most fragile artifacts (and along with the skeleton, the rarest organic materials recovered from la Pérouse's disaster), the *Banksia* seeds were nevertheless sacrificed for a smaller relic they were imagined to contain—the living tissue within their kernel and, within that, the DNA. No longer visible, tangible, or displayable, the twenty-first-century relics of La Pérouse were now only accessible through the biotech laboratories, their

---

[62] A. Martin, 'Introduction: Surfing the Revolution: The Fatal Impact of the Pacific on Europe', *Eighteenth-Century Studies* 41.2 (2008) 141–7.

electron microscopes, and magnetic resonance imaging. The publicly circulated photographs of the *Banksia* seeds had combined the sterile surfaces and containers of the lab with the yellowed envelope and wax seal meant to evoke eighteenth-century authenticity, at once reassuringly sterile and imbued with a historical aura (Fig. 6.3).

The Conservatoire investigators reasoned that the lessons learnt from the failed experiment would be helpful for their future attempts to regenerate rare or extinct plants from materials preserved in herbaria. Cook's *Banksia* specimens, like one at the Natural History Museum in London, are examples of such meticulously preserved botanical relics (Fig. 6.4). Type specimens (holotypes), meaning the first specimen associated with the naming of a species, as Lorraine Daston has argued, are "unique and irreplaceable"[63]—the botanical equivalent of a sacred relic, as in this case of the pictured Cook *Banksia ericifolia*. A unique type specimen would not be subjected to the all-consuming investigation that la Pérouse's *Banksia* seeds underwent. Nevertheless, the *Banksia* experiment reveals how different our threshold for materiality and visibility is from those of previous recuperations of La Pérouse's legacies for modernity.

In addition to being botanical specimens, objects of indigenous exchange, disaster relics, and tourist souvenirs, La Pérouse's seeds are now also technological

Fig. 6.3 La Pérouse *Banksia ericifolia* seeds in Conservatoire botanique national de Brest. Photograph by Charlotte Dissez.

---

[63] L. Daston, 'Type Specimens and Scientific Memory', *Critical Inquiry* 31 (2004), 153–82, on 160.

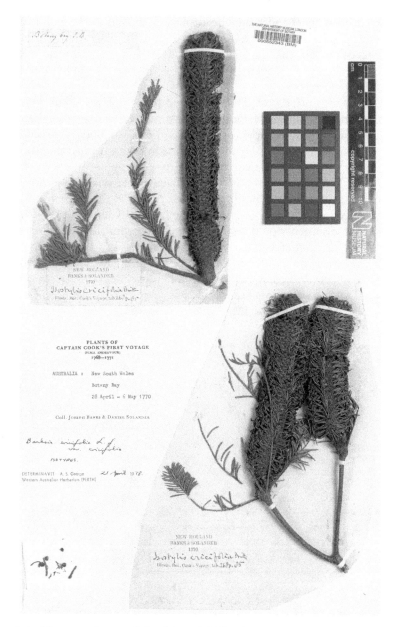

Fig. 6.4 Type specimen of *Banksia ericifolia* from *Endeavour*, Natural History Museum, London

projects, a problem to be solved, and, finally, pure information. Because the information turned out to be absent, the seeds are, as the Conservatoire lamented in its press release, empty envelopes.[64] Of course, this absence of information is only visible, as Latour has argued, through "the local, material and practical networks that accompany artifacts through the whole duration of their lives."[65]

La Pérouse's *Banksia* seeds are unusually rich examples of the historicity of objects. In the regulated spaces of national museums, biotech laboratories, and the "gardens of the explorers" that they eventually reached, we saw briefly the possibility that nothing can escape our will to know, not even in death. La Pérouse's seeds may have been "mobiles" recruited in this particular vision of Enlightenment science, but they proved mutable, taking a surprising series of turns in their long lives—as gifts, relics, specimens, souvenirs, and, ultimately, information. In the end, they turned out to be not only mutable but, thankfully, mortal.

[64] C. Le Guen, 'La Pérouse: Les graines de banksia n'ont pas parlé' (*Le Telegramme*, 5 July 2012).

[65] B. Latour, 'On the Partial Existence of Existing and Nonexisting Objects', in Daston (ed.), *Biographies of Scientific Objects* (Chicago: University of Chicago Press, 2000) 247–269, on 250.

PART II

Tools and Travels

A Bird in the Hand, or, Manufacturing Credibility in the Instruments of Enlightenment Science

Richard Dunn

I was secured from any errors in the construction of the quadrant, by the known skill of the artist... (Nevil Maskelyne 1762)[1]

This essay concerns questions of authorial ownership and consumer trust in the manufacture of scientific instruments, focusing in particular on maker–retailers of the mid to late eighteenth century. One type of instrument they produced was for precision measurement. Instinctively, one might expect the quality of these instruments to have been assessed primarily in terms of observational precision and accuracy. While this is one part of the story, it is also clear that special trust was placed in the perceived skills of specific makers, often identified as 'artists'.[2] The belief that there were individuals who had unique skills and/or techniques that raised them above other makers could, therefore, be a significant factor contributing to commercial and reputational standing and to the trust placed in the instruments they produced. Looking first at the general background and at some of the issues surrounding the concept of 'maker' in this period, this essay moves on to examine the work of a small number of makers of bespoke instruments for astronomical observatories. In their

---

[1] Nevil Maskelyne, 'A Letter from the Rev. Nevil Maskelyne, M.A. F.R.S. to the Rev. Thomas Birch, D.D. Secretary to the Royal Society: Containing the Results of Observations of the Distance of the Moon from the Sun and Fixed Stars, Made in a Voyage from England to the Island of St. Helena', *Philosophical Transactions* 52 (1761–1762), 558–77, on 559.

[2] While a number of makers were singled out as 'artists' in this way, the term was still not so exclusively tied to the fine arts as it would be a century later; see Raymond Williams, *Keywords* (London: Flamingo, 1983), 40–3.

R. Dunn (✉)
Royal Museums Greenwich, London, UK
e-mail: rdunn@rmg.co.uk

© The Author(s) 2016
A. Craciun, S. Schaffer (eds.), *The Material Cultures of Enlightenment Arts and Sciences*, Palgrave Studies in the Enlightenment, Romanticism and the Cultures of Print, DOI 10.1057/978-1-137-44379-3_7

work, it seems, trust lay as much as anything in assumptions about their manual skill, something seen as so valuable that it was worth attempting to codify and publish it.

Instruments and Their Makers

It is best to begin by introducing the objects on which this essay focuses. Strictly speaking, one should not use the term 'scientific instrument' when writing about the eighteenth century. Rather, one should think of three categories of instrument: mathematical, philosophical and optical. Mathematical instruments generally had some sort of divided scale, linear or circular, and were used for number-based measurements—they were instruments of quantity. Philosophical instruments, such as air pumps or electrical machines, were used to investigate, but not necessarily to quantify, natural phenomena (that is, they were instruments of quality), while optical instruments made use of lenses, mirrors or prisms to facilitate observation. These demarcations were not absolute, however, with overlap between the three, such as the use of both telescopes and graduated scales on instruments like theodolites, and with many makers and retailers including all classes of instrument in their stock.[3]

It is important to recognize that these were manufactured commodities much like other products. Subcontracting was commonplace. 'Makers' were coordinators of networks of artisans dispersed throughout London and beyond, who between them made the parts from which the final instruments were assembled. As Campbell's *London Tradesman* noted in the middle of the century, 'the Optical-Instrument-Maker ... executes very little of the Work, except grinding the Glasses [lenses] ... The Cases and Machinery of his Instruments are made by different Workmen, according to their Nature, and he adjusts the Glasses to them'. These other workmen included the shagreen case maker, the box maker, the cabinetmaker and turners of ivory, wood and silver.[4] A potential ambiguity of this culture of subcontracting was that the named maker–retailer could be seen as removed from the process. The French astronomer Jean Bernoulli could knowingly and pejoratively write in 1769 of the flourishing firm established by Peter Dollond:

---

[3] Deborah Warner, 'What Is a Scientific Instrument, When Did It Become One, and Why?', *British Journal for the History of Science* 23 (1990), 83–93; Liba Taub, 'On Scientific Instruments', *Studies in History and Philosophy of Science* 40 (2009), 337–43, on 337–8. J.R. Millburn, *Adams of Fleet Street, Instrument Makers to King George III* (Aldershot: Ashgate, 2000), 362–82, illustrates the range offered by one retailer.

[4] R. Campbell, *The London Tradesman* (London: T. Gardner, 1747), 253–4; see also G.l'E. Turner, 'The London Trade in Scientific Instrument-Making in the Eighteenth Century', *Vistas in Astronomy* 20 (1976), 1–21, especially 8; G.L'E. Turner, 'Decorative Tooling on 17th and 18th Century Microscopes and Telescopes', *Physis* 8 (1966), 99–128; Anita McConnell, 'From Craft Workshop to Big Business—The London Scientific Instrument Trade's Response to Increasing Demand, 1750–1820', *The London Journal* 19 (1994), 36–53.

We should note, however, that brass instruments are made more or less by the dozen and that those outside London make a big mistake if they suppose that an astronomical instrument that bears the name Dollond must be excellent in every respect. Should an instrument of this quality be received, that is a sign that it had not been finished by one of Dollond's workmen; often, to maintain his reputation, he has the mountings, the divisions etc, made by his brother in law Ramsden who passes for one of the best craftsmen in London of this type.[5]

The need to maintain a link between the name on the instrument and its supposed quality may equally explain George Adams's claim about the products his firm sold: 'That their *Exactness* may be particularly attended to, I always inspect and direct the several Pieces myself, see them all combined in my own House, and finish the most *curious* Parts with my own Hands.'[6] Adams, somewhat defensively, was eager to emphasize that although he had not made each and every part, his role in the creation of the final product was active and personal, the quality guaranteed. Similar questions and concerns were equally prevalent in other areas of specialized precision-instrument production. In the early nineteenth century, for example, two London watchmakers, William Parkinson and William James Frodsham, wrote to Edward Sabine, by then a Commissioner of Longitude, to defend their status as the named 'makers' of the marine chronometers recently trialled on Captain Parry's voyage to the Arctic. While the production of these complex devices required the input of around 40 specialist artisans, Parkinson and Frodsham asserted their right to be identified as the makers because 'The whole of the chronometrical parts were made in our House under our direction by Workmen articled to us for the purpose of instructing them in that branch of the business and the final corrections and adjustments were completed by ourselves personally on a method peculiarly our own'.[7] Thus their claim rested on personal supervision and the unique nature of their manufacturing methods.

Cultures of subcontracting, and attendant issues of authorship/ownership, were not, of course, restricted to the manufacture of precision instruments, but extended across all fields, including the decorative and fine arts.[8] In the field of painting, for example, Britain's leading portraitist and first President of the Royal Academy, Joshua Reynolds, is well documented in his use of assistants and subcontracted workers. As Joseph Farington noted, Reynolds's 'school … resembled a manufactory, in which the young men who were sent

[5] Jean Bernoulli, 20 June 1769, quoted in Anita McConnell, *Jesse Ramsden (1735–1800). London's Leading Scientific Instrument Maker* (Aldershot: Ashgate, 2007), 20.

[6] George Adams, *Micrographia Illustrata* (London: Printed for the Author, 1746), 244 (original italics).

[7] Parkinson and Frodsham to Captain Sabine, 26 March 1821, Cambridge University Library (hereafter CUL) RGO 14/24, fols. 383–4, quote on fol. 383r; Eóin Phillips, 'Making Time Fit: Astronomers, Artisans and the State, 1770–1820', Unpublished PhD Thesis (University of Cambridge, 2014), Chap. 1. See also Campbell, *The London Tradesman*, 250.

[8] Giorgio Riello, 'Strategies and Boundaries: Subcontracting and the London Trades in the Long Eighteenth Century', *Enterprise & Society* 9 (2008), 243–80.

to him for tuition were chiefly occupied in copying portraits, or assisting in draperies, and preparing backgrounds.'[9] Nonetheless, while this use of a team of artisans facilitated a prodigious rate of production, Reynolds retained his identity as painter or maker of the finished product, just as Adams or Parkinson and Frodsham claimed, by virtue of having trained or overseen the work of the assistants and having executed key stages in the process. With that control of authorship, he could keep prices high.

George Adams provides a good example among instrument makers of this period, since he established one of the most widely known firms of the eighteenth century. Adams sold to many different (generally affluent) clients, whether as maker to the king, supplier to the Ordnance or retailer to the genteel London public at his shop in Fleet Street.[10] For some of these customers, indeed, Adams self-consciously operated in a context and mode much like other suppliers of high-end decorative arts. Most conspicuously and ostentatiously, for example, two surviving silver microscopes, one made for George III, took advantage of the skills of sculptors, model makers and silversmiths more typically involved in the production of other showy silverware.[11]

Precision, Accuracy and the Artist's Hand

Moving away from general, albeit prolific and prosperous, retailers like Adams, the central discussion of this essay focuses on a handful of makers of large astronomical instruments, whose work included commissions for high-status institutions like the Royal Observatory, Greenwich. These were mathematical instruments for precise observations in positional astronomy, devices whose performance and errors could be, and were, exhaustively checked, quantified and rechecked.

The key to the desired quality of these instruments lay above all in the division of their degree scales. Thus a crucial element of the maker's art lay in the accuracy and precision that could be achieved in marking off the graduations of the scale. Scale division for large instruments was a highly skilled and laborious manual art, and remained primarily a manual skill well into the nineteenth century. In this field, it was George Graham (c.1673–1751) who stood out among the makers of the first half of the eighteenth century. Trained as a clock and instrument maker, Graham is credited with taking the art of scale division

[9] Joseph Farington, *Memoirs of the Life of Sir Joshua Reynolds* (London: Cadell and W. Davies, 1819), quoted in M. Kirby Talley Jr., ' "All Good Pictures Crack": Sir Joshua Reynolds's Practice and Studio', in Nicholas Penny (ed.), *Reynolds* (London: Royal Academy of Arts/Weidenfeld and Nicolson, 1986), 55–70, on 57–8.

[10] Millburn, *Adams of Fleet Street*; Roy Porter, Simon Schaffer, Jim Bennett and Olivia Brown, *Science and Profit in 18th-Century London* (Cambridge: Whipple Museum of the History of Science, 1985).

[11] 'New Universal' microscope, by George Adams, London, 1761, Science Museum, London, 1949–116; microscope, made for George III, by George Adams, London, about 1763, Museum of the History of Science, Oxford, 35086.

to new levels by refining the method and introducing cross-checking mechanisms for observation.[12]

Before Graham's time, scales had been divided using a knife and a ruler. *The Edinburgh Encyclopedia* later described the knife in memorable terms: 'Had we, indeed, been inclined to describe it as found in the workshop of an ordinary divider, we should only have occasion to say, that it exactly resembles the butcher's cleaver; and perhaps we might add, is commonly directed with about equal science.'[13]

Graham, however, was no 'ordinary divider'. Dispensing with this apparently crude tool, he used a beam compass (see Fig. 7.1), which was capable of being handled with far greater finesse when marking the divisions of a scale.[14] He also introduced (although he had not invented) a second scale on the largest of his observing instruments, his great mural quadrants.[15] This was divided, by repeated bisection, into 96 parts along an arc of 90 degrees and could be used to cross-check the readings of the more conventional degree scale. This was significant, since bisection was a more exact process, but could not be used to produce a conventional 90-degree scale. These innovations underpinned Graham's success and established him as the leading maker for angle-measuring observatory instruments, notably mural quadrants and zenith sectors.[16]

It is worth noting too the credit that contemporary astronomers accorded him. Writing of the discovery of the aberration of light (the first observational evidence of the Earth's orbit around the Sun), for instance, James Bradley, by then Astronomer Royal at Greenwich, enthused:

> If my own Endeavours have, in any respect, been effectual to the Advancement of Astronomy; it has principally been owing to the Advice and Assistance given me by [Graham]...whose great Skill and Judgement in Mechanicks, join'd with a complete and practical Knowledge of the Uses of Astronomical Instruments, enable him to contrive and execute them in the most perfect manner.[17]

[12] Allan Chapman, 'The Accuracy of Angular Measuring Instruments Used in Astronomy Between 1500 and 1850', *Journal of the History of Astronomy* 14 (1983), 133–7, on 133. See also Allan Chapman, *Dividing the Circle. The Development of Critical Angular Measurement in Astronomy 1500–1850* (Chichester: Ellis Horwood, 1990); Richard Sorrenson, 'George Graham, Visible Technician', *The British Journal for the History of Science* 32 (1999), 203–21.

[13] 'Graduation', in D. Brewster (ed.), *The Edinburgh Encyclopedia*, 18 vols. (Edinburgh: Printed for William Blackwood and others, 1808–30), vol. 10, 349.

[14] Chapman, *Dividing the Circle*, 68–9.

[15] The first of Graham's mural quadrants, completed in 1725, is in the National Maritime Museum, Greenwich, AST0970. It is displayed in the Royal Observatory, Greenwich.

[16] Sorrenson, 'George Graham'; J.A. Bennett, 'The English Quadrant in Europe—Instruments and the Growth of Consensus in Practical Astronomy', *Journal for the History of Astronomy* 23 (1992), 1–14; Jeremy Lancelotte Evans, 'Graham, George (*c.*1673–1751)', *Oxford Dictionary of National Biography* (Oxford: Oxford University Press, 2004); online edition [http://www.oxforddnb.com/view/article/11190, accessed 20 March 2012]. Graham also made precision regulators for the Royal Observatory and other customers.

[17] James Bradley, 'A Letter to the Rt. Hon. George, Earl of Macclesfield, Concerning an Apparent Motion in Some of the Fixed Stars', *Philosophical Transactions* 45 (1748), 1–43, on 2. One could

Fig. 7.1   John Bird, engraved and published by Valentine Green, after a painting by Lewis, published 2 December 1776. A beam compass lies on top of the copy of Bird's *Method of Constructing Mural Quadrants* and his drawing of a large mural quadrant from the *Method of Dividing Astronomical Instruments*. Mezzotint; 426×321 mm (National Maritime Museum, PAF3435. © National Maritime Museum, Greenwich)

Bradley's enthusiasm in acknowledging Graham's very individual skills and qualities is notable, and echoes George Adams's insistence on the personal touch. Moreover, it was not just Bradley who appreciated what Graham as an individual brought to the instruments made under his name. Pierre-Louis

compare this rare acknowledgement of an artisan with René Antoine Ferchault de Réaumur's praise for the artist Hélène Dumoustier de Marsilly; see Lorraine Daston and Peter Gallison, *Objectivity* (New York: Zone Books, 2007), 84.

Moreau de Maupertuis, for example, wrote of a zenith sector taken on an expedition to Lapland to measure the length of a degree of meridian arc: 'It was made at *London* under that ingenious Artist Mr. *Graham*, a Fellow of the *Royal Society*, who had exerted himself to give it all the Advantages and all the Perfection that could be wished for. He had even taken the trouble to divide its Limb with his own hands.'[18] Like Bradley, Maupertuis foregrounded the extent to which Graham was personally involved in production, particularly the division of the scales.

This notion of the manual skill of an individual as crucial can be explored fruitfully in the work of John Bird (1709–1776), whom Graham trained in the art of instrument making and scale division. Bird, indeed, was Graham's natural successor in almost every way, becoming the main supplier of large astronomical instruments to observatories in Britain and overseas.[19] The title of an engraved portrait (Fig. 7.1) acknowledges this fulsomely:

> JOHN BIRD of LONDON, who furnished the Chief Observatories of the World, with the most Capital Astronomical Instruments divided by him after an improved method of his own, in a manner superior to any executed before, for which, and many other Improvements in the Construction of Astronomical Instruments, he was honoured with a considerable Recompence from the Commissioners of Longitude.

It is also worth noting the prominence the portrait gives to Bird's beam compass, his principal tool of inscription (as taught to him by Graham), which lies close to his hand.

Like Graham's customers, those purchasing instruments from Bird set great store by the touch of his hand. In 1768, for instance, Benjamin Franklin wrote from London to John Winthrop, Professor of Mathematics and Natural Philosophy at Harvard College, to apologize for not having sent several instruments he was helping to procure for the college. These included commissions from Bird and from James Short, a renowned supplier of reflecting telescopes. In both cases, it was clear what their own manual skills brought:

> You must needs think the time long that your instruments have been in hand. Sundry circumstances have occasioned the delay. Mr. Short, who undertook to make the telescope, was long in a bad state of health, and much in the country for the benefit of the air. He however at length finished the material parts that required his own hand, and waited only for something about the mounting that was to have been done by another workman; when he was removed by death. I have put in my claim to the instrument, and shall obtain it from the executors as soon as his affairs can be settled. It is now become much more valuable than it

---

[18] Pierre de Maupertuis, *The Figure of the Earth* (London: Printed for T. Cox and others, 1738), 65–6.

[19] Anita McConnell, 'Bird, John (1709–1776)', *Oxford Dictionary of National Biography* (Oxford: Oxford University Press, 2004); online edition [http://www.oxforddnb.com/view/article/2448, accessed 20 March 2012]; Chapman, *Dividing the Circle*, 71–6.

would have been if he had lived, as he excelled all others in that branch. The price agreed for was 100l [£100].

The equal altitudes and transit instrument was undertaken by Mr. Bird, who doing all his work with his own hands for the sake of greater truth and exactness, one must have patience that expects any thing from him. He is so singularly eminent in his way, that the commissioners of longitude have lately given him 500l [£500] merely to discover and make public his method of dividing instruments.[20]

As Franklin remarked, and as the posthumous print noted, Bird's skills were so valued that he had recently been granted a reward by the Board of Longitude to disclose his methods publicly.[21] The resulting publications—*The Method of Dividing Astronomical Instruments* (1767) and *The Method of Constructing Mural Quadrants* (1768)—offer telling accounts of the laborious, often individual, nature of dividing scales and building large observatory instruments.

For the purposes of this essay, the 1767 work is worthy of particular focus. As Adrian Johns has pointed out, publication in print was a common strategy for asserting authority for artists and craft workers of all types, with authorial rights becoming an increasingly prominent issue during the eighteenth century.[22] Bird's *Method of Dividing Astronomical Instruments* reflects these concerns. In his preface, Bird moves to assert his claim to be the acknowledged author of the printed work, of (some of) the methods described and of the instruments made, by outlining a distinctive textual strategy:

> The following Method of dividing Astronomical Instruments, &c. is collected principally from the experience which I have gained in thirty-four years, and, in some part, from the instructions I received from the late Mr. Jonathan Sisson.
>
> What I call my own, I have distinguished by Italic characters: If any other Instrument-makers have used the same method, it is unknown to me; and shall, therefore, pay no regard to any pretensions unsupported by evidence: I mean, pretensions, without producing Astronomical Instruments superiour, or at least equal to, those which I have made.[23]

Bird's italic/roman differentiation is used throughout the ensuing description, which draws on the techniques of his 'late worthy friend', George Graham, while carefully detailing the extent to which the author has developed additional techniques all his own.[24] This careful delineation of the origins—

[20] Benjamin Franklin to John Winthrop, 2 July 1768, in William Temple Franklin (ed.), *Memoirs of the Life and Writings of Benjamin Franklin*, 3 vols. (London: H. Colburn, 1818), vol. 3, 370–4, quote on 370–1.

[21] Derek Howse, 'Britain's Board of Longitude: The Finances, 1714–1828', *The Mariner's Mirror* 84 (1998), 400–17, especially 407.

[22] Adrian Johns, *Piracy. The Intellectual Property Wars from Gutenberg to Gates* (Chicago: University of Chicago Press, 2009).

[23] John Bird, *The Method of Dividing Astronomical Instruments* (London: Commissioners of Longitude, 1767).

[24] Bird, *The Method*, 5.

crucially, the authorship—of different parts of the *Method* perhaps reflects the fact that Bird's right to call particular techniques his own was being challenged as the work came towards completion. At a meeting of the Board of Longitude on 14 March 1767, the London instrument maker Jeremiah Sisson presented a memorial claiming that Bird's method was identical to his own and derived principally from Jonathan Sisson, his father. He requested that the Board compare their respective methods and reward him accordingly.[25] It is presumably no coincidence that Bird's preface, dated 14 March 1767 (although the whole work was not delivered until 21 March), did give credit—'at least in some part'—to the elder Sisson.[26] After consideration, however, the Board told Sisson junior that they could not adequately judge his claim and would not be rewarding him as they had Bird. Implicitly, the Board identified Bird as the legitimate author and owner of text and method, and left the often struggling Sisson without recompense.[27]

What becomes evident in reading Bird's *Method* is that it describes techniques of the hand, in particular of Bird's hands, the embodiment of his expertise and artistic skill. Touch is crucial in detecting and correcting error, he writes: '*if the said impression be not too faint, feeling, as well as seeing, will greatly contribute to make the points properly.*' Bird seems to deploy his tools as an extension of the hands, recommending '*holding the Beam Compass a small while in the hand*, previous to the cutting', this to allow hand and compass to come to thermal equilibrium. Elsewhere, he instructs readers: '*Lodge that point of the Beam Compass next your right hand...press gently with your finger upon the screw-head...and, with the point towards the right hand, cut the divisions*'.[28] The well-trained hand, Bird's text suggests, is the key to quality and accuracy.

TRUTH SEEKING: CONSIDERATIONS ETERNAL AND CONTINGENT

Bird's *Method* concerns the attempt to manufacture instruments that will help uncover truths about the operations of the universe, and Bird finishes his description with thoughts on this very question. Citing the very similar observational results produced by Tobias Mayer with a 6-foot mural quadrant at the University of Göttingen and by James Bradley with an 8-foot quadrant in Greenwich, both of which had been constructed under his supervision and inscribed by him, he concludes:

---

[25] Board of Longitude, 'Confirmed minutes', 14 March 1767, CUL RGO 14/5, 147.

[26] Nevil Maskelyne, 'Preface', in Bird, *The Method*, iii–iv, notes on iv that the writing and plates were delivered on 21 March 1767.

[27] Board of Longitude, 'Confirmed minutes', 21 March 1767, CUL RGO 14/5, 150; Derek Howse, 'Sisson, Jeremiah (*bap.* 1720, *d.* 1783/4)', rev. *Oxford Dictionary of National Biography* (Oxford: Oxford University Press, 2004); online edition [http://www.oxforddnb.com/view/article/37969, accessed 24 November 2014].

[28] Bird, *The Method*, 5, 6, 11 (original italics).

That two different observers, with instruments of different radii, and in different parts of Europe, should so nearly agree, is matter of no small astonishment; and sufficiently proves, that a mean of several observations, made by good observers with accurate instruments, properly adjusted, will always lead us either to the truth, or extremely near to it.[29]

Truth is an important word here and its use can be related to similar concerns in other scientific and artistic endeavours. Daston and Gallison, for example, have argued that a new Enlightenment ideal of 'truth-to-nature' saw a shift in emphasis towards 'the quest for regularities glimpsed behind, beneath, or beyond the accidental, the variable, the aberrant in nature'. In scientific illustration, this manifested itself in the 'reasoned image', which looked for the 'typical', 'ideal', 'characteristic' or 'average'.[30] They identify similar moves in painting, quoting Reynolds in his assertion that

amongst the blades of grass or leaves of the same tree, though no two can be found exactly alike, the general form is invariable: a Naturalist, before he chose one as a sample, would examine many; since if he took the first that occurred, it might have been an accident or otherwise such a form as that it would scarce be known to belong to that species; he selects as a Painter does the most beautiful, that is the most general form of nature.[31]

A 'convergence of artistic and scientific vision', they suggest, 'arose from a shared understanding of mission: many observations, carefully sifted and compared, were a more trustworthy guide to the truths of nature than any one observation.'[32] One can draw parallels with eighteenth-century astronomical investigation, in the quest to assimilate vast numbers of observations into coherent patterns and predictive models of the universal motions. Nowhere was this more urgently sought or challenging than in the attempt to pin down the motions of the Moon, among other things as part of the attempt to come up with workable methods for finding longitude at sea.[33] This was something in which both Bradley and Mayer had specific interests, and for which the mural quadrants by Bird, and by extension his manual skills, were essential.

[29] Bird, The Method, 14. Both instruments survive—Mayer's is in the University of Göttingen, C.001; see Helmut Grosser, Historische Gegenstände an der Universitäts-Sternwarte Göttingen (Göttingen: Akademie der Wissenschaften zu Göttingen, 1998), 24–5. Bradley's is on display in the Royal Observatory Greenwich (National Maritime Museum, Greenwich, AST0971).

[30] Daston and Gallison, Objectivity, 66–7.

[31] Joshua Reynolds, Discourse Delivered to the Students of the Royal Academy (1769), quoted in Daston and Gallison, Objectivity, 81; on Reynolds and the need to extract generalized characteristics in portraiture, see Celina Fox, The Arts of Industry in the Age of Enlightenment (New Haven & London: Yale University Press, 2009), 299.

[32] Daston and Gallison, Objectivity, 82.

[33] Richard Dunn and Rebekah Higgitt, Finding Longitude (Glasgow: Collins, 2014), 51–7, 95–9.

Bird's quote, like Daston and Gallison's analysis, suggests that observational agreement and the perception of truth-to-nature might have offered the principal means to assess quality. There is evidence, however, that there was more going on than this, and that peculiarly contingent trust in individuals and their personal skills and techniques (in this case, the parts Bird has in italics) could be equally powerful. Two examples in which Bird's individual skills as perceived by others were critical serve to illustrate this point.

The first took place a decade earlier and concerned the fate of an angle-measuring instrument devised by the Hanoverian astronomer Tobias Mayer, for determining a ship's longitude at sea. Having trained as a cartographer, Mayer became interested in understanding the Moon and its motions for the improved determination of terrestrial coordinates, and, following his appointment at the University of Göttingen, in ways of accurately determining longitude at sea by lunar distances. This required not only the production of good tables of the Moon's future positions, but also the creation of an instrument capable of accurate and precise observations from the deck of a ship. His proposal was a circular instrument that operated on the principle of double reflection, allowing the observer to sight two targets at once in order to measure their angular separation; in other words, it operated on the same principle as the octant, which first came to use in the 1730s and of which Mayer had read a description. Mayer originally hoped that just a description of his instrument could be submitted to the British Board of Longitude with his astronomical tables and associated method, rather than an actual instrument. In his view, it would be best that a trusted London craftsman such as Bird (whose work he knew well) make the instrument for testing. In the end, however, Mayer's acquaintances persuaded him that a craftsman from Göttingen should make a wooden prototype, and it was Mayer himself who divided its scale before it was sent to England in 1755.[34]

The instrument's circularity was fundamental to Mayer's conception. The observer was to make successive observations by moving the two arms around the scale, alternately fixing one then the other to make each new reading, then averaging the readings obtained (see Fig. 7.2). Mayer claimed that this reduced errors to plus or minus 10–15 seconds of arc. So the instrument and its operation used the circle as a certain principle with which to improve accuracy. The axiomatic certainty that a circle comprises 360 degrees guaranteed that the final (averaged) readings were true (or at least truer) than if relying solely on a shorter arc, which might have undetected division errors or even be of the wrong angular length.

What happened once the instrument reached London is revealing. In 1756, James Bradley, Astronomer Royal (and *ex-officio* Commissioner of Longitude)

---

[34] Eric G. Forbes, *Tobias Mayer (1723–62) Pioneer of Enlightened Science in Germany* (Göttingen: Vandenhoeck und Ruprecht, 1980), 162–9. The circle sent to England is probably the one illustrated in Tobias Mayer, *Tabulae Motuum Solis et Lunae* (London: W. & J. Richardson, 1770), Tab. II.

commissioned John Bird to make a brass version (Fig. 7.2). This was used for tests of Mayer's lunar tables the following year under the supervision of Captain John Campbell while on blockade duty off Cape Finisterre (during the Seven Years' War). Campbell found the large circular instrument cumbersome, however, and reported that only a third of its scale was usable. He therefore worked with Bird, who produced a more manageable instrument, a sextant, the scale of which was just a sixth of a circle (Fig. 7.3).[35] A point of particular interest in this development emerged in a letter written subsequently by Bradley, when he noted:

> as the principal use of this [circular] construction is to obviate the inconvenience proceeding from the inaccurate division of instruments and as that might be sufficiently removed by the care and exactness with which Mr. *Bird* is known to execute those that he undertakes to make; a sextant of a radius, twice as long as that of the circular instrument, was made by him, and afterwards used by Capt. *Campbell* in taking several observations on board the *Royal George* in different cruises near *Ushant* in 1758 and 1759.[36]

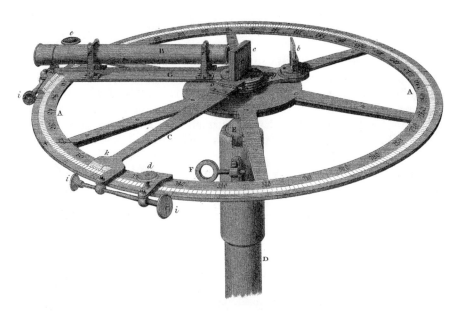

Fig. 7.2 Tobias Mayer's reflecting circle, as constructed by John Bird in 1757 for testing by John Campbell (From Abraham Rees, *The Cyclopaedia; or, Universal Dictionary of Arts, Sciences, and Literature* (London, 1820). © National Maritime Museum, Greenwich)

---

[35] William Pearson, 'Circle', in Abraham Rees (ed.), *Cyclopaedia*, 39 vols. (London: Printed for Longman, Hurst, Rees, Orme, & Brown and others, 1802–19), vol. 8; W.F.J. Mörzer Bruyns, *Sextants at Greenwich* (Oxford: Oxford University Press, 2012), 37.

[36] James Bradley to Mr. Clevland, Secretary of the Admiralty, 14 April 1760, reproduced in Mayer, *Tabulae*, cxi–cxv, on cxiii–cxiv.

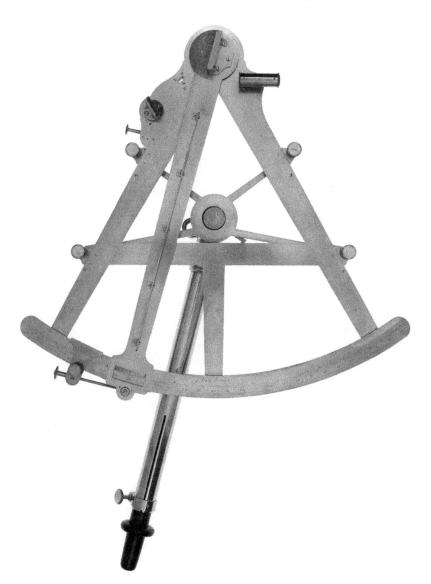

Fig. 7.3 Marine sextant, by John Bird, London, about 1758. Radius 18¼″ (464 mm); brass, glass, wood (National Maritime Museum, NAV1177. © National Maritime Museum, Greenwich)

In other words, the move from circle to sextant discarded the axiomatic certainty of the circle for the contingent guarantee of accuracy provided by the manual skills of one man, John Bird. Such was Bird's credibility that the guarantee of geometry could be discarded for pragmatic convenience. While this is a notable incident, it does not seem to have been unique. A key issue for Bradley and other observers lay in the attempt to identify and quantify instrumental error, then either eliminate or accommodate it. Dealing with such errors, indeed, remained fundamental to astronomical and navigational work. This was certainly the case in the work of Nevil Maskelyne during further trials of longitude methods and technologies in the 1760s.[37] It is notable in this context of legitimation from trust in contingent skills and techniques that Maskelyne's publications from these voyages were careful to name specific makers to confer credibility on the observational results. In a published letter on determining longitude by lunar distances on a voyage to St Helena in 1761, for instance, Maskelyne emphasized that his Hadley quadrant (octant) was by Bird. He was, therefore, 'secured from any errors in the construction of the quadrant, by the known skill of the artist'. It was not just Bird's hands and skills that Maskelyne relied on, however, since he also noted that the octant's mirrors and coloured glass filters 'were ground by Mr. Dollond, by a particular method of his own, by which he is certain of making the two surfaces of a glass truly parallel to each other'.[38] Issues of parallelism were a known source of error that Bradley, Maskelyne and others sought to identify and eliminate. Indeed, Maskelyne came back to parallelism and error at the end of the letter, when he made reference to Nicolas Louis de Lacaille's account of the difficulties of achieving accurate results even on land:

> I find myself at a loss to account for the great difference found by the Abbé De La Caille, in the result of several observations taken by himself, and a friend of his, at land, which ought to agree still nearer with one another than those made at sea. I cannot conceive that such able observers could be liable to an error of 5′ in measuring the distance of a star from the Moon's limb, if their instruments were not faulty. The most likely and the most common cause of error lies in the speculums and dark glasses; for if these are not ground truly parallel, which I am afraid they very often are not, by the common methods, they may easily produce a refraction of some minutes.[39]

Those 'common methods', the reader was to understand, stood in contrast to Dollond's presumably error-free 'particular method'.

There could, of course, be some connection here with a notion of 'brand' (to use a modern term) that was developing in the work of Josiah Wedgwood and others, yet there do seem to be distinctions to be made.[40] The Dollond name was certainly well known by the early 1760s as a result of John Dollond's

---

[37] Maskelyne, who became Astronomer Royal in 1765, was a protégé of Bradley; see Rebekah Higgitt (ed.), *Maskelyne: Astronomer Royal* (London: Robert Hale, 2014), 12–3, 90–1, 170. For his involvement in testing longitude methods, see Dunn and Higgitt, *Finding Longitude*, 98–103.

[38] Maskelyne, 'A Letter', 559.

[39] Maskelyne, 'A Letter', 576–7. A letter by 'Verax', including a translation of Lacaille's comments on the inaccuracies inherent in lunar-distance observations, appeared in *The Gentleman's Magazine* 37 (1757), 544–6; see also Mayer, *Tabulae*, cxxviii.

[40] N. McKendrick, J. Brewer and J.H. Plumb, *The Birth of a Consumer Society* (London: Hutchinson, 1983), 100–45, especially 137–40; Hilary Young (ed.), *The Genius of Wedgwood* (London: Victoria and Albert Museum, 1995), 9–20.

patent of the achromatic lens, which his son Peter aggressively protected.[41] In 1768, for instance, Jean Bernoulli wrote from London 'You know very well the name of M. DOLLOND, the celebrated artist', acknowledging the spread of the firm's name overseas.[42] By the end of the century, moreover, the firm's name had become synonymous with the telescope more generally, as became clear in a ballooning poem by Thomas Hood:

Ah me! my brain begins to swim!—
The world is growing rather dim;
The steeples and the trees—
My wife is getting very small!
I cannot see my babe at all!—
The Dollond, if you please![43]

Nonetheless, this appears to be different from Maskelyne's specific identification of Peter Dollond as the individual who executed the particular methods that conferred credibility on a measuring instrument. Likewise, it seems reasonable to suggest that Maskelyne's note in another paper, that he had observed the beginning and end of a lunar eclipse 'with an opera glass of Dollond's construction', is emphasizing the nature of Dollond's 'construction', rather than the name of the firm.[44] Again, there are parallels to be drawn with other fields; for instance, with Adrian Johns's discussion of medical cures and other pharmaceutical substances. 'In short,' he 'writes, authenticating substances generally meant authenticating people, and when people could not be authenticated serious problems arose.'[45] Credibility, in other words, resided in the 'maker'. Charisma, whether gained through recognized manual skill, persuasive rhetoric or the testimony of others, was key.

It is also possible to see this reliance on the guarantee provided by the personal touch extending into and beyond the end of the eighteenth century. As noted above, a significant change in instrument production in the 1770s was the introduction of mechanical scale division through Jesse Ramsden's development of dividing engines. Ramsden (1735–1800; Fig. 7.4) began working on this idea in the 1760s, but only after completing his second engine in 1774

[41] Brian Gee, Anita McConnell and A.D. Morrison-Low, *Francis Watkins and the Dollond Patent Controversy* (Farnham: Ashgate, 2014).

[42] Jean Bernoulli, *Lettres Astronomiques* (Berlin, 1771), quoted in J.A. Bennett, 'Shopping for Instruments in Paris and London', in Pamela H. Smith and Paula Findlen (eds.), *Merchants and Marvels. Commerce, Science, and Art in Early Modern Europe* (New York & London: Routledge, 2002), 370–95, quote on 370.

[43] Thomas Hood, 'Ode to Mr Graham, the Aeronaut', in *Odes and Addresses to Great People*, 2nd ed. (London: Printed for Baldwin, Cradock, and Joy, 1825), 1–13, on 2. For the Dollond firm and its reputation, see Richard Dunn, *The Telescope: A Short History* (London: National Maritime Museum, 2009), 72–82.

[44] Nevil Maskelyne, 'Astronomical Observations Made at the Island of Barbados', *Philosophical Transactions* 54 (1764), 389–92, on 391.

[45] Johns, *Piracy*, 103.

Fig. 7.4 Jesse Ramsden, engraved by John Jones, after a painting by Robert Home; published by Molteno, Colnaghi & Co., 1 January 1791. Mezzotint; 530×375 mm (National Maritime Museum, PAG6438. © National Maritime Museum, Greenwich)

did he inform the Board of Longitude of his new 'Instrument for dividing Sextants &c, the construction of which is such as leaves no dependance upon the Workman, as a Boy can use it with the same exactness as the most experienced hand; and in the most speedy manner.'[46] For handheld instruments,

[46] Board of Longitude, 'Confirmed minutes', 25 June 1774, CUL RGO 14/5, 262. This dividing engine is in the Smithsonian, Washington, MA*215518. His first engine of the 1760s is in the Musée des arts et métiers, Paris, 00100.

such as marine sextants and octants, this important development allowed the production of smaller, cheaper instruments on a sufficiently large scale to meet naval and merchant seafaring needs. The Board of Longitude recognized and rewarded Ramsden's innovation and encouraged other makers to build their own engines or use Ramsden's (at a fee) for dividing their scales.[47]

For the larger scales of bespoke observatory instruments, however, the artist's hand remained essential. From the mid-1770s, Ramsden ran a factory-style workshop in Piccadilly, with a range of specialist workers under one roof, something that was unique in the London trade. Nonetheless, it remained crucial for the individual maker to be seen as actively involved in the production of the instruments that bore his name, particularly in the production of high-end precision instruments for astronomy and navigation. The perception of personal skills still carried great weight; (literally) hands-on involvement was expected. In an echo of George Adams's comments of the 1740s, the *European Magazine* noted in 1789: 'That every part of his instruments may be fabricated under his own inspection, Mr Ramsden has in his workshops men of every branch of trade necessary for completing them'.[48] At the very least, the watchful eye of the master could reassure customers of the reliable quality of the instruments sold in his name. Further than this, the extent to which the very personal and individual skills of specific makers continued to be valued was still obvious in one plaintive cry, with Ramsden's unreliability already painfully obvious to a number of would-be buyers:

> My heart is set more than ever on M. Bergeret's mural quadrant; having been its legitimate owner for twelve hours, I cannot allow it out of my mind, and in one or other manner, I must have one by Ramsden, and even were I to own one by Bird, I would never surrender pride of owning one by Ramsden. And sadly there is but one Ramsden in this world, because if he was not there, and if there were another craftsman able to make one as perfect as that Arch-liar is capable of, I assure you my dear Count, I should long ago have resorted to that man.[49]

Robert Home's portrait of Ramsden, subsequently issued as a print by Valentine Green (Fig. 7.4), ties together these two seemingly divergent strands. Ramsden is shown leaning on his second dividing engine. Behind him, however, is the large observing circle he designed and made for Palermo Observatory, which, like Graham's mural quadrant, became a model for similar instruments in observatories elsewhere.[50] The engine hints at one future—the reproduction of identical instruments by machine. The circle nods to a second—innovation in large, bespoke instruments that still embodied and relied on the manual skills of their maker.

---

[47] McConnell, *Jesse Ramsden*, 39–51; Howse, 'Britain's Board of Longitude', 411; Dunn and Higgitt, *Finding Longitude*, 172–5.

[48] *European Magazine* 15 (1789), 96, quoted in McConnell, *Jesse Ramsden*, 53.

[49] Duke Ernst II von Sachsen-Gotha-Altenberg to Count Brühl, 26 September 1786, quoted in McConnell, *Jesse Ramsden*, 127.

[50] McConnell, *Jesse Ramsden*, 131–5.

Conclusion

In considering a very particular class of objects—precision instruments for astronomical and navigational observation—this essay has touched on some of their potentially unique aspects. Makers and users thought long and hard about instrumental accuracy and error in a way that may distinguish such artifacts from other manufactured items. Running somewhat counter to this was the notion that specific makers might have contingent and local skills as 'artists' that could in themselves provide some guarantee as to instrumental performance and quality. While this could tie up with what we might today call brand identity, in several instances it seems clear that a more specific argument was being made about the legitimation provided by 'the known skill of the artist', and that this is something that was still evident even as techniques of large-scale production began to be introduced.

Acknowledgements I would like to thank all those who attended the *Things* workshops in which earlier versions of this paper were discussed and enriched. Particular thanks are also due to Molly Dorkin for highlighting Joshua Reynolds, to Nicky Reeves and Jenny Bulstrode for their thoughts on John Bird's *Method*, and to Eóin Phillips and Katy Barrett for many comments and examples of enormous value to this chapter.

CHAPTER 8

Mapping New Spaces

Patricia Seed

Spurred by newly discovered coastlines on both sides of the Atlantic, map making had made huge strides during the sixteenth century. Thousands of miles of shorelines were recorded at tremendous speed and equally rapidly assimilated into enormous maps depicting three-quarters of the world's coasts. After this initial sprint, the pace of new discoveries slowed. So too did innovations in map making, which experienced a century-long lull.

As the eighteenth century began, innovations in mapping once again started to gain momentum. Encouraged once again by efforts to find a new route to Asia (Columbus's original ambition), this second wave of innovations focused on finding new routes across the Pacific, the vast ocean that Columbus had never breached.

Towards the end of the seventeenth century, French officials in the New World as well as in France launched efforts to compete against Spain in the China trade. Convinced that the Mississippi emptied into the Sea of California, in 1672 Jean Talon, the intendant of New France, sent Louis Jolliet and Jacques Marquette to find the Pacific Ocean. The pair only managed to reach Arkansas before turning back. Ten years later, Robert de La Salle undertook a more successful expedition, navigating through the mouth of the Mississippi heading westward towards the Pacific before foundering on the coast of Texas. While the route to China through the middle of the United States proved to be a chimera, France successfully founded a colony near the mouth of the Mississippi in 1699. French royal cartographer Guillaume Delisle, whose map is exhibited here, first gained recognition for his precision in mapping these French possessions in North America.

P. Seed (✉)
Department of History, University of California, Irvine, CA, USA
e-mail: seed5@uci.edu

© The Author(s) 2016

91

A. Craciun, S. Schaffer (eds.), *The Material Cultures of Enlightenment Arts and Sciences*, Palgrave Studies in the Enlightenment, Romanticism and the Cultures of Print, DOI 10.1057/978-1-137-44379-3_8

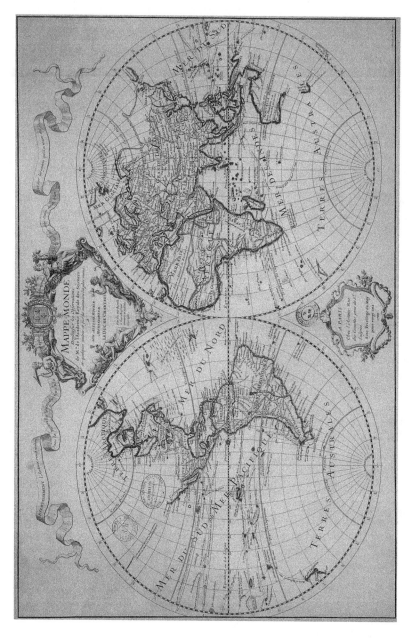

Guillaume Delisle, World map Drawn from Observations Made at the Academy of Sciences. Copperplate by Claude-Auguste Berey. Paris, 1700.
© De Agostini/The British Library Board

With the North American shortcut to Asia precluded, in 1700 French merchants and leaders turned their attention to potentially crossing the Pacific by sailing west from South America or east from the Indian Ocean. To persuade a royal as well as a mercantile audience of the feasibility of such trans-Pacific French journeys, Delisle portrayed previously successful Spanish and Dutch voyages from the west coast of South America and a Dutch voyage from the Indian Ocean, thus illustrating the potential of both approaches.

Absent logbooks recording the exact path of each ship, Delisle's map approximates the Pacific path of Magellan's ships in 1520, and three subsequent journeys from Peru: Álvaro de Mendaña y Neira's expeditions to the Solomon Islands (1567) and Marquesas (1595), together with Fernandes de Queirós's attempted return to the Solomon Islands in 1605, which discovered Vanuatu and the Pitcairn Islands instead. Two Dutch journeys appear. Jacob Le Maire's 1615–16 voyage proved that ships could sail around the southernmost tip of South America, far from the reach of Spanish ships. Abel Tasman's dramatic crossing of the southern Indian Ocean around the blustery shores of southern Tasmania in 1642 proved that China could be reached from that direction as well.

Although he first sketched his classic double-hemisphere map in 1700, Delisle continued to improve on it until his death. When he added the first trans-Pacific round trip by a Frenchman, Captain Nicolas de Frondat's 1708–11 circuit from Cape Horn to China and return via Guam and the Marianas to Peru, Delisle demonstrated that a French navigator could sail the Pacific from South America. However, the map maker omitted Frondat's name, noting only that of his ship, the *Saint-Antoine*.[1]

In order to reach the South American departure point for the Pacific, French pilots needed to travel to the south of the well-traversed sea lanes guarded by their Iberian competitors in the South Atlantic. To this end, Delisle sketched two southern-hemisphere crossings to reassure French pilots of the alternative routes in this region. He added Edmund Halley's journey that mapped changes in the magnetic fields in this region, rendering the magnetic compass more reliable in those waters. With Halley's information, a pilot could change course to evade pursuers and still arrive safely at his destination. Finally, Delisle illustrated the feasibility of the most extreme dodge against Iberian attacks of the South Atlantic journey of the *Saint-Louis* from Cape Horn to the Cape of Good Hope.

In addition to his encouraging guidance concerning Pacific crossings, Delisle also realized how important accurate longitude would be. For sailors on long exploratory forays across thousands of miles of nearly land-free open ocean, the technically easy but previously unimportant science of longitude would need to find a solution. While lacking scientifically precise information on the location of the island kingdoms of the Pacific, Delisle did use the most accurate techniques available at the time

---

[1] Gabriel Marcel, 'Les navigations des Francais dans la mer du sud au xviiie siècle,' *La Géographie (1900): bulletin de la Société de géographie* pp. 490–2.

to fix the longitude of French possessions in North America. While at least half a century would pass before technically correct longitude could be established for the Pacific, Guillaume Delisle's cognizance of the importance of this problem earned him a place as one of the finest European map makers of the early eighteenth century. His double-hemisphere maps, with their emphasis on the Pacific, retained their popularity for most of the first half of that century.

CHAPTER 9

By Hand or By Engine

Richard Dunn

Towards the end of the eighteenth century, the sextant and octant were becoming established as essential and iconic instruments of navigation (Fig. 9.1). Changes in training, practice and production methods underpinned this, the last allowing more, and more affordable, instruments to be made.

An inscription on this instrument's crossbar reads:

> This Sextant was presented to Admiral Sir John Ommaney [*sic.*] (then a Midshipman) by Ramsden himself in 1792; being graduated by his own hand, and afterwards given by Sir John to Capt. Blackwood, in 1851

The words look back nearly 60 years and were presumably inscribed for Captain Blackwood, perhaps a son of Sir Henry Blackwood.[1] What stands out is the emphasis on Ramsden and the graduation 'by his own hand'. In 1792, Jesse Ramsden was Britain's leading instrument maker. His fame and fortune derived in part from his development of mechanical 'dividing engines' for marking the scales of measuring instruments, an enterprise for which the Board of Longitude gave him a substantial reward.[2] These engines increased production rates and helped reduce the size and cost of sextants, octants and other instruments.

---

[1] J.K. Laughton, 'Blackwood, Sir Henry, First Baronet (1770–1832)', rev. Andrew Lambert, *Oxford Dictionary of National Biography* (Oxford: Oxford University Press, 2004); online edition [http://www.oxforddnb.com/view/article/2548, accessed 23 October 2012].

[2] Anita McConnell, *Jesse Ramsden (1735–1800). London's Leading Scientific Instrument Maker* (Aldershot: Ashgate, 2007), 39–51.

R. Dunn (✉)
Royal Museums Greenwich, London, UK
e-mail: rdunn@rmg.co.uk

© The Author(s) 2016
A. Craciun, S. Schaffer (eds.), *The Material Cultures of Enlightenment Arts and Sciences*, Palgrave Studies in the Enlightenment, Romanticism and the Cultures of Print, DOI 10.1057/978-1-137-44379-3_9

Fig. 9.1 Marine sextant, by Ramsden, London, about 1792. Radius 10″ (254 mm); brass, glass, wood (National Maritime Museum, NAV1140. © National Maritime Museum, Greenwich)

Given that the new dividing engines were meant to replace the vagaries of manual scale division with mechanical accuracy, there is some irony in the desire to place Ramsden's hand on this instrument. The hand of the artist could still, in an age of mechanical production, elevate and validate an instrument. A later testament to the sextant's perceived quality is that it was considered worth certifying at Kew Observatory in the nineteenth century, by Blackwood or by Herbert Edward Purey-Cust, the Admiralty surveyor from whom it passed to the National Maritime Museum.[3]

Ommanney's ownership throws up other interesting readings. As an 18-year-old midshipman in 1792, it would be unusual to own a sextant – the

[3] W.F.J. Mörzer Bruyns, *Sextants at Greenwich* (Oxford: Oxford University Press, 2012), 172; R.O. Morris, 'Cust, Sir Herbert Edward Purey- (1857–1938)', *Oxford Dictionary of National Biography* (Oxford: Oxford University Press, 2004); online edition [http://www.oxforddnb.com/view/article/41230, accessed 23 October 2012].

cheaper wooden octant was more common among junior officers. Perhaps it signalled Ommanney's prosperity and professional ambitions. That year, he joined the crew of the *Lion*, on which Lord Macartney led an ill-fated embassy to China, hoping to open up trade. Optical and mathematical instruments by Ramsden and others took pride of place as the cream of British workmanship. It is intriguing to speculate as to whether Macartney might have considered purchasing this high-quality sextant as he sought to augment the stock of gifts during the voyage outwards.[4]

Many readings accrue to this item, then: precision instrument; professional tool; mark of rank; valuable gift; jewel fashioned by a master's hand; product of mechanization; museum object.

[4] J.K. Laughton, 'Ommanney, Sir John Acworth (1773–1855)', rev. Andrew Lambert, *Oxford Dictionary of National Biography* (Oxford: Oxford University Press, 2004); online edition [http://www.oxforddnb.com/view/article/20757, accessed 23 October 2012]; J.L. Cranmer-Byng and Trevor H. Levere, 'A Case Study in Cultural Collision: Scientific Apparatus in the Macartney Embassy to China, 1793', *Annals of Science* 38 (1981), 503–25; Simon Schaffer, 'Instruments as Cargo in the China Trade', *History of Science* 44 (2006), 217–46.

CHAPTER 10

The Ship as Object: The Launch of the *Queen Charlotte*

James Davey

The launch of the naval ship *Queen Charlotte* was a remarkable occasion that drew thousands of people to Deptford (Fig. 10.1). *The Morning Post* went to great lengths to describe the event's extraordinary popularity:

> the Kent Road was filled by Persons repairing to Deptford to witness the launch. Great numbers of chariots coaches and carts, crowded with company, graced the road, while a corresponding number of pedestrians thronged the paths … the number of people collected in every part, where a view of the launch could be expected or hoped, was much greater than has been witnessed on a similar occasion for many years, and it must be confessed that the grandeur of the spectacle furnished an ample excuse for the curiosity of the populace.[1]

In a similar vein, the *Naval Chronicle* spoke of over 100,000 spectators.[2] The print vividly captures the public excitement that surrounded the launch. In doing so it offers a very different perspective to the many other prints produced at the height of the Napoleonic Wars that celebrated the Royal Navy. Depictions of heroic commanders and their glorious actions were commonplace, but prints representing naval launches celebrated the very fabric of the ship itself and shed light on one of the most important naval spectacles of the era. Images like this allow us to consider the ship as an object; one that was viewed and commented on by the broader British population. Thinking of the

---

[1] *The Morning Post*, 18 July 1810.
[2] *Naval Chronicle*, IIIV, 1810, 35–7.

J. Davey (✉)
National Maritime Museum, Royal Museums Greenwich, London, UK
e-mail: JDavey@rmg.co.uk

© The Author(s) 2016
A. Craciun, S. Schaffer (eds.), *The Material Cultures of Enlightenment Arts and Sciences*, Palgrave Studies in the Enlightenment, Romanticism and the Cultures of Print, DOI 10.1057/978-1-137-44379-3_10

Fig. 10.1 A view of the launching of his Majesty's Ship Queen Charlotte from Deptford Yard July 17th 1810 (Published by G. Thompson, 7 August 1810. Hand-coloured etching. NMM, PAH0775 © National Maritime Museum, Greenwich, London)

ship in this way helps to us to consider a range of social and cultural attitudes towards the navy, to technology, and to national identity.

There were many reasons why naval vessels attracted such popular interest. The ship was the largest and most sophisticated 'object' in existence, seen by many people as a technological wonder and an example of engineering brilliance. Descriptions of the *Queen Charlotte* emphasized its technical qualities, with *The Times* describing it as 'one of the finest models of naval architecture ever produced in this country'. The newspaper discussed the ship's 'grand and simple' proportions and the 'bold plainness' of its decorations, noting that the vessel conveyed 'a perfect idea of massive and majestic strength'.[3] *The Morning Post* commented on its aesthetic power: the *Queen Charlotte* was 'supposed to exceed in beauty, as it does in size any vessel that was ever launched on the Thames'. Commentators also noted its 'immense magnitude' and its 'stupendous size' that excited 'astonishment'.[4] As these reports testify, ship launches were meticulously staged to show off these objects to the public in the most

[3] *The Times*, 18 July 1810.
[4] *The Morning Post*, 18 July 1810.

positive way. Some were advertised in newspapers to maximize the audience, and by the 1790s launch notices had become part of the daily news cycle.

Care was also taken to ensure that these vessels reinforced popular ideas about the navy and the nation it represented. Ships were given their own names, as these magnificent objects were presented with their own identity and history. The largest ships, such as the 104-gun *Queen Charlotte*, were named after royalty, a living embodiment of crown and constitution. There was also a reference back to an earlier ship of the same name: built in 1790, this predecessor had been Admiral Howe's flagship at the Battle of the 'Glorious First of June', a notable British naval victory. As the print suggests, ship launches were also very patriotic events. One observer described a scene 'covered in flags and banners', and noted the 'general effect of this superb spectacle'. Bands played 'God Save the King', guns were fired and the ship 'rushed into the water, amidst the shouts of twenty thousand persons'.[5] *The Morning Post* commented on the 'strikingly grand' combination of flags, naval trophies and patriotic music, and recorded the sound of the 'assembled thousands' rending 'the air with loud huzzas, and closed a scene so noble with merited eclat'.[6] In this way the ship, at the moment of its launch, played a crucial role in presenting the navy to the public, and further reinforced the nation's preoccupation with its navy.

[5] *The Times*, 18 July 1810.
[6] *The Morning Post*, 18 July 1810.

CHAPTER 11

The *Nautical Almanac*: Instrument of Controversy

Sophie Waring

Old Nautical Almanacs are like rotten pineapples, once the very apex of astronomy, or gastronomy, and now only fit for the paper vat or the pigs. (Francis
Beaufort, 1848)[1]

The first *Nautical Almanac* was published in January 1767, followed quickly
by the 1768 edition, under the editorship of the Astronomer Royal, Nevil
Maskelyne. Captain Cook took the almanacs for 1768 and 1769 on his first
voyage of exploration (1768–71). The edition in this image is the *Nautical
Almanac* for 1822, and is the first edition produced, in 1820, under the
superintendency of Thomas Young, a doctor, mathematician and Admiralty-
sponsored civil servant in the period following the Napoleonic Wars (Fig. 11.1).
A book very similar to others produced in this period, the *Nautical Almanac*
was published annually and cost five shillings. Its main purpose was to simplify
attempts to find the longitude of a ship at sea; each annual volume contained all
the necessary tables and instructions to simplify both the taking of astronomical readings and the complex calculations of the 'lunar distance method', so
that seamen could conduct the calculation quickly and efficiently with minimal
error, securing their longitude.

After the first two editions were produced, Maskelyne was authorized by the
Board of Longitude to continue preparing the volumes. The annual editions
were published in advance of the years for which they predicted the movement

---

[1] Francis Beaufort to—Stratford, 27 June 1848, Hydrographic Office, UKHO LB15:242.

S. Waring (✉)
Modern Collections Curator, Museum of the History
of Science, University of Oxford, Oxford, UK
e-mail: sophie.waring@mhs.ox.ac.uk

© The Author(s) 2016
A. Craciun, S. Schaffer (eds.), *The Material Cultures of Enlightenment
Arts and Sciences*, Palgrave Studies in the Enlightenment, Romanticism
and the Cultures of Print, DOI 10.1057/978-1-137-44379-3_11

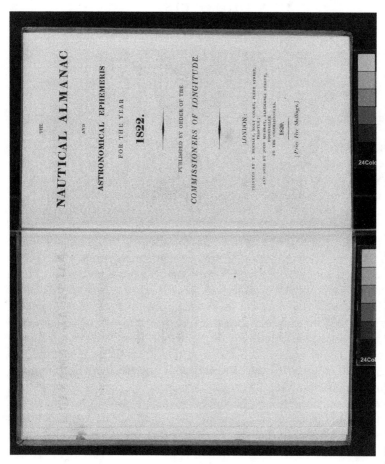

Fig. 11.1 The Nautical Almanac and Astronomical Ephemeris for the year 1822, published by order of the Commissioners of Longitude (Printed by T. Bensley, Sold by John Murray (London, 1820) © National Maritime Museum, Greenwich)

of the heavens, and they became standard issue on naval voyages. By the early nineteenth century, both chronometers and the lunar distance method were commonly employed for finding longitude at sea. The *Nautical Almanac* was essential to the lunar distance method and in this sense was an instrument in its own right, used in combination with a sextant, rather than simply being a reference text or book. The *Nautical Almanac* turned astronomical observations into meaningful data for finding a ship's longitude and transformed sextants into practical, rather than theoretical, tools for navigation and astronomy. The tables in the almanac were entirely functional and interactive: without them the readings from a sextant were useless. The *Nautical Almanac* was not passive; it functioned as one of many instruments that astronomers and navigators employed in their ambition to chart the stars or sail the oceans. The sailor performing the longitude calculation required no particular knowledge of the theory behind it; he just had to follow the instructions within the almanac. Importantly, the use of the almanac was finite, lasting only for the year that it described, and excess or out-of-date almanacs quickly became problematic for the Admiralty. This difficulty of excess copies resulted in the Hydrographer to the Navy, Francis Beaufort, commenting on the ephemerality of their usefulness and comparing them to rotten pineapples.

As the *Nautical Almanac* became an essential instrument for navigation, the problem of errors in the publication's calculations grew ever more serious. The astronomer John Herschel commented in 1842: 'An undetected error in a logarithmic table is like a sunken rock at sea yet undiscovered, upon which it is impossible to say what wrecks may have taken place.'[2] Herschel was writing in support of further funding for the mathematician Charles Babbage's analytical engine. Babbage's plans for calculation by steam would remove the potential for human error that apparently plagued the calculations done in the preparation of the *Nautical Almanac*. Herschel argued that calculating engines either worked or they did not, but that they never produced mistakes and therefore could overcome the human capacity for, or the inevitability of, error.

The presence and implications of errors in the *Nautical Almanac* place it at the centre of reform debates in Regency scientific circles. This rather unassuming book shaped debates about the place of science in society, and its funding, during the formative years of the early nineteenth century. The necessity of maintaining and safeguarding the quality of the *Nautical Almanac* was, for both astronomers and navigators, a significant motivating factor in the fluctuations of the reform movement that shaped the metropolitan scientific community. Thomas Young, the superintendent of this volume, his first, was condemned and his character publicly attacked in pamphlets and periodicals. The *Nautical Almanac* did not affect merely how longitude readings were produced, understood and utilized in this period, but also how the scientific

---

[2] John Herschel writing to the Chancellor of the Exchequer, Henry Goulburn, 16 September 1842, Royal Society Archive, RH:HS B27.51.

community interacted and evolved; it had a social as well as a scientific impact. Remaining editions of the *Nautical Almanac* offer historians insight into both the practical nature of navigation and the politics that swamped scientific endeavour in the Regency period. The book serves as a reminder that scientific instruments can also function as instruments of controversy.

CHAPTER 12

The Navy's New Clothes

Amy Miller

During the French Revolutionary and Napoleonic Wars (1792–1815), the Royal Navy held an iconic place in British society (Fig. 12.1). The Navy was the largest employer in Britain and advancement within it differed from the Army, being achieved through merit (although connections were desirable). There were great naval victories: the Battle of Trafalgar in 1805 forced Napoleon to abandon his maritime ambitions, and Britain held supremacy over the seas. The Navy was the saviour of trade and empire. Nevertheless, Trafalgar came at a cost—the loss of the man considered to be Britain's greatest naval hero, Horatio Nelson. The officers of the Navy were viewed as heirs to his genius, a legacy that proved a burden in the ensuing years, which saw a public crisis of confidence in Britain's Navy.

By the 1820s, the public perceived the Navy to be in decline in terms of both sea power and morality. Sir John Barrow, Second Secretary at the Admiralty, had launched a new programme of naval polar exploration in 1818, in part to remedy this crisis. In 1827, the Lord High Admiral, the future William IV, radically altered uniform regulations, dramatically changing the appearance of the Navy and creating a streamlined modern look. No records survive in regard to the motivations behind the uniform change; in their absence, it must be examined in its cultural context. In 1824, one pamphleteer, 'An Old Naval Surgeon', questioned 'why their Lordships have not, at a time like the present, turned their attention to the moral improvement of the Navy.'[1] He referred to

---

[1] Anon., *An Address to the Officers of His Majesty's Navy, by an Old Naval Surgeon* (London: Hatchard and Son, 1824), 4.

A. Miller (✉)
National Maritime Museum, Royal Museums Greenwich, London, UK

© The Author(s) 2016
A. Craciun, S. Schaffer (eds.), *The Material Cultures of Enlightenment Arts and Sciences*, Palgrave Studies in the Enlightenment, Romanticism and the Cultures of Print, DOI 10.1057/978-1-137-44379-3_12

Fig. 12.1 Commander James Clark Ross (1800–62) dubbed by Lady Franklin 'the handsomest man in the Navy' (Painted by John Robert Wildman in 1834 shortly after Ross's return from an expedition in the Arctic. BHC2981, in the collection of the National Maritime Museum, Greenwich, London, Caird Fund)

the transition from sail to steam and felt that strides forward on one front were at odds with what was popularly viewed as outmoded moral laxity. The novelist Frederick Marryat, who served in the Napoleonic wars, highlighted the damaging moral environment of the ship in his novel *Frank Mildmay* (1829), which focused on the moral decay of the eponymous character, a naval officer.

Mildmay cites 'sensual education in the cockpit'[2] while still a young midshipman for his decline. To change the uniform meant visually severing the 'old Navy' from the new. The new, correct dress was pared of excesses and denoted the moral rightness not only of the wearer, but of the organization he represented.

Some people thought that the new uniform linked to the effeminate masculinity of the dandies—flamboyantly fashionable men of the 1830s—rather than a reshaped morality. This association with dandyism, paired with the phasing out of ships of the line (part of the transition to steam power), engendered a public hysteria, a new public perception of a downsized and vulnerable Navy manned by dandies. *The Navy* (1838), a privately published pamphlet, warned that the loss of the old ships of the line meant that 'the wooden walls are thrown down; the country is laid open; ... and defenceless must England remain unless her walls are set up again.'[3]

Polar exploration proved an antidote to these fears. These expeditions were not new; even Nelson as a young midshipman was on Phipps's Arctic expedition, attempting to capture a polar bear for its skin, an event depicted in popular prints. These voyages were eclipsed by naval achievements in the Arctic and Antarctic from the 1820s–1840s. Polar exploration contributed to the expansion of empire and intellectual and cultural cachet, and in this sphere the Navy surpassed the legacy of Nelson.

The 1834 portrait of James Clark Ross, who discovered the magnetic north pole in June 1831, embodies the new naval hero, resplendent in his dress uniform, swathed in bearskin and surrounded by the attributes of his discovery. His immaculate full dress is tempered by the bearskin, implying that the masculinity of the *arctic* explorer is a foil to the overly refined dandy. Where Nelson failed, Ross got his bearskin.

---

[2] Frederick Marryat, *The Naval Officer; or, Scenes and Adventures in the Life of Frank Mildmay*, 3 vols. (London: Henry Colburn, 1829), vol. 3, 256.

[3] Edward Hawker, *The Navy, Letter to His Grace the Duke of Wellington, K.G., upon the Actual Crises of the Country in Respect to the State of the Navy* (London: A. Spottiswoode, 1838), 2.

CHAPTER 13

Unwrapping Gods: Illuminating Encounters with Gods, Comets and Missionaries

Maia Nuku

In London in October 1818, an engraving announcing 'The family idols of Pomare' (Fig. 13.1) appeared in the widely circulated evangelical publication *Missionary Sketches III*.[1] Seven Tahitian gods (or *to'o*) feature in a numbered series along the top, hovering rather sinisterly over two carved wooden figures (known as *ti'i*, a derivative of the more familiar *tiki*). These flank a still more unusual carving, identified simply as no. 9, an upright baton with rounded finial and tip that appears to have a series of curiously arched canopies punched along its length. These, it is explained, were the family idols of the Tahitian chief Pomare, 'relinquished, and sent to the Missionaries at Eimeo, either to be burnt, or sent to the Society'.[2] This gathering of oddly shaped forms, replete with feather attachments and coconut fibre bindings, loom over a pair of squat wooden effigies beneath. The larger carving in particular has odd proportions: distorted facial features and a pair of stumped arms. Descriptions in the accompanying legend reinforce the overall visual perplexity of the image, 'the relation of different elements suggest[ing] no manifest form ... which pre-

---

[1] The London Missionary Society (subsequently LMS) was a non-denominational missionary society, largely Congregationalist in outlook, formed in 1795 by evangelical Anglicans and Nonconformists, which established missions in the Pacific, India, Africa and China. Original correspondence, reports and journals along with edited publications relating to the transactions of the LMS are housed in the archive of the Council for World Mission (subsequently CWM), Archives and Special Collections, School of Oriental and African Studies (SOAS), University of London.

[2] *Missionary Sketches III* (Oct 1818), CWM, 3.

M. Nuku (✉)
Metropolitan Museum of Art, 1000 Fifth Ave, New York, NY 10028 USA
e-mail: M.nuku@metmuseum.org

© The Author(s) 2016
A. Craciun, S. Schaffer (eds.), *The Material Cultures of Enlightenment Arts and Sciences*, Palgrave Studies in the Enlightenment, Romanticism and the Cultures of Print, DOI 10.1057/978-1-137-44379-3_13

THE FAMILY IDOLS OF POMARE,

Which he relinquished, and sent to the Missionaries at Eimeo, either to be burnt, or sent to the Society.

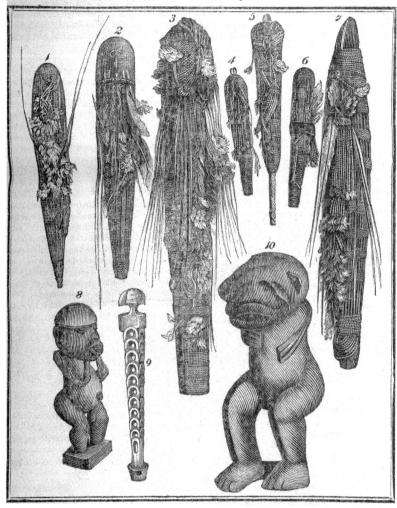

Fig. 13.1 The Family Idols of Pomare, *Missionary Sketches III* (October 1818). Council for World Mission archive, SOAS Library (CWML U156)

sumably aroused disquiet and fear in the viewer'.[3] Alien and unknowable, missionaries were alleged to have been rather disturbed by their strangeness: the accompanying text explained 'they differ from anything we remember to have seen or read of, which has been used by idolaters for the purpose of worship'.[4]

In general, missionaries had struggled to grasp the sheer significance of these baton-shaped gods, control of which had caused Tahiti and its neighbouring islands to descend into warfare. They were described variously as grotesque, rude and featureless. Captain Wilson, who had settled the first missionaries on Tahiti in 1797, pondered their significance: 'Yet to these wooden representatives the[y] seemed to pay little respect'.[5] To missionaries, who expected gods to look anthropomorphic, *to'o* seemed pretty insubstantial:

> The image of their god is nothing more than a piece of hard wood called Eito [*aito*], about 6 ft. long, without any carving, wrapt up in sundry cloths, and decorated with red feathers &c[.] Into this log of wood the natives confidently affirm Oro [the god] ... enters at peculiar times.[6]

Their unexpected shapelessness conformed to missionary expectations about idolatry and reinforced already considerable misgivings about the state of barbarism in the islands. In short, these idolatrous images became vessels onto which missionaries might project their own fears and anxieties.

Almost 30 years earlier, Joseph Banks had written of his own encounter with a *fare atua*, a chest or 'god house' in which precisely this order of sacred objects were kept. Banks had joined HMS *Endeavour* under the command of Captain James Cook, whose principal objective was to observe the Transit of Venus on Tahiti. Anchoring briefly off the coast of Huahine in 1769, Banks took to exploring the island, leaving us this journal entry for July 18:

> One end of the chest was open with a round hole within a square one, this was yesterday stopd up with a piece of cloth which least I should offend the people I left untouched, but to day the cloth and probably the contents of the chest were removd as there was nothing at all in it.[7]

Two days later, having arrived at the neighbouring island of Ra'iatea, a small party including Banks were led by the high-ranking *Arioi* priest Tupaia[8]

[3] N.Thomas, *Entangled Objects: Exchange, Material Culture and Colonialism in the Pacific* (Cambridge, MA: University of Harvard Press, 1991), 154.

[4] *Missionary Sketches III* (Oct 1818), CWM, 2.

[5] J.Wilson, *A Missionary Voyage to the Southern Pacific Ocean in the Years 1796, 1797 and 1798, in the Ship 'Duff', Commanded by Captain James Wilson* (London: T. Chapman, 1799), 166.

[6] Jefferson, 20 April 1801, South Sea Journals, CWM; also cited in C. Newbury (ed.), *History of the Tahitian Mission 1799–1830* (Cambridge: Hakluyt Society, 1961), xliii.

[7] J.C. Beaglehole, *The Endeavour Journal of Joseph Banks 1768–1771*, 2 vols. (Sydney: Angus and Robertson, 1962), I, 316.

[8] Tupaia was a high-born Ra'iatean chief schooled in the ritual arts, navigation and oratory. Tupaia accompanied Captain Cook onboard HMS *Endeavour* as the expedition continued from

to Taputapuatea, the most sacred (or *tapu*) ritual precinct in central Polynesia. Banks encountered up to four or five of these *fare atua* and now conjured up the courage to explore inside at least one of them. He wrote:

> One of these I examind by putting my hand into it: within was a parsel about 5 feet long and one thick wrapped up in matts ... These I tore with my fingers till I came to a covering of mat made of plattd Cocoa nut fibres which it was impossible to get through so I was obligd to desist, especialy as what I had already done gave great offence to our new friends.[9]

Banks was trying to get to grips with one of these *to'o* that comprised a heavy wooden shaft encased in a finely plaited covering made of woven coconut fibre cords, known as sinnet. These intricate bindings were often knotted and wound around the wooden core of such artifacts to create a fibre encasement. Further layers of highly potent materials (including feathers, plaited lengths of human hair and small strips of the finest white barkcloth) might then be knotted and bound into this outer wrapper, usually to the accompaniment of rhythmic chanting by ritual practitioners, the steady recital of which was an important means of activating their potency.[10] Designed to encourage the presence of gods so that they might enhance the efficacy of ritual procedure, *to'o* continued to be added to over time, the accretion of bindings serving as a useful aid to assist in the seamless delivery of chanting, for this had to be fluid and faultless to be fully effective.[11] Esoteric knowledge was intricate and complex, a series of formulas that flowed one into the other. Repeated in steady motion, each consecutive phrase built on the foundation of the former to create a continually evolving rhythm whose momentum may have been intended to mimic

---

Tahiti to New Zealand and beyond, proving himself invaluable as an intermediary during Cook's various encounters and negotiations with islanders and Maori. He did not survive the voyage, dying unfortunately in Batavia in November 1770, but his remarkable visual legacy remains, which includes his own chart of the Polynesian islands, a facsimile of which is in the British Library ('Tupaia's Chart of the Society Islands with Otaheite in the centre, July-August 1769', British Library 21592C). A suite of further pencil and watercolour illustrations, also held in the British Library (*Maori bartering a crayfish*, Tupaia, 1769, BL, Add. MS 15508, f. 11; *Chief Mourner*, Tupaia, 1769, BL, Add. MS 15508, f. 9), give us unique and invaluable insights into the ritual and daily life of eighteenth-century islanders. Refer also to Anne Salmond, *The Trial of the Cannibal Dog: Captain Cook in the South Seas* (London, 2003).

[9] Beaglehole, *Endeavour Journal*, I, 318.

[10] Refer to T. Henry, *Ancient Tahiti*, Bishop Museum Bulletin No. 48. (Honolulu: University of Hawaii, 1928); A. Babadzan, *Les dépouilles des dieux: essai sur la religion tahitienne a l'époque de la découverte* (Paris: Maison des sciences de l'Homme, 1993), 89–41; A. Kaeppler, 'Containers of Divinity', in S. Hooper (ed.), *Polynesian Art: Histories and Meanings in Cultural Contexts*, Special Issue, *Journal of Polynesian Society* 116, 2 (2007), 97–130.

[11] LMS missionary J.M. Orsmond devoted a full 20 pages of his manuscript 'Tahitian Texts' to entries concerning '*aha* which explained the binding techniques associated with coconut fibre cord, red feathers and the chanting of prayers. The dynamic process of assemblage was as crucial as the thing itself'. According to Orsmond, *aha atua* did not only refer to the sennit used to make a god, but to 'the whole round of prayers offered to him' (Sydney: Mitchell Library, 1862).

the original phases of creation and evolution, conceived of as a process of unin-
terrupted and continued growth (or *tupu*).

To'o were commonly referred to as batons or posts, and the term was an apt
one since they were literally intended as posts or support with which to prop
up the sky. Cosmological accounts described Ta'aroa, the earliest creator god,
as conjuring forth gods in the night. Finding himself in a void of darkness,
Ta'aroa had pushed against the limits of the space surrounding him and pecked
his way through the shell in which he found himself encased. Overturning this
empty dome, he raised it up to form the canopy of the sky, creating a world of
light from the void of darkness.[12] *Te po* was the realm associated with darkness
and the night, with ancestors, gods and spirits. Conceived not so much as a
cold or empty void, it was a vital and active space that pulsed with the force of
regeneration. Its corresponding realm was a world of light and life, known as
te ao, in which ordinary human endeavour took place. For islanders who dwelt
in the everyday, artefacts such as *to'o* were a means of engaging with their gods,
the spirits and ancestors who dwelt on the other side of their existence in *te po*.

This link to the divine was instantiated in the materiality of the *to'o* itself.
Expertly prepared and plaited coconut fibre cordage was highly valued throughout central Polynesia, where it was associated with the god Tane. Red and yellow
feathers were valued for their extreme rarity as well as their association with the
earliest creator god Ta'aroa, for, having escaped the dark void of *te po* and raised
up the canopy of the sky, Ta'aroa now stepped into the light, shedding the feathers from his body, which became the trees, plants, rivers and landscape of Tahiti.
Feathers were charged quite literally with the potency of *te po*, the night realm
in which gods resided. They did not represent or symbolize divinity, they were
literal instantiations of it.

While the gods illustrated in the engraving that announced the family idols
of Pomare were deeply problematic to early voyagers and missionaries—for they
failed of course to 'look' like gods in any representational or anthropomorphic
sense—islanders accepted that they instantiated core principles of divinity. When
activated with word and gesture, they enabled interaction between gods and men,
acting as a dynamic link between two complementary realms. Islanders embraced
the unique materiality of their gods, a crucial aspect of the gods' make-up. The
highly convoluted surface textures of *to'o* enhanced their ability to captivate and
transform, for binding signified a change in status that enabled the breaching of
significant thresholds during ritual. Wrapping and binding—the attachment of
cord, hair and feathers—were directed towards the effective capture and harness-
ing of potency, which enabled humans to access the charged *mana tapu* of gods.[13]
Crucially, it was precisely the *material* aspect of god images that secured transcen-
dence to the *immaterial* or, as Europeans understood it, the spiritual domain.

---

[12] T. Henry, *Ancient Tahiti*, 336–8.

[13] Refer to A. Gell, *Art and Agency. An Anthropological Theory* (Oxford: Clarendon Press,
1998).

MISSION MUSEUM, LONDON

By 1818, London missionaries had been resident in Tahiti for over two decades and the published engraving served as a public announcement of recent missionary success in the region. Pomare II had forwarded his ancestral gods to missionaries in the settlement at Papetoai with a letter, dated Feb 1816, explaining his motives:

> Friends … I wish you to send those idols to Britane for the Missionary Society, that they may know the likeness of the gods that Tahiti worshipped… If you think proper, you may burn them all in the fire; or, if you like, send them to your country, for the inspection of the people of Europe, that they may satisfy their curiosity, and know Tahiti's foolish gods![14]

These ten idols came to form the original core of the Mission Museum collection and were displayed in a series of galleries alongside the secretariat of London Missionary Society headquarters in Austin Friars, within the City's square mile. Public admission to the museum was limited in 1826 to one day a week—Wednesday—and was subject to an individual procuring a signed ticket from one of the Society's officers. Each week a small group of interested parties was admitted and guided by a member of the Society through the extraordinarily diverse collections that missionaries had amassed during their various missions to Africa, India, China and the Pacific. A catalogue of the Museum's principal attractions was published in 1826 and promised that alongside 'specimens in natural history [were to be found the] various idols of heathen nations'[15] as well as their 'dresses, manufactures, domestic utensils, instruments of war, &c.'[16]

Betraying the underlying structure of missionary collecting practice, the various categories and classifications inscribed within the catalogue are a useful means of isolating the diverse strategies by which London missionaries sought to make sense of the heathen (or *etene*) populations they set out to convert. Deeply cynical about the system of religion they were attempting to dismantle, missionaries targeted the various orders of ritual practitioners—referred to loosely as 'priests'—and accused them of colluding with Satan in support of a system of superstition 'wonderfully adapted to debase the mind, and keep the people in the most abject subjection'.[17] Priests were 'sorcerers' charged with ensnaring gods with their 'conjuring implements',[18] their 'cruel and wicked practices … b[inding islanders] in the chains of their superstition'.[19]

---

[14] *Missionary Sketches III* (Oct 1818), CWM, 3.

[15] W. Phillips, *Catalogue of the Missionary Museum* (London: London Missionary Society, 1826), frontispiece.

[16] Ibid.

[17] W. Ellis, *Polynesian Researches*, 4 vols. (Rutland: Tuttle, 1831 [1969]), I, 406.

[18] J. Davies, in Newbury, *History of the Tahitian Mission*, 177.

[19] Ibid., 101.

An *Advertisement* preceding the 1826 catalogue outlines the Society's keen ambition that a view of the gods and trophies of Christianity might inspire zeal and continued commitment to the missionary cause. Explaining that articles in the collection are 'calculated to excite … feelings of deep commisseration [*sic.*] for the hundreds of millions of the human race, still the vassals of ignorance and superstition',[20] it hoped that a public encounter with the varied manufactures of these countries might also 'prove how capable even the most uncivilized of mankind are of receiving that instruction which it is the study of the Missionaries to communicate'.[21] With each turn of the page, galleries unfolded: shelves, cabinets and vitrines line the walls, each harbouring unimaginable diversity, a myriad artifacts from overseas shores. Alongside Indian idols and graven images from China are a 'model of the large Church, 712 feet long, built by Pomare, for the worship of Jehovah'[22] in Tahiti. This was a visual marker of the mission's apparently startling progress to date, while a 'globe, representing the religion of the different countries',[23] functioned as a visual aid to mapping out future expansion. Surrendered idols expertly conveyed a narrative of triumph. As an index of the former heathenism of islanders, they usefully evidenced the spiritual transformation in which islanders now appeared to be engaged and acted as philanthropic incentives to support the continued work of the mission.

VISUAL METAMORPHOSIS: DARKNESS TO LIGHT

During the course of their long-term residency in Tahiti, English missionaries had enacted a kind of visual metamorphosis[24] on the island landscape of Tahiti and its surrounding archipelagos. White limestone churches and organized settlements saw gardens enclosed for cultivation. The wearing of hats, sober garments and attendance at church brought about a reorganization of safely domesticated life that was central to the material and ideological revolution that missionaries hoped to bring about. Evangelical rhetoric employed not only metaphors of light seeping into darkness, but ideas of parched, arid deserts (by implication, a reference to the soul) described as flourishing into lush, fertile pastures. A landscape transformed in synch with converted souls—this was wild, lush nature tamed.

A handful of tantalizing references in the archive also suggest that missionaries played out their metaphorical understandings of this transition from darkness to light through the instructive use of philosophical apparatus and instruments, playing out visual experiments, described as 'ocular demonstrations', for the benefit of islanders. Exhaustive lists of gifts and donations bequeathed to the

---

[20] Phillips, *Catalogue of the Missionary Museum*, iv.

[21] Ibid., iii.

[22] Ibid., 19.

[23] Ibid., 45.

[24] S. Sivasundaram, *Nature and the Godly Empire: Science and Evangelical Mission in the Pacific, 1795–1850.* (Cambridge: Cambridge University Press, 2005).

Missionary Society in support of the Tahitian mission were printed in evangelical publications with specific requests for further items to assist in the speedy establishment of a South Seas Academy for the instruction of young converts. Reporting on the progress of the mission as part of the LMS Deputation to the South Seas (1821–24), Revd Daniel Tyerman and George Bennet strongly urged 'the religious public to send contributions of both books and philosophical apparatus for the use of both these important Institutions'.[25] As well as requests for slates, pencils, alphabet wheels and globes to assist in teaching geography, missionaries suggested items that would assist them in their efforts to articulate notions of intellectual and spiritual development to islanders. Focusing on mathematics, astronomy and a useful knowledge of the 'Heavenly Bodies' (the planets, their magnitudes, motions and eclipses), Tyerman and Bennet note the special donation of an orrery, a clockwork model of the planetary system. This visually demonstrated for islanders the phenomenon of the seasons and the various orbits of the moon, earth and sun. In 1825, David Darling was thrilled to report the further donation of 'an air-pump and apparatus, an orrery, a camera obscura, a box of magnetism nearly complete, [and] a pair of valuable globes'.[26]

Scientific apparatus that encouraged the diffusion or refraction of light in particular were used as props to illustrate sermons and lectures—a visual reinforcement acknowledged to be a highly persuasive means of encouraging islanders to embrace the new religion. Missionaries continued to use the analogy extensively in their own rhetoric and the Society's former chairman and co-founder was no exception. Although the energetic Revd Dr Haweis had never himself visited Tahiti, he was its staunchest supporter and patron. Having argued strongly in 1797 for Tahiti to be the initial site for missionary settlement, Haweis was able to reflect almost 20 years later on this apparently strategic success: 'As from the beginning was my hope ... [that] if the light was collected in this focus, from thence the diverging rays would spread, till the multitude of the isles should be illumined.'[27]

These dramatic displays seem also to have been favoured by converted islanders, 'native ministers' known as deacons, who were spreading the message to outlying island groups. In Rurutu, for example, Threlkeld and Williams reported that 'the two native teachers made very suitable addresses to the congregation and the ocular demonstration of the powers of Christ overturning the kingdom of Satan ... raised sensations of joy and gratitude which men of the world are strangers to'.[28]

---

[25] Extract of a Letter of Messrs Tyerman and Bennet, *Quarterly Chronicle of Transactions of the Missionary Society (TMS)*, III, CWM, 146.

[26] Report to Directors, 1825, CWM, 162.

[27] Letter Thomas Haweis to George Burder, 6 August 1819, CWM, South Seas Incoming.

[28] Report from Threlkeld and Williams, 11 November 1822, CWM, South Seas Incoming, Box 3 Folder 8.

The reference is instructive and alerts us to the fact that islanders appear to have responded with equal vigour to missionary narratives that underscored a relationship between light and and a state of enhanced spirituality, not least because these satisfied already current ideas about the *tapu* (or sacred) nature of light and luminosity. Thunder, bolts of lightning, the tail of a comet streaking through the sky were all portentous signs of gods alerting their arrival and presence in *te ao*, the light-filled realm inhabited by humans. Encouraged to fly through the sky, gods were literally beckoned into the light from the dark reaches of *te po*, the shadowy realm in which they dwelt alongside ancestral spirits. God images were specifically designed to instigate this transition across the fluid boundaries between the two opposing realms. Unwrapped and brought out of storage for the occasion, they were re-presented for ritual, anointed with oils, bathed in the smoke of burned offerings and bound anew with cords of sinnet and feathers.

In his *Narrative of Missionary Enterprises* (1841), John Williams leaves his own account of a display instigated by islanders that saw a host of surrendered idols presented to missionaries in the chapel at Ra'iatea. As the evening drew in on 9 August 1821, Williams recalls:

> A meeting was held in our large chapel, to communicate the delightful intelligence to our people, and to return thanks to God for the success with which he had graciously crowned our first effort to extend the knowledge of his name ... In the course of the evening the rejected idols were publicly exhibited from the pulpit. One in particular, Aa, the national god of Rurutu, excited considerable interest; for, in addition to his being bedecked with little gods outside, a door was discovered at his back, on opening which, he was found to be full of small gods; and no less than twenty-four were taken out, one after another, and exhibited to public view.[29]

Here now exhibited from the pulpit, the islanders of Rurutu stage-managed a dramatic rejection of their former gods by opening up the back of A'a to release dozens of smaller gods, described as 'little gods ... the family gods of the old chiefs, the points of spears, old slings, &c., of ancient warriors',[30] which may well have referred to the simple wooden and sinnet-bound armature of *to'o* and *tahiri*.

This public exhibition of idols in the missionary chapel was an open and public declaration by Rurutuan islanders of their recent decision to embrace the new religion, with the unique figural sculpture of A'a perhaps its ultimate trophy. Presented by islanders at LMS missionary headquarters in Ra'iatea, A'a

[29] J.Williams, *A Narrative of Missionary Enterprises in the South Seas; with Remarks upon the Natural History of the Islands Origin, Languages, Traditions, and Usages of the Inhabitants.* (London: J. Snow, 1841), 37–8.

[30] J. Montgomery, *Journals of Voyages and Travels by Revd. Daniel Tyerman and George Bennet* (London: F.Westley and A.H.Davis, 1831), I, 507–8.

was given up to missionaries, or 'cast off',[31] just north of Taputapuatea, the most revered and sacred site in the whole of Polynesia; the epicenter, if you will, of island religion.[32] Slippage occurs in the diverse accounts relating the capture of this 'Great God Aa from Rurutu'.[33] An extract purporting to be an eye-witness account gives the name of the idol as 'the great national god, Taaroa',[34] and this is the name cited in the engraving published three years later in *Missionary Sketches XXIV* (January 1824; Fig. 13.2). The reference to Ta'aroa is apt given that that he is the creator god from whom all others descend, and appropriate given the sculpture's very explicit instantiation of creativity and divinity: 30 small figures sprout forth to stud the entire surface of the sculpture, which is itself an erect phallus. This effect is diminished rather in the published illustration, where a loose belt or *maro* has been added to protect its dignity.

There were certainly established precedents in Polynesia for the replacement (or 'casting off') of ineffectual gods. These entailed making an exhortation to the rejected god to return to *te po*, the domain of Ta'aroa, the original creator god, god of all gods: '*Te va atu nei au ia 'oe. E haere roa 'oe i te Vai-tu-po, i te aro o Ta'aroa, to 'oe na metua, Ta'aroa, te metua o te mau atua 'atoa'*.[35] After this proceeding, 'another god was chosen to take its place … [and a] new image … was made and inaugurated'.[36] In this context, the efforts of London missionaries to establish their own Christian god in Tahiti from 1797 onwards can be understood as the latest incursion in a ritual landscape that could accommodate the repeated attempts of competing constituencies to position their own god(s) at the head of the religious and political hierarchy.

The dramatic display of these idols in the depth of night also echoed the gatherings of high-status *Arioi*, which had formerly taken place at night in large shelters illuminated by lamps incorporating numbers of candles manufactured from *tutui*, or candlenuts. When lit in fulsome quantity, the light could be so abundant as to create day in the night, which was known as *rehu arui*, literally 'night-day', and was particularly auspicious.[37] Tyerman and Bennet

---

[31] Henry, *Ancient Tahiti* (Honolulu: Bishop Museum, 1928), 178.

[32] The suffix to Ta'aroa—Upo'o Vahu—refers to 'eight heads', which may have been a reference to the eight political units or chiefly districts that formerly made up the regional landscape. In a fascinating convergence, eight noticeably raised knots in the grain of the wood turned out in fact to be eight iron nails, driven into the sculpture in several places (noted by Steven Hooper and Maia Nuku on close examination of the sculpture in 2006; refer to S. Hooper 2007, 'Embodying Divinity: The Life of A'a', in S. Hooper (ed.), *Polynesian Art: Histories and Meanings in Cultural Contexts*, Special Issue, *Journal of the Polynesian Society* 116, 2), 179, f. 24. See also *A'a: a deity from Polynesia*; Julie Adams, Steven Hooper and Maia Nuku. The British Museum Press (2016).

[33] Letter Threlkeld to LMS directors, 8 July 1822, South Seas Incoming, CWM.

[34] Letter from Threlkeld and Williams dated 18 October 1821; cited in Montgomery, *Journals and Voyages*, I, 507–8.

[35] Henry, *Ancient Tahiti*, 178.

[36] Ibid.

[37] Candlenuts (*Aleurites moluccana*) have a high oil content; when threaded onto the stalk of the coconut palm leaf, they made effective candles complete with wick; refer to Henry, *Ancient Tahiti*, 246; C. Orliac, *Fare et habitat à Tahiti* (Marseille: Éditions Parenthèses, 2000), 94.

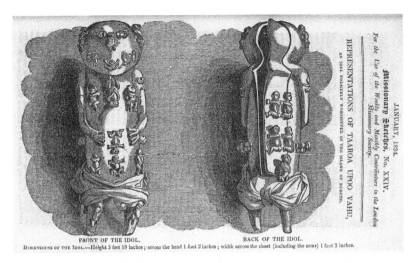

Fig. 13.2   Representation of Taaroa Upoo Vahu, *Missionary Sketches XXIV* (Jan 1824). Council for World Mission archive, SOAS Library (CWML U156)

witnessed a further gathering of islanders in May 1821, where missionaries had organized the manufacture of

> chandeliers made of wood, turned with cocoa-nut shells for lamps. The middle one sustained eighteen lights, the others ten or twelve each; besides which, branches, holding double lights were fixed along the walls. When these ... were blazing out, they presented to the natives such a spectacle of artificial brilliance as had never before been conceived, much less seen, among them, and called forth expressions of astonishment.[38]

The notion of light defeating darkness, the sharp focus of Christianity reducing idols to dust, was a powerful metaphor—'before it every idol hath mouldered into dust'[39]—which missionaries would continue to use to great effect. Citing Tuahine, one of the newly converted native ministers, Williams reports that he cried out:

> Thus the gods made with hands shall perish. There they are, tied with cords! ... Formerly they were called '*Te mau Atua*' ... the gods; now they are called '*Te mau Varu[a] ino*', or evil spirits ... look! it is birds' feathers, soon rotten; but our God is the same for ever.[40]

---

[38] Montgomery, *Journals of Voyages and Travels*, I, 512.

[39] J. Wilson, *A Missionary Voyage to the Southern Pacific Ocean in the Years 1796, 1797 and 1798, in the Ship 'Duff', Commanded by Captain James Wilson* (London: T. Chapman, 1799), 345.

[40] Williams, *A Narrative of Missionary Enterprises*, 37–8.

Using a stylistic device common to much missionary literature of the period, Williams reports the dialogue in the form of direct speech as if quoting Tuahine verbatim. Designed of course to render the text more authentic, this operation allowed missionaries to put unlikely-sounding speeches into the mouths of native informants. Although it aimed principally at eliding their presence, ironically it was a rhetorical device that tended to betray their own concerns and anxieties. In this case, Williams unwittingly inserted himself into the narrative, his preoccupation with the troublesome materiality of idols laid bare.

The fragile ephemerality of god images that incorporated organic material and the feathers of birds 'soon rotten'[41] were clearly disturbing to evangelicals who taught that 'there was One living and true God',[42] in opposition to the 'gods of wood, and stone, and feathers, the works of their own hands'[43] that the heathen worshipped. Questioning the potency of gods 'made with hands' alone,[44] missionaries assumed that these must necessarily be devoid of sanctity, rather missing the point that they were vessels that could be invested with potency during ritual practice at specific times.

The sheer diversity of gods encountered was a further area of concern. Noting the extraordinary variety of images and gods worshipped by islanders, Williams noted that these

> were different in almost every island and district. I do not recollect to have seen two precisely similar representations of the same deity ... Some were large, and some were small; some were beautiful, while others were exceedingly hideous. The god-makers do not appear to have followed any pattern, but were left to display their folly according to their own fancy.[45]

This general lack of uniformity puzzled observers. Unique and different, the variety of god images was in part exaggerated by distinctive styles of manufacture and binding. For while the construction and assembly of god images might conform to a general template, each in practice looked very different from the other; since they were not intended as representations of gods, form was never an end in itself.

PROPPING UP THE SKY

The single whalebone carving illustrated in the engraved 'Family Idols of Pomare'[46] (Fig. 13.1) is a case in point. Now identified as LMS 57 (Fig. 13.3) in the British Museum following its transfer there from the London Missionary Society (LMS) in 1890, it is now stripped of any former attachments. Carved

[41] Ibid.
[42] Ellis, *Polynesian Researches*, II, 184.
[43] Ibid.
[44] Williams, *A Narrative of Missionary Enterprises*, 47.
[45] Ibid., 47–8.
[46] *Missionary Sketches III* (Oct 1818), CWM.

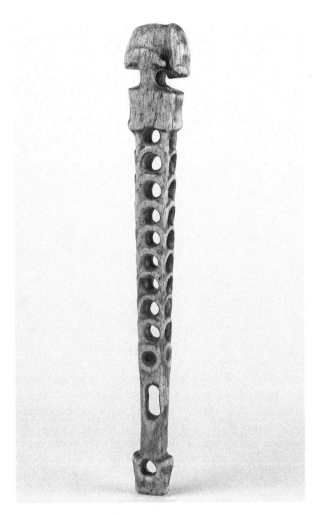

Fig. 13.3 Whalebone *tahiri* (flywhisk), Austral Islands. Oc, LMS 57 British Museum, London. Length 24.2 cm © The Trustees of the British Museum. All rights reserved

from a single section of whalebone, it is easily manipulated in the hand and large perforations at its base would likely have incorporated fibre bindings extending below in a tail or 'whisk'. The highly sculptural finial is in fact a figure, now heavily eroded—a clue to the fact that it has been handled extensively over time. Raised features indicate an oval face with two crescents for eyes and subtly discerned contours reveal a backwardly arched figure with thighs flexed to expose the vagina, in counterpoint to the phallic tip referencing the glans of the penis, at its opposite end. The arching female figure was likely a reference to birthing, or more specifically transition across thresholds.

Missionaries described these flywhisks, used to attract, or beckon, gods (or *atua*) into the light, as being turned and danced in bold gestural movements. Certainly not intended as static instruments of worship, they were waved vigorously in order to create channels, currents of air through which a god could descend. Recalling the frenzied fanning of the chief Vehiatua by those who attended him during a late-night vigil to try to stem a protracted fever, the Spanish soldier Máximo Rodriguez was informed that fanning in this way enabled 'their deity ... to descend—for they say that he comes down in a whirlwind'.[47]

Another example in the Metropolitan Museum of Art, New York (Fig. 13.4) has a similarly distinctive, yet far more discernible, backward-arching figure. Balanced on a wide collar at one end, the figure infers a hollow space or canopy from which the central stem extends in a series of openwork sections bound into the whole. The carving on these varies from angular sections with minimal intervention to more complex sections incorporating highly stylized figures that support each corner, those with outstretched arms giving way to a series of simple incisions that indicate facial features on highly abstracted figures. Most strikingly, the tip remains largely uncarved, the final series of carved detail fading into the smooth, creamy surface of whale ivory.

Coveted for their rarity, whalebone and ivory were particularly potent. Whales in particular were deemed to be the *ata*, the shadow or embodiment of Ta'aroa, the original god from whom all others derived. Their bones were not merely symbolic or ornamental, they were relics quite literally fused with the essence of Ta'aroa, in the same way as red feathers. Strong and lasting, they were his *iho* (or essence) made permanent. Since the bones of one were also deemed to be the bones of all, this whalebone or ivory worked metonymically to index the entire lineage and all its members. The serial canopies painstakingly hollowed along its length were therefore intended as a highly abstracted, visual expression of fundamental genealogical principles. Much of the detailed carving is now heavily eroded, suggesting that it was much handled over time, perhaps even rubbed and anointed with oils during ritual practice. When wielded dramatically by chiefs and their priests during ritual, these rare and prestigious items were an effective means of dramatically asserting divine sanctity and legitimacy to title. Accompanied by the steady recital of genealogical chants, they were an accessory that enabled ritual experts (known as *haere po*) to approach and actually transcend (from the verb *haere*) the dangerously potent threshold with the other side (*te po*) in order to draw down the presence of the god (or *atua*) into the realm of human existence.

Intriguingly, a further five whale ivory *tahiri* have been identified in museum collections[48] and each incorporates some indication of this arched component

[47] B.G. Corney (ed.), *The Quest and Occupation of Tahiti by Emissaries of Spain During the Years 1772–6.* (Cambridge: Hakluyt Society, 1916), I, 50.

[48] M. Jessop [Nuku], 'Unwrapping Gods: Encounters with Gods and Missionaries in Tahiti and the Austral Islands, 1797–1830' (Doctoral thesis, Sainsbury Research Unit, University of East Anglia, 2007), 161–98.

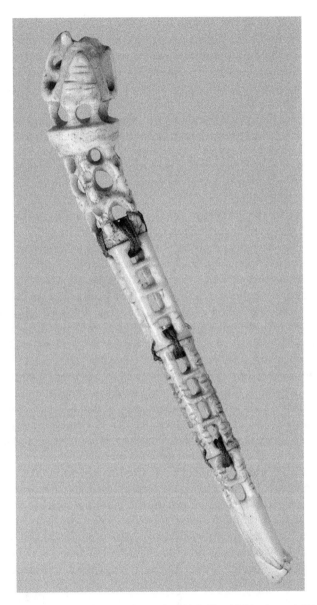

Fig. 13.4 Whale ivory and sinnet-bound *tahiri* (flywhisk), Austral Islands. 1978. 412.875, Metropolitan Museum of Art, New York. Length 27.9 cm Image © The Metropolitan Museum of Art (www.metmuseum.org)

that creates a canopy at the summit with a series of hollowed crescents extending below. In terms of Polynesian cosmology, the canopy inferred by this arched figure is a reference to a point of origin in terms of space and time, since the raising of the first sphere to form the sky immediately preceded the creation of humans.[49] Islanders imagined the universe as a vast immensity that surrounded and enclosed them. Ellis reported in more detail, explaining that 'they imagined that the sea which surrounded their islands was a level plane, and that at the visible horizon, or some distance beyond it, the sky, or *rai* [*ra'i*], joined the ocean, enclosing as with an arch, or hollow cone, the islands in the immediate vicinity'.[50] Human existence was played out in this fragile sphere of light and ritual protocols aimed at keeping the potentially engulfing darkness at bay.

Luminosity and sound were other devices used in this regard, attracting as well as announcing the imminent arrival of gods. The arrival of the god Oro was said to be accompanied by the dynamic arching of a rainbow that stretched from the dome of the sky to the land below amid flashes of lightning and thunder. The missionary Jefferson even compiled a list identifying the divine attributes of Oro that found their chiefly instantiation in Pomare, which included *Aora'i* (lit. sky pierced with light), the house in which Oro was said to dwell; *Anuanua* (rainbow), the double-hulled canoe that bore him across the threshold into *te ao*, armed with *U'ira* (lightning), 'the torch that gives him light at night'; and *Patire* (thunder), 'the drum that beat … for his amusement'.[51] A note in the legend accompanying the 'Family Idols of Pomare' (Fig. 13.1) identifies the proper name for the whalebone god (Fig. 13.3) as 'Tahi[r]i Anunaehau'[52]—a particularly compelling detail given the paramount chief's strong association with Oro. Likely a composite term combining *anuanua* (rainbow)[53] with *hau* (the term for wind or air),[54] the latter can also serve as a qualifying adjective meaning to move beyond, in terms of something greater, larger and more significant.[55] In this sense, the name would infer the greatest, most magisterial rainbow.

The lustre and brightness inferred in the name, and indexed materially in the selection of whalebone and ivory, surely aimed at establishing conditions appropriate for ritual. Certainly, the names of islands integral to the ritual landscape of Polynesia referred specifically to this aspect of clarity and brightness in the sky (*ra'i*), allied to the notion of a vast expanse (*atea*). Ra'iatea—the focal point of all ritual endeavour within central Polynesia—was a case in point. Perhaps it was no coincidence after all that this was the site selected by islanders as most appropriate for the deliverance of their former gods to missionaries in the night. While Banks and other early visitors to Tahiti had first encountered

[49] Henry, *Ancient Tahiti*, 161.

[50] Ellis, *Polynesian Researches*, III, 168.

[51] J. Jefferson, 26 May 1799, South Sea Journals, CWM; cited in Newbury, *History of the Tahitian Mission*, xliii.

[52] *Missionary Sketches III* (Oct 1818), CWM.

[53] J. Davies, *A Tahitian and English Dictionary* (Tahiti: LMS Press, 1851), 99.

[54] Ibid., 24.

[55] Ibid., 99.

these objects in wood, referring to them rather flatly as flywhisks or 'fly-flaps', we now begin to see that they were in fact highly sophisticated and complex cosmological artifacts that supported the landscape literally and conceptually.

'TAHEITE WAS STRICKEN BY THAT COMET'

In the same way that gods were encouraged to bear down on the wind, the streaking tail of a comet in the sky signalled imminent arrival. Islanders observed these formidable events with extreme unease, reading shooting stars or comets as ominous warnings. In her manuscript on *Ancient Tahiti*, Teuira Henry clarified that 'a comet was supposed to be a god forerunning war or sickness',[56] and Davies reported an occasion when a fiery meteor flew across the island, prompting the anxious cries of those who witnessed it: 'He atua! He atua! [It is god! It is a god!]'.[57] Taking this to be a clear sign of ill luck, Davies added that 'soon afterwards the high chief Tamatoa fell down in a fainting fit, [when] the people made prayers and offerings to appease the *atua*'.[58]

Remarking that 'the old people say that meteors were formerly much oftener seen from these islands than they are now',[59] Tyerman and Bennet related another incident involving a 'magnificent meteor, whose train, in its flight, measured ninety or a hundred degrees'.[60] Described as the tail of the god Tane, it was said to have become caught on 'a remarkable stone, set on end ... when, from the top of it, he attempted to mount into the air'[61] once again. The tail itself was deemed to be of 'celestial origin' and so *tapu* that anything that came into contact with it, such as 'various trees, in the boughs of which it had been entangled ... have become sacred in consequence of being touched by it'.[62]

While missionaries had deployed the apparatus of natural science to convince island populations of the primacy and omniscient presence of the new Christian god, Pomare II now also turned to the divine potency of astronomical phenomena to account for the eclipse in status of Tahiti's former gods. He described the advent of the new religion as the breaking of a spell of enchantment in which the islands had long been held captive:

> Taheite was stricken by that comet...The star is still flying and at the time appointed by the Lord that it should [a]light on a country the spell of that country will be dissolved, until the enchantment be broken in all Lands by the word of the Lord.[63]

[56] Henry, *Ancient Tahiti*, 227.
[57] D. Oliver, missionary card index, card 255; cited in Newbury, *History of the Tahitian Mission*.
[58] Ibid.
[59] Montgomery, *Journals of Voyages and Travels*, I, 283.
[60] Ibid.
[61] Ibid.
[62] Ibid.
[63] Pomare to Haweis, Tahiti, 3 October 1818, CWM, South Seas Incoming, Box 3A Jacket B Folder 7.

While the letter, like so much of the missionary record, betrays the heavy influence of missionary advisers who clearly assisted the chief in his personal letter writing, the choice of cosmological phenomenon in the exegesis was thoroughly Polynesian.

CONCLUSION

the Sun & Moon are the original parents of all the Stars, and when they are in eclipse they say they are in the act of Generation and that evry thing on earth is produced in the same Manner.[64]

For Polynesians, the darkness associated with *te po* was deemed to be vital and regenerative and, gently reverberating with the steady pulse of creation, the phenomenon of the eclipse was its most potent expression. Clearly, there were both synergies and distinctions in the approaches of eighteenth-century Tahitians and evangelical missionaries to notions of dark and light, to ideas about the universe, its diverse planetary and celestial embodiments and their varied meteorological manifestations. Examining the boundaries and oppositions of each is just one way to draw out their vigorous potential; close attention to 'things' themselves—the artifacts and instruments that were embodiments of these understandings—allows us to get even closer to the precise ideologies embedded at their core.

In his discussions of the navigational and astronomical hardware that accompanied early expeditions to the Pacific, Schaffer has wondered what scientific instruments were taken to be.[65] What embodiment of the divine did Europeans perceive in the mechanics of their own precision instruments? And how did these instruments, whose design aimed at perfection, fit in the overall scheme of understanding nature and the divine? Coveted by islanders, valuable items such as quadrants, sextants and almanacs often proved so irresistible a temptation that they were frequently pilfered and stolen, perhaps in a bid to secure some of their raw potential for themselves.[66] Did islanders also perceive in the complex design and intricate mechanics of these navigational and astronomic 'novelties' a means by which they might mediate their own transit into the various spheres they knew to exist beyond their immediate horizon—the realm from which these vessels had travelled?

If instruments of precision chronometry allowed Europeans to create a grid enabling the measurement of movement through space and time, Polynesians

---

[64] J Morrison [1791], in V. Smith and N. Thomas (eds.), *Mutiny and Aftermath* (Honolulu: University of Hawaii, 2013), 197.

[65] S. Schaffer, ' "On Seeing Me Write": Inscription Devices in the South Seas', *Representations*, 97 (Winter 2007), 90–122.

[66] J. Newell, 'Irresistible Objects: Collecting in the Pacific and Australia in the Reign of George III', in K. Sloan (ed.), *Enlightenment: Discovering the World in the Eighteenth Century* (London: British Museum, 2003), 246–57.

were equally invested in the design of a range of complex cosmological artifacts that enabled the collapse of spatial and temporal boundaries. Designed for mobility and efficacy, these too were a study of the cosmos in miniature, and allowed ritual experts to track an equivalent motion through space and time in order to approach the potent realm of their ancestors. Even the term for a god, *a-tua* (to turn or revolve on itself), reinforced their essential and dynamic premise. Repeating a turn or revolution around a single axis forced an interplay of dimensions from the here (this side) to the beyond (further, that side). Conceived literally as columns or posts, when spun or twirled *to'o* and *tahiri* operated like live channels linking land and sky, light and dark, past and future. In that respect these manufactured 'gods' were instruments of a very unique kind. They were not just 'things' but creative technologies[67] with the capacity to manage always uncertain transition across thresholds, most notably the boundary between the ordinary (earthly) and the extraordinary (or spiritual) realm.

[67] A. Gell, 'The Technology of Enchantment and the Enchantment of Technology', in J. Coote and A. Shelton (eds.), *Anthropology, Art and Aesthetics* (Oxford: Oxford University Press, 1992), 40–63.

PART III

Artificial Curiosities

CHAPTER 14

Persons and Things

Jonathan Lamb

In Roman law the person was someone entitled to hold property: the person was the antithesis of a slave, who could own nothing. A residue of this distinction is found in the slave law of the American South, where slaves were neither personate nor propertied except when accused of a serious crime, whereupon they were invested in a temporary personhood that would last the length of their trial. A parallel metamorphosis was achieved by pain in ancient Rome, where slaves were required by law to be tortured before they gave evidence. In civil society the person—as opposed to the fool, madman, child, slave, bondservant, idol or thing—has a definite function as a representative of authority, one whose testimony may be relied on and whose goods are to be defended from misappropriation. Pufendorf divided this figure into the political person and the moral person:

> Moral Persons ... are either particular Men, or several join'd in one Body by some moral Tie, consider'd with the State and Office which they maintain in common Life. ... There is likewise a peculiar Species of politick Persons, which we may stile Representatives because they sustain the Character of other Persons.[1]

The political person, like the 'Actor' defined by Thomas Hobbes in *Leviathan*, is the individual who joins the vast web of representations that constitutes the commonwealth, becoming in effect one of the many persons of the person of the king. The moral person is constituted like the person defined by John Locke in the *Essay Concerning Human Understanding* as one fit to own a personal history and to

---

[1] Samuel Pufendorf, *Of the Law of Nature and Nations*, 2 vols., trans. Basil Kennett (London: J. Walthoe et al., 1729), 1.7.

J. Lamb (✉)
Department of English, Vanderbilt University, Nashville, TN, USA
e-mail: jonathan.lamb@vanderbilt.edu

© The Author(s) 2016
A. Craciun, S. Schaffer (eds.), *The Material Cultures of Enlightenment Arts and Sciences*, Palgrave Studies in the Enlightenment, Romanticism and the Cultures of Print, DOI 10.1057/978-1-137-44379-3_14

take responsibility for it. Locke's moral person arises from the union of self and consciousness, just as the political person arises from the union of the sovereign and the multitude; but each is endowed with property and has a claim on justice that ensures every person keeps their own.

What is peculiar about both these unions is that they must already exist before they can take place. The covenant that binds the multitude to the king has force, says Hobbes, only provided that the contract is confirmed by the sword of the sovereign; but of course, the sovereign is not created until the contract has been made, so the product of that agreement cannot be enforced except by what is strictly a preposterous fiction. Similarly, Locke's moral person is assumed to exist before it has come about, for as he says:

> That which consciousness of this present thing thing [i.e. the self] can join it self, makes the same Person, and is one self with it, and with nothing else, and so attributes to it self, and owns all the Actions of that thing, as its own, as far as the consciousness reaches, and no farther.[2]

You will observe that the subject of that sentence is in fact the same as its predicate, and so what makes the person is none other than the person, just as Leviathan (Hobbes's arche-person) originates in nothing but itself.

I stress the tautologous and fictive origin of the person in order to explain one of Hobbes's more astonishing claims for the extent of personation in a civil state, when he says, 'There are few things, that are uncapable of being represented by Fiction. Inanimate things … may be Personated … Likewise, Children, Fooles, and Mad-men … may be Personated'. There is no difference between the legal fiction that made a slave fit to stand trial in antebellum America and this sort of fiction that Hobbes describes, for anything may be made to speak as a person if it is properly represented as such. His only reservation is that 'things Inanimate, cannot be Authors, nor therefore give Authority to their Actors'.[3] Pufendorf thought this a pointless refinement, 'it being more natural to say in plain Terms, that particular Men are empower'd by the Community, to collect the Revenue, settled for the preserving of such Places, or Things'.[4] But he missed the twin advantages that Hobbes assigned to fiction, the first being that power is not held in the repository of the community, rather that it flows through a system of delegation; the second being that the system is held together by fiction, and that it is belief in fiction alone that ensures its future.

As for Locke's moral person, it is an attribution of identity impossible to sustain, Hume said, without a fiction, 'or at least [without] a propensity to such

---

[2] John Locke, *An Essay Concerning Human Understanding*, ed. Peter H. Nidditch (Oxford: Clarendon Press, 1975), 341 (2.27.17).

[3] Thomas Hobbes, *Leviathan*, ed. Richard Tuck (Cambridge: Cambridge University Press, 2004), 113.

[4] Pufendorf, *Of the Law of Nature*, 1.8.

fictions'.[5] When he challenged Hobbes's claim for the power of fiction to create what he called artificial persons, Pufendorf said, 'Whatever such a fictitious Actor says or does, leaves no moral Effect behind it, and is valu'd only according to the Dexterity and Artifice of the Performance'. Hobbes could not have disagreed more, for while he freely confessed that his account of the origin of civil society was a fiction, he argued vigorously that we are all creatures of it, and subsist in the historical narrative that derives from it. Similarly, Locke's fiction of personal identity has its source in a simulacrum, not the thing itself, and it is responsible for a probable (not a certain) history of an individual's actions. So Leviathan and personal identity have a common origin in stories of how the individual and the community gave birth to themselves, a conjecture that Immanuel Kant compared to 'drawing up a plan for a novel'.[6] Nevertheless, it guaranteed (and still does) the rights to property and a history—what we own in the sense of holding, and own in the sense of telling.

One of the effects of the fiction of persons was a radical revision in the relation of citizens to property. Under feudal systems of tenure, personal property, or personalty, had very little importance, because there was no formal way of owning it; you could not be seized in it as you could be seized in a fee. So land or realty was the main issue, and it was never settled in terms of absolute ownership, since it was held provisionally from the crown and descended through a succession of tenurial inheritors. However, with the expansion of trade and the multiplication of commodities, priorities were reversed, and the acquisition of personal property became the chief concern of individuals and an important focus of the law; so much so that William Blackstone defined ownership not as a conditional tenure of things, but as 'that sole and despotic dominion, which one man exercises over the external things of the world, in total exclusion of the rights of any other individual in the universe'.[7] That such a tight grip on things is no more than a legal velleity is evident from Locke's second *Treatise of Government*, where he supposed such unconditional possession to be the happiness of the primitive huntsman, whose prey is his, and so much his, that it can be no one else's. Yet ever since the advent of civil society a combination of fiction and contract ('fancy and agreement') had hastened what he called the 'partage' or alienation of our property, making exchange of goods the business of life, for everything is bought and sold, and everything is on the move.[8] Even David Hume, who, like Lord Shaftesbury and Immanuel Kant, found the fiction of the original contract risible, believed that the 'looseness and easy transition' of material goods was a worrisome development. He thought that 'the situation of external objects' might

[5] David Hume, *Treatise of Human Nature*, ed. L.A. Selby-Bigge and P.H. Nidditch (Oxford: Clarendon Press, 1978), 255.

[6] I. Kant, 'Conjectures on the Beginning of Human History' [1786], in *Kant: Political Writings*, ed. H. Reiss, trans. H.B. Nisbet (Cambridge: Cambridge University Press, 1991), 22–34, 221.

[7] W. Blackstone, *Commentaries on the Laws of England*, 4 vols. (Cambridge: Clarendon Press, 1773), 2.2.

[8] John Locke, *Two Treatises of Government*, ed. Peter Laslett (New York: New American Library, 1963), 328, 342.

best be stabilized 'by putting these goods, as far as possible, on the same footing with the fix'd and constant advantages of the mind and the body'.[9] Personal property, that is to say, should be regarded in the same light as personal attributes: your pocket watch ought to belong to you as securely as your wits.

There is plenty of evidence to suggest that property owners agreed with the tendency of all these propositions concerning the ideal fixture of things. In terms of realty, the seventeenth-century innovation in feudal law called entail was an attempt to satisfy the immoderate desire of owning a thing both completely and forever. It allowed the owner of an estate not only to nominate the line of its descent, but also to occupy the fee as long as it might exist, leaving subsequent inhabitants of it merely tenants for life. The further the descent of realty stood from the original donor, long since dead but still nominally seized in it, the more capriciously it was likely to move from tenant to tenant, with exasperating results well illustrated in the novels of Jane Austen. The only way to put an end to this grotesque bid for tenurial immortality was by the legal fictions of entry, recovery and settlement, where the tenant of an entailed estate colluded with the next in line in a pretence of occupying and then alienating it from the defunct donor, who was no longer in a position to object to the injury—a remedy proving, if any proof were needed, that real estate was more 'real' than the fictions of owning it.

Nevertheless, there is an instructive equation to be drawn from the despotic bid for absolute mastery of property and the freedom of movement that this imparts to the property itself. The more human beings desire to attach things to their persons, the more errant those things are likely to become. Henry Fielding's Jonathan Wild, an expert in organizing this kind of mobility, studies the first book of Aristotle's *Politics* with great attention in order to mark the difference between those whose grip on things is less than tight, and those men of many hands such as himself who can hold lots of property very close indeed. Wild discovers that the greatness of any agent is proportionate to the numbers of living tools—slaves in Aristotle's terms and 'hands' in Wild's—under his thumb. Wild has no time for Hobbes's system of delegation nor for the subtleties of Locke's self-reflection. Instead, he hews to Blackstone's principle of the 'sole and despotic dominion' possible for an individual to exert over the external things of the world, in total exclusion of the rights of anybody else. Wild situates himself in Hobbes's state of war; that is to say, where rights are asserted and defended by force and fraud, and contracts mean nothing. Certainly this is not an enterprise in which the laws of England meant to conspire, but Locke understood how the invention of money was responsible for huge inequities in the ownership of property, defended as savagely by the law as Wild defends his monopoly of metropolitan theft and information. Moreover, Wild boldly exploits the paradoxes of commercial society, drawn from the odd state of affairs where vice furthers the public interest and good springs up and pullulates from evil: he is a criminal benefactor.

[9] Hume, *Treatise*, 489.

He is also what Hobbes calls an Author, someone who has found it unnecessary to cede his rights to whatever he chooses to seize. That is to say, he is not an Actor, one who has made that concession and now functions only vicariously as an agent. In Hobbes's civil society there are in fact no Authors left, for authority exists only in the circulating serial fiction of its representation, not in Pufendorf's community chest of central authority, nor even in the sword of the sovereign, since that is wielded only by another person in the chain of personate substitutions. Hobbes has inanimate things represented within that circuit not because they embody the inalienable properties of their owners, but because they may be personated. If someone like Wild, or perhaps like the ambitious framer of an entail, exits civil society in pursuit of despotic dominion, he dismantles what Hobbes calls 'Dominion of Persons'; that is, the system of distributed power in a commonwealth.[10] He breaks the circuit of representation by reinstalling the possibility of total ownership and unreflective self-absorption that Locke and Jean-Jacques Rousseau variously ascribe to individuals in the state of nature; but he does so by relying on, or precipitating, the maximum mobility among things. So it seems that things enjoy the circumstances attending human ambition, happy to exchange the weak form of expression supplied by representation for the meatier pleasures of unauthorized agency. After all, Locke seriously entertained the hypothesis that things might think, 'it being impossible for us ... to discover, whether Omnipotency has not given to some Systems of Matter fitly disposed, a power to perceive and think'.[11] And what would it be like to witness such a phenomenon?

Aristotle briefly handles this topic in the *Politics* when he mentions Homer's war-mad man as someone detached entirely from social life, lacking family, law and home: 'He is a non-cooperator, like an isolated piece in a game of draughts'.[12] Reinforcing his argument for the natural priority of the state, he uses the metaphor of amputation for the bloody-minded man, or anyone else who imagines that it is possible to live like a singleton, which has a sort of punning relevance to the ambitions of Fielding's Wild:

> Separate hand or foot from the whole body, and they will no longer be hand or foot except in name, as one might speak of a 'hand' or 'foot' sculptured in stone. That will be the condition of the spoilt hand, which no longer has the capacity and the function which define it. So, though we may say they have the same names, we cannot say that they are, in that condition, the same things.[13]

Scenes of war provide the most dramatic setting for observing how extreme circumstances force the pace of change from functionality to disintegration,

---

[10] Hobbes, *Leviathan*, 113.
[11] Locke, *Essay*, 540 (4.3.25).
[12] Aristotle, *The Politics*, trans. T.A. Sinclair (London: Penguin, 1992), 60.
[13] Ibid., 60–61.

equally affecting animate and inanimate matter as portions of bodies literally are divided from each other and dwellings and tools are destroyed, or almost so. Laurence Sterne's Uncle Toby is the first character in literature to exploit the aesthetic possibilities of ruin, first carefully putting his toy fortifications in a condition to be bombarded and then, in a rapture, beholding their collapse. Edmund Blunden, a close reader of *Tristram Shandy*, is especially attentive to what Félix Vallotton called the 'décor' of half-achieved devastation. The large church at Richebourg he found astonishing because it exhibited 'that state of demi-ruin which discovers the strongest fascination'. Demi-ruin requires an equilibrium between what the building had been and what it has now been reduced to, such as the line of village dwellings 'where thatch and brick and lath hung together still in no mean likeness of houses'. When that balance is lost the sight is horrifying, and it is hard to distinguish disgust from the malign intention of its object. The mill at Hamel was 'a sordid cripple, it hated us all'.[14] In the meantime, Blunden becomes a collector, loitering as he says too long among little things—old rifles, damaged helmets and even unexploded bombs—and his friend Sergeant Worley begins to draw pictures, remarkable for a frightful and indiscriminate accuracy, of the fragments of things surrounding them, as if he were constructing an endless inventory of ruin. Blunden's and Worley's war is like William Hogarth's *The Bathos*, a sort of anti-sublime where the foreground is filled with broken tools, a church tower is tottering in the distance, and Phaeton (the only human in the picture) is about to be blown to bits in an explosion.

The aesthetics of lost property was at the core of the historical Wild's innovation in the art of crime. Having personal property stolen and then sold back to its owner was an improvement in felonious enterprise that he was able to organize because he understood before anyone else the advent of sentimental value. People who found the disappearance of their watch, snuffbox or cane intolerable, either because of the fineness of its workmanship, or because it was a present from a valued friend, or because it was as dear to them as the attributes of their own minds, entered into a bargain that had nothing to do with the law of supply and demand, concerning as it did a value lodged in a thing for which an extremely private market had a price but as yet no name. This was a bargain that was not only illegal, since it required the injured party to compound a felony, but it was also subversive of the idea of property, since it involved owners in the purchase of what was already theirs. The same revision of the entity of Aristotle's amputated hand applies here. All genuine social pleasure in things, he had argued, arose from two impulsive reflections, 'This is my own' and 'This is a delight'.[15] Yet now there was an extra frisson to be derived from the reflection, 'This is no longer my own', followed by another, 'On that account it is delightful beyond measure'. In the zone of theft this was something like demiloss, analogous to demi-ruin in the zone of war. The purloined thing, having

---

[14] E. Blunden, *Undertones of War* (New York: Doubleday, 1929), 83, 125.
[15] Aristotle, *Politics*, 111.

been removed for no matter how short a period from its customary uses, gained that kind of sculptural independence that Aristotle identifies in the thing that is called a hand without acting like one. The owner is introduced via loss to an intuition of that species of satisfaction shared by despotic devisers of entails and others whose ideas of dominion were absolute and non-personate. And this intuition circumscribed a value that no public market was fit to calculate, since the re-purchaser had already decided that its object, or rather its thing, was priceless.

In describing the subsequent history of sentimental value, Deidre Lynch has suggested that the gift of keepsakes such as rings, lockets, bits of gold and snuffboxes was the safest and certainly the most amiable way of holding inalienable things as one's very own. Sentimental and Gothic fiction is filled with such memorials of undying friendship and love, intended to refine the article from the grossness of a commodity while reducing its looseness and easy transition to a minimum. The trouble with undying love is that it is subject to the same vagaries as other passions, and its tokens are prone to the same accidents as other things: loss, destruction, misapplication, amnesia. Narratives of keepsakes, as Lynch points out, record loss as often as preservation, suggesting that the dream of absolute possession is as wistful in the world of sentiment as it is elsewhere.[16] Death, however, provides a punctum. 'Sentimental fiction's morbid moments', says Lynch, 'might owe something to the recognition that death conveniently resolves the difficulties characters have in calling property their own'.[17] She means that a gift received from a person who is dead, and who is therefore a person no longer and will never demand reciprocation, is the purest token of all, a focus for the survivor's unconditional devotion, as long as she or he may live.

Before taking a look at the development of the fiction of keepsakes, I want very briefly to point out that it was out of the primal soup of civil and legal fictions that the novel itself took rise, along with a host of resuscitated and newly discovered genres such as the animal fable, spy literature (*The Turkish Spy, The Jewish Spy, The London Spy*), the oriental tale, stories of metamorphosis such as Apuleius's *The Golden Ass*, secular biographies such as Francis Kirkman's and John Dunton's, and modern satires such as Swift's *Tale of a Tub*. They were the inspiration for a brand new departure in fiction, namely the it-narrative, the biography or autobiography of things—animals, artifacts, clothes, money and vehicles. This began in 1709 with *The Golden Spy* by Charles Gildon, a collection of first-person stories whispered to the author in bed, at night, by golden coins from various quarters of Europe. It was clear from the outset that things did not have much in common with the priorities of social life, for the author confesses that he had to edit the more scandalous episodes from the memoirs

---

[16] Deidre Lynch, 'Personal Effects and Sentimental Fictions', in Mark Blackwell (ed.), *The Secret Life of Things*. (Lewisburg: Bucknell University Press, 2007), 73.

[17] Ibid., 86.

of his golden spies, 'for fear the Sense of Things should destroy all Confidence betwixt Man and Man, and so put an End to human Society'.[18]

In other it-narratives the author–things often accuse humans of inhumane treatment of living creatures, as well as cruelty to their own kind in the form of avarice, violence and lust. The only way to sympathize with a rodent, says the author of *The Life and Peregrinations of a Mouse*, is to endure the identical sensation of pain inflicted on it by its human enemies. The reports of Claude-Prosper Jolyot de Crebillon's sofa, Denis Diderot's jewels and Charles Johnstone's guinea placard the same perversity and cruelty in human conduct towards things; and when Lemuel Gulliver, stunned by the inferences he is obliged to draw from the observations of his hosts on the nature of civil society, to all intents and purposes is transformed from a human into a horse, his estrangement from his human reader is dramatic and total.

If Hobbes had supposed that by fiction a thing endowed with a voice would peaceably take its place within the representational system of the civil state, then the fictions springing from that hypothesis were for the most part quite contrary in tendency: things are antagonistic to their former owners and, as Theodor Adorno says, implacable.[19] They do not seek any of the reconciliations that their owners pursue. When Robinson Crusoe spots the three hats, one cap and two non-matching shoes washed up on the shore, he stares at belongings that seem to stare back, knowing they will never be owned again. His agitation is extreme: 'This threw me into terrible Agonies of Mind, that for a while I run about like a Mad-man'.[20] Crusoe's moment of madness arrives when the principles of possession and self-possession are shaken by an event that cannot be told, when the transition of things is extreme and irreversible and the person stops being a person because he is incapable, however briefly, of owning anything. In Sarah Scott's novel *The History of Sir George Ellison*, the hero's uncle goes mad and all his property is removed by a commission of lunacy; so his faithful nephew gives him pet pigs, birds and rabbits, wistful but useless tokens of personhood, ownership and sanity. As humans lose life, agency and sanity, things acquire it. When the whale that he thought he had made his own fights free from Captain Ahab, taking off his leg as it goes, Ishmael explains the resulting mania as follows: 'That before living agent, now became the living instrument. If such a furious trope may stand, his special lunacy stormed his general sanity, and carried it, and turned all its concentred cannon upon its own mad mark'.[21] There is no finer fable of this reversal of agency than Maupassant's short story about a man returning from the opera who sees his furniture and curiosities making their way out of his house. When

[18] Charles Gildon, *The Golden Spy* (London: J. Woodward, 1709), 116.

[19] T. Adorno, *Minima Moralia*, trans. E.F.N. Jephcott (Norfolk: Verso, 1974), 40.

[20] Daniel Defoe, *The Life and Surprizing Adventures of Robinson Crusoe*, ed. J. Robert Crowley (Oxford: Oxford University Press, 1983), 47.

[21] Herman Melville, *Moby-Dick; or, The Whale*, ed. Harold Beaver (Harmondsworth: Penguin, 1978), 284.

they reappear in a seedy second-hand shop run by a monstrous dwarf, the man tries to repurchase one or two pieces; but nothing is sent home and he commits himself to an insane asylum, whereupon what were his goods reoccupy the house that was once his house.[22]

Dickens's interest in cast-off clothes probes the extremes of this sort of divestment, where the personate owning of a thing and a life breaks down and the emancipation of the thing is proportioned to the nakedness, distraction and death of someone who is no longer a person. In his *Sketches by Boz* he includes 'Meditations in Monmouth Street', a place near Holborn that then functioned as the premier market for second-hand garments. Boz looks at them hanging up and imagines the lives of their owners: 'We have gone on speculating in this way, until whole rows of coats have started from their pegs, and buttoned up, of their own accord, round the waists of imaginary wearers'. Clothes are the jolly instruments of the restoration of human agency and human history. 'A black suit and the jacket changed into a diminutive coat' tells the tale of those who wore them: 'His father had died, and the mother had got the boy a message-lad's place in some office'.[23] When the genial trope of thingly agency is reversed in *Oliver Twist*, the effect is much more disturbing. As Fagin reflects (rather like Mr Peachum) on how many thieves he has seen end their lives on the gallows, he remembers 'how suddenly they changed from strong and vigorous men to dangling heaps of clothes'.[24]

The same unsettling reversal of the alignment between humans and things takes place in *Great Expectations* when Pip asks Wemmick about the mourning rings, seals and brooch ornamenting his watch chain, 'as if he were quite laden with the remembrances of departed friends'. Wemmick's unsentimental explanation is that the gifts of men about die are to be husbanded: 'They're curiosities. And they are property ... they're property and portable'.[25] The security of possession that might have been expected from keepsakes is undermined by Wemmick's contempt for the dead whose gifts they are, and by his insistence on their portability. At the same time, their mobility seems to be limited to the motions of the body they adorn, since Wemmick shows no sign of trading in them or losing them. What he insists on, however, is the distinction between the deceased owner, the person who is no longer a person and can own nothing, and the survival of the thing. Hence his attitude to Magwitch's pocketbook: 'You don't know what may happen to him. Don't let anything happen to the portable property'.[26] When Pip says piously, 'What I think of, Wemmick, is the poor owner of the property', Wemmick retorts, 'I do not

[22] Guy de Maupassant, 'Who Knows?' in *A Parisian Affair and Other Stories*, trans. Sian Miles (London: Penguin, 2004), 275–87.

[23] Charles Dickens, 'Meditations in Monmouth Street', in *Sketches by Boz* (London: Odhams, 1836), 72–82.

[24] Charles Dickens, *Oliver Twist* (London: Odhams, 1932), 362.

[25] Charles Dickens, *Great Expectations*, ed. Margaret Cardwell (Oxford: Oxford University Press, 2008), 169, 199.

[26] Dickens, *Great Expectations*, 368.

think he could have been saved. Whereas, the portable property certainly could have been saved. That's the difference between the property and the owner, don't you see?'[27] You might think that Wemmick was telling Pip to seize and utilize the fortune the pocketbook contains, but nowhere in his doctrine of portable property are the principles of use or exchange to be discerned; and even if they were, how could they be reconciled with a criminal act? Like the mourning rings and items on the mantelpiece of Jaggers's office, the pocketbook appears to be proposed by Wemmick as a curiosity like the others, a material trace of a criminal life, of despotism successfully resisted by a thing whose portability expresses mobility purely on its own account. Wemmick's waistcoat in this reading is the frame or vitrine of things triumphantly memorializing human deaths, his own not excluded.

Wemmick has invented a category of which Blackstone never thought, namely ownerless property, rather like the clothes seen by Crusoe on the beach and by Fagin on the gallows: the shreds of lost humans. While standing in the dock, seized by a paroxysm of fear and wrath so severe he loses all sense of his situation, Fagin tries to align what he has left of his life with a thing when he stares first at a broken pencil and then falls 'to counting the iron spikes before him, and wondering how the head of one had been broken off, and whether they would mend it or leave it as it was'.[28] The superlative indifference of pencil and spike to the predicament of the human who appears to take such an interest in their injuries looks like implacability: as if they were saying, 'What are you to us?' Fielding's Wild enters into a similarly brief and futile relationship with a corkscrew shortly before his own death.

'Ownerless Jewish property' was the Nazi definition assigned to the valuables sequestered from their Jewish owners in Austria after the *Anschluss*, and it provides the focus of Edmund de Waal's memoir published in 2010, *The Hare with the Amber Eyes*. This is a story of the loss and recovery of a family heirloom, a collection of 264 Japanese netsuke. These tiny figures of people, creatures and things carved from ivory or boxwood were the property of the rich banking house of Ephrussi in Vienna. The netsuke are saved by a servant, Anna, who remains in the house, hiding them by twos and threes in her pocket until she has stored the entire collection in her mattress. When de Waal's grandmother arrives after the end of the war to assemble the scant remnants of the vast estate, Anna is able to say, 'I have something to return to you'. De Waal grants that for Anna each one of the netsuke may be 'a resistance to the sapping of memory ... a story recalled, a future held on to'. But that is emphatically not how they strike him: 'The survival of the netsuke in Anna's pocket, in her mattress, is an affront. ... Why should they have got through this war in a hiding-place, when so many hidden people did not? I can't make people, places, and things fit together any more'.

---

[27] Ibid., 446.
[28] Dickens, *Oliver Twist*, 360.

This shocking moment has been carefully advertised by the narrator when he talks of the heaviness acquired by things during an *Umsturz* in civil society, when 'ownership seemed transposed … a process that could send you towards mania' –mania that reminds him of Maupassant, who said, 'The bibelot is not only a passion, it is a mania'.[29] Do things weep for their dispossessed owners? wonders Viktor Ephrussi, the former great collector; for his part, de Waal is deeply suspicious of nostalgia and the things that appear to provoke and cherish it, remaining equally doubtful of the value of sentimentalized curiosities and of sentimentalized history.

It is surprising, therefore, to observe the confidence of those historians of material culture who assume, like Neil MacGregor, that things in museums provide such a commodious vehicle for the annals of human agency. *The History of the World in 100 Objects* operates, it seems to me, on two vulnerable assumptions. The first is that things 'speak of whole societies' in a helpful and constructive way, and the second is that in speaking thus socially things give humans a voice.[30] Things emancipated from ownership have no interest at all in society, or in the fates of the political and moral persons who comprise it; and when things start speaking, persons shut up. The two philosophers in the third book of Gulliver who have elected to give up their voices to the things they carry in sacks on their backs, convinced that the effort of speaking corrodes their lungs and shortens their lives, are now neither rational nor articulate, having delegated their rights of representation to things that are not persons and will represent nothing.

Let me give a final example of the implacable agency of things, taken from one of John Banville's detective stories, *The Silver Swan*:

> Over every scene of violent death there hung a particular kind of silence, the kind that follows after the last echoes of a great outcry have faded. There was shock in it, of course, and awe and outrage, the sense of many hands lifted quickly to many mouths, but something else as well, a kind of gleefulness, a kind of startled, happy, unable-to-believe-its-luckiness. Things … even inanimate things, it seemed, loved a killing.[31]

[29] Edmund de Waal, *The Hare with the Amber Eyes: A Hidden Inheritance* (London: Vintage Books, 2010), 279, 283, 57.

[30] Neil MacGregor, *The History of the World in 100 Objects* (London: Penguin, 2012), xv, xvii.

[31] Benjamin Black (John Banville), *The White Swan* (London: Pan Macmillan, 2007), 294.

CHAPTER 15

The Fabric of Domestic Life: Rethinking the Humble Painted Cloth

Tara Hamling

This exhibit is a set of painted cloths in 'Queen Margaret's Chamber' at Owlpen Manor, Gloucestershire.[1] They are painted in distemper (a tempera technique where earth pigments are bound with glue size) on 42-inch unbleached canvas-linen strips, with an expansive stylized landscape of trees, foliage, conical hills and white buildings (Fig. 15.1). Within this landscape setting are figures and animals representing scenes from the biblical story of Joseph (Genesis 37:1–36). Duty stamps on the reverse side are consistent with a date between 1712 and 1719. The cloths were acquired for another of Owlpen's rooms with similar dimensions but later repositioned in this space, so their current presentation retains a sense of their original form and appearance as expansive wall coverings.

Painted cloths have been neglected as an art form, partly because so few survive, but also because of a general disdain for decorative crafts and the domestic context within traditional art historical scholarship. They have generally been treated in terms of their content or iconography, thus neglecting the qualities and effects of their material form, and their absence within conventional accounts of art and design arises from the mistaken assumption that they were a cheaper alternative to tapestry or a crude

---

[1] My thanks to Nicholas Mander for permission to feature these cloths and represent his research, published most recently as 'The Painted Cloths at Owlpen Manor, Gloucestershire', in Nicola Costaras and Christina Young (eds.), *Setting the Scene: European Painted Cloths from the Fourteenth to the Twenty-First Century* (London: Archetype Publications, 2013), 24–32.

T. Hamling (✉)
Department of History, University of Birmingham, Birmingham, UK
e-mail: T.J.Hamling@bham.ac.uk

© The Author(s) 2016
A. Craciun, S. Schaffer (eds.), *The Material Cultures of Enlightenment Arts and Sciences*, Palgrave Studies in the Enlightenment, Romanticism and the Cultures of Print, DOI 10.1057/978-1-137-44379-3_15

Fig. 15.1 Painted cloth in 'Queen Margaret's Chamber' at Owlpen Manor, Gloucestershire

antecedent to wallpaper. In fact, recent research has established that painted cloths were a prominent and instrumental element of early modern material culture, with a central place in religious ceremony, pageantry, domestic interiors and scenic art throughout the period *c.*1400–1800.[2]

The ubiquity of painted cloths in domestic interiors as decoration and insulation is attested to by probate documents of the fifteenth and sixteenth centuries. In the 1570s William Harrison described the effect of such hangings in making rooms 'not a little commended, made warm, and much more close than otherwise they would be'.[3] Yet very few examples survive and most are in a fragmentary condition. This makes the Owlpen cloths particularly special, and they have served as a template for replica hangings in recreated interiors of *c.*1590 at Blakesley Hall in Birmingham. This assumes that the Owlpen cloths are a late, and representative, example of a much older tradition. It is important, however, not to gloss over the significant changes in the character and function of the painted cloths popular in Elizabethan England compared with those of the eighteenth century.

Shakespeare mentions the type of cloths common in his lifetime as painted with sentences to keep people 'in awe'; this was part of a widespread vernacular tradition of domestic decoration with religious content that

[2] As represented by the 2012 conference at the Courtauld Institute of Art, resulting in the publication just referenced.

[3] William Harrison, *The Description of England* (1587), ed. Georges Edelen (New York: Dover, 1994), 197.

went out of fashion in the seventeenth century.[4] John Aubrey described in *c.* 1640 a 'dark old-fashioned house': 'The hall after the old fashion, above the wainscot, painted cloath, with godly sentences out of the Psalmes, etc., according to the pious custome of old times'.[5] By around 1600 this native production had been undermined by imported wares. In 1601 a bill in the Commons mentioned that 'Painting of Cloth is decayed, and not *One Hundred* Yards of new Painted Cloth made here in a Year, by reason of so much painted *Flanders* pieces brought from thence.'

It appears, therefore, that the painted cloths of early modern England can be separated into two traditions, vernacular and imported, separated by a hiatus in the seventeenth century. While the biblical theme of the Owlpen cloths preserves the earlier interest in didactic content, here the design favours landscape over narrative. This distinction is important, because eliding these two traditions obscures a sense of the changing role of domestic decoration as part of wider cultural trends and risks misrepresenting historical interiors when they are dressed to offer a synchronic window on the past.

---

[4] Tara Hamling, *Decorating the Godly Household: Religious Art in Post-Reformation Britain* (New Haven: Yale University Press, 2010).

[5] John Aubrey, *Brief Lives*, ed. by Richard Barber (Woodbridge: Boydell, 1998), 123.

CHAPTER 16

The Willdey Telescope: Instrument for Fashion, Learning and Amusement

Alexi Baker

By the eighteenth century, London was the largest and most esteemed centre for the trade in optical, mathematical and philosophical instruments—now anachronistically called 'scientific'. Hundreds of metropolitan makers and sellers outfitted Great Britain, Europe and their colonies. In addition to activities that would today be viewed as scientific, these technologies were employed in diverse careers including the naval and military, surveying, architecture, teaching and art. They could also be everyday wares such as vision aids and basic drawing tools, or fashionable and entertaining accoutrements.

George Willdey made and sold this telescope at his shop near St Paul's Churchyard between the first decade of the eighteenth century and his death in 1737 (Fig. 16.1).[1] It is a portable instrument with a main body measuring about 365 millimetres (14.37 inches) long, strikingly covered in black rayskin (shagreen) and accented by ivory rings. This blooms into four vivid drawtubes of green leather detailed in gold, one of which was signed by Willdey. All of the glass lenses are now missing. There are similar telescopes, fashionable and luxurious but not technologically complex, in museums around the world. These include a similar Willdey telescope at the Museumslandschaft Hessen Kassel, and a similar telescope by Willdey's one-time partner Timothy Brandreth at the Whipple Museum. Such instruments were often used as spyglasses, which is why many early modern naval officers are depicted hold-

---

[1] Alexi Baker, 'Willdey, George (bap. 1676, d. 1737)', in *Oxford Dictionary of National Biography* (Oxford University Press, 2015). Available at www.oxforddnb.com/view/article/50906 (accessed 29 September 2015).

A. Baker (✉)
Centre for Research in the Arts, Social Sciences and Humanities (CRASSH),
University of Cambridge, Cambridge, UK
e-mail: alexi.baker@cantab.net

A. Craciun, S. Schaffer (eds.), *The Material Cultures of Enlightenment Arts and Sciences*, Palgrave Studies in the Enlightenment, Romanticism and the Cultures of Print, DOI 10.1057/978-1-137-44379-3_16

Fig. 16.1 Telescope by George Willdey, London, *c.* 1710, object #NAV1522. © National Maritime Museum, Greenwich, London, Gabb Collection

ing them in portraits—much as contemporary office holders brandished a staff of office.

This specific telescope and its counterpart in Germany tell a more unusual and highly important tale given their maker. George Willdey was a well-known and successful luxury retailer (or 'toyman') and optician in eighteenth-century London. He has been ignored in the history of instruments because he was a diversified and fashionable retailer and not thought to have made his own wares.

I overturned these assumptions by tracing the paper trail that Willdey left, including shop accounts that are the only account books known to have survived from the first 250 years or so of the British instrument trade.[2] The optician also left behind hundreds of newspaper advertisements, many surviving pictorial advertisements and maps, and globes and telescopes.

This evidence suggests that Willdey made his own lenses, and more importantly shows that he sold or bartered tens of thousands of small fashionable telescopes as well as large numbers of eyeglasses and other vision aids—almost unbelievable sums. His individual and wholesale customers hailed from across Britain and many parts of Europe, and included other instrument makers. Optical instruments always remained a key element in the toyman's self-identity, and were also the main currency with which he bartered with other craftsmen

[2] Alexi Baker, "This ingenious business": the socio-economics of the scientific instrument trade in London, 1700–1750', PhD dissertation, University of Oxford, 2010.

and wholesalers in order to continue diversifying. This reflects how saleable fashionable and everyday instruments were across early modern Europe.

Willdey's career shows how large swathes of the preindustrial instrument trade, which have largely been ignored by historians as too 'unscientific' or retail, need to be reintegrated into our modern understanding. They produced a large proportion of the instruments sold across Britain and Europe and often intertwined socioeconomically with the better-studied and more 'scientific' actors. The two telescopes so far attributed to George Willdey make these dynamics manifest.

Additionally, the telescopes emphasize the multiple roles such instruments could play. They were fashionable and everyday accoutrements, but also utilitarian, and were sometimes purchased for more professional or mathematical activities. The telescope now in Kassel was likely purchased for the 'scientific' college there. Such findings show the value of interpreting early modern crafts and retail specialties as contemporary actors experienced and perceived them, rather than through the lenses of narrower modern definitions.

CHAPTER 17

Cataloguing Curiosities: Whitby's Barkcloth Book

Billie Lythberg

In a seventeenth-century house on Whitby's harbor, in which Captain James Cook lodged as a young apprentice, there is a curious vellum-bound book, the pages of which fairly bulge with 'artificial curiosities' from the South Sea. Its hand-lettered title page announces 'A COLLECTION of Various Specimens of CLOTH &CC, Obtained in the THREE VOYAGES of CAPT, COOK, 1768–1779'. There follow 59 well-preserved barkcloth samples from Tonga, Tahiti and Hawai'i, snippets of cordage, a 'necklace curiously formed of small shells', and a bundle of the red feathers so valued throughout Polynesia that they were used for the most sacred and potent chiefly regalia. This is a jewel in the collection of Whitby's Captain Cook Memorial Museum, a *mise-en-scène* of Polynesia produced for an eighteenth-century English audience very familiar with viewing the world in miniature.

The aficionado of Pacific voyaging art might single out a sample of cloth with bamboo-stamped circles, like that worn by the Tahitian Omai in a portrait produced during his stay in England 1774–76, when he beguiled London's high society.[1] Others will admire bold abstract patterns, bright pigments, corrugations and striations, thick felting and the finest of gauzes. Yet more may

---

[1] Francesco Bartolozzi, *Portrait of Omai, a native of Huahine* (1774). Engraved by Nathanial Dance (1775). British Library Add. Ms. 23921, f.45.

B. Lythberg (✉)
Mira Szászy Research Centre, University of Auckland,
Auckland, New Zealand

Cambridge University Museum of Archaeology
and Anthropology, UK
e-mail: b.lythberg@auckland.ac.nz

© The Author(s) 2016
A. Craciun, S. Schaffer (eds.), *The Material Cultures of Enlightenment Arts and Sciences*, Palgrave Studies in the Enlightenment, Romanticism and the Cultures of Print, DOI 10.1057/978-1-137-44379-3_17

153

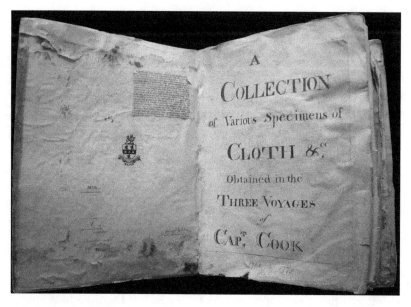

Fig. 17.1 A COLLECTION of various specimens of CLOTH &CC, obtained in the THREE VOYAGES of CAPT, COOK, 1768–1779 (Photograph by Billie Lythberg (2012) © Captain Cook Memorial Museum, Grape Lane, Whitby, YO22 4BA)

despair at the reduction of bales of cloth (some Tongan examples were 30 m in length) to mere 'ethnographic fragments'[2]: the diminution of the vast Pacific.

Although the book's barkcloth samples are unreliably attributed in handwritten descriptions to almost every place visited by Cook—some of which neither produced nor used barkcloth—they match or are similar to other eighteenth-century examples, including some of those collected and published by Alexander Shaw in 1787.[3] Shaw's famous books are prefaced 'with a particular account of the manner of manufacturing the same in the various islands of the South Seas; partly extracted from Mr Anderson and Reinhold Forster's observations', and a printed catalogue promising 39 specimens 'properly arrainged'. In reality, the specimens vary widely throughout the extant catalogues; no two are exactly alike; and only one has so far been recognized that adheres strictly to Shaw's list of contents.[4]

[2] B. Kirschenblatt-Gimblett, *Destination Culture: Tourism, Museums, and Heritage* (Berkeley and Los Angeles: University of California Press, 1998), 18.

[3] M. Larkin, 'Tales and Textiles from Cook's Pacific Voyages', *Bulletin of the Bibliographical Society of Australia and New Zealand* 28 (2004), 20–33; Ian Morrison, 'The Cloth, the Catalogue, and the Collectors', *Bulletin of the Bibliographical Society of Australia and New Zealand* 27 (2003), 48–59.

[4] State Library of New South Wales DL 78/64; Maryanne Larkin, 'Tales and Textiles from Cook's Pacific Voyages', *Bulletin of the Bibliographical Society of Australia and New Zealand* 28 (2004), 21.

The book in Whitby is a manuscript, not a Shaw. Whence it came and by whom it was assembled are unclear, but its inside cover bears the Clive family crest and a small cutting from a newspaper article announcing its inclusion in an unnamed exhibition in Bilston (UK). Partial and undated, the article offers only tantalizing hints about the exhibition it describes and the barkcloth book it includes. Yet it records the English public's interest in these samples and snippets from another world, made immediate and intimate through their domestication within the pages of an eighteenth-century book by someone with a penchant for cataloguing curiosities, even as it betrays the writer's prejudices: 'because in the great variety of the qualities, and especially of the colours and patterns of the cloths, is seen that innate love of art which is found to pervade the mind of even the untutored savage'.

CHAPTER 18

Art and Things: Fragonard's Colour Box

Hannah Williams

A shallow wooden box, 46 centimetres wide, 37 centimetres deep and 10 centimetres high when closed. The inside is divided into nine small compartments. The six at the back contain eighteen cork-stoppered glass bottles, varying in shape, each hand-labelled with the name of the pigment that fills it: *bleu de Prusse, sienne brûlée, carmin*, and so on. The three compartments at the front are designed for tools, with central dividers curved so that utensils can rest without rolling away. The items left include an ebony stick, some blending stubs and a fine brush darkened at the tip.

This unassuming colour box is thought to be one of the few remaining traces of Jean-Honoré Fragonard, one of the best- and least-known artists of eighteenth-century France.[1] Fragonard is famous today because his celebrated painterly paintings have secured him a place in the canon of European art, but still surprisingly mysterious in the sense that so little has been retrieved about his personal life.[2] His colour box therefore offers a rare connection to this man and a vivid insight into his artistic practice.

As eighteenth-century colour boxes go, Fragonard's was a fairly simple piece of kit. Unlike more elaborate boxes, some of them substantial pieces of furniture with legs and drawers, this small, transportable version was most likely

---

[1] Chemical analysis indicates that the box was used by an artist active in the late eighteenth century; its provenance via Fragonard's family suggests a fairly conclusive attribution. François Delamarre and Bernard Guineau, 'La boîte de couleurs dite "de Fragonard": Analyse du contenu des flacons', in *Jean-Honoré Fragonard, peintre de Grasse*, exh. cat. (Grasse: Villa-Musée Fragonard, 2006), 25–31.

[2] Pierre Rosenberg, *Fragonard*, exh. cat. (New York: Metropolitan Museum of Art, 1987), 15.

H. Williams (✉)
School of History, Queen Mary University of London, London, UK
e-mail: hannah.williams@qmul.ac.uk

© The Author(s) 2016
A. Craciun, S. Schaffer (eds.), *The Material Cultures of Enlightenment Arts and Sciences*, Palgrave Studies in the Enlightenment, Romanticism and the Cultures of Print, DOI 10.1057/978-1-137-44379-3_18

Fig. 18.1 Colour box presumed to have belonged to Jean-Honoré Fragonard, eighteenth century, 10 x 46 x 37 cm. Collection of Musée Fragonard, Grasse, France (Photo © Musée Fragonard, Grasse)

a travelling box.[3] Physical evidence confirms a life outside the studio. Two metal clips punched through the lid once attached a presumably leather handle (now perished) so that the box could be carried without upsetting the contents. Yet traces of bright red pigment indelibly staining the wood inside the lid nevertheless suggest some mishap, perhaps a jostled explosion of *cinabre*. Chips and scratches also bear witness to active use, the splintering and detached joint at one of the corners recalling another accident in transit.

[3] On painters' tools see the plates for 'Peintures en huile', in Denis Diderot and Jean le Rond d'Alembert (eds.), *Encyclopédie, ou dictionnaire raisonné des sciences, des arts, et des métiers* (University of Chicago: ARTFL Encyclopédie Project, 2011), Robert Morrissey (ed.), http:// encyclopedie.uchicago.edu (accessed: 26 September 2013).

Fragonard undertook two substantial journeys in his lifetime: the first in 1756, travelling to Rome as a student and returning to Paris in 1761; and then between 1773 and 1774, travelling along the Mediterranean coast to Italy, through Central Europe and back via Germany.[4] It is tempting to speculate that this well-travelled box accompanied Fragonard on one or both of these journeys, and even that it was acquired during that first trip. According to the regulations of the French Academy in Rome, its young artists, known as *pensionnaires*, were presented on arrival with the necessary tools of their trade: two palettes and a colour box.[5]

The contents of the box are also revealing. Materiality of paint is what Fragonard is known for, but these neat bottles of raw pigment form a counterpoint to the rich, creamy surfaces of his canvases. This figurative before-and-after attests to both the economies and labours of eighteenth-century artistic practice: to the complex commercial ecosystem involved in manufacturing and retailing colours; and to the artist's physical, time-consuming daily tasks of grinding and preparing paint.[6] This powdered assortment reminds us of the commerce, industry, technological innovations and frankly messy work that underpinned the aesthetic creations of eighteenth-century French painters.

Fragonard's colour box was an ordinary thing, a commonplace item in the studio. Yet it has become, thanks to its survival, an extraordinary thing: a witness to the practices of an artist's everyday life and a relic bearing the trace of its elusive owner in the memory of its use.

[4] Rosenberg, *Fragonard*, 70–71, 366–367.

[5] These regulations were issued later under the directorship of Joseph-Marie Vien in 1775, but it is likely that this was ratifying an established custom. Article IV, 'Règlemens qui doivent être observés par les pensionnaires de l'Académie de France à Rome', in Anatole de Montaiglon and Jules Guiffrey (eds.), *Correspondance des directeurs de l'Académie de France à Rome avec les surintendants des bâtiments*, vol. 13 (Paris: 1887–1908), 159.

[6] On the eighteenth-century colour trade see Sarah Lowengard, *The Creation of Colour in Eighteenth-Century Europe* (New York: Columbia University Press, 2006), http://www.gutenberg-e.org/lowengard/ (accessed: 26 September 2013).

CHAPTER 19

Keep Within Compass

Katy Barrett

Society was a minefield for an eighteenth-century lady. The temptations of gambling, fashion and drink easily led to a spiral of financial, social and physical ruin ending in prostitution and imprisonment. Such was the moral of an earthenware plate produced by John Aynsley in Staffordshire in the 1790s.

It features a black enamel transfer print, with colour hand-painted over the glaze, based on one of a pair of mezzotints produced by Robert Dighton in 1765.[1] These featured a man and a woman displaying exemplary moral and immoral behaviour along the lines established by William Hogarth's *Progresses*.[2] Dighton's woman avoids social peril by focusing on 'The Pleasures of Imagination' in the book in her hand, within an idyllic rural setting. She is physically restrained within a pair of compasses opened just wide enough to reveal the engraved advice 'Fear God'.

The accompanying verses connect the 'virtuous and prudent way' that this woman should follow to the compasses that define it, concluding: 'When Women once o'erstep the bounds Of decency and cares,—A crowd of folly quick surrounds, And nought but woes she shares.' Scientific instruments were often used throughout the eighteenth century to establish such social bounds. Authors advised on a 'moral compass' guiding towards heaven, used the gridded map of latitude and longitude lines to delineate social bound-

---

[1] Robert Dighton, *Keep Within Compass, Industry Produceth Wealth* and *Keep Within Compass, Prudence Produceth Esteem* (1765).

[2] William Hogarth, *A Harlot's Progress* (6 plates, 1732); *A Rake's Progress* (8 plates, 1735); Ronald Paulson, *Hogarth's Graphic Works* (London: Print Room, 1989), 76–83, 89–98.

K. Barrett (✉)
Royal Museums Greenwich, London, UK
e-mail: kbarrett@rmg.co.uk

© The Author(s) 2016
A. Craciun, S. Schaffer (eds.), *The Material Cultures of Enlightenment Arts and Sciences*, Palgrave Studies in the Enlightenment, Romanticism and the Cultures of Print, DOI 10.1057/978-1-137-44379-3_19

161

Fig. 19.1   John Aynsley, Plate (1790) featuring a version of a print by Robert Dighton, *Keep Within Compass, Prudence Produceth Esteem*. Plate: 24.4 cm diameter. © Victoria and Albert Museum, London

aries, or suggested the loadstone as a means of 'weighing' character.[3] The volatile nature of female emotions was compared to magnetic forces or to sensitive metrological instruments.[4]

Yet the prudent woman within her compass is accompanied by her frolicking dog, an established reference to uncontrollable female sexuality, and the reward for her virtue is a chest overflowing with money and jewels. Such conspicuous consumption was one of the key dangers of eighteenth-century

[3] John Flavel, *Navigation spiritualiz'd: or, A new compass for seamen* (London: M. Fabian, 1698); Anon., *A New and Exact Map of Toryland* (1729); John Clubbe, *Physiognomy* (London: R. and J. Dodsley, 1763), with Hogarth frontispiece.

[4] Patricia Fara, 'A Treasure of Hidden Vertues': The Attraction of Magnetic Marketing in *The British Journal for the History of Science* 28:1 (1995), pp. 5–35; Terry Castle, *The Female Thermometer: Eighteenth century Culture and the Invention of the Uncanny* (New York: Oxford University Press, 1995).

society.[5] Female consumption included just such elegant scientific toys as compasses or loadstones and it was particularly dangerous for women to consume literature. Female novel reading was compared to masturbation and female writing to prostitution.[6] The very book held by our woman references Mark Akenside's poem *The Pleasures of Imagination*, which bemoaned the social obsession with appearance.[7]

As a transfer print, this image adorns an earthenware plate produced in Staffordshire as a cheaper competitor to expensive French porcelain or fashionable Wedgwood ceramics.[8] It would have featured at tea parties or adorned the mantelpiece of a boudoir. Thus, while warning against the perils of consumption, Aynsley's plate was also an object that encouraged that very behaviour.

[5] John Brewer, '"The most polite age and the most vicious": Attitudes towards culture as a commodity, 1660–1800' in Ann Bermingham and John Brewer (eds.), *The Consumption of Culture 1600–1800: Image, Object, Text* (London: Routledge, 1995), pp. 353–8.

[6] Deborah Needleman Armintor, 'The Sexual Politics of Brobdingnag,' in *Studies in English Literature* 47:3 (2007), pp. 619–640; John Brewer, *The Pleasures of the Imagination: English Culture in the Eighteenth Century* (London: Harper Collins, 1997), xxii–iii.

[7] Mark Akenside, *The Pleasures of Imagination. A poem in three books* (London: R. Dodsley, 1744).

[8] Maxine Berg, *Luxury and pleasure in eighteenth-century Britain* (Oxford: Oxford University Press, 2005), pp. 117–53.

CHAPTER 20

Perfected Thing: A Lay Figure by Paul Huot

Jane Munro

From the middle of the eighteenth century, French mechanical ingenuity applied itself in the service of art, and artists, as never before. Parisian makers cornered the niche market of *mannequins d'artiste*, or 'lay figures', full-scale articulated human surrogates that were standard pieces of workshop equipment from at least the Renaissance onwards. Intended primarily as a support for drapery or clothing, the inanimate figure allowed artists to create more naturalistic effects of the texture and fall of fabric over a notionally human form. Like the living model, the mannequin could be manipulated and posed at will, but with the supra-human ability, once keyed into position, to remain fixed and motionless for as long as the artist required.

Few historical accounts of mannequin making have survived, but what scant evidence remains shows how, for over a century, French mannequin makers were engaged in the quest to create the 'naturalistic' mannequin, a figure that simulated the human body in ever more lifelike ways.[1] Top-of-the-range 'perfected' mannequins (*mannequins perfectionnés*) had two leading characteristics: a 'skeleton' or articulated internal mechanism made of metal and wood, constructed so as to allow the figure to move with all the fluidity of a human being; and an external finish or *garniture* that replicated muscle, flesh, skin and facial features.

Undoubtedly the most renowned Parisian mannequin maker in the early years of the nineteenth century was Paul Huot, whose figures were highly

---

[1] The term *'mannequin naturaliste'* appears in E.J. Barillet in *Sur le Mannequin* (Paris: Au Bureau des Annales du Musée, 1809), 16.

J. Munro (✉)
Keeper of Department of Paintings, Drawings and Prints, Fitzwilliam Museum
Cambridge, Cambridge, UK
e-mail: jm115@cam.ac.uk

© The Author(s) 2016

A. Craciun, S. Schaffer (eds.), *The Material Cultures of Enlightenment Arts and Sciences*, Palgrave Studies in the Enlightenment, Romanticism and the Cultures of Print, DOI 10.1057/978-1-137-44379-3_20

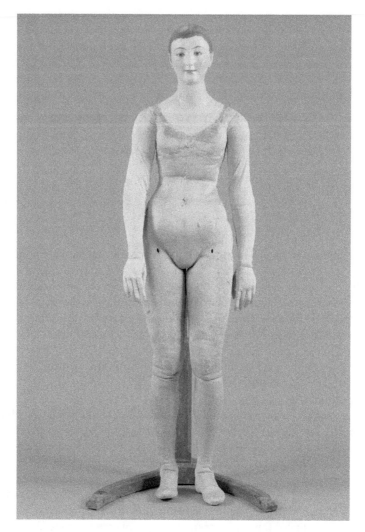

Fig. 20.1   Paul Huot (fl. 1790s–1820s). Female mannequin, *c.* 1816. Wood, metal, horsehair, silk, cotton and painted papier mâché. Height: *c.* 163 cm. Museumslandschaft Hessen Kassel, Sammlung Angewandte Kunst

sought after throughout Europe and commanded high prices even at second hand; for decades after his death, loyal disciples proudly claimed that they continued to work in the *système Huot perfectionné*. As early as the 1790s, one of Huot's figures is recorded as being sent from Paris to St Petersburg at the request of a miniature painter who clearly needed to think big in order to paint small.[2] Regular use—and, doubtless, abuse—in the studio have prevented many of these so-called Parisian stuffed mannequins from surviving in anything like their original condition. A rare exception (although itself partly restored) is the figure made by Huot for the now all but unknown genre painter August von der Embde (1780–1862; Fig. 20.1), who in 1817 had one sent to Kassel from Paris at the significant cost of 1000 francs (transport included). It was accompanied by a three-page pamphlet of instructions that contained such important advice as how to mount the mannequin on its stand and fix the arms and thighs in position, how to protect it from dust and, in a final paragraph, how to make the figure pose like the Venus de' Medici; special attention should be paid to the hair, it was advised, which ought to be regularly combed so as to prevent moths from laying their eggs in it.[3]

Huot's mannequin may have been 'perfected', but to be perfect in artistic terms, it had to negate its existence and become conspicuously absent in the finished painting; without that, it destroyed the very illusion of naturalism the artist had set out to create. It was a thing that was most fully realized as a thing by becoming a replica person. Nineteenth- and twentieth-century artists would explore with psychological depth the paradoxes of this interaction. Ultimately, the mannequin was an artifact whose purpose was to appear as anything other than itself.

[2] The mannequin was intended for use by the Swiss painter Henri-François-Gabriel Viollier (1750–1829). See Johann Georg Wille, *Mémoires et journal de J.-G. Wille*, ed. George Duplessis (Paris : Ve Jules Renouard, 1857), 245.

[3] Heinrich von Bezold, *Explication pour le mannequin*, n.d. (c. 1817), 3.

PART IV

Exotic Goods

CHAPTER 21

A Home Away from Home: Sophie Magdalene's Clockwork Chinoiserie

Josefine Baark

Introducing several beautifully crafted mechanical models, known as *Zimingzhong,* to the scholarly canons of both chinoiserie and automata, this essay argues that the Danish Queen Sophie Magdalene's Chinese-made model houses and their mechanical occupants were not only exceptional, their roles in the Danish royal interior reflected the increasingly unstable relationship between possessing what the East had to offer and imitating a European-made fantasy of a Far Eastern court. Furthermore, these houses symbolically invert the economic premise of trade between China and Europe, wherein clockwork was one of the few types of European artifacts that intrigued the Chinese.[1]

---

[1] The assumption that Chinese-made clockwork was not imported into Europe is widespread. Most significantly, perhaps, it features prominently in Cathrine Pagani's otherwise excellent overview of the 'clocks of Imperial China'. Her first paragraph states: 'In 1987, thirty timepieces from the Palace Museum, Beijing travelled to Florida and were placed on display for the first time outside of China in the Chinese pavilion of the World Showcase at EPCOT Centre … Clocks made in China were at last exhibited in the West next to the European pieces that had served as their inspiration'. The Danish mechanical houses may not be timepieces, but they represent an instance in which automata made in China were exhibited in the West. Pagani seems unaware of these pieces' existence. C.Pagani, *Eastern Magnificence European Ingenuity: Clocks of Late Imperial China,* (Ann Arbor: The University of Michigan Press, 2001), 1. Furthermore, it is interesting to note that the production of these houses and their export to Denmark occurred when the import of opium into China was still in its early stages. The status accorded to clockwork as an import to, rather than an export from, China cannot therefore be overstated. For more on the import of opium see J.Lovell, *The Opium War: Drugs, Dreams and the Making of China* (London: Picador, 2011).

J. Baark (✉)
Department of Visual Studies, Lingnan University, Hong Kong
e-mail: jbaark739@gmail.com

© The Author(s) 2016
A. Craciun, S. Schaffer (eds.), *The Material Cultures of Enlightenment Arts and Sciences,* Palgrave Studies in the Enlightenment, Romanticism and the Cultures of Print, DOI 10.1057/978-1-137-44379-3_21

Even in the European context of a chinoiserie fantasy, the model houses do not fit neatly into the accepted conventions of exotic-looking clockwork.[2]

The Enlightenment emphasis on mechanics, automata and androids is well documented.[3] There was also increasing European interest in exotic goods. Since the establishment of a Danish East India Company in 1620, Danish royalty had created a theatre of the world on which to stage themselves as purveyors of trade and beautiful craftsmanship. Yet the combination of these two trends, whereby chinoiserie-designed houses produced in China entered a European court, has never been seriously researched.[4]

From early on, Danish royalty had displayed an intense interest in mechanical artifacts and 'automata'.[5] Tycho Brahe's mechanical globe found a permanent home 'amongst the other rare artefacts in [the King's] Kunstkammer ... [which he] often since took great pleasure in watching'.[6] In addition, Ole Worm's collection contained important and unique pieces of Chinese workmanship, focused not solely on luxury but also on 'scientific' innovations, for instance a Chinese geomantic compass.[7]

---

[2] This section has benefited from extensive discussion with Professor Simon Schaffer at the University of Cambridge.

[3] The most famous example of royal interest in automata is perhaps King Frederick the Great of Prussia's intense obsession. His father had a close friendship with Frederick IV of Denmark and, moreover, he was a contemporary of Sophie Magdalene. The history of automata has deep roots in antiquity and has played a significant role in European conceptions of craftsmanship, wealth, magic, pranks and religious beliefs. A.Marr, 'Gentille curiosité: Wonder-working and the Culture of Automata in the late Renaissance' in R.J.W. Evans and Alexander Marr (eds.) *Curiosity and Wonder from the Renaissance to the Enlightenment* (Aldershot: Ashgate, 2006) 149–170. See also W.B.Hyman, *The Automaton in English Renaissance Literature* (Farnham: Ashgate, 2011).

[4] Little reference is generally made to the explosion of mechanical craftsmanship in China after the advent of direct trade with Europe, and no references are to be found to these particular examples of mechanical invention and design in Denmark, even in the most recent overviews of the history of automata or of the role of automata in the Enlightenment. For examples of generally useful recent studies that omit any such reference, see A.Voskuhl, *Androids in the Enlightenment: Mechanics, Artisans, and Cultures of the Self* (Chicago and London: The University of Chicago Press, 2013); J.Riskin (ed.) *Genesis Redux: Essays in the History and Philosophy of Artificial Life* (Chicago and London: University of Chicago Press, 2007); M.Kang, *Sublime Dreams of Living Machines: the Automaton in the European Imagination* (Cambridge Mass. and London, Harvard University Press 2011).

[5] Also, as early as 1690, Bendix Grotschilling (Royal Ivory turning master) was paid for an ivory contour or desk containing a clockwork mechanism, which was given to the queen ('for et contoir af elfenben, hvori var et urverk, som dronningen bekom'). E.Marquard, *Kongelige Kammerregnskaber fra Frederik III.s og Christian V.s tid* (Copenhagen: G. E. C. Gad, 1918), 20.

[6] 'Mesling forgyldt Globus, som han selv havde forarbeidet, hvorudi var et Hjul-Værk, hvilket saaledes blev Sol og Maane ... bød han Kongen, at hand Majestat vilde tage den med sig og unde den Plads blandt andre rare sager udi hans KunstKammer, hvilket Kongen med Nåde antog, og forlystede sig ofte siden med at se derpaa' (translation the author's). L.Holberg, *Danmarks Riges Historie* (Copenhagen, n.p., 1763.), 551.

[7] O.Worm, *Museum Wormianum, seu, Historia rerum rariorum: tam naturalium, quam artificialium, tam domesticarum, quam exoticarum, quae Hafniae Danorum in aedibus authoris servantur* (Leiden: John Elsevir, 1655), 372.

In the 1700s, a small group of moving dolls and musical pavilions created by Chinese craftsmen became wondrous parts of Danish castle interiors. Belonging mostly to the chinoiserie collection of Queen Sophie Magdalene, their exotic origins of production, rarity and significance in a world that was increasingly filled with Chinese artifacts is little understood. They embody impressive skill and invention sourced in the craftsmanship available and the technological advances made in both Europe and Asia.[8] Ultimately, they are the marvellous exception to the dominant scholarly European perception of the Sino-European trade: that Europeans traded automata to China and *not* vice versa.

The model houses are early examples of Chinese artifacts to be brought directly from China by the Danish Asiatic Company's new direct trade route in 1732.[9] Yet, despite the novelty to the Danes of an increased and more or less steady and direct influx of artifacts from China, Chinese objects had been available to the affluent Danish consumer for some time. The establishment of direct trade merely solidified a trend whereby, increasingly, what had previously been available only to collector princes or curious men of science had become accessible to a broad spectrum of people.

THE MECHANICAL MODELS IN DANISH COLLECTIONS

A mechanical two-storey house, a mechanical boat, two pagodas, a model shop-house and a court of nodding-head dolls were bequeathed to the Kunstkammer collection in 1772 from the estate of Queen Sophie Magdalene. The model houses are the focus of this chapter, while the mechanical boat models and nodding-head dolls must be left for later study.

The mechanical house contains a large figure on the ground floor and two smaller figures on the top floor (Fig. 21.1). The larger figure moves both arms to hit the drum and the two top figures swing one arm each to hit the drum from either side. The shop signs on the sides of the portal are written in Chinese 'seal script', which had risen to prominence during the Ming dynasty and was still commonly used in the Qing. This confirms their Chinese origins, as the characters are correct and do not resemble the nonsensical imitations found, for instance, in Rosenborg. The third character on the left side is *Ke* (客), meaning guest.[10]

[8] At this time, the questionable time-telling abilities of clocks were secondary to their social importance 'as status symbols, as decorative items, and as personal adornments', both in Europe and in China. Pagani, *Eastern Magnificence*, 6. These pieces' inability to function as timekeepers should not therefore render them irrelevant to the discussion of the exchange in technology between East and West.

[9] Some of these figures nod their head and some do not; Tønder, van Hurck and Bonsach do not. B.Dam-Mikkelsen and T.Lundbæk, (ed.) *Etnografiske Genstande i det Kongelige Danske Kunstkammer 1650–1800 / Ethnographic Objects in the Royal Danish Kunstkammer 1650–180* (Copenhagen: Danish National Museum, 1980) and B.Gundestrup, *Det Kongelige Danske kunst-kammer 1737 / The Royal Danish Kunstkammer 1737* (Copenhagen: Nyt Nordisk Forlag Arnold Busck: Nationalmuseet, 1991).

[10] Translation by Erik Baark, 2014.

Fig. 21.1 Anonymous artist, *Chinese Mechanical House from the Collection of Sophie Magdalene*, pre-1772. Painted ivory and interior mechanism, 32 cm. Copenhagen, Danish National Museum. The inventory caption reads: 'inside … a woman beating a kettledrum, a clockwork to set the same in motion but damaged' (Dam-Mikkelsen and Lundbæk, *Etnografiske Genstande*, 206). Photographs by Josefine Baark, 2012

The second model house in Sophie Magdalene's group is made of painted ivory and occupied by a European man in the front and two figures, potentially a European man and a Chinese woman or two Europeans, at the back (Fig. 21.2). Despite not being a mechanized model, it is still unusual for its age on two accounts: it is an incredibly astute and exacting replica of a traditional South Chinese storefront *and* it contains European merchants rather than the Chinese figures that occupy the other mechanical models.

Sophie Magdalene's collection also contained two model pagodas made of ivory and covered with glass beads, standing higher than a meter (Figs. 21.3 and 21.4). In themselves they are not very rare, not being mechanical. Yet they have clear visual links to the two pagodas from the Kunstkammer collection, which were produced in China between 1723 and 1732.[11]

The last unique mechanical artifact in the royal Kunstkammer collection originates from another source: the collection of Olfert Fas Fisher, the second director of the Danish Asiatic Company (1739–52). This stunning model of a house features four floors under a pagoda-like tiered roof structure and is populated by a myriad of figures (Fig. 21.3).

Olfert Fas Fisher also bequeathed several unique pieces of lacquer furniture to the royal collection, but his assemblage hardly rivals Sophie Magdalene's vast contribution. Her collection of houses and boats was accompanied by a vast number of nodding-head dolls of Chinese figures. These dolls are far less rare in current collections, but no less fascinating.[12]

Mechanical marvels were not unheard of in European courts. Nor is the personal association between a queen and musical clockwork devices something new. The most famous instance is that of the dulcimer player who purportedly represents the French Queen Marie Antoinette and was presented to her as a gift by David Roentgen and Peter Kinzing in 1785. This automaton succeeds those discussed here by at least 13 years and is far more complicated than the figures occupying the Chinese houses. Furthermore, it has a detailed provenance, which is entirely European in origin, execution, history and social significance.[13]

The playfulness of automata was not long unexamined by science. Yet much as with the critical treatises that expounded the social advances of the East, these theories soon felt a literary backlash.[14]

[11] Dam-Mikkelsen and Lundbæk, *Etnografiske Genstande*, 207–8.

[12] T.Clemmensen and M.B.Mackeprag, *Kina og Danmark 1600–1950: Kinafart og Kinamode.* Copenhagen: Nationalmuseet, 1980), 212; Dam-Mikkelsen and Lundbæk, *Etnografiske Genstande*, 174–175.

[13] This musical instrument–playing automaton is discussed in depth alongside a harpsichord player from 1772–74, to show that they 'replicate mechanically a comprehensive scenario of cultural and political activity of their time', in Voskuhl, *Androids in the Enlightenment.*

[14] Particularly by notables in France, such as Cyrano de Bergerac (1619–55), who attacked Descartes, and Giles Morfouace de Beaumont, who pointed out the impossibility of a generative machine. J.Cohen, *Human Robots in Myth and Science* (London: Allen & Unwin, 1966), 73.

Fig. 21.2 Anonymous artist, *(Non-mechanical) Model house with European figures-from the Collection of Queen Sophie Magdalene* and details, pre-1771. Ivory and tortoiseshell, 25 cm. Copenhagen, Danish National Museum. Photographs by Josefine Baark, 2012

Fig. 21.3 Anonymous artist, *Mechanical House from the estate of Olfert Fas Fischer*, 1762. Lacquer wood and ivory, mechanical, 82 cm. Copenhagen, National Museum of Denmark. Photograph by Josefine Baark, 2012

The Production of Automata in China

Meanwhile, in China, automata had been a key element of philosophical discussion for centuries.[15] A first-century Taoist text tells the story of a life-sized human machine equipped with perfect internal organs and capable of song, dance and flirtation:

> The king stared at the figure in astonishment. It walked with rapid strides, moving its head up and down, so that anyone would have taken it for a live human being ... The king was delighted. Taking a deep breath he exclaimed, 'can it be that human skill is on par with that of the great Author of Nature [*tsao hua che*]?'[16]

What is particularly striking is the way in which the nodding head seems to definitively indicate perfect human attributes, more so even than the song and dance. Both music and the nodding head are characteristics of Chinese automaton design that persisted through the export of figures to Europe and even the return export of clockwork devices to China.[17] And yet, despite this early Chinese proficiency and interest in automata, by the seventeenth century the study of mechanics had advanced further in the West.

Some writers suggest that the Jesuit missionaries, so influential in bringing mechanical knowledge to the Chinese court, may have educated craftsmen in the hinterlands of Canton, since theatrical automata had long been used in

[15] Mechanical engineering was, as already noted, not unknown in China. However, previous pieces had primarily been water driven, for instance the *Xinyixiang fayao*, an eleventh-century clock by the astronomer Su Song, and the mechanical, rotating celestial globe and two clocks made by Guo Shoujing for Kublai Kahn in the 1260s. Y.Zheng, *China on the sea: how the maritime world shaped modern China* (Leiden; Boston: Brill, 2012), 139–141; Pagani, *Eastern Magnificence*, 6–14; J.Needham, L.Wang and D.J.de Solla Price, *Heavenly Clockwork: the Great Astronomical Clocks of Medieval China* (Cambridge: University Press, 1960). Moreover, as early as the fourteenth century the French ironsmith Guillaume Boucher purportedly constructed 'an elaborate clock with fountains' for the first Yuan emperor. Boucher entered the court of Emperor Mangu (1250–59) through a Mongol raid into Hungary. None of his instruments has survived and all information on them relies on the account of the Franciscan friar William of Rubruck (1253–55). L.Olschki, *Guillaume Boucher: a French Artist at the Court of the Khans* (Baltimore: The Johns Hopkins Press, 1946); S.Harcourt-Smith, *A Catalogue of Various Clocks, Watches, Automata: and Other Miscellaneous Objects of European Workmanship dating from the XVIIIth and the Early XIXth Centuries, in the Palace Museum and the Wu ying tien* (Beijing: Palace Museum, 1933), 1; for original Chinese clock-making skills, see J.Needham, *Clerks and Craftsmen in China and the West: Lectures and Addresses on the History of Science and Technology* (Cambridge: Cambridge University Press, 1970), 203–38.

[16] This same text mentions a flying automaton/kite built by Mo Ti (Mo Tzu), which it can be presumed was a war machine. J.Needham, *Science and Civilization in China: Volume 2.* (Cambridge: Cambridge University Press, 1986), 53.

[17] A 1760 musical timepiece by Chas. Plummer, produced in London, features a squatting Chinese figure whose head nods in time to music. The small watch is supported on an urn surrounded by four oriental figures, in turn supported by a nécessaire with Chinese silver mounts, carried on the backs of small elephants. Harcourt-Smith, *Catalogue of Various Clocks*, 24.

Europe to surprise, astound and teach the lessons of Christianity.[18] However, I believe this is very unlikely, since it has recently been discovered that the first clocks imported into China through Macao and Canton were gifts for local officials, and it was only later at the Qing court that the Jesuits taught local artisans to repair and maintain the clocks.[19]

Another similarity that may strike the casual observer is also worth mentioning briefly: the similarity in dimension between these model houses and the ancestor altars that were common in Chinese households.[20] However, there is no direct evidence of a link between these two practices, as architectural models were not uncommon outside of the production of ancestral altars.[21]

Nevertheless, there is no denying that the status of intricate clockwork at the Chinese court, after the arrival of the Jesuits, was so great that it spawned an imperial workshop in Beijing, one in Canton and several smaller workshops in the Guangzhou region, where courtiers could buy locally produced mechanical marvels to present to the emperor.[22] Catherine Pagani has suggested that 'both the European and the Chinese clocks made for Chinese consumption followed Western aesthetics',[23] yet the Danish examples suggest that some (and these may easily have been unsuccessful exceptions) may have been made entirely according to Chinese aesthetics.

Moreover, in 1627, Wang Zheng (1571–1644) published *Yuan xi qi qi tu shuo, Illustrated Explanations of the Strange Implements of the Far West*, to explain the complicated mechanical devices being introduced to the Chinese at the time. This treatise was published at a time of surging scholarly interest

---

[18] Athanasius Kircher—a correspondent of Ole Worm—apparently produced several automatons for the Jesuits, including a statue that spoke and listened via a 'speaking tube'. H.Flachenecker, 'Automaten und lebende Bilder in der höfischen Kultur des Spätmittelalters' in Klaus Grubmüller und Markus Stock (ed.) *Automaten in Kunst und Literatur des Mittelalters und der frühen Neuzeit*, 172–195 (Wiesbaden: Harrassowitz in Kommission, 2003), vol.3, 177–8.

[19] Zheng, *China on the Sea*, 142–8.

[20] This similarity is in fact emphasized by the current display in the Danish National Museum, where these houses are placed next to nineteenth-century Javanese spirit houses.

[21] Indeed, a model of the *kuaixuetang* (Hall of Eternal Snow) garden and pavilions in Beihai was produced in the late eighteenth century from a combination of paper, millet, stalks and wood. See illustration in N.Z.Berliner, *The Emperor's Private Paradise: Treasures from the Forbidden City* (New Haven, Conn.: Peabody Essex Museum in association with Yale University Press, 2010), 127.

[22] The province to which Canton belonged was then known as Liang Kwang. However, for clarity I refer to it hereafter as Guangdong, its modern name. W.E.Cheong, *The Hong Merchants of Canton: Chinese Merchants in Sino-Western Trade* (Richmond: Curzon, 1997), 329.

[23] She very rightly observes that the Chinese collectors who acquired European-style chinoiserie clocks were interested in them 'not for their Chinese-style motifs, since they also collected clocks in neoclassical style when chinoiserie had begun to fall out of favour in Europe. ... it was only coincidental that they began to consume European goods at a time when chinoiserie was popular'. Pagani, *Eastern Magnificence*, 164–5. For a discussion of the European taste in chinoiserie clocks and the export of these to China, see ibid., 135–52; for a discussion of Chinese tastes in Chinese-made clocks, see ibid., 152–70.

in artifacts and their production.[24] A print, now at the Peabody Essex Museum in Salem, Massachusetts, shows a watchmakers' shop in Canton (Fig. 21.4). These men belonged to the *Zhongbiao hangshang hui* or Commercial Clock Guild Association, which had been active since the arrival of the Jesuits.[25]

The collection of elaborate gilded clocks in the imperial palace is now one of the most well-preserved remains of the Chinese empire's former glory.[26] Containing not only the items brought by Lord Macartney's Embassy to China in 1792–94 (and rejected for its perceived inferior quality by the emperor), it also contains clocks imported throughout the eighteenth century and displayed in the Summer Palace's Exhibition Hall of the West.[27]

Fig. 21.4   Anonymous artist, *Watchmaker Shop, c.* 1825. Gouache on paper. Peabody Essex Museum, Salem, MA

[24] The same author also published *Zhu qi tu shuo* [*Illustrated Explanations of the Various Implements*], while in 1631 Song Yingxing published *Tian gong kai wu*]. *Heaven's Craft in the Creation of Things.* C. Clunas, *Superfluous Things: Material Culture and Social Status in Early Modern China* (Cambridge: Polity, 1991), 166–7.

[25] Pagani, *Eastern Magnificence*, 78–81.

[26] To view one of these wonderful clocks in motion, see the video of the 'Working Chinese Automaton Clock' in the Peabody Essex Museum temporary exhibition 'The Emperor looks West' (online exhibition, since 2006). Imperial Palace Workshop, *c.* 1790, gold and enamel, Peabody Essex Museum, Salem, MA. http://www.pem.org/collections/7-chinese_art?autovideo=Clock (accessed 20/08/2014).

[27] Berliner, *Emperor's Private Paradise.*

As mentioned, centres of mechanical expertise began to develop in the regions of Guangdong and Suzhou as a consequence of ever-increasing demand from high government officials and other members of the Chinese court.[28] These patrons of the mechanical arts were motivated mainly by the favour shown to those who were able to give such elaborate and amusing machines to the emperor as tribute. In 1692, an imperial workshop, the *zaozongchu*, was set up in the Forbidden City to cater to these needs.[29] Many of these pieces are still to be found in the National Palace Museum, although they have also trickled into other elite Beijing households.[30]

Recently, several pieces produced by the court workshop during the Qianlong period (1711–99) have surfaced; the wide span of that period makes these particular artifacts very difficult to place in relation to Sophie Magdalene's collection. Still, structural similarities and a small figure grasping a miniature model of a pagoda close to his top hat, next to another European figure, can be found in the *Clock with the decoration of pavilion swimming ducks and revolving figures and detail* from the Qianlong period. Made in Guangzhou, the little European figures and their even smaller Chinese companions are later versions of those in the model shop house.

However, the most exciting piece found in the imperial collections is the pavilion-shaped clock made in Canton and showing what appears to be the workmen themselves engaged in building a model pagoda, similar to the ones bought by both Olfert Fas Fisher and Sophie Magdalene. This could, however, also be a reference to the Su Song astronomical clock tower, which it resembles in form although not in size.[31]

The final clue pertaining to the Chinese-produced clocks is that while those produced at the imperial workshop tend to be made of wood, the chiming clocks brought in from Guangzhou were covered in the colourful enamel produced in that city. The Danish examples are made almost exclusively of ivory, but certain areas are painted and some even have enamel. The intricacy and details of the towers must have appealed a great deal to Danish royalty, who were known for their extensive abilities in the art of ivory turning and carving.[32] Sophie Magdalene in particular was known to be enthusiastic and skilful in her artistry—the complicated woodturning table that enabled her to be so is still kept in Rosenborg Castle.

---

[28] Other less-productive centres existed around Shanghai, Ningbo and Nanjing as well. C.Pagani, 'Clockmaking in China under the Kangxi and Qianlong Emperors' in *Arts asiatiques* (1995) 50: 76–84, on 28.

[29] Zheng, *China on the Sea*, 150–54; Pagani, 'Clockmaking in China', 78.

[30] Pagani, 'Clockmaking in China', 29.

[31] Pagani, *Eastern Magnificence*, 7–13; Needham et al., *Heavenly Clockwork*.

[32] Many of the pieces carved in ivory and amber by Christian IV are now in the treasury collection in Rosenborg Castle. The tutelage of Lorenz Spengler, who arrived at the Danish court in 1743, cannot be understated regarding the increased interest shown by Danish royalty in this craft. From 1770 onwards he was in charge of the royal Kunstkammer.

Overall, however, we can conclude that interest in miniature versions of houses, palace structures and pagodas was common to both the Danish and Chinese courts.[33]

EUROPEAN CLOCK MAKING FOR CHINESE CLIENTS

By the time of the Macartney Embassy, it was remarked that the collection of automata in the imperial treasury outshone any in Europe.[34] Unfortunately, only 11 mechanical clocks from the period prior to 1760 have been identified: a 1715 enamel watch with Cupid and Venus by Joseph Williamson, a 1755 musical timepiece by Robert Sellers, two 1755 musical timepieces by William Shutter, a 1750 'half-vase' by Thomas Rayment, a 1740 Cartel clock by Henry Padeval, a 1740 enamel watch by George Pembroke, a 1750 'half-vase' by John Halstead, a 1740–50 chinoiserie bronze-gilt musical timepiece by Fromanteel and Clark, a 1750 'half-vase' inspired by Chinese *hua p'ing* by G. Duck, and a small 1734 enamel watch by Thomas Broome.[35] Very few of these late eighteenth-century pieces bear any similarity in form to those found in Denmark and, without exception, all of them were produced in Europe.

European clockmakers and artists had in fact already begun to target the distant Chinese market by 1700.[36] However, early pieces in the imperial collections produced in China were probably made in the workshops at the palace, while later examples were produced in the workshops near Canton; both were prohibited from being sold to buyers outside the imperial court. The Chinese provenance of the Danish pieces is thus even more remarkable.

Some resemblance in the architectural theme of the pieces can be found to that of later European examples in the imperial collection. The most convincing similarity is to the pair of 1780 bronze-gilt musical clocks whose clock case supports a five-tiered pagoda hung with bells and decorated with paste flowers. The lowest tier is occupied by soldiers in British uniform, who march as the tiers rotate and music plays.[37]

Another pair of bronze-gilt musical clocks also support pagoda-like tiered roofs and moving figures. These clocks, from 1775, have very complicated interior mechanisms, but apart from their pagoda roofs they are Western in style. A bronze-gilt timekeeper from 1765 found in the Wu Ying Tien Museum has a Chinese figure under an umbrella supported by an architectural structure resting on dolphins, which was most likely produced in France. The formal similarity and later dates of these European-produced clocks might suggest that they were inspired by the Chinese-made clocks that had arrived in Europe;

[33] X.Guan, 'Chinese Timepieces' in The Palace Museum (ed.), *Timepieces in the Imperial Palace.* (The Imperial Palace Museum: The Forbidden City Publishing House, 2007).

[34] Harcourt-Smith, *Catalogue of Various Clocks*, 1.

[35] Ibid.

[36] Zheng, *China on the Sea*, 159–61. S.Schaffer, 'Instruments and Cargo in the China Trade' in *The British Journal for the History of Science*, (2006) 44: 217–46, on 235–40.

[37] Harcourt-Smith, *Catalogue of Various Clocks*, 6.

however, until other examples of Chinese export clockwork are discovered, this seems a tenuous supposition.

Only one piece in the Beijing collection appears to have been produced in Copenhagen: a small gold watch, about one inch in diameter with a white enamel face and a very fine flower painting in rococo arabesques, made by Isaac Berger in 1760.[38] The whole is attached to a chain and key.[39] This piece is one of the smaller, less elaborate clocks in the collection, which contains clocks with moving dragons, musicians and goatherds, paintings, bells, and a menagerie of elephants, rhinoceroses and birds. Some of the pieces have even been improved on by Chinese craftsmen (much like the astronomical instruments of the Jesuits). For example, a 1780 bronze-gilt timepiece containing a watch set in a gilt rock and a smaller watch set in the heart of a rose, produced by Thomas Larrymore in London, had its painted rustic scenes overpainted later with Chinese designs.[40]

Unquestionably, the production and use of automata formed an area of intense interest in both Europe and China.[41] Yet, while it is very likely both that automata were made in Europe for the Chinese market and that automata were made in China with the Chinese court in mind, these Danish examples are the first evidence to come to light that automata were produced in China for the European market.

It must be remembered that producing these delicate, intricate mechanisms—whether in Europe or China—was so difficult and time-consuming that 'the only people able to afford to construct such artefacts were well-to-do artisans, artisans in employment or under the patronage of a court, or artisans who could expect members of the nobility to buy their products'.[42]

So the mechanical houses travelled from China to Europe and the Europe in which they arrived was not unprepared. At the turn of the eighteenth century, Renaissance experiments had improved mechanical skills as well as stimulated increasing interest in these artifacts. The fashion for mechanical beings is perhaps most notoriously expressed in the automata produced by the French *mécanicien* Jacques Vaucanson.[43] Without going into great detail, Vaucanson's flutist automaton, the tambourine player and the digesting duck (considered

---

[38] 'Berger, Isach (Isaac), Copenhagen. Became master in 1753 and specialized in gold watches with enamelling'; Pagani, *Eastern Magnificence*, appendix C, 188. See also G.H.Baillie, *Watchmakers and Clockmakers of the World* (London: NAG Press, 1969).

[39] Harcourt-Smith, *Catalogue of Various Clocks*, 12.

[40] Ibid., 22.

[41] The production of clockwork dolls took root more firmly in Japan than in China, as early as 1662, when Takeda Omi—inventor of the first Karakuri (mechanical) dolls—performed at Osaka's Dotonbori. M.Hillier, *Automata & Mechanical Toys: an Illustrated History* (London: Jupiter, 1976), 36.

[42] Voskuhl, *Androids in the Enlightenment*, 25.

[43] The use of the term *mécanicien* rather than *artiste* to designate the designers of these intricate pieces has a deprecatory ring to it. Yet it was the most commonly used term at the time. A.Marr, 'Understanding Automata in the Late Renaissance' in *Journal de la Renaissance* (2004) 2: 205–22, on 207.

the world's first successfully built biomechanical automaton and put on public display in Paris in 1738) were all recognized as exceptionally skilful creations, above and beyond what others were capable of doing at the time.[44]

The increase in automata production—with its baggage of entertainment value and facetiousness—led to social derision of the craft by the end of the eighteenth century. Despite having been used as useful illustrations of human ability and even of human metaphysical origin, European-made mechanized 'toys' were no longer considered as any more than mere foolishness by the beginning of the nineteenth century. The mechanical houses of Queen Sophie Magdalene appeared on the scene just before this last juncture, at the height of mechanical invention, when the limitations of automata as scientific examples were beginning to manifest.[45]

Indeed, royals experienced a rising proficiency and popularity of automata in European courts, famously that of Frederick the Great, King of Prussia,[46] or Maria Theresa of Austria, for whom a chess-playing Turk was constructed in 1770.[47] In fact, the association between the powerful, 'magical' mechanical devices and royal power was strong. As Helmut Flachenecker has observed, 'ownership of machines or the ability to have them manufactured formed a central part of the aura of power and dominion'.[48]

Furthermore, as we have seen, it was only later in the eighteenth century that chinoiserie mechanical clocks meant to appeal to the Chinese court began to appear on the market in earnest, produced by such men as the illustrious English inventor James Cox.[49] Cox moreover also advertised these pieces in Europe. Here, they appealed to the market for purchasing whatever the Chinese emperor was buying, so that wealthy Europeans could simultaneously

---

[44] The Digesting Duck did not in fact digest anything; it contained an internal sack containing green dye and breadcrumbs, which were expelled when the duck was 'fed'. Such abilities fed into the literary debate on society and the human condition—in particular, the Digesting Duck seemed to endorse Cartesian ideas that animals are no more than machines. Vaucanson would, however, soon switch to inventing industrial machinery in state service. Marr, 'Understanding Automata', 209–21.

[45] Automata would soon become the butt of satirical jokes and songs. Marr, 'Gentille curiosité', 163–64.

[46] Michel Foucault has commented, 'The great book of Man-the-Machine was written simultaneously on two registers: the anatomico-metaphysical register, of which Descartes wrote the first pages and which the physicians and philosophers continued, and the technico-political register, which was constituted by a whole set of regulations and by empirical and calculated methods relating to the army, the school and the hospital, for controlling or correcting the operations of the body ... The celebrated automata [of the eighteenth century] were not only a way of illustrating an organism, they were also political puppets, small-scale models of power.' M.Foucault, *Discipline and Punish* (New York: Vintage Books, 1979), 136.

[47] The Turk, 1770 by Wolfgang von Kempelen. Destroyed in 1854.

[48] 'Der Besitz von Automaten bzw. die Möglichkeit, diese herstellen zu lassen, bildete einen Bestandteil der die Herrschaft umgebenden Aura' (translation by the author). Flachenecker, 'Automaten und lebende Bildern', 191.

[49] R. Smith, 'James Cox (c. 1723–1800): A Revised Biography' in *Burlington Magazine* (2000) 142: 353–61.

imitate the practice of the emperor and possess a European-made fantasy of the East with some authority.

In February 1781, John Henry Cox travelled to Canton to collect on some of his father's debts. Moreover, he set up a workshop to cater to the desire for automata at the Chinese court, although he apparently avoided the expensive, elaborate clocks that earned his father his reputation and cost him his business.[50] Some of his constructions had been sent along with the Macartney Embassy, and although the emperor had generally derided the British gifts, these mechanical marvels had met with approval.

AT THE COURT OF SOPHIE MAGDALENE

The next problem these houses present involves tracking their journey from Canton to Copenhagen. Unfortunately, no records have been found of their commission by or purchase for the Danish East India Company, nor is there any record of their being sold by the Company. The material point at which we can pick up the story once more is in the domestic households of the aristocracy.

Therefore, we must look more closely at how these mechanical marvels were displayed in the royal collection of Queen Sophie Magdalene.[51] As a member of the royal court, she had access to many of the illustrated works sent back by the Jesuits, as well as to the beautifully painted porcelain that inspired so much interior design at the time and was available in the royal household.[52] Yet in these small figures, the moving, playing, dancing, wider world represents even more exquisitely a court geographically far removed from her own.

The artifacts were first officially described in the inventory of the royal Kunstkammer from 1772.[53] However, in the 1754 inventory taken of Sophie

[50] Schaffer, 'Instruments and Cargo', 217; S.Schaffer, 'Enlightened Automata' in William Clark, Jan Golinski, and Simon Schaffer (ed.) *The Sciences in Enlightened Europe*, 126–165 (Chicago, Ill. and London: University of Chicago Press, 1999), 139. Also R.Altick, *The Shows of London* (Cambridge, Mass. and London: Belknap Press of Harvard University Press, 1978), 350–51; D.S.Landes, *Revolution in Time: Clocks and the Making of the Modern World* (Cambridge, Mass.: Belknap Press of Harvard University Press, 1983), 37–52, 401.

[51] Sophie Magdalene was the wife of Christian VI (m. 1721) and had previously lived in Bayreuth and attended Queen Christine Eberhardine, wife of August the Strong. J. Hein, *The Treasure Collection at Rosenborg Castle, the Inventories of 1696 and 1718, Royal Heritage and Collecting in Denmark-Norway 1500–1900* (Copenhagen: Museum Tusculanum Press, 2009), Vol. I, 107–10. See also E.Jørgensen and J.Skovgaard, *Danske Dronninger, Fortællinger og Karakteristikker* (Copenhagen: H. Hagerup, 1910); H.Willemsen, *Norske reise anno 1733: beskrivelse af kong Christian 6. og dronning Sophie Magdalenes rejse til Norge 12. maj-23. September: faksimileudgave af håndskrift i Hendes Majestæt Dronningens håndbibliotek*, Poul Kristensen Herning and Klaus Kjølsen (eds.), (Copenhagen: Hendes Majestæt Dronningens håndbibliotek, 1992).

[52] It is interesting to note that this region was the main site of porcelain production, for both imperial use and export. R.Finlay, *The Pilgrim Art: Cultures of Porcelain in World History* (Berkeley, Calif.: University of California Press, 2010).

[53] Their late date of registration may suggest to some that these automata are connected with the production of such famous pieces as the Turk, a 'mechanical' chess-player (in reality operated by a concealed person), created by Wolfgang von Kempelen in 1769, or the mechanical tiger that eats

Magdalene's home at Sophienberg—now emptied and made into a business retreat—several 'Chinese figures' (sometimes explicitly porcelain and sometimes without a designated material) are repeatedly mentioned, displayed in nearly every room, on specially produced lacquered or japanned consoles.[54] They are particularly numerous in the bedrooms assigned to visiting family members from Germany.

This inventory gives us a narrow but important insight into Sophie Magdalene's home and the position that chinoiserie artifacts occupied not only in the familial and domestic sphere, but also in the political sphere. Often the objects are grouped by size irrespective of whether they are figures or vases. Furthermore, the inventory lacks reference to other fixtures in the rooms, except when it comes to special, often lacquered, furniture. Instead, it includes references to groups of figurines, the colour and material of the curtains and the paintings hung on the walls. It is by no means exhaustive, yet this brevity in itself could indicate a coherent scheme whereby function (references to the necessary, ordinary furniture) is removed so as to foreground the aesthetic (and expensive) experience.[55] What is certainly clear is that the Chinese or Chinese-like objects are integral to the design and experience of the rooms, each one containing at least one Chinese artifact, be it a vase, a figure or a gold-inlay lacquered screen. One room, for instance, contained around 75 porcelain figures and pots in addition to being dotted with portraits of queens and their children.[56]

Moreover, the first hall on the second floor contained a 'Dining Table covered in Chinese printed cloth'.[57] It seems that the exotic experience was also immersive. The musical abilities of the mechanical houses and the travelling,

a British soldier commissioned by Tippu Sultan around the same time. However, I believe that they precede both of these automata. The Turk has now disappeared and Tippu's Tiger is on display in the Victoria and Albert Museum, London. Dam-Mikkelsen and Lundbæk, *Etnografiske Genstande*; Kongehuset Christian 6, Dronning Sophie Magdalene, *Dødsbo (officielt)* (1757–72).

[54] Sophienberg has previously been the focus of only a very basic study; see B.Bramsen, *Sophienberg, Bygning og Beboere gennem 250 år* (Copenhagen: Gymnasieskolernes Lærerforening, 1994).

[55] Naturally, inventories often record only the most precious elements of a household. Yet in the case of Sophienberg's inventory, the scarcity is especially striking, and as the castle was a royal residence and a site of diplomatic entertainment, it is therefore unlikely that the inventory yields comprehensive insight into the entirety of the precious furnishings. Slott-, Meubels- og have-Inventarium, af det kongelige Lyst-Slott Sophienberg, 1755 in Finanskollegiet, Sekretariatet, *Sager vedrørende Sophie Magdalenes bo* (1771–72).

[56] Slott-, Meubels- og have-Inventarium, af det kongelige Lyst-Slott Sophienberg, 1755 in Finanskollegiet, Sekretariatet, *Sager vedrørende Sophie Magdalenes bo* (1771–72). See also Partikulærkammeret, Dronning Sophie Magdalene, *Hofholdningssager* (1739–66).

[57] '*Taffel Okule med Chinessisch Zitz betrukan*' Slott-, Meubels- og have-Inventarium, af det kongelige Lyst-Slott Sophienberg, 1755 in Finanskollegiet, Sekretariatet, *Sager vedrørende Sophie Magdalenes bo* (1771–72). Using exotic cloth in the context of eating or sleeping shows how increasingly commonplace it had become. The experience of the East was highly sensory and included spiced food, tablecloths, *nef* model ships and perhaps even the tinkling of mechanical chinoiserie musicians.

table-top boats served to add to the overall ambience of the rooms and their social function.[58]

Thus, it is possible partially to reconstruct the palace rooms, since the inventory also lists the paintings adorning the walls, such as a view of Frederiksberg Castle, a Christ on the Cross, an Ecce Homo and a Christ and the Samaritans.[59] The *Christ on the Cross* painting by Peter Paul Rubens, bought for the Royal Kunstkammer in 1735 and now in the State Museum of Art, gives an idea of the visual context in which these chinoiserie pieces were viewed (Fig. 21.5).

It is not altogether surprising to find a Rubens within the context of Asian exchange. Rubens had close ties to the Jesuit order, particularly in Ghent, and he sought subject matter from its missions in Asia for several significant works. In addition, his studies of Asian costumes—completed in the early seventeenth century—may not have been unknown to the Danish royal family, which had close connections to the Netherlands, if not directly to Belgium, and which possessed so striking a piece of religious art by the master.[60] Still, it is unusual to find a devotional depiction of Christ's body in the Northern, Lutheran court of a queen whose piety was well known. Is it going too far to suggest that the Lutherans perceived the same magic in the Orient that they saw in the Eucharist?

It appears, moreover, that the attention lavished on the chinoiserie goods at Sophienberg was not unique. The 'Inventory of Linens and Bedcovers' (1754) from Hirchholm Castle, where the Queen often resided, refers to 'Her Majesty the Queen's Brown Lacquered Bed Chamber'.[61] The castle has now been demolished after extended disuse, so the chamber has disappeared. However, the reference certainly recalls the other, earlier chinoiserie rooms created for Queen Sophie Amalie at Rosenborg Castle.

In a more geographically far-reaching context, Sophienberg Castle was by no means the only place in Scandinavia drowning in chinoiserie. In 1753, the Swedish King Adolf Fredrik had a series of Chinese pavilions built for

---

[58] The desire for musical machines at court has roots in medieval literary works such as the *Floire et Blanchefleur* (version a), where a joust between two mechanical knights is described as being accompanied by figures playing music. Flachenecker, 'Automaten und lebende Bilder', 180.

[59] The inclusion of the prospect of Frederiksberg may be of significance. In 1699 Frederik IV built an Italianate palace just outside Copenhagen. In 1791, his grandson started planning an English garden, begun by Marcus Frederich Voigt in 1797. The garden included a 'Chinoiserie' pavilion on an artificial island, created by Andreas Kirkerup. Its design is certainly inspired by those of William Chambers, yet it has also been suggested that the pavilions built by the Swedish King Adolf Frederik in 1753 for his Queen, Lovisa Ulrika, at Drottningholm Castle also influenced the building.

[60] See also Rubens's *Portrait of Nicolas Trigault in Chinese Costume*, 1617, The Metropolitan Museum of Art, New York. Purchase, Carl Selden Trust, several members of The Chairman's Council, Gail and Parker Gilbert, and Lila Acheson Wallace Gifts, 1999.222; *Man in Korean Costume*, c. 1617, Black chalk with touches of red chalk in the face, 40 × 24 cm, Los Angeles, The J. Paul Getty Museum; and his *Miracles of Saint Francis Xavier*, c. 1617, Kunsthistorisches Museum, Gemäldegalerie, Vienna.

[61] Inventarium over Sengeklæder og Linn Tog ... ved Hirschholm Slott 1754 in Finanskollegiet, Sekretariatet, *Sager vedrørende Sophie Magdalenes bo* (1771–72).

Fig. 21.5 Peter Paul Rubens, *Christ on the Cross*, 1592–1633 (acquired 1750). Oil on wood, 74 × 105 cm. Copenhagen, State Museum of Art. Photograph by Josefine Baark, 2012

his Queen, Lovisa Ulrika, at Drottningholm Castle, influenced by William Chambers' designs.[62] The rooms of this pavilion are dotted with nodding-head

[62] The pavilion was first built in 1753, and then again in 1769. W. Chambers, *Designs of Chinese Buildings, Furniture, Dresses, Machines, and Utensils / Engraved by the best hands, from the originals drawn in China by Mr. Chambers, architect, … To which is annexed, a description of their temples, houses, gardens, &c.* (London: published for the author, 1757); W. Chambers, *A Dissertation on Oriental Gardening* (London: W. Griffin, 1772); G.Alm, (ed). *Kina Slott* (Stockholm: Byggförlaget, 2002).

dolls, keeping silent court. These pavilions are separated from the castle by the park and exhibit a chinoiserie style throughout. Hence, the pavilion does not contain any significant classical European painting.

Sophie Magdalene did not have at her disposal the funds to build a chinoiserie pavilion, but she did import the next best thing: miniature life-like figures in Chinese spaces, playing music and enacting the exoticism that other royals could only pretend to know. Her political position, her entertaining of foreign diplomats and her family connections made her an integral, albeit smaller part of the social and economic discussion playing out among the royal European houses and, as Olfert Fas Fisher's automaton reveals, the Danish aristocracy. Automata were almost unfailingly amusing, regardless of their scientific merit. This also accounts for the integration of so many of her rare artifacts into the Kunstkammer collection at her death.

Although the level of knowledge of the East in Europe had risen substantially during the seventeenth century, it had not rendered these cultures more easily commensurable. The conditions in the trading ports, the only places where many travellers left boats, continued to be restricted. Moreover, even after launching their third trade delegation, the Danes were slow to acquire the new (often Jesuit) publications about Asian religions, languages and cultures, and continued to rely on artifacts for information and inspiration. Yet the void of value generated by a limited cultural exchange was creatively constructed in commercially minded interiors.

In addition, as contact increased and direct trade grew, opportunities for communication between producers and consumers also multiplied. Artifacts could be produced for foreign consumption, aided by instructions from the consumers themselves. Nevertheless, the imaginative and innovative impulse was not stifled and the producers continued to improve on, and add to, the aesthetic orders they received or the technological aspirations they encountered. There was universal appeal in acquiring the means to display the opulence and leisure necessary in diplomatic circles and easily recognizable symbols of profit and power to ensure continued trade. This cultural exchange therefore continued to evolve and change. The level of fantasy and invention present in the interim between the first fumbling attempts at a global trade network and a fully fledged economic plan increased exponentially. Chinoiserie courtiers nodded along to the music of chinoiserie drummers, watched over by a crucified Christ.

Ultimately, the visual confusion and misunderstanding born of early economic globalization were creative—they freely marshalled contemporary political and economic concerns alongside fashionable aesthetic templates to promote trade. None of the efforts to include a living, knowledgeable version of the East into royal interiors was accompanied by any sustained wish, as Ole Worm had wanted for the Danes, to 'replace persuasion with evidence, debate with research, belief with knowledge', yet they all resulted in a creative, innovative artistic production, whose consistent disregard of new cultural knowledge enabled it dynamically to change form, if not content.

CHAPTER 22

The Chinese Tallow Tree: From Asset in Asia to Curse in Carolina

Charles Jarvis

During the last quarter of the seventeenth century, commerce was increasing between Europe and China. In England, demand for Chinese goods, notably tea, porcelain, lacquerware and silk, was strong, and the English East India Company (EIC) responded by sending ships to the East, trying to establish trading posts on the Chinese islands of Amoy (Xiamen) and Chusan (Zhoushan). For connoisseurs and natural philosophers this raised the possibility of obtaining items of considerable interest from far-flung, exotic locations. James Cuninghame (*c.* 1665–1709), a Scottish surgeon, travelled to Chusan with the EIC and would prove invaluable to keen collectors of specimens of animals and plants (of potential economic, ornamental, 'scientific' or curiosity value) in England.

Among Cuninghame's London acquaintances were collectors such as the apothecary James Petiver (1665–1718), the Royal gardener Leonard Plukenet (1642–1706) and the physician and Secretary of the Royal Society Hans Sloane (1660–1753). Petiver, in particular, went to great lengths to cultivate people whom he thought might supply him with rare specimens, particularly plants, insects and shells. In 1698, learning that Cuninghame intended to travel ('Being assured you design for China …'), Petiver sent Cuninghame a list of 80 botanical desiderata,[1] which included ginseng, rhubarb, tea, 'great long nutmeg', 'lichi' and 'candle tree'. Cuninghame proved to be a remarkable recruit, collecting and sending to England many hundreds of carefully pressed Chinese plants. While

---

[1] J. Petiver to J. Cuninghame, 1698, Sloane MSS, British Library, 3333, 113–116.

C. Jarvis (✉)
Department of Life Sciences, Natural History Museum, London, UK
e-mail: c.jarvis@nhm.ac.uk

© The Author(s) 2016   191
A. Craciun, S. Schaffer (eds.), *The Material Cultures of Enlightenment Arts and Sciences*, Palgrave Studies in the Enlightenment, Romanticism and the Cultures of Print, DOI 10.1057/978-1-137-44379-3_22

Fig. 22.1 A dried specimen of the Chinese Tallow Tree (*Triadica sebifera*), collected by James Cuninghame in Chusan (1700–1703). His own, highly informative label is mounted to its left in one of Leonard Plukenet's bound herbarium volumes (now in the Sloane Herbarium, Natural History Museum, London, HS 94, 192)

stationed in Chusan between October 1700 and February 1703, Cuninghame collected the specimen of the Chinese Tallow tree (*Triadica sebifera*) shown in this exhibit, which may have been the sought-after 'candle tree' from Petiver's list.

A number of Cuninghame's specimens of this species survive in the huge collection of dried plants assembled by Hans Sloane, and now housed at the Natural History Museum in London. Containing an estimated 120,000 specimens collected between about 1600 and 1750 and mounted in bound volumes,[2]

---

[2] J.E. Dandy, *The Sloane Herbarium: an annotated list of the* Horti Sicci *composing it; with biographical accounts of the principal contributors* (London: The British Museum, 1958).

the herbarium reflects both patterns of trade and the intellectual networks that Sloane and his contemporaries developed and used.

This specimen, the basis for a published engraving,[3] exemplifies Cuninghame's meticulous approach. The carefully pressed branchlet shows both upper and lower leaf surfaces and a cluster of mature, three-part fruits, split open to reveal the three large wax-encased seeds that each contains. Cuninghame's original label is on the left, with slits near its base through which the branchlet was slipped to keep plant and label together during the long voyage home. The label provides an exemplary description in Latin, also noting the months of flowering and fruiting, and the vernacular names of both the tree ('Kiū-tze') and its wax ('Kiū-yēu').[4]

Chinese tallow is a useful tree in the Asian subtropics, grown chiefly for seed oil. In England in the mid-eighteenth century, there was interest in the potential of Eastern plants for improving the agriculture of the North American colonies. Chinese tallow seeds were accordingly sent from England to the colonies in the 1760s. Embracing the warm climate of its new continent enthusiastically, and having escaped its natural Asian pests and diseases, Chinese tallow spread easily and became naturalized across the southern Atlantic and Gulf coasts, where it is now a major invasive pest.

The Chinese tallow specimens that James Cuninghame, that 'learned and most industrious Promoter of Natural Philosophy',[5] sent to his friends in London galvanized the interest of the latter and paved the way for other introductions of interesting and valuable plants. Few of them, however, have wrought the unexpected havoc that Chinese tallow unleashed in the United States.

---

[3] L. Plukenet, *Amaltheum botanicum* (London: for the author, 1705), t.390, f.2.

[4] Sloane Herbarium, Natural History Museum, London, HS 94, 192.

[5] J. Petiver, *Musei Petiveriani* (London: S. Smith & B. Walford, 1699), 44.

CHAPTER 23

Global Connections: Punch, Porcelain and Maritime Material Culture

John McAleer

For over two centuries, the commercial and cultural relationship between Europe and Asia was mediated through the agency of various East India companies. As trading ventures chartered by their respective governments, these companies were, at their most basic, organizations interested in objects. Their main business involved the transportation of huge quantities of commodities—principally spices, tea and textiles in the British case—back to Europe for sale, fundamentally altering ideas of taste and fashion in the process. Ironically, however, the physical items on which they based their commercial power and success were ephemeral and few have survived. However, other artifacts, such as the porcelain bowl in Fig. 23.1, were more durable and stand as eloquent testimony to the extraordinary range of global connections and maritime trading networks that characterized the period.

The bowl was made in China in about 1785, specifically for export to Europe. The circumstances of its production, its decorative imagery and even its intended usage encapsulate the global commercial connections of the eighteenth-century world. On one level, the bowl highlights the movement of material culture and exchange of ideas between Asia and Europe. Although access to Chinese markets was jealously controlled, East India companies managed to procure highly sought-after commodities—such as tea, silk, jade and porcelain—from Canton, the only Chinese port open to Europeans. Porcelain was greatly prized for its fine, translucent quality, the result of a manufacturing technique that had yet to be mastered in Europe.

J. McAleer (✉)
Department of History, University of Southampton, London, UK
e-mail: j.mcaleer@soton.ac.uk

© The Author(s) 2016   195
A. Craciun, S. Schaffer (eds.), *The Material Cultures of Enlightenment Arts and Sciences*, Palgrave Studies in the Enlightenment, Romanticism and the Cultures of Print, DOI 10.1057/978-1-137-44379-3_23

Fig. 23.1 Punch bowl, *c.* 1785, object #AAA4440. © National Maritime Museum, Greenwich, London

The inscription on the interior of the bowl—'Success to Mr Barnard's Yard'—demonstrates the importance of maritime connections in facilitating Britain's burgeoning commercial relations with the rest of the world. William Barnard, for whom this bowl was probably commissioned, was born into a Suffolk shipbuilding family. In 1763, he moved to the River Thames where he leased an extensive yard in Deptford. Britain's expanding maritime trade and the seemingly incessant wars of the eighteenth century, all of which necessitated the building and maintenance of large fleets of ships, meant that William Barnard prospered.

The decoration of the bowl highlights the ways in which Chinese craftsmen adapted their style to suit European aesthetic preferences. The buildings, scenery and river are distinctively Chinese, but many of the decorative elements are more European than Asian. And the line drawings of ships, painted in grisaille, are based on European engravings sent with the original commission. In this instance, the inspiration probably came from Fredrik Henrik af Chapman's *Architectura Navalis Mercantoria*, first published in Stockholm in 1768. As an object that combines Asian and European elements, the bowl represents the cultural exchange that went hand in hand with commercial endeavours.

The bowl was intended to contain punch. The word is derived from the Hindi *panch* or *paantsch*, meaning 'five', because the drink was originally made with five ingredients. A variety of wines or liquors could be used, which were then mixed with hot water or milk, and flavored with sugar, lemons or spices to complete the concoction. As its etymology suggests, 'punch' was another phenomenon that came to Europe from Asia, via the same East India Company channels as the porcelain bowl. In 1662, John Evelyn visited 'an East India vessel that lay at Black-Wall, where we had Entertainment of several curiosities:

among other spirituous drinks, as Punch'.[1] By the end of the eighteenth century, when this bowl was commissioned, one of the 'spirituous liquors' regularly used to make punch was rum. Produced from sugar cane grown in Britain's slave-holding Caribbean colonies, rum offers another example of the way in which global trade and empire shaped British culture and consumer habits. In many ways, the bowl and its intended contents stand as a symbol of Britain's global commercial reach, as well as the impact and importance of Asian and American commodities in British culture and society.

---

[1] J. Evelyn, *The Diary of John Evelyn*, edited by W. Bray, 2 vols (New York and London: M. Walter Dunne, 1901), vol. 1, 356.

CHAPTER 24

A Damaged and Discarded Thing

Anne Gerritsen

The two-storey building on display here is a rather grand building. It has a finely curved roof on each of the two floors, carved panels and latticework on either side of the doors, steps leading to the front entrance, and a setting with trees, plants and a panelled fence. All this appears in fine shades of cobalt blue on a white surface. The decorative edge running along the top of the object consists of simple circular, hatched and swirly patterns. Evidence of damage, however, partially obscures the drawing of the building. Soil and grit have been burnt into the glaze, leaving traces all over the surface of the object, and its shape has been distorted. The very top edge of the object shows traces of a rust-coloured line, similar in shade to the soil attached to the glaze. Although the object sustained serious damage during the firing process, it was clearly intended to be a cup with a single handle, about 6 cm high and perhaps 4 cm in diameter, although its squashed shape makes this difficult to ascertain. That much is clear from looking at the image.

Much more we cannot see, but can deduce from historical contextualization. Such straight-sided coffee cups were made in late eighteenth-century China for the European market. The Chinese did not drink out of such tall cups with handles, and the pattern, with a multi-storey pavilion set in a garden near a lake with a boat, was mainly produced for overseas consumers. This global production was concentrated around the inland city of Jingdezhen, where Chinese merchants conveyed the orders of the port-based overseas customers for specific shapes, styles and designs. Mass-production methods meant that local potters could largely meet the demand, although the damage on this

A. Gerritsen (✉)
Department of History, University of Warwick, Coventry, UK
e-mail: a.t.gerritsen@warwick.ac.uk

© The Author(s) 2016   199
A. Craciun, S. Schaffer (eds.), *The Material Cultures of Enlightenment Arts and Sciences*, Palgrave Studies in the Enlightenment, Romanticism and the Cultures of Print, DOI 10.1057/978-1-137-44379-3_24

Fig. 24.1 Blue and white porcelain kiln waster. Jingdezhen, late eighteenth century. H 6 cm. Author's collection. Photograph by Jane Jones, http://www.janejonesimages. co.uk

little cup suggests that they placed items too closely together in the kiln when it was fired, causing it to fuse partially with another object. The cost of such failures was high. In a tightly packed kiln, unexpected fluctuations in the temperature or falling objects could mean that thousands of damaged items had to be discarded, and scores of workers did not get paid. Today, the steady stream of damaged items found in mounds and digs around the city and offered for sale in the illegal shard market testifies to this high failure rate, just as the absence of control over such excavations suggests the strength of the ceramics trade.

So why should we be looking at such a damaged and discarded thing? The fine pieces of ceramics that fill museums and grand homes all over the world tell a global success story: the blue-and-whites of Jingdezhen were sent throughout Afro-Eurasia and the Americas from their first production in the fourteenth century onwards. However, the growth of global demand meant an increase in local pressures in Jingdezhen. The vast labour force, entirely dependent on a single industry, faced growing competition from other production centres, in Canton, Japan and industrializing Europe. The beauty of perfect things distracts us from the grittiness of local production visible on the surface of this discarded thing. Its appearance here reminds us of the local story behind global connections, in the past, when the locality bore the brunt of the cost of global production, and in the present, when the traces of that local past are sold in the market and in danger of disappearing.

CHAPTER 25

Sarah Sophia Banks, Adam Afzelius and a Coin from Sierra Leone

Catherine Eagleton

In 1792, this penny for use in Sierra Leone was struck in Birmingham, UK, on the new steam-powered coining presses at the Soho Mint. This method of manufacturing coins, developed through a partnership between Birmingham entrepreneur Matthew Boulton and Scottish engineer James Watt, revolutionized the production of small change—a constant problem throughout the history of money—since it meant that large numbers of identical low-denomination coins could be produced cheaply and quickly, for the first time.[1]

Large quantities of coinage were certainly needed in Freetown, Sierra Leone, since the new West African colony was precarious, both in practical and financial terms.[2] The currency and accounting systems of the colony were complicated, and near-constant shortages of coin meant that local issues of paper money supplemented the official coinage.[3] Pennies like this one were minted

---

[1] On coins for Sierra Leone, see David Vice, *Coinage of British West Africa and St Helena, 1684–1958* (Birmingham: Peter Ireland, 1983), chapter 3 (19–35). On Matthew Boulton, see for example George Selgin *Good Money: Birmingham button makers, the Royal Mint, and the beginnings of modern coinage, 1775–1821* (Ann Arbor and Oakland: University of Michigan Press, 2008), and Richard Clay (ed), *Matthew Boulton and the art of making money* (Studley: Brewin, 2009).

[2] A first-hand account of early Freetown is in A. Falconbridge, *Narrative of two voyages to the river Sierra Leone during the years 1791–1792–1793*, edited by Christopher Fyfe (Liverpool: Liverpool University Press, 2000), 85.

[3] The complex currency system is discussed in A. P. Kup, 'John Clarkson and the Sierra Leone Company', *The International Journal of African Historical Studies* 5:2 (1972), 203–229. On the early paper money, see Peter Symes, 'The colonial paper money of Sierra Leone' at http://www.pjsymes.com.au/articles/SierraLeone.htm (accessed 25 November 2014).

C. Eagleton (✉)
Asian and African Collections, British Library, London, UK
e-mail: catherine.eagleton@bl.uk

© The Author(s) 2016
A. Craciun, S. Schaffer (eds.), *The Material Cultures of Enlightenment Arts and Sciences*, Palgrave Studies in the Enlightenment, Romanticism and the Cultures of Print, DOI 10.1057/978-1-137-44379-3_25

Fig. 25.1 Penny, dated 1791 but struck in 1792, Sierra Leone, with original ticket (registration number SSB,154.27). © Trustees of the British Museum

to try to improve the currency situation at Freetown, and featured a design of a lion on one side, in reference to the name 'Sierra Leone'. On the other side was a design of two hands—one white and one black—reflecting the ideals of the founders of Freetown, who had included abolitionist campaigners and freed African Americans.[4]

From 1792, Freetown's residents included the Swedish botanist Adam Afzelius, who collected natural specimens and assembled a collection of ethnographic objects from Sierra Leone.[5] Collecting in and around Freetown was no easy task, because of shortages of appropriate preserving and packing materials, as well as regular raids on the colony.[6] Returning briefly to London in 1793, Afzelius visited the London home of his friend and supporter Sir Joseph Banks. The two men shared interests in botany and collecting, and Banks had significant collections at his house at 32 Soho Square, as well as supporting the development of the collections of the British Museum.[7] Banks was also actively

[4] See, for example, Deirdre Coleman, *Romantic colonization and British anti-slavery* (Cambridge: Cambridge University Press, 2005).

[5] Adam Afzelius's ethnographic collections are now in the National Museum of Ethnography, Stockholm, and are one of the most important early collections of material from Sierra Leone: Ezio Bassani, *African art and artefacts in European collections 1400–1800* (London: British Museum Press, 2000), 203–8.

[6] On 17 February 1795, Sir Joseph Banks wrote to Adam Afzelius in Freetown, expressing his 'horror [at] the enormities committed by the Buccaneers who attack'd you', but reassuring Afzelius he was sending botanical supplies including 'bottles for your spirit collections'. State Library, New South Wales, Series 73.047, copy of a letter received by Adam Afzelius from Banks, 17 February 1795, accessed online at http://www2.sl.nsw.gov.au/banks/series_73/73_047.cfm, 25 November 2014.

[7] On Joseph Banks's collecting see, for example, John Gascoigne, *Science in the service of empire: Joseph Banks, the British state and the uses of science in the age of revolution* (Cambridge: Cambridge University Press, 1998); Neil Chambers, *Joseph Banks and the British Museum: the world of collecting, 1770–1830* (London: Pickering & Chatto, 2007); and Patricia Fara, *Sex, Botany and Empire: the story of Carl Linnaeus and Joseph Banks* (New York: Columbia University Press, 2004).

involved in promoting and supporting the exploration of West Africa, through the Association for Promoting the Discovery of the Interior Parts of Africa, of which he had been a founding member in 1788.[8]

Joseph Banks's sister, Sarah Sophia, also lived at 32 Soho Square, and shared her brother's interest in collecting, assembling an important collection of coins and tokens from around the world. On 25 September Afzelius gave this penny to her, and she recorded the gift in a manuscript, 'List of coins &c. Presents to me & of Do. that I have bought'. The provenance of this penny was clearly of importance to her, since Sarah Sophia noted that it had been 'brought from Sierra Leone', distinguishing it from the other Sierra Leone penny already in her collection, which had been given to her earlier in 1793 by Matthew Boulton, and had come directly from the Soho Mint.[9]

Tracking the story of this rather ordinary-looking penny, then, links together several topics that are often considered separately when looking at the late eighteenth century. Minted on some of the earliest steam-powered coining presses at the heart of the industrial revolution, shipped out to an early African colony founded on abolitionist ideals, taken out of circulation by a botanist, before being given to a coin collector—this penny traces a network that links together Birmingham, Freetown and London, and the histories of industrialization, of imperial expansion, of the abolition of the slave trade, and of collecting.

[8] Tim Fulford and Debbie Lee discuss Joseph Banks and his involvement with the African Association: 'Mental traveler: Joseph Banks, Mungo Park, and the romantic imagination', in *Nineteenth-Century Contexts: an interdisciplinary journal* 24:2 (2002), pp. 117–137.

[9] British Museum, Department of Coins and Medals Archives, SSB I.21. On Sarah Sophia Banks and her collecting of African coins, see C. Eagleton, 'Collecting African money in Georgian London' in *Museum History Journal*, 6 (2013), 23–38.

CHAPTER 26

A Pacific Macrocosm: 'Les Sauvages de la mer Pacifique'

Billie Lythberg

'Les Sauvages de la mer Pacifique', produced in Mâcon between September 1804 and September 1805, is a 20-panel wallpaper based on eighteenth-century voyages of exploration to the Pacific. The largest panoramic wallpaper of its time, and a product of French neoclassical culture, it depicts the 'noble savages' of the Pacific in utopian surroundings. Once installed on parlour walls, it recreated for its observer—within a papered room—an exotic world that owed at least as much to the imaginations of Europeans as it did to its professed subjects. Tellingly, the wallpaper cast the observer at the centre of this macrocosm, leaving its Pacific subjects on the periphery.

The paper was designed by Jean-Gabriel Charvet. Charvet was a known admirer of the philosopher Jean-Jacques Rousseau, who influenced French Enlightenment perceptions of Otherness and whose *Discourse on the Origin of Inequality* (1755) discussed the happiness of man in the state of nature. Charvet designed for wallpaper manufacturers from 1795 to 1810, but his romantic sympathies were surely never better expressed than by 'Les Sauvages de la mer Pacifique'.

Despite being often referred to as 'Les Voyages du Capitaine Cook' (a figure whom manufacturer Joseph Dufour repeatedly mentions in his accompanying catalogue), this artwork draws also on accounts from French-led expeditions for its depictions of Pacific peoples. It is delightfully ahistorical, collapsing voyages, people and events into a chronoclasm. All are set against the paradisiacal

B. Lythberg (✉)
Mira Szászy Research Centre University of Auckland, Auckland, NZ

Cambridge University Museum of Archaeology and Anthropology, United Kingdom
e-mail: b.lythberg@auckland.ac.nz

© The Author(s) 2016   207
A. Craciun, S. Schaffer (eds.), *The Material Cultures of Enlightenment Arts and Sciences*, Palgrave Studies in the Enlightenment, Romanticism and the Cultures of Print, DOI 10.1057/978-1-137-44379-3_26

Fig. 26.1 Joseph Dufour & Cie, Jean-Gabriel Charvet, 'Les Sauvages de la mer Pacifique (The Native Peoples of the Pacific Ocean)', *c.* 1804. Woodblock and gouache on paper, 2200×1800 mm (three-panel section of panoramic wallpaper approximately 2500×10500 mm). Courtesy Mackelvie Trust Collection, Auckland Art Gallery Toi o Tāmaki, M1995/3

backdrop of Tahiti, first reached by Louis Antoine de Bougainville in 1768, who named the island New Cythera after the home of Aphrodite. Redolent with papaya, coconut and banana palms, this lush dreamland is an apt milieu for the neoclassical figures it contains. A hierarchy is evident. Within the Tahitian panel itself, Aphrodite's maidens appear as the Three Graces; elsewhere 'Kings' and 'Queens' and their most elegant subjects occupy the foreground, while less beguiling events and encounters are relegated to the fringes. A scene depicting the death of Cook is placed strategically in the middle distance, able to be excised to accommodate, say, a doorway, should this detail be undesirable in domestic environs.

Panels XV–XVII, in post-production frame, depict (left to right) the King of Tongatapu, Tu'i Tonga Pau as Cook met him in 1777, resplendent in a feathered headdress, armed with bow and arrow, and accompanied by his favourite wife and dog. Their clothes are fanciful interpretations of draped barkcloth, their laced shoes a blend of ballet slipper and gladiator sandal; she wears what can only be a painted coconut shell bra. Before them a wrestling match takes place; to the right, the King and Queen of Tahuata, the Marquesas Islands, engage in conversation as guests of this imaginary fête, staged for Cook's reception. To the rear, Cook's Tahitian guide and interpreter Omai watches from beneath a tamarind tree.

Dufour's paper allowed 'parlour travellers' to imagine themselves as companions to the world's foremost explorers—including London-going Omai himself. Created using a combination of woodblock, stencils and handpainting, the wallpaper was cleverly designed to work both as a seamless panorama when installed in its entirety, and in smaller, discrete scenes. Its large sky further permitted copious trimming to fit within walls of different sizes. This allowed it to be used in upper-class *and* middle-class homes, where Dufour's professed educational goals—he claimed that lessons could be learnt from his work about history, geography and plants, as well as Pacific peoples—were construed as meeting certain requirements of social and self-improvement. In hindsight, however, the work speaks more of Charvet's desire for a utopian Europe, based on the Enlightenment vision of the noble savage, than of the realities of Pacific lives, whether past or contemporary.

CHAPTER 27

'Columen Vitae': Pharmaceutical Packaging, 1750–1850

Jennifer Basford

Medical products, predominantly sold by newspaper and book printers, became the most heavily advertised branded good throughout the eighteenth century.[1] Proprietary medicines were big business and so counterfeits were rife; protecting the brand was crucial. Proprietors aimed to convince consumers of the medicine's authenticity, its reliability and, on occasion, its safety and efficacy. This was in part achieved in the physical fabric of the product and its packaging, as well as through controlled distribution and marketing of the medicine.[2]

Packaging encompassed a broad range of media: it included the design and colour scheme of bottles, pots and boxes, wrapping materials and the marks embossed, stamped or handwritten on these items. One such example where proprietors sought to communicate trust and efficacy through their branding was with Dalby's Carminative, formerly a patent remedy for stomach problems in children, whose popularity had led to its manufacture by number of medicine proprietors. Such genericization was not unusual with patent nostrums—as many kitchen and household books demonstrate, they were often created at home.[3] Dalby's Carminative was produced and marketed by a number of pro-

---

[1] J. Styles, 'Product innovation in early modern London', *Past & Present* 168 (2000), 150.

[2] J. Basford, '"A commodity of good names": the branding of products, c.1650–1900' (PhD thesis: University of York, 2012).

[3] E. Leong, 'Making medicines in the early modern household', *Bulletin of the History of Medicine* 82:1 (2008), 145–168.

J. Basford (✉)
St George's, University of London, London, UK
e-mail: jbasford@sgul.ac.uk

© The Author(s) 2016
A. Craciun, S. Schaffer (eds.), *The Material Cultures of Enlightenment Arts and Sciences*, Palgrave Studies in the Enlightenment, Romanticism and the Cultures of Print, DOI 10.1057/978-1-137-44379-3_27

Fig. 27.1 Dalby's Carminative bottle. Medicine bottle (1820–30). York Museums Trust, YORCM: AA10239. Image courtesy of York Museums Trust, http://yorkmuseumstrust.org.uk, CC BY-SA 4.0

prietors throughout the early nineteenth century, and bottles with the marks of at least three different proprietors embossed on them have been uncovered.[4]

The bottle pictured in Fig. 27.1 was simply marked 'DALBY'S // CARMINATIVE'. Although this may have been the production of proprietor James Dalby, it is just as likely to have been a generic bottle created for multiple vendors. Proprietors thus needed to use additional methods to reassure potential consumers about the credibility and efficacy of their particular brand. Labels that bore the signatures of proprietors were often placed around bottles or boxes of medicines. Likewise, wrapping material frequently featured the handwriting of the 'trusted' producer, whose medical knowledge and link to the inventor were trumpeted by testimonials and endorsements from satisfied customers, in conjunction with strict directions on where to buy the 'genuine' medicine. In doing so, the makers of Dalby's Carminative demonstrated an awareness of innovations in packaging, as well as a keen understanding of how trust and credibility could be enhanced through the physical aspect and materiality of a product's branding.

Finally, producers reinforced the ties between the wrapping and advertising material and the steeple-shaped bottle, which was uniquely used by makers of Dalby's Carminative in this period. On their wrapping and promotional materials, two leading proprietors of the remedy, Anthony Gell and James Dalby, used the advertising motto 'Columen Vitae' ('pillar of life').[5] The use of an unusually long bottle, then, can be interpreted both symbolically as a physical representation of this 'pillar of life', and more practically as making it an instantly recognizable medicine. Testimonies and endorsements worked in tandem with the physical product and in so doing, reinforced the branding and messages that were expressed by the material fabric of the medicine's packaging itself.

[4] Basford, 'A commodity of good names', 49–51.
[5] Reproductions of these fliers appear in P.G. Horman, B. Hudson, and R.C. Rowe, *Popular Medicines. An Illustrated History* (London: Pharmaceutical Press, 2008), 60–63.

CHAPTER 28

Tropical Lifestyles, Luxury, and the Health of Britain's Global Power, 1793–1825

Jonathan Eacott

Park Street Cemetery in Calcutta provides grim evidence for the rate at which Britons died in tropical climates, and for their belief that they died for something grand and impressive. Greek- and Roman-inspired monuments like those in Park Street projected wealth, power, and a sense of imperial genealogy. A few tombs, like that for Charles "Hindoo" Stuart, show significant South Asian influences.[1] The rarity of such tombs, on the surface, seems to suggest that British responses to Indian material culture were largely negative at the turn of the nineteenth century. Yet the monumental tombs of Park Street not only projected a particular image of imperial power, they intentionally obscured many material aspects of the lifestyles of the people on whom that power depended. The design of the monuments in Park Street reflected a basic problem that Britons perceived in the governance of their empire: how to rule in their own moral terms without succumbing to foreign luxury and corruption, and without killing the Britons administering and defending the empire abroad. Solutions to this problem required a complex calculus of politics, gender, science, and material culture—a calculus profoundly influenced by the demographics of imperial competition. The global

---

[1] Robert Travers, 'Death and the Nabob: Imperialism and Commemoration in Eighteenth-century India', *Past & Present*, no. 196 (August 2007), 83–124. On cemeteries as overwhelming evidence of high mortality rates among Europeans in India, see, for example, Richard Harlan, 14 April 1816, Richard Harlan Journal, American Philosophical Society, Philadelphia, Mss.B.H228, 33.

J. Eacott (✉)
Department of History, University of California, Riverside,
Riverside, CA, USA
e-mail: jeacott@ucr.edu

© The Author(s) 2016
A. Craciun, S. Schaffer (eds.), *The Material Cultures of Enlightenment Arts and Sciences*, Palgrave Studies in the Enlightenment, Romanticism and the Cultures of Print, DOI 10.1057/978-1-137-44379-3_28

Fig. 28.1   Greek- and Roman-inspired British tombs, Park Street Cemetery, Calcutta

contest with France from 1793 to 1815, particularly the need to counter the Levée en Masse, created demands on Britain's population greater than during earlier contests. Britain's demographic disadvantage as well as the need to protect an empire that had become not only larger but more tropical after the American Revolution created considerable interest in lowering mortality rates by rethinking the supposed dangers and benefits of what was known as Asiatic luxury.[2]

India, with its large population and variety of cultures, provided the main source of both products and practices debated not just by medical professionals but by a broad cross-section of Britons interested in reducing mortality in tropical climates. As the East India Company pursued territorial expansion requiring ever larger numbers of soldiers and administrators, the high mortality rates of Britons

---

[2] Linda Colley, 'The Reach of the State, the Appeal of the Nation: Mass Arming and Political Culture in the Napoleonic Wars', in Lawrence Stone (ed.), *An Imperial State at War* (London: Routledge, 1994), 165–184. On the war in the West Indies, see Michael Duffy, *Soldiers, Sugar, and Seapower: The British Expeditions to the West Indies and the War Against Revolutionary France* (New York: Oxford University Press, 1987); Roger Norman Buckley, *The British Army in the West Indies: Society and the Military in the Revolutionary Age* (Gainesville: University Press of Florida, 1998). On the East Indies, see Randolf G. S. Cooper, *The Anglo-Maratha Campaigns and the Contest for India: The Struggle for the Control of the South Asian Military Economy* (New York: Cambridge, 2003); Maya Jasanoff, *Edge of Empire: Conquest and Collecting in the East, 1750–1850* (London: Fourth Estate, 2005), esp. 164–184.

in much of India made the pursuit of well-being a growing preoccupation.[3] The Company had an official establishment of 234 surgeons and assistant surgeons in 1785, increasing to 630 by 1824.[4] The expanded wartime navy, too, provided many surgeons with tropical experience. Historians of science and medicine have shown that the experience and knowledge gained by these and other medical practitioners shaped professional debates over theories of disease and treatment, as well as conceptions of race.[5] At the turn of the nineteenth century, however, the definition and qualifications of medical professionals remained hazy, and many people still did not seek guidance and care only from professionally trained surgeons or physicians.[6] Family members, friends, and writers who were not, and did not claim to be, healthcare professionals actively debated treatments for tropical illness, but they primarily debated appropriate prophylaxes. These debates over not getting sick in tropical climates were particularly important due to the limited effectiveness of much medical care. Hopes of staying healthy through lifestyle and consumption choices were more promising than hopes of getting healthy through treatment.

The answers to the question of whether Indian goods increased or decreased the risk of mortality depended on the extent to which Britons believed that the environmental conditions of place and the supposed physiological differences of race changed the useful and moral qualities of objects. Eighteenth-century Britons did not buy and consume every new or foreign good that became available to them, and they debated the consequences of owning and using specific Indian goods such as hookahs, palanquins, umbrellas, and curries.[7] Many Britons

[3] Peter Marshall, 'The Whites of British India, 1780–1830: A Failed Colonial Society?' *International History Review* 12, no. 1 (February 1990), 26–44, on 26.

[4] D. G. Crawford, *A History of the Indian Medical Service, 1600–1913* (London: W. Thacker, 1914), vol. 1, 197–221.

[5] See in particular Mark Harrison, *Climates and Constitutions: Health, Race, Environment and British Imperialism in India, 1600–1850* (New York: Oxford University Press, 1999), 2–3; Mark Harrison, *Medicine in an Age of Commerce & Empire* (New York: Oxford University Press, 2010), 3–13. On the "dual engagement—with the environment and with culture" in shaping the transmission of Western medicine eastward as opposed to Indian practices westward, see David Arnold, *Science, Technology and Medicine in Colonial India* (Cambridge: Cambridge University Press, 2000), 57.

[6] Roy Porter, 'The Patient's View: Doing Medical History from Below', *Theory and Society* 14, no. 2 (March 1985), 175-198; especially for a somewhat earlier period see Leigh Whaley, *Women and the Practice of Medical Care in Early Modern Europe, 1400-1800* (London: Palgrave, 2011). On the continuing negotiation over the make-up of the medical profession, see Alison Winter, *Mesmerized: Powers of Mind in Victorian Britain* (Chicago: University Of Chicago, 2000), esp. 34.

[7] On the luxury debates and foreignness more broadly, see Maxine Berg, 'From Imitation to Invention: Creating Commodities in Eighteenth-Century Britain', *Economic History Review* 55, no. 1 (2002), 1–30, on 2–3; Maxine Berg, 'In Pursuit of Luxury: Global History and British Consumer Goods in the Eighteenth Century', *Past & Present*, no. 182 (February 2004), 85–142, on 94–5. On luxury and Britons returned from India, or nabobs, see James Raven, *Judging New Wealth: Popular Publishing and Responses to Commerce in England, 1750-1800* (Oxford: Clarendon Press, 1992), 160-64; Tillman Nechtman, *Nabobs: Empire and Identity in Eighteenth-Century Britain* (New York: Cambridge 2010).

had long associated India, as well as arch-enemy France, with effeminate and corrupting luxury. As a character in 1785's *The Maternal Sister, A Drama in Three Acts* exclaimed, "few constitutions can stand against *East Indian luxury*. Their *chaian pepper*, their *spices*, and other *instruments of death*."[8] Such resistance to Indian goods whether a Briton lived in a temperate or a tropical climate dovetailed with James Lind's popularization of the argument that Europeans who did not die immediately in India would become "seasoned" to the tropical heat and then experience similar mortality to Britons at home. Lind saw no major physical benefits from Indian material culture. At the turn of the nineteenth century, however, many Britons with experience in India countered that elite Indians knew the appropriate activities, objects, and schedules that any person needed to survive in the local climate. A growing belief in racial difference could make such Indian prophylaxes even more important for Britons—ironically encouraging the use of Indian luxury, not discouraging it.[9] In the context of the struggle with France, supporters of elite Indian material culture employed arguments based on the necessary, healthful, and manly qualities of Indian objects for the survival of the empire to strike back successfully against critics claiming Indian goods and objects to be effeminate, immoral luxuries.

Throughout the middle of the eighteenth century, debates over the need to use some of the habits and goods of wealthy Indians to reduce mortality ebbed and flowed, but support was generally strongest among Britons with experience on the subcontinent. Nevertheless, in the 1750s the prime architect of British expansion in India, Robert Clive, attempted to regulate more strictly the use of several Indian goods by Britons in the East India Company's employ. In response, many others with experience in India pointed out that while limiting luxury was a noble sentiment, restricted goods such as palanquins and sun umbrellas were vital necessities for the protection of health. Several petitioners wrote to Clive explaining "the manifest prejudice which our healths and constitutions must sustain from the being obliged to lay aside palanquins." Others wrote that unseasoned new arrivals who could least afford palanquins and umbrellas had the most pressing need for them. They required such protections from the sun to avoid fevers and death.[10] These arguments appeared frequently throughout the 1770s. Clive's edicts and

---

[8] *The Maternal Sister, A Drama in Three Acts* (1785).

[9] James Lind was not the first to make this claim. His text, however, appeared in frequent reprints and new editions and was a major source for information on European health in tropical climates for approximately a century after its first publication in 1768. James Lind, *An Essay on Diseases Incidental to Europeans in Hot Climates* (London: T. Becket and P. A. de Hondt, 1768), 146. For more on seasoning and the potential of racial difference to "alienate the British from their new domains," see Harrison, *Climates and Constitutions*, 11, 17, 45, 88–92. For more on Lind, see Harrison, *Medicine in an Age of Commerce & Empire*, 69–77.

[10] Petition to Lord Clive and his Reply, Governor and Council, Fort William, 27 November 1758, Papers from Bengal and Madras, British Library (hereafter BL), IOR/H/805/25, 855–6; Edward Ives, *A Voyage from England to India, in the Year MDCCLIV. And an Historical Narrative of the Operations of the Squadron and Army in India* (London: Edward and Charles Dilly, 1773), 21–2; Charles Caraccioli, *The Life of Robert Lord Clive, Baron Plassey* (London: T. Bell, [1775–77]), vol. 1, 283.

later Company attempts to restrict the habits and goods of its employees went largely unheeded and unenforced. Many who arrived in India expecting to avoid goods, such as palanquins, that they saw as luxuries soon changed their minds. Philip Stanhope, for instance, derided the palanquin as an "effiminate luxury." He associated the Indian object with notions of emasculating vice. Shortly, however, he testified to using his "palanquin when the heat renders the exercise of riding inconvenient."[11] Apparently, he realized, it was the climate, not the palanquin, which threatened his manly vigor.

In 1777, N. E. Kindersley, a British woman who had lived in India for over three years, argued for the necessary utility of Indian goods among Britons in India on the basis of racial difference, preceding such claims by medical professionals.[12] She explained that the Indian climate, while fatal for Europeans, was healthful for Indians. She set up her understanding of racial difference by claiming that the hot sun made Indian children mature quickly and peak early, like desert plants sprouting under the sun after rain. "The wisdom of Providence" had made Indian children able to raise themselves, since, she claimed, they had naturally weak, lazy, and incompetent mothers. Furthermore, she explained that Indian children healed more easily than Europeans. Through her descriptions of limited mothering, quick healing, and a sort of photosynthesized growth, Kindersley positioned Indians as not quite human or even animal, but plant-like in nature. The sun nourished young Indians, while it killed Europeans. Kindersley's racist derision of Indians made her more, not less willing to accept many aspects of elite Indian culture. Since Europeans were not physically designed for the Indian climate, the health of their race in India depended on adopting an apparently luxurious Indian lifestyle. As a result, Kindersley argued, large numbers of servants, many changes of Indian-style clothing, palanquins, and other concessions to the hot climate formed a system of material culture necessary to the survival of Europeans in India. Her definition of utility shifted depending on race and place. For Kindersley, what were necessities to Britons in India could be problematic and effeminate luxuries to both Britons and Indians in their home environments.[13] Back in Britain, however, the Parliament and the public attacked both Clive and Warren Hastings, who had continued the process of expanding British rule in India, for embracing and encouraging the corrupt practices and luxurious goods that Britons associated with Asiatic cultures, despite Clive's earlier attempts to the contrary.[14]

In 1782, the influential anti-slavery activist and Anglican evangelical Granville Sharp, for instance, argued strongly against adopting the goods or

[11] Philip Dormer Stanhope, *Genuine Memoirs of Asiaticus, in a Series of Letters to a Friend, During Five Years Residence in Different Parts of India* (London: G. Kearsley, 1784), 36, 73.

[12] For the development of racial ideas among medical professionals in the 1820s and 1830s, see Harrison, *Climates and Constitutions*, 11–19.

[13] N. E. Kindersley, *Letters from the Island of Teneriffe, Brazil, the Cape of Good Hope, and the East Indies* (London: J. Nourse, 1777), 194, 234–7, 291–2.

[14] Nechtman, *Nabobs*, 92–183.

supposed habits of elite Indians. Sharp had not been to India.[15] Nevertheless, he wrote a letter of advice on living in India to Lieutenant Alcock. Considerable edits to the draft letter show that Sharp put much thought into this advice. He warned that in India, Alcock must overcome "frequent Communication … with Persons of very opposite Principles as also the general prevalency of corrupt Fashions among the European Settlers, & the frequent temptations in which the lawless Customs of the East will of course involve you." Many Europeans, he believed, enslaved young women in India to their passions, ruining the innocent. This, he explained, not only led to death for Europeans, but made one unworthy to die. Europeans fell to the sin of gluttony in India, which "encreases the difficulty of controuling human passions … of every kind, insomuch as that the Man who does not keep his Body in strict Temperance, can very seldom preserve it in such purity and Chastity as the Christian Religion absolutely requires." He encouraged "abstemiousness," and although he generally disdained Indian cultures, he approved of the simple rice-and-fish diet of the Malays as healthful.[16]

Additionally, British debates over using Indian goods in Britain, particularly cotton cloth, had been ongoing for centuries, driven in part by fears of Asian competitive advantages in production. Parliament restricted the importation of India's dyed, stained, and printed cotton fabric in the early eighteenth century on the grounds that it cast England's vaunted woolen workers out of employment, drained bullion to India, and corrupted English women with Indian and supposedly French luxury.[17] By the 1790s, advances in mechanization had transformed Britain into a major cotton cloth producer and consumers eagerly embraced the domestically made cloth. Nevertheless, some continued to criticize the fabric. British etiquette author John Armstrong wrote, "Cotton stands in the middle between animal … [fur] and linen; it increases warmth and perspiration, retains the latter to the injury of the wearer, on account of its compactness, and like wool readily attracts infectious matter." He rated customary English wool as the best clothing fiber, followed by linen, cotton, and finally fur as the worst. He disparaged popular cotton and silk stockings for absorbing perspiration and degrading health.[18] Indeed, Britain's military continued to wear woolen and linen. The increasingly tropical empire, however, could no longer absorb incidents such as that in 1780 when four regiments in Jamaica

---

[15] Edward Charles Ponsonby Lascelles, *Granville Sharp and the Freedom of Slaves in England* (Oxford: Oxford University Press, 1928), esp. 16–34, 50–55, 69–80.

[16] Granville Sharp to Lieutenant Alcock, 28 August 1782, Lieutenant Alcock Papers, Gloucestershire Archives, Gloucester, D3549/13/1/A5.

[17] For an excellent review of the woolen makers' response to cotton cloth, see Beverly Lemire, *Fashion's Favourite: The Cotton Trade and the Consumer in Britain, 1660–1800* (Oxford: Oxford University Press, 1991), 23–42.

[18] John Armstrong, *The Women's Guide to Virtue, Economy, and Happiness* … 6th ed. (Newcastle upon Tyne: MacKenzie and Dent, 1817?), 407–10.

lost nearly 50 percent of their men to disease within six months.[19] The growing demands for men to administer, defend, and expand the empire in the tropics under the pressure of a global war with France encouraged novel responses.

Many experts and many in the British military argued for cotton fabric as well as the cut of South Asian banians, not as dangerous luxuries but as fortifications for a manly British constitution. In 1795 an anonymous author recommended to the Pitt administration a reduction in the complexity of officers' uniforms in the West Indies, as well as the replacement of linen in soldiers' uniforms with "Good cotton or calico."[20] A few years later in his major study of troop mortality in the West Indies, McLean similarly argued for the use of cotton clothing. Woolen flannels made troops feel "incumbered, hot, and uneasy," and risked drawing disease into the skin. He advocated, moreover, that West Indian army shirts be cut as part-sleeve cotton shirts modeled on the banian shirts that East Indians had developed for a similar tropical climate. In addition to the healthful qualities of cotton, soldiers could carry many more of these lightweight shirts. They could change more frequently and spend more time in dry, uninfected clothing, thereby maintaining their vigor.[21] William Lempriere, in his work on the mortality of troops in St. Domingo during the 1790s, recommended new large-brimmed hats to provide shade from the sun, as well as thin flannel shirts, but only if dry ones were readily available. Flannel wetted with perspiration may "give rise to disease" and troops would therefore be better off wearing cotton calico. He also quoted at length from Dr. Gordon, whose experience with the 13th Regiment in Jamaica in 1793 led him to believe that cotton was better than flannel for garrison duty, while flannel should still be worn on campaign, when men were apt to get wet from rain and cold in the night.[22] The Army itself remained in two minds on the issue. The Navy, meanwhile, began issuing cotton banians to some sailors in the mid-1790s. By 1804, Thomas Trotter recommended in *Medicina Nautica* that the Navy adopt cottons universally. Woolens, he wrote, made the men "walking stinkpots" and caused them to "lose the hardiness of constitution that fits them for duty."[23]

[19] On the losses in Jamaica, see John Hunter, *Observations on the Diseases of the Army in Jamaica; and on the Best Means of Preserving the Health of Europeans in that Climate* (London: G. Nicol, 1788), 13. For additional developments in hygiene and hospitals, see Harrison, *Medicine in an Age of Commerce and Empire*, 18–24.

[20] "Clothing Proper for the West Indies," 1795, William Pitt, 1st Earl of Chatham Papers, UK National Archives, PRO 30/8/351, f120. Hunter had said little about uniforms; Hunter, *Observations on the Diseases of the Army in Jamaica*.

[21] Hector McLean, *An Enquiry into the Nature, and Causes of the Great Mortality among the Troops at St. Domingo: With Practical Remarks on the Fever of That Island* (London: T. Cadell and W. Davies, 1797), 269–70.

[22] William Lempriere, *Practical Observations on the Diseases of the Army in Jamaica, as They Occurred Between the Years 1792 and 1797* (London: T. N. Longman and O. Rees, 1799), vol. 1, 279, 289–90; vol. 2, 17.

[23] Adm. 49/35, UK National Archives, cited in Lemire, *Fashion's Favourite*, 104; Thomas Trotter, *Medicina Nautica* (London: Longman, Hurst, Rees, and Orme, 1804), vol. 3, 93–4.

On land in the West Indies, too, East Indian luxury might help defend the health of planters locked in nationally important economic competition with the French, at least for those non-abolitionists who thought planters worth defending at all. James Sayers's 1800 print *Johnny New-come in the Island of Jamaica* (Fig. 28.2) captured a common theme of the rapid deterioration of the health of young English gentlemen in Jamaica. Sayers showed the typical young newcomer making no concessions to the tropical climate, which quickly led to his death. Sayers drew attention to the dangers of the tropics and the poor adjustments of Britons in meeting those dangers. He did not specifically advocate for a more East Indian lifestyle, although many others did. Henry Brougham, for instance, noted that "A residence in the West Indies tends to debase the European character. A residence … in the East, mixes it with a character completely different, both in a moral and a political view." Unlike the Johnny Newcomes in the West Indies, Britons in the East Indies had beneficially encountered and emulated "polished" Asian lifestyles. Such manners when in England could be luxurious, effeminate, and frivolous, although they did increase employment opportunities. Brougham found Asiatic manners in a temperate climate to be "infinitely less injurious" than Caribbean ones, but Asiatic modes of government and religion "unquestionably much more hurtful."[24]

Meanwhile in India, the pursuit of territorial power that Clive and Hastings had developed continued through war with French-allied Mysore and then the Maratha empire, requiring yet more soldiers, planters, merchants, and administrators. Thomas Williamson's *East India Vade Mecum*, first published in 1810 with the support of the East India Company, became the seminal work for these Britons heading to India. Williamson was not a health professional, but he was likely the single most influential provider of health advice to individuals heading east. He cautioned, "We must coincide with the habits of the natives, to a certain extent, if we mean to retain health," and explained, "I do not mean to say that we should imitate, much less adopt, without discrimination, all we see; but it may be considered an axiom, that, by taking the general outline of indigenous customs for our guide, if we err, it will be on the safe side." Focusing on health gave Williamson the opportunity to advocate for the many aspects of Indian culture he admired, while rebutting charges that Indian culture promoted frivolous or enervating luxury. He told his readers that "however absurd many practices may at first appear, it will ordinarily result that necessity was their parent." Aware that many young men would arrive in India conditioned with disgust for Indian material life, Williamson flipped the script, arguing that "Nothing can be more preposterous than the significant sneers of gentlemen on their first arrival in India; meaning, thereby, to ridicule, or to despise, what they consider effeminacy, or luxury." Trusting to their pride and moral judgments, these men walked the streets "without *chattahs*, (*i.e.* umbrellas,) during the greatest heats." Readers who ignored his advice could look forward to "cold shiverings, and

[24] Henry Brougham, *An Inquiry into the Colonial Policy of the European Powers* (Edinburgh: Balfour, Manners & Miller; and Constable, 1803), vol. 1, 80–83.

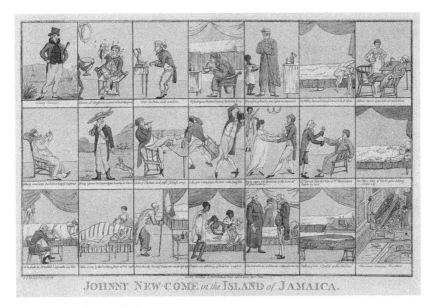

JOHNNY NEW-COME *in the* ISLAND *of* JAMAICA.

Fig. 28.2 James Sayers, *Johnny New-come in the Island of Jamaica* (1800). Courtesy of The Lewis Walpole Library, Yale University

bilious vomiting" and, he continued, "delirium speedily ensues" and "putrefaction advances." Within a week, or perhaps a few days, "we too often are called upon to attend the funeral of the self-deluded victim!" For Williamson, life under the Indian sun, and not the local defenses from it, were the real risks to British manhood.[25]

A man's health and virility in India depended on following Indian customs and using Indian objects. Williamson applauded Britons in India for their ever-increasing use of umbrellas and large verandahs for shade, and their use of wetted tatties (screens) in the windows to cool the air. He recommended that readers model their eating habits on Indian curry and rice to fortify themselves against the extreme heat. Outside of the British enclave in the city, moreover, Williamson stressed that "a man may be next to starving" if he refused to eat like Indians. For those many soldiers, sailors, and Company officials in India outside of the leading British settlements, curry was hardly a luxury. McLean likewise recommended a change in diet for Britons in the tropics, pointing to European diets as the damaging luxury compared to "savage" models. Increasing the consumption of rice

[25] Thomas Williamson, *East India Vade-Mecum; or Complete Guide to Gentlemen intended for the Civil, Military, or Naval Service of the Hon. East India Company* (London: Black, Parry, and Kingsbury for the Honorable East India Company, 1810), vol. 2, 2. Williamson's work was revised and reissued as John Borthwick Gilchrist, *The General East India Guide and Vade Mecum: for the Public Functionary, Government Officer, Private Agent, Trader or Foreign Sojourner, in British India* (London: Kingsbury, Parbury, & Allen, 1825).

and limiting that of meat and liquor would improve overall health and reduce the heightened risk of bile caused by hot climates. Yet, Williamson warned, even local foods could be a threat to health if one overindulged. Excessive mango consumption, for example, apparently caused dreadful boils on the skin. These were warnings against intemperance, however, not against Indian material culture itself. Indeed, for Williamson, when in India one was at far greater risk living in a fully European style than in a mixed Anglo-Indian one. Significantly, he did not claim that Indians and Europeans possessed innately different abilities to endure the Indian climate. It was the suitability of one's objects and habits for the environment that determined health.[26]

A few years later, James Johnson published his *Influence of Tropical Climates on European Constitutions,* which remained the most widely circulated professional medical guide regarding the tropics through the middle of the nineteenth century, and which supported much of Indian material culture as essential to health in both the East and West Indies on a racial basis. Johnson brought to print his experience as a surgeon in the Royal Navy gained from war with France.[27] In his 1807 guide to tropical Asia, he had written that Britons and Indians shared "the human constitution," but in 1812 he placed more emphasis on racial difference. His clearer argument that Europeans were less able to withstand heat than Indians and Africans strengthened his case in both of his major works that to survive in tropical climates Britons needed to adopt several supposedly luxurious aspects of Indian material culture. This racial argument followed the ideas of earlier non-medical writers with experience in India, such as Kindersley. Johnson acknowledged that the "untravelled cynic" would argue that "the palankeen, the budgerow [a river boat], the punka [a swinging fan], the tatty, and the light, elegant, and cool vestments of India" were effeminate, Asiatic luxuries. He countered that "the medical philosopher will be disposed to regard them as rational enjoyments, or rather as salutary precautions, rendered necessary by the great difference between a temperate and torrid zone." The "powerful shields" that Indians had developed offered vital protection from a "burning climate." Young arrivals who stuck to European conventions in India, much like Johnny Newcome in the West Indies, suffered severely compared to their companions who chose to wear the "light, cool, and elegant vesture of the East."[28]

[26] Williamson, *East India Vade-Mecum,* vol. 2, 5–14, 198, 153; Gilchrist, *General East India Guide,* 77; McLean, *Enquiry into the Nature, and Causes of the Great Mortality,* 270–90.

[27] For more on Johnson's life, see 'A Sketch of the Life, and Some Account of the Works, of the late Dr James Johnson', *Medico-Chirurgical Review and Journal of Practical Medicine* 48 (1846), 1–48.

[28] Harrison described James Johnson's pessimistic views of Europeans in tropical climates as helping to lead the shift to more racial understandings of health; Mark Harrison, '"The Tender Frame of Man": Disease, Climate, and Racial Difference in India and the West Indies, 1760-1860', *Bulletin of the History of Medicine* 70, no.1 (1996), 68–93, on 78–9. James Johnson, *The Oriental Voyager; or, Descriptive Sketches and Cursory Remarks, on a Voyage to India and China* (London: James Asperne, 1807), 89; James Johnson, *The Influence of Tropical Climates on European*

Johnson saw "tyrant custom" imposing unsuitable and dangerous fashions brought from England, thereby inverting the usual association of tyranny and Indian luxury. He spoke out against the "luxuries of linen," which was a European fiber, instead of against cotton, which was not. Similar to those advocating cotton fabric for the military, Johnson concluded that "cotton from its slowness as a conductor of heat" and its ability to absorb sweat was ideal in the hot tropics, and he also favored it for cooler climates. Cotton beat traditional woolen flannel by providing lighter weight, cooler wearing, and less excitement to the skin. For Johnson, a tropical climate also inverted the gendered associations of objects that might be seen as effeminate luxuries in temperate Britain or America—in India they were manly.[29]

Johnson also intervened in a pre-existing debate over the qualities of Indian foods among Britons back home, writing that "In India, and I believe in Europe, rice and curry will be found a salutary dish." He continued, "Rice is, without exception, the most un-irritating, nutritious, and easily digested vegetable, which the bountiful bosom of the earth produces." Spicy curries provided a healthful "stimulus ... very different from that of spirits or wine." Medical practitioners in Europe had long ascribed medicinal qualities to many Asian spices, and curry had been promoted as healthful in Britain decades earlier.[30] Sorlie's Perfumery Warehouse in London, for example, celebrated curry powder in 1784 as "invaluable ... exceeding pleasant and healthful." It "renders the stomach active in digestion—the blood naturally free in circulation—the mind vigorous." Playing on the associations of spice, sex, and India's large population, the advertisement continued that curry "contributes most of any food to an increase of the human race."[31] In his 1808 *New Family Cook*, Duncan MacDonald recommended curry and rice in his "Bills of Fare" for May and December. He claimed that his work "is founded upon *English*, and not upon *French* culinary culinary principles." This claim reflected the current war as well as long-standing British associations of France with corruption and luxury. Indeed, MacDonald went on that his was a "more economical plan ... more conducive to health than any other." He was not alone: many cookery

Constitutions: Being a Treatise on the Principal Diseases Incidental to Europeans in the East and West Indies, Mediterranean, and Coast of Africa (1813; Reprint, London: J. Callow, 1815), 104–5, 426.

[29] Johnson, *Influence of Tropical Climates*, 423–6. For a similar argument from a medical professional that many aspects of Indian material culture were essential and not effeminate luxuries, see Charles Curtis, *An Account of the Diseases in India, as they Appeared in the English Fleet, and in the Naval Hospital at Madras, in 1782 and 1783, with Observations on Ulcers and the Hospital Sores of that Country* (Edinburgh: W. Laing, 1807), 281.

[30] Johnson, *Influence of Tropical Climates*, 314. Medicines imported from Asia went in and out of fashion like other commodities; Peter Boomgaard, 'Dutch Medicine in Asia, 1600-1900', in David Arnold (ed.), *Warm Climates and Western Medicine: The Emergence of Tropical Medicine, 1500–1900* (Atlanta: Rodopi, 1996), 49–51.

[31] *The Morning Herald and Advertiser*, 1784.

authors included curry recipes in their books by the end of the Napoleonic Wars.[32]

Additionally, Johnson advocated that many aspects of East Indian material culture be transferred to the West Indies. He explained that without the guide of a native example, many young Britons in the West Indies died unnecessarily. He praised the effect of turbans and Indian cummerbunds as prophylactic and "highly deserving of imitation." He championed the benefits of a vegetable diet in the West Indies, noting that Hindu legislators had wisely fused religion and health when they banned meat. He commented acerbically that many Britons seemed to think it far better to get one of "those fashionable Oriental diseases" than to "turn Hindoo and live upon rice." He also criticized Britons in the West Indies for dancing, noting "in the East there are *wise men* still, for instead of dancing themselves they employ the *nautch-girls*" who take the brunt of the exercise. Bungalows, verandahs, tatties, and punkahs too should be transferred to the West Indies to improve the health of British colonists. Johnson was astonished to read that palanquins were not in use in Jamaica (they actually were), and could only imagine that there was some difficult or costly problem of making slaves do such work. He exclaimed, with sarcasm about the idea that such things were effeminate, "It would be well if several other Asiatic effeminances were more generally adopted in the trans-atlantic islands."[33]

In the 1821 third edition of the *Influence of Tropical Climates*, James Johnson's relation Daniel Johnson argued that so-called Indian luxuries would broadly protect the health of the empire, building on arguments from the previous three decades. Daniel Johnson had served as a surgeon in the Company's Bengal service and thus spoke from a position of experienced authority. From the outset of his work, he attempted to mollify critics of Indian culture by invoking the popular orientalist understanding that ancient India had been one of the world's greatest civilizations. He argued that "the prevailing customs of the natives ... have been handed down to them by their forefathers, who were more enlightened then the present inhabitants." Daniel Johnson carefully explained that British power depended on using a different calculus to evaluate luxury in tropical climates unsuitable to "European Constitutions." Although James Johnson disagreed, Daniel Johnson followed the long-standing claims of Britons in India that smoking offered benefits in hot climates, "particularly

---

[32] Duncan MacDonald, *The New London Family Cook: Or, Town and Country Housekeeper's Guide* (London: J. Cundee, 1808), iv, 62, 87, 208–17; for another example of a cookery author indicating the healthfulness of his recipes and including curry, see R. House, *Family Cookery, Combining Elegance and Economy: with Various Receipts for Making Gravies, Soups, Sauces, and Made Dishes, Directions for Roasting and Boiling Game, Poultry, Meat, Fish, &c.* (London: J. Bailey, [1810]), i, 101.

[33] Johnson, *Oriental Voyager*, 89; Johnson, *Influence of Tropical Climates*, 422, 458–63. A decade later Fredrick Accum similarly wrote, "It appears to be the effect of climate and religion that makes the Hindoo adopt vegetable rather than animal food"; Fredrick Accum, *Culinary Chemistry* (London: Ackermann, 1821), 11.

if not indulged in to excess, or poisoned by the introduction of intoxicating ingredients." Smoking pure tobacco, he explained, "acts as a gentle stimulus to the intestines, and causes regular evacuations." Most of all, it was imperative that Europeans follow the habits of wealthier Indians who already had the advantage of a physiology more suited to their environment. If Britons in India wore loose silk or cotton, for example, instead of woolen jackets, they could avoid "perspiring at every pore to the great injury of their constitution, and eventually of the Government by whom they are employed." The health of the British empire in India, Daniel Johnson asserted, depended on the health of its colonial agents, whose own health, compromised by the alien environment, depended on accepting the usefulness of the habits and fashions of Indians.[34]

Bolstered by such prominent arguments about health, initially from non-medical professionals but now from medical professionals as well, consumption rates of many so-called Asiatic luxuries in Bengal either remained high or went up. Historians have assumed that hardening attitudes of racial superiority made Britons less inclined to own Indian goods in India. Probate inventories for the Bengal Presidency show that for goods frequently mentioned as healthful, ownership levels were high and often increasing through the 1820s. Palanquin ownership levels, for instance, fluctuated between one-third and two-thirds of decedents. The ownership of banians, meanwhile, hovered at between 50 and 60 percent from the 1760s through the 1820s. Umbrella ownership increased from a few percent to approximately 20 percent in the 1790s, although for the 1820s changes in inventory practices towards more frequent use of the broad category "wearing apparel" make it difficult to determine ownership levels. Most strikingly, hookah pipe and curry dish ownership continued to increase, from only a few percent in the 1760s up to nearly 50 percent for hookahs and nearly 40 percent for curry dishes by the 1820s. Fan, or punkah, ownership increased from 2 percent to over one-third of all decedents over the same period.[35]

Back in Britain, however, the calculus of West and East Indian mortality and morality had shifted again as Britain secured its power during the Napoleonic

---

[34] Daniel Johnson, 'Miscellaneous Observations on Certain Indigenous Customs, Diseases, and Remedies in India', in Johnson, *Influence of Tropical Climates*, 3rd ed. (Philadelphia: Dobson, 1821), vol. 1, 365, 368, 374; Johnson, *Influence of Tropical Climates* (1821), vol. 2, 273. On orientalism, see David Kopf, *British Orientalism and the Bengal Renaissance: The Dynamics of Indian Modernization, 1773–1835* (Berkeley: University of California Press, 1969), 102; Thomas Trautmann, *Aryans and British India* (Berkeley: University of California Press, 1997), 64–85. On smoking, see also McLean, *Enquiry into the Nature, and Causes of the Great Mortality*, 262–3; Samuel Bagshawe to his uncle, 10 February 1756, Colonel Samuel Bagshawe Papers, John Rylands Library, Manchester, 2/3/172.

[35] This analysis draws on a database created by the author that includes 272 inventories from the Bengal Presidency for the periods 1760–65, 1790–99, and 1820–29. 1760s inventories from Inventories of Deceased Estates, Bengal, BL, IOR/P/154/62–69. 1790–99 and 1820–29 inventories from Inventories and Accounts of Deceased Estates, Bengal (1780–1840), BL, IOR/L/AG/34/27/13–22, 69–93. Few inventories exist for the thousands of British army privates and other lower-sort British individuals with few possessions who died in Bengal.

Wars. In the West Indies, British victories as well as the Haitian Revolution reduced the French threat, and the success of British abolitionists against the slave trade reduced support for Britain's planters.[36] Increasingly wide and deep discomfort in Britain with West Indian slavery and the moral failings of slave owners fitted easily with accusations that the latter had adopted Eastern vices—not for health but to further their corrupt lifestyles. In 1812, a new series of Johnny Newcome prints by William Elmes (Fig. 28.3) attacked the East Indian products and practices that Williamson and the Johnsons recommended. Elmes associated the East Indian-inspired umbrellas and palanquins that Johnny adopted on his arrival with Johnny's despotic and barbaric treatment of his slaves. Elmes built on long-standing British associations of palanquins and umbrellas with Asiatic despotism. During Hastings's impeachment trial in 1788, for instance, William Dent depicted Hastings being carried in a palanquin by lawyers treading on the lord's heads. Lord Thurlow thrusts up a sword capped by a hat, like an umbrella, blocking out the pummeling burst of Edmund Burke, who led the impeachment.[37] In the East Indies, the threat of Napoleon invading from Egypt had been eliminated in 1798, and by 1803 the British had defeated Napoleon's main allies in India, the rulers of Mysore, and achieved victory in the second Anglo-Maratha war. By the time of the third Anglo-Maratha war in 1817, peace with France and global British dominance had reduced the importance of mortality in India for geopolitics. Mark Lewis's *Adventures of the Tenth!*, which took a paneled form similar to that of the Johnny Newcome prints, depicted the movement of the 10th Huzzars to India. In the fourth panel, an officer is debauched while smoking a hookah, which does little to save him as he becomes more fully Indian in dress and complexion, grows ill, and dies.[38]

Many Britons argued, much as they had in the eighteenth century, that so-called climatic protections in India were simply frivolous and dangerous excuses for luxury. On assessing the luxurious lifestyle of Europeans in India in 1817, Eliza Fay decided that decadence, not heat, caused illness: "I see very plainly that the same mode of living, would produce the same effects, even 'in the hardy regions of the North.'" The need to practice moderation, particularly in India, was a dominant theme in Thomas Moore's 1817 *Lalla Rookh*, one of the early nineteenth century's most popular poems. In 1828, William Peacock wrote home to his family from India that "you need not fear me being sick in this climate, there is nothing more delightful than the heat here."[39] John Harriott likewise suggested in his published advice to his

---

[36] Duffy, *Soldiers, Sugar, and Seapower*; Christopher Leslie Brown, *Moral Capital: Foundations of British Abolitionism* (Chapel Hill: University of North Carolina for the Omohundro Institute, 2006), esp. 26–30, 152–60, 239–58.

[37] William Dent, *A Slow and Sure Deliverance* (London, 1788).

[38] Mark Lewis, *Adventures of the Tenth!* (London, 1824).

[39] Eliza Fay, *Original Letters from India* (1817; Reprint, New York: Harcourt, Brace & Co., 1925), 170. At least one critic, however, thought that *Lalla Rookh* surreptitiously celebrated "gorgeous showy objects" and "bad morals and taste"; Review of *Lalla Rookh*, *North American Review*, 6 (November 1817), 1–25; for more on *Lalla Rookh* and moderation, see George Bearce, *British*

sons leaving for India that the climate of India was not to be feared. The fundamental risks in India were excessive laziness and spending. Economy was central to all of Harriott's advice. Everywhere in the world idleness and debauchery "will rot thy body, and prove a cancer in thy mind." An early nineteenth-century board game entitled *The New Game of Virtue Rewarded and of Vice Punished* captured this idea, and used a depiction of a large man eating a huge, meaty meal to represent the vice of overindulgence. Moyle Sherer warned that if they were not careful, Britons would lose their empire in India, like the "gay careless Frenchmen, who lived only the life of pleasure and indulgence."[40]

Other Britons in India aligned their growing belief in racial difference with such older concerns with luxury. For the devout evangelical David McFarlan, for example, the health of "Hindoos" and Britons alike depended on maintaining synchronicity between lifestyle and race. Unlike many authors, he differentiated between Muslims and Hindus in India. Hindus were, he claimed, "a weak and silly race of people, imbecile in mind and feckless in body." It made sense, in McFarlan's mind, for such people to wear scanty clothing on their bodies, and "a great bundle of cloth upon their heads by way of a hat viz to prevent the sun's rays _____ their brains too much." Such clothing would not suit Europeans, who he claimed were not ill suited to the tropics but in fact were racially stronger and more vigorous. McFarlan doubted too the common advice to eat like Hindus when in India. Muslims ate much more meat than Hindus, yet he found them stronger and more durable. He imagined that race and diet must be in harmony:

> Give us a Hindoo constitution such as I presume they derive from their fathers and mothers, feed us upon rice all our infancy and youth up and then tell us to go on with it and not to take to flesh—but do not say to a man whose habit has been formed upon the gross food of a cold climate whose "limbs were made in Scotland or in England either"—that he is to withdraw its customary support.

The secret to health in any climate, according to McFarlan, was avoiding foreign luxury, eating food appropriate to one's race, and regular exercise.[41] Nevertheless, support for local diets still did not line up easily along religious or political divisions. Reverend James Cordiner wrote, as had Sharp before him,

Attitudes towards India, 1784–1858 (Oxford: Oxford University Press, 1961), 108–9. William Peacock to Anna, 7 July 1828, William Peacock Papers, BL, MSS Eur. C180.

[40] John Harriott thought that dancing girls were a far better class of people than European prostitutes. John Harriott, *Struggles Through Life, Exemplified in the Various Travels and Adventures in Europe, Asia, Africa, & America, of Lieut. John Harriott* (New York: Inskeep and Bradford, 1809), vol. 2, 233–5. T. Newton, *The New Game of Virtue Rewarded and of Vice Punished, for the Amusement of Youth of Both Sexes,* Collection 121, Winterthur Museum and Library, Delaware, 74×438.781. An Officer for Fire-Side Travellers at Home [Moyle Sherer], *Sketches of India* (London: Longman, Hurst, Rees, Orme, and Brown, 1821), 151.

[41] David McFarlan to John McFarlan Jr., 19 August 1817?, Letters to and from David MacFarlan, BL, MSS Eur. C315/1. Rule denotes illegible text.

Fig. 28.3   William Elmes, *Adventures of Johnny Newcome* (1812), Plate 1. Courtesy of The Lewis Walpole Library, Yale University

that "all classes of European society here live sumptuously" with great spreads of food. In contrast, he explained, "rice and curry … form all the repasts of the natives … those who wish to enjoy good health in a tropical climate will follow their example."[42]

Indeed, with limited numbers of missionaries sent to India at considerable trouble and expense, the growing early nineteenth-century evangelical missionary movement sharply felt the tension between the moral problem of luxury and the physical problem of survival. British victories in India had dovetailed with evangelical interests in spreading the gospel, despite the East India Company's frequent objections.[43] On the one hand, popular evangelical works such as Mary Sherwood's *The History of George Desmond* railed against Indian palanquins, hookahs, punkahs, dress, and curries as the devil's own devices to bamboozle poor Indians and foolish Europeans alike. The missionary Nathaniel Forsyth and Mr. Powell wrote separately from India

---

[42] James Cordiner, *A Voyage to India* (Aberdeen: Brown and Co.; London: Longman, 1820), 100.

[43] For more on the missionary movement and the Company, see Penelope Carson, *The East India Company and Religion, 1698–1858* (Woodbridge, UK: Boydell and Brewer, 2012), esp. 52–182.

claiming that the climate was not unhealthy and that those who died were either already sickly in Britain or had not lived "as they ought to," although precisely what that entailed was not spelled out. The missionary William Ward advised that "A simple and light diet, a tranquil mind, caution against sudden changes in the air, and moderate exercise, seem to be the most necessary things in Bengal to preserve health."[44] The Baptist Missionary Society's early instructions disdained palanquins and explained that Britons need not find life in India expensive. On the other hand, they must hire a native cook to make curries, as well as having an umbrella carrier. These two concessions to the climate were absolutely necessary even if they seemed luxurious and morally corrupting in Europe. The Church Missionary Society explained in its quarterly newsletter that European women teaching natives the gospel in India needed to ride in palanquins to avoid death in the "hot and exhausting climate." And the Scottish Missionary Society wrote to its missionaries in India: "Be careful of your health ... we entreat you carefully to follow the practice, and to attend to the maxims of those Europeans who have been resident in the country. Beware of treating their representations with incredulity."[45] The evangelical community that had contributed so much to the ending of the slave trade, and effectively criticized the corrupt luxury of slave owners, now found its missionaries adopting some of the same Indian goods to preserve their own health and missions.

CONCLUSION

The fight to achieve victory in the Napoleonic Wars and the contemporaneous growth of the empire's territory created a fertile moment for the adoption of East Indian lifestyles to safeguard the physical health of the empire's soldiers, sailors, administrators, and increasingly missionaries. As the Navy in the West Indies outfitted men with cotton banians adopted from the East Indies, official writers for the East India Company encouraged Britons in the East and West Indies to buy many Indian goods and follow many Indian practices. Most Britons on the ground in the colonies saw a sharper difference between physical health and moral health than people in the metropole

---

[44] William Staughton, *The Baptist Mission in India: Containing a Narrative of its Rise, Progress, and Present Condition, A Statement of the Physical and Moral Character of the Hindoos, their Cruelties, Tortures and Burnings, with a Very Interesting Description of Bengal, Intended to Animate to Missionary Co-operation* (Philadelphia: Hellings and Aitken, 1811), 265–6; William Ward, *View of the History, Literature, and Mythology of the Hindoos: Including a Minute Description of their Manners and Customs, and Translations from their Principal Works* (1822; Reprint, Port Washington, NY: Kennikat Press, 1970), 118.

[45] *Baptist Missionary Society Periodical Accounts Relative to the Baptist Missionary Society*, Vol. I (Clipstone, 1800), 30; *Missionary Papers for the use of the Weekly and Monthly Contributors to the Church Missionary Society* (Lady Day, 1826), 41; *Letter of Instructions from the Directors of the Scottish Missionary Society to their Missionaries Among the Heathen* (Edinburgh: Scottish Missionary Society, 1828), 63, 68–9.

without colonial experience. Physical health in the tropics simply could not be subjected to all of the moral norms of Britain. Indeed, such subjection could lead to the end of the empire itself. The intensified pressure against calls for adopting Indian lifestyles in the tropics signified the strength and success of such calls, the reality of increasing consumption of many aspects of Indian material culture among Britons in India, and the newfound stability of the empire against France and indigenous powers alike. Arguments against elite Indian material culture underscored the continued importance of the threat of luxury in British thought. Belief in racial difference, meanwhile, need not lead to broader rejections of India's material culture as inferior or degenerate; for many it continued to lead to the belief that several aspects of that culture were more important for Britons than for Indians.

Charting the debate over luxury outwards from India instead of outwards from the metropole suggests that many Britons in the tropics reframed the luxury debates on their own terms, arguing that they must choose between luxury and death. In 1822, Fanny Parkes wrote with exasperation, "I wish much that those who exclaim against our extravagances here, knew how essential to a man's comfort, to his quiet, and to his health it is, to have every thing good about him." She went on to defend hookahs, sun umbrellas, local Indian cots instead of bedsteads to keep cool, curries, and many other aspects of Indian material culture.[46] She was not alone. Yet celebrating one's Indian lifestyle in death, as Charles "Hindoo" Stuart did with his Indianesque tomb, exposed one's conversion to the supposedly corrupt pleasurable luxury of South Asian culture as more than just a healthful concession. The last panel of the *Adventures of the Tenth!* depicts a classical tomb and urn. The urn is surmounted by a statue of a monkey in a military uniform, while live monkeys sob, and the epithet concludes "monkey's mourn around their tomb," suggesting that the stoic classical tomb was a sham and did not reflect the corrupted Asiatic lives of those buried beneath it. Classical monuments literally covered over the bodies of those who had lived by adopting varying degrees of the supposedly luxurious material culture of the people they ruled. The vigor with which these monuments stressed a sense of superior European and British ideals reveals not necessarily the strength of Britons' belief in the superiority of these ideals, but their uneasy dependence on South Asian knowledge, goods, and practices to defend against their own mortality and that of their empire.

---

[46] Fanny Parkes, *Wanderings of a Pilgrim in Search of the Picturesque* (1850; Reprint, London: Oxford University Press, 1975), 37–8, 46–7, 146, 149, 393.

PART V

Worlds on Paper

CHAPTER 29

Extra-illustrations: The Order of the Book and the Fantasia of the Library

Luisa Calè

Can this cockpit hold
The vasty fields of France? or may we cram,
Within this wooden O, the very casques,
That did affright the air at Agincourt?
(William Shakespeare, *Henry V*)

The imaginary is not formed in opposition to reality as its denial or compensation; it grows among signs, from book to book, in the interstice of repetitions and commentaries; it is born and takes shape in the interval between books. It is a phenomenon of the library. (Michel Foucault, 'The Fantasia of the Library')

This essay defamiliarizes the book as an object of knowledge through an eighteenth-century practice that subverts its bibliographical codes. Extra-illustration challenges the stability and homogeneity identified with the codex as a commodity and as a condition of possibility for the production and circulation of knowledge. In *Bibliomania; or Book-Madness: A Bibliographical Romance in Six Parts* (1811), Thomas Frognall Dibdin associates its rise in the last quarter of the eighteenth century with the publication of James Granger's *Biographical History of England* (1769). A catalogue of prints of English heads, Granger's book invites readers to visualize history by documenting the people, monuments and places mentioned on the page with prints and other kinds of illustration that

L. Calè (✉)
Department of English and Humanities,
Birkbeck, University of London, London, UK
e-mail: l.cale@bbk.ac.uk

© The Author(s) 2016
A. Craciun, S. Schaffer (eds.), *The Material Cultures of Enlightenment Arts and Sciences*, Palgrave Studies in the Enlightenment, Romanticism and the Cultures of Print, DOI 10.1057/978-1-137-44379-3_29

235

capture their existence outside the book.[1] Two extra-illustrated Shakespeares are described in some detail in Dibdin's *Bibliomania*.[2] Both were gifts to John George Earl Spencer, acquired at the time when his collection at Althorp, Northamptonshire, was becoming the most important private library in Europe (between 1790 and 1820).[3] One was assembled by Shakespeare editor George Steevens, who extra-illustrated the text with printed portraits of Shakespeare, his editors and commentators, as well as characters and places mentioned in the plays; the other by Spencer's mother-in-law, Margaret Bingham, Lady Lucan, whose watercolour inserts harked back to the aristocratic world of illuminated manuscripts. Each shored up an alternative archive: Steevens inscribed the edition with the agency that established the text as an unstable and ever-expanding accretion of documents and critical voices; Lady Lucan carefully refashioned the eighteenth-century antiquarian archive in mock fifteenth-century form. In their different social and aesthetic choices, the two interventions reclaim Shakespeare from the identity of a commercial print run. Customized as unique association objects, Steevens's and Lady Lucan's Shakespeares find a place alongside the unique copies of fifteenth-century books in Earl Spencer's library. Building on Michel Foucault's notion of the fantasia of the library and Roger Chartier's discussion of the orders of books,[4] I will explore what extra-illustration says about the book, its uses and modes of inscription in the orders and imaginaries of the library.

Extra-illustration activates the performative power of language. The text becomes a script whose performance requires a material practice of collecting. The collector's act of reading is broken down into a series of steps in Dibdin's 'Recipe for Illustration':

> Take any passage from any author—to wit; the following (which I have done, quite at random) from SPEED: '*Henry Le Spenser*, the warlike *Bishop of Norwich*, being drawne on by *Pope Vrban* to preach *the Crusade*, and to be General against

---

[1] On the rise of extra-illustration, see L. Peltz, 'Engraved Portrait Heads and the Rise of Extra-Illustration: The Eton Correspondence of the Reverend James Granger and Richard Bull, 1769-1774', *Walpole Society* 66 (2004), 1–161; L. Peltz, 'Facing the Text: the amateur and commercial histories of extra-illustration, c. 1770-1840', in Robin Myers, Michael Harris, and Giles Mandelbrote (eds), *Owners, Annotators, and the Signs of Reading* (New Castle, DE and London: Oak Knoll Press and The British Library, 2005), 91–135; L. Peltz, 'A Friendly Gathering. The Social Politics of Presentation Books and their Extra-Illustration in Horace Walpole's Circle', *Journal of the History of Collections*, 19:1 (2007), 33–49.

[2] T.F. Dibdin, *Bibliomania; or, Book Madness: A Bibliographical Romance, In Six Parts. Illustrated with Cuts* (London: Printed for the Author, by J. McCrerry, 1811), 571n, 667–8n.

[3] A. A. Renouard, *Annales de l'imprimerie des Alde, ou Histoire des trois Manuce et de leurs Éditions* (Paris, 1803), II, 8; T.F. Dibdin, *Bibliotheca Spenceriana; or A Descriptive Catalogue of the Books Printed in the Fifteenth Century, and of many Valuable First Editions, in the Library of George John Earl Spencer*, 4 vols (London: Bulmer, 1814), vol. I, vi.

[4] M. Foucault, 'The Fantasia of the Library', in *Language, Counter-Memory, Practice*, ed. and trans. by Donald Bouchard (Ithaca: Cornell University Press, 1977); R. Chartier, *The Order of Books: Readers, Authors, and Libraries in Europe between the Fourteenth and the Eighteenth Centuries*, trans. Lydia G. Cochrane (Stanford: Stanford University Press, 1994).

Clement (whom sundry *Cardinals* and great *Prelates* had also elected Pope) having a fifteenth granted to him, for that purpose by *Parliament, &c. Historie of
Great Britaine*, p. 721, edit. 1632.' Now let the reader observe, here are *only four*
lines; but which, to be PROPERLY ILLUSTRATED, should be treated thus: 1st; procure
all the portraits, at all periods of his life, of *Henry Le Spenser*, 2dly; obtain every
view, ancient and modern, like or unlike, of the city of *Norwich*, and, if fortune
favour you, of *every Bishop of the same see*; 3rdly; every portrait of *Pope Vrban* must
be procured; and as many prints and drawings as can give some notion of *the
Crusade*—together with a few etchings (if there be any) of *Peter the Hermit* and
Richard 1st, who took such active parts in the Crusade: 4thly; you must search
high and low, early and late, for every print of *Clement*. 5thly; procure, or you will
be wretched, as many fine prints of *Cardinals* and *Prelates*, singly or in groups,
as will impress you with a proper idea of the *Conclave*; and 6thly; see whether
you may not obtain, at some of our most distinguished old-print sellers, views of
the *house of Parliament* at the period (A.D.1383.) here described!!! The result,
gentle reader, will be this: you will have work enough cut out to occupy you, for
one whole month at least.[5]

Dibdin's bibliomaniac recipe literalizes the classical etymology of reading as
a form of collecting: 'to read in the classical sense of the word, LEGERE',
argued anthologist Vicesimus Knox, is 'to *pick out*, to select the most valuable
and worthiest objects'.[6] Knox was concerned to provide an anthological selection for a busy middle class overwhelmed by the exponential multiplication of
books produced by the art of printing; Dibdin multiplies the book's dimensions. Activating the text as a set of operations means relating the words on
the page to the classes, series and categories to which they belong. In Dibdin's
account, reading fuels the indexical drive of antiquarian, topographical and
bibliographical practices. New referential worlds open up within the space of
four lines.

Gathering the evidence involves repurposing the book as a repository. When
the text acts as a prompt for collecting, the book's function can shift from a
support for reading to an ordering device for the collection. The multifarious
accumulation of specimens collected to account for the words on the page
tests the limits of the book's operations as a reading tool. Reaching out to the
words' material referents might end up breaking down the continuity between
words across pages. In such acts of supplementation, words turn into 'pegs' on
which to hang materials culled from other books and introduced within this
book's leaves.[7]

[5] Dibdin, 'Recipe for Illustration', *Bibliomania*, 665–6n.

[6] V. Knox, *Winter Evenings; or, Lucubrations on Life and Letters*, 3 vols (London, 1788), vol. II,
224.

[7] I am adapting to the role of words in the practice of extra-illustration what Dibdin says about
the fiction of characters and dialogue in his bibliographical writing: 'The worthy Gentlemen, by
whom the Drama is conducted, may be called by some, merely wooden machines or pegs to hang
notes upon', Dibdin, *Bibliomania*, vii.

Granger's work seems to have sounded the tocsin for a general rummage after, and plunder of, old prints. Venerable philosophers, and veteran heroes, who had long reposed in unmolested dignity within the magnificent folio volumes which recorded their achievements, were instantly dragged forth from their peaceful abodes, to be inlaid by the side of some clumsy modern engraving, within an *Illustrated Granger!* Nor did the madness stop here. Illustration was the order of the day; and *Shakespeare* and *Clarendon* became the next objects of its attack.[8]

The plunder of collecting takes the form of a profanation of the dead, as 'Venerable philosophers, and veteran heroes' are disturbed, disinterred, disbound from their dignified repose in magnificent folios. The new currency they gain from being inlaid in extra-illustrated books involves a bibliographical, aesthetic and social upheaval. Steevens announces that the extra-illustrated pages of his Shakespeare 'exhibit engravings of very discordant value; from such as are known to have been sold at five or ten guineas each, down to those for which the possessors were ashamed to ask even the most trivial sum'.[9] The logic of extra-illustration privileges the identity of sitters or their occupation over artistry in levelling acts of juxtaposition that place beside one another objects coming from different aesthetic domains.

Sourcing and adding the portraits of people mentioned in the text on the facing page of a book literally defaces other books. Holes and stubs in one volume mark what has been cut out to beautify another. Horace Walpole sounded the alarm as early as 1772, criticizing extra-illustrators Richard Bull and Joseph Gulston for 'cutting books to pieces for a single print or two'.[10] About a decade later, Steevens foresaw the defaced future of illustrated books: 'in the course of a few years, no ancient English Portraits will be met with in the books they originally belonged to, unless where they have sculked in hereditary libraries, and escaped the consequences of publick sale'. He blamed book destruction on commercial forms of exchange and the unrestricted circulation that auctions fostered. Binding, like hereditary libraries, protects the book as an archive where portraits are preserved 'in a state of lasting confinement; or, if set at liberty, would only exchange one prison for another', and enter 'Clarendon, Burnet, Rapin, and County Histories, or collectors' series of their relations, or of our poets, painters, statesmen, ecclesiasticks'. Complementary to the barren

---

[8] Dibdin, *Bibliomania*, 667–8.

[9] G. Steevens, 'Advertisement', in *The plays of William Shakspeare. In fifteen volumes. With the corrections and illustrations of various commentators. To which are added, notes by Samuel Johnson and George Steevens. The fourth edition; Revised and augmented (with a glossarial index) by the editor of Dodsley's collection of old plays*, 15 vols (London, 1793), University of Manchester, John Rylands Library, Spencer 22347, manuscript annotation in the preliminary papers of vol. 1.

[10] Horace Walpole, 'Of collectors of English portrait-prints', 'Book of Materials', 3 vols, vol. II (1772), 2, Yale University, Lewis Walpole Library, 492615; on Joseph Gulston's compilation of an appendix to Granger documenting the portraits of foreigners in England, his collection of 23,500 English portraits, and the sale of his books in 1784 and his prints in 1786, see L. Namier and J. Brooke, *House of Commons 1754–1790* (London: Secker, 1964), vol. I, 562; John Nichols, *Illustrations of the Literary History of the Eighteenth Century*, vol. V, 1–60.

future of the defaced book is the cornucopian expansion of the extra-illustrated book, whose binding may be 'taken to pieces and recompacted'. The series may be completed as 'vacant leaves are inserted for the admission of portraits known to have been engraved', but the future may also require a more radical disbinding and rebinding, for 'no forecast could adjust receptacles for those which may be hereafter published from originals as yet undiscovered by the most diligent among the numerous disciples of *Ames, Walpole, Granger* and *Bromley*'.[11] Another decade later, Robert Southey famously complained that 'you rarely or never meet an old book here with the author's head in it; all are mutilated by the collectors'.[12] Book destruction is the other side of extra-illustration,[13] an iconoclastic act that disturbs not only the physical identity of books, but also the boundaries between books. So how did this practice work?

The extra-illustrated book can be distinguished from the scrapbook as an intervention on a particular edition, which is altered by pasting additional materials onto blank or inserted leaves or on the margins of the letterpress, for instance on copies printed on large paper.[14] Alternatively, the gatherings of the book are disbound and each page is inlaid in a window frame cut through a larger leaf to enable both sides of the page to be read. Then text and images need to be collated and the new pages numbered to avoid displacement during binding. As the book is extended, inlaid, collated and newly bound, its dimensions can multiply from octavo to folio and so does the number of volumes, hence the need for new title pages—a paratext that often records the collaborative work of different agents: collector, inlayer and binder may join author and publisher on the threshold of the newly bound extra-illustrated book.

Added materials can be verbal as well as visual. Another type of extra-illustration that Dibdin identified consists 'in bringing together, from different works, [including newspapers, magazines, and by means of the scissors, or otherwise by transcription] every page or paragraph which has any connexion with the character or subject under discussion'.[15] While this scrapbooking activity adds layers of context and commentary, the original text is also sometimes presented through different specimens of letterpress, for extra-illustrators collect within one book alternative examples of typeface. As a result, the book may house the visual history of the text as well as its iconographical world.

Such specimens show the heterogeneous practices associated with the complementary rise of book history and extra-illustration, which Jon Klancher calls

[11] Steevens, 'Advertisement' penned in the preliminary papers of *The plays of William Shakspeare,* Spencer 22347, vol. 1.

[12] Manuel Alvarez Espriella [Robert Southey], *Letters from England,* 2nd edn, 2 vols (London, 1808), vol. I, 235.

[13] Lucy Peltz discusses a satirical woodcut vignette featuring the extra-illustrator's workshop as 'The Destruction Room' in 'Facing the Text', 91–3.

[14] For a discussion of the extra-illustrated book as a 'methodized scrapbook', see J.M. Bulloch, *The Art of Extra-illustration* (London: Treherne, 1903), 11.

[15] Dibdin, *Bibliomania*, 669.

'wild bibliography'.[16] Establishing the text *ne varietur*, restoring the original, or producing an eclectic ideal text, involves compiling and collating different editions of the same work to reconstruct its publication history. The editor's inclusiveness turns the extra-illustrated book into a bibliographical microcosm, which juxtaposes sample specimens from other editions within the expanded bounds of an individual copy. Such a hybrid emphasizes the paradox at the heart of bibliographical practices. Ideal textual stability and its ideal textual forms depend on an eclectic material practice. The extra-illustrated book exhibits a work's multiple, fluid and accidental forms. Tracing the metamorphoses of an object re-engraved, repurposed and supplemented by alternative acts of framing emphasizes its mobile inscriptions. As Klancher argues, 'dismantling the codex form itself', and thus destroying the very objects that the emerging discipline sets out to investigate, bibliomaniac editors and 'collectors performed extraordinary acts of authorship in their own right. What resulted were effectively multi-authored, multimedia concoctions'.[17]

Extra-illustrating Shakespeare was an established practice. The print market responded to the demand of collectors by producing ready-made series of prints to illustrate key texts with or without the accompanying letterpress, taking account of subscribers who might prefer to insert prints in editions they already owned. Series of prints illustrating Shakespeare were published in numbers to respond to the demand of extra-illustrators. John Bell's 'acting' and 'literary' editions of Shakespeare (1774, 1788) could be bound in the same volume, arranging the plates in varying sequences according to the taste of the reader, as Stuart Sillars has shown.[18] The flexibility of such series can be evinced from the advertisements of *The Picturesque Beauties of Shakespeare*, published in ten numbers between 1783 and 1787, which pointed out the paper and size options available for purchasers wishing to insert prints in their editions.[19] John and Josiah Boydell's Shakespeare Gallery, launched in 1786 and open as a gallery from 1789, was presented as an 'encouragement to the arts of painting, engraving, and printing', combining the new commission of paintings and the serial publication of prints with a text established by George Steevens and

[16] J. Klancher, 'Wild Bibliography', in I. Ferris and P. Keen (eds), *Bookish Histories* (Palgrave, 2009).

[17] Ibid., 28–9.

[18] S. Sillars, 'Reading Illustrated Editions: Methodology and the Limits of Interpretation', *Shakespeare Survey* 62 (2009), 162–81, on 167.

[19] A slip of paper dated 1 June 1783 announces: 'To accommodate those Gentlemen who wish to insert the Prints of this Work into Quarto Editions of Shakspeare, a Number of Proof Impressions are Printed upon a Royal Paper for the Purpose, Price Seven Shillings and Sixpence. Any Gentleman who desires it, may change small Paper Prints of As You Like it for the Larger, by Application to the Publisher', inserted between the cover and the first print, *The picturesque beauties of Shakespeare, being a selection of scenes, from the works of that great author; intended to contain the most striking incidents and descriptions of Each Play; in Oval Prints, six inches by four and a half wide* (London: Taylor, 1783–87), No. II, University of Oxford, Bodleian Library, Johnson d.832.

printed 'with a Set of new Types cast by Mr. Caslon'.[20] Buyers were also offered the option to subscribe for the prints only and insert them into editions they already owned. Much as Boydell stressed the gallery's distance from theatrical portraiture and emphasized its role in establishing an English school of historical painting,[21] John Bell's advertisements addressed 'Shakspearean Collectors and Admirers', inviting them to insert prints from his acting and literary editions into Boydell editions despite their different formats and aesthetics.[22]

The first extra-illustrated Shakespeare that Dibdin mentions in the Althorp Library is one of 25 copies printed on large paper of an octavo edition published in 1793 in 15 volumes, edited and extended to 18 by Steevens.[23] Long footnotes in *Bibliomania* celebrate Steevens's work as a draughtsman and collector, his hunting for rare portraits, sketching them and delivering them to print sellers to make prints for extra-illustrators. His formidable library of early modern books is recorded in long extracts from the posthumous catalogue of his library, *Bibliotheca Steevensiana* (1800).[24] Steevens's collection included many first editions of the quartos, some of which were inlaid on large paper. The expanded margins obtained by mounting each page onto larger sheets of paper turned the book into an interim object, which functioned as a laboratory for inscribing collations, remarks and other editorial changes in the transition from one edition to another.[25] *Bibliotheca Steevensiana* also lists a second Folio owned and annotated by Charles II and a copy of the First Folio, 'with a manuscript title, and a fac-simile drawing of the portrait by Mr. Steevens'.[26] Like the copies inlaid on large paper, this late eighteenth-century hybrid illu-

---

[20] *The Times*, 5 December 1786, 2; Prospectus dated 28–29 November 1786, *The Times*, 2 Dec 1786, 1; 'The Preface', *A Catalogue of the Pictures in the Shakspeare Gallery, Pall-Mall* (London, 1789) mentions the letterpress being printed by 'Mr Nicol, his Majesty's Bookseller' with 'Types ... made in his own house', and the editorial expertise of George Steevens's 'national Edition of the Works of Shakspeare', xv–xvi.

[21] On the Shakespeare Gallery in the context of the British School, see R. Dias, *Exhibiting Englishness: John Boydell's Shakespeare Gallery and the Formation of a National Aesthetic* (New Haven and London: Yale University Press, 2013); S. Sillars, *Painting Shakespeare: The Artist as Critic* (Cambridge: Cambridge University Press, 2006), 254–99.

[22] 'Sets of Prints, fine Impressions, adapted to each of Shakspere's Plays ... may be bound up with any Edition of his Works'—including 'Boydell's Edition, or any of the smaller Publications'—'or added to them as a Supplementary Volume of Embellishments', *The Oracle*, 8 April 1793; also quoted in R. Dias, 'John Boydell's Shakespeare Gallery', PhD Thesis, University of York, 2003, 270n.

[23] Dibdin, *Bibliomania*, 571n, 668n; see also T.F. Dibdin, *Aedes Althorpianae; or an Account of the Mansion, Books, and Pictures, at Althorp: the Residence of George John Earl Spencer* (London: Nicol, 1822), 206.

[24] Dibdin, *Bibliomania*, 571–85.

[25] For instance, a first edition of *The Merchant of Venice* inlaid on large paper 'with the autograph of L. Theobald and carefully collated by him with the other edition of the same date', see *Bibliotheca Steevensiana*, 87, no. 1279, and inlaid first quartos of *Midsummer Night's Dream* (no. 1285), *The Taiming of the Shrew* (no. 1302) and *Titus Andronicus* (no. 1304).

[26] *Bibliotheca Steevensiana. A Catalogue of the Curious and Valuable Library of George Steevens, Esq. Fellow of the Royal and Antiquary Societas, (Lately Deceased.)* (London, 13–23 May 1800), no. 1313, quoted in Dibdin, *Bibliomania*, 581.

minates the convergent material cultures of Shakespeare editing, collecting and extra-illustrating.

Steevens's modern Shakespeare text articulates a contradictory relationship with pictures. The 'Advertisement' announces that 'the reader may observe that, contrary to usage, no head of Shakspeare is prefixed to the present edition of his plays'.[27] What follows is an analysis of the evidence, supposed originals and reproductions, with the conclusion that no portrait can be considered authentic; hence 'we boast of no exterior ornaments except for those of better print and paper'. Yet the logic of the text is contradicted by a footnote, which redirects the reader to a complementary publication: 'they who wish for decorations adapted to this edition of Shakspeare, will find them in Sylvester Harding's Portraits and Views'.[28] *Shakspeare Illustrated, by an Assemblage of Portraits and Views, Appropriated to the whole suite of that Authors Historical Dramas; to which are added Portraits of Actors, Editors*, published in 30 numbers also in 1793, reprints plates already 'published separate a short time back'. By indicating a ready-made series of prints and printing directions to the binders to control the placement of Harding's prints in the text, Steevens's edition advertises and at the same time regulates the complementary practice of extra-illustration.[29] Engraved portraits of editors and critics Rowe, Hanmer, Pope, Warburton, Johnson, Malone, Reed, but also Mrs Lennox and Mrs Montagu, among others, join actors and views that will bring Shakespeare to the eye of the reader, documenting the work of historical and philological reconstruction. The visual canon produced for public and commercial consumption celebrates Shakespeare as a layered corpus assembled by the collaborative and complementary work identified by an assemblage of the faces of those who have contributed to establishing, emending and performing the text. Against the selection of prints gathered together and reissued in a publication for extra-illustrators, Steevens's extra-illustrated copy of Shakspeare stands out as a unique association object.

How Steevens's relationship with portraiture is played out in his extra-illustrated copy of Shakespeare is noted in an obituary published in the *Gentleman's Magazine* in May 1800: 'He never would sit for his picture, but had no objection to illustrate his own Shakspeare with 1500 portraits of all the persons in the notes and texts, of which he could make drawings or procure engravings.'[30] Yet an engraving after a portrait painted by the fashionable Royal Academician Johan Zoffany in 1773, published in September 1800 and bearing Steevens's dates of birth and death, faces the title page to the first volume

[27] Steevens, 'Advertisement', *The plays of William Shakspeare*, vol. I, i,

[28] Ibid., vi.

[29] Ibid., v and footnote; newly paginated section after the Advertisement, i–viii; *Shakspeare Illustrated, by an Assemblage of Portraits and Views, Adapted to the whole series of that Author's Historical Dramas; to which are added Portraits of Actors, Editors, &c* (London: S & F Harding, 102 Pall Mall, 1793).

[30] *Gentleman's Magazine* 70 (May 1800), 178–9, on 178.

of his extra-illustrated copy of the 1793 edition.[31] Against the title page, the engraved portrait issued to commemorate the editor on the occasion of his death marks the posthumous expansion of the work posthumously bequeathed to Lord Spencer, First Lord of the Admiralty.[32]

Steevens's presentation copy is elegantly bound with his gold-tooled initials on the upper cover, gilt Greek key rolls tooled in the turn-ins, and a gold-lettered leather insert inscribed 'Bibliotheca Spenceriana' in the pastedown end paper.[33] The binding expresses the social relation between the editor and the aristocratic collector through the 'fantastic form of a relation between things'.[34] The double inscription records the book's transfer of ownership, subsuming the name of the owner and editor under the sign of the *Bibliotheca Spenceriana*. Read together with the posthumous catalogue of the *Bibliotheca Steevensiana* in May 1800, the posthumous bequest articulates the relation between the book and the library. The extra-illustrated Shakespeare inscribes the world of prints let loose of their bindings, the commercial world of the auctioneer and the work of the editor 'bound up ... into a state of lasting confinement'. The handwritten advertisement that Steevens adds to his presentation copy suggests that the extra-illustrated Shakespeare will be safe from 'the consequence of publick sale' in the Spencer Library. The binding will add Steevens's extra-illustrated Shakespeare to the aesthetic economy of the aristocratic collection. Yet it could also spell out a different story of acquisitive consumption, in which Shakespeare joins other bibliographical treasures that had come up for sale with the dispersal of aristocratic libraries in the late eighteenth century and the revolutionary period. In this case, Steevens's tooled initials spell out the value of the object in terms of its provenance, evidence for the growing 'memoirs of libraries'.[35]

Steevens's extra-illustrated copy is a microcosm of Shakespeare illustration, which includes the series of illustrative plates from Rowe's edition of 1709.

[31] 'Painted by Zoffanii, Esq R.A. The face engraved by W. Evans | Engraved from a Portrait Painted by Zoffanii in'774 | Published Sep 1 1800 by S. Harding no 127 Pall Mall, BM 1868,0822.2470.

[32] A handwritten note pasted on the flyleaf of the first volume leaves posthumous directions: 'On my death, I request my Executrix, Miss Elizabeth Steevens, to send these eighteen Volumes of the edition of Shakspeare 1793, to the Right Hon.ble Earl Spencer, first Lord of the Admiralty.—they are, in this manner, bequeathed to his Lordship (as a sincere though inconsiderable mark of regard) by George Steevens | Hampstead Heath, Aug. 30. 1795.'

[33] The Index volumes bear the stamp of Charles Lewis in the top left corner of the turn-in. H.M. Nixon, 'English Bookbindings X', *Book Collector* 3 (Summer 1954) dates Charles Lewis's first binding to 1812; on Charles Lewis, see T.F. Dibdin, *The Bibliographical Decameron*, VIII; C. Ramsden, *London Book-binders 1780–1840* (London: Batsford, 1956), 14–16.

[34] Karl Marx, 'The Fetishism of the Commodities and the Secret Thereof', *Capital*, trans. S. Moore and E. Avelling, ed. Frederick Engels (London: Lawrence and Wishart, 1954), 77.

[35] The foundation of Spencer's collection of fifteenth-century books dates to his acquisition of Count Revickzky's library in 1790; see Dibdin, *Bibliotheca Spenceriana*, vol. I, i–ii. Spencer acquired an outstanding collection of early printed books by Aldus Manutius. On the dispersal of libraries, see Edward Edwards, *Memoirs of Libraries* (London: Trübner, 1859), vol. II, 121–32, and 147–51 on Spencer's acquisitions.

Taken singly, this act of repurposing points to the flexible practice of inscription that adapts series of illustrations to different editions. Steevens's library also included a copy of the second edition of Shakespeare that he edited with Samuel Johnson, with Edmond Malone's Supplement 'and the plates from Bell's edition'.[36] Yet as part of an assemblage that includes frontispieces and title pages from earlier editions of Shakespeare and other works mentioned in footnotes, such a gathering of specimens turns the book into 'an archival survey of past responses',[37] a portable library in which collected fragments point to virtual wholes to be activated in the mind of the reader, or found in the library of the extra-illustrator.

Steevens's dealings with Rowe's frontispiece illuminate his dialectic of illustration. The intersection of the order of books with the orders of painting, engraving and antiquarian protocols of collecting is spelt out by the sequence of engravings inserted in the first volume. Portraits of Royal Academy President Sir Joshua Reynolds and engraver George Vertue face the 'Advertisement' to mark their intervention in the debate about Shakespeare's likeness, and Vertue's repeated impressions of the Chandos portrait.[38] As Margreta de Grazia notes, the allegorical composition adopted in Michael van der Gucht's frontispiece to Rowe's edition draws on a portrait of the French dramatist Pierre Corneille, which was reproduced as a frontispiece in the Rouen edition of 1660: 'by appropriating its ornate apparatus in order to crown Shakespeare, ... the modern portrait of the English contender had usurped the classical bust of his French co-rival.'[39] However, Steevens's act of extra-illustration destabilizes van der Gucht's monumental portrait and calls into question Rowe's judgement:

> on vague and dubious authority this head has hitherto been received as a genuine portrait of our author, who probably left behind him no such memorial of his face. As he was careless of the future state of his works, his solicitude might not have extended to the perpetuation of his looks.[40]

Rowe's frontispiece no longer anchors the author's words as a stand-in for the presence of the author. Transferred to its new extra-illustrated location, it anchors an alternative text, which overwrites and supersedes Rowe's edi-

---

[36] *Bibliotheca Steevensiana*, 86, no. 1334.

[37] S. Sillars, 'The extra-illustrated edition', *The Illustrated Shakespeare, 1709–1875* (Cambridge: Cambridge University Press, 2008), 216.

[38] The first portrait presented to the National Portrait Gallery on its opening in 1856, the Chandos portrait of Shakespeare (NPG 1), takes its name from its late eighteenth-century owner James Brydges, 3rd Duke of Chandos, who acquired it in 1789. The portrait was engraved in Rowe's 1709 edition, and has been the key point of reference for the likeness of Shakespeare; see Vertue's Notebook entries in 1719, quoted in Tarnya Cooper, *Searching for Shakespeare* (London: National Portrait Gallery, 2006), 54, 57; on Shakespeare editors and Shakespeare's likeness, see also Margreta de Grazia, *Shakespeare verbatim: the reproduction of authenticity and the 1790 apparatus* (Oxford: Clarendon, 1991), 78.

[39] De Grazia, *Shakespeare Verbatim*, 82.

[40] Steevens, 'Advertisement', *The plays of William Shakspeare*, vol. I, ii.

tion. Validating Steevens's words, the portrait acts as a negative presentation: it denounces itself as an unreliable record, points to the impossibility of capturing Shakespeare's likeness, and deconstructs the author's portrait as a means of stabilizing the text.

Despite Steevens's position on Shakespeare's portraits, his dismissal prompts a whole gallery of likenesses of Shakespeare to be inserted between the leaves. The proliferation of engravings after the Chandos portrait exhibits differences in size, decoration and framing devices, from the most monumental and allegorical to the less ornate, emphasizing the range of social and aesthetic inflections of a technically reproduced image. Placed one after the other, such a spectrum of variations confirms Steevens's point and undermines the status suggested by van der Gucht's classical allusion, as the allegorical attributes of Rowe's frontispiece are revealed to be less durable stage props, when followed by three versions of Vertue's engraved portrait, Duchange's after Artaud, Hubert Gravelot's, Jacobus Houbraken's, 'a tail-piece to Mr Capell's Shakspeare',[41] John Hall's frontispiece of Johnson for Steevens's *Works of Shakespeare* (1785), Thomas Cook's frontispiece to John Bell's *Plays of William Shakespeare* (1788), Charles Knight's frontispiece to Malone's *The Plays and Poems of Shakespeare* (1786)[42] and Harding's Shakespeare for *Shakespeare Illustrated*. After such a cornucopia of likenesses, the reader has to leaf through two portraits of John Aubrey, Sir William Davenant, several of Gulielmus Lilius Astrologus and a William Faithorne before getting to page iii of the Advertisement, where the last four characters are justified as part of the ensuing argument about genealogical uncertainty transferred from Shakespeare's likeness to the question of his offspring. 'The verification of portraits was so little attended to, that both the Earl of Oxford, and Mr. Pope, admitted a juvenile one of King James I as that of Shakspeare,' Steevens concludes, criticizing a previous Shakespeare editor.[43] Yet if his charge against portrait appreciation indicates the imperfect early stages in the artistic and antiquarian work of verifying portraits, looking at Steevens's work as a Shakespeare scholar alongside his practice as extra-illustrator adds a further point to his critique of the interface between the orders of prints and books: instead of marking the threshold of the text, stabilizing the boundaries of the book and the author function as a 'principle of thrift in the proliferation of meaning', portraiture exhibits the desire and

---

[41] Edward Capell's *Mr William Shakespeare: his Comedies, Histories, and Tragedies*, 10 vols (1768–69), followed by *Notes and Various Readings to Shakespeare*, 3 vols (1779–83). Capell's crucial role in Shakespeare criticism is discussed in S. Jarvis, *Scholars and Gentlemen: Shakespearean Textual Criticism and Representations of Scholarly Labour, 1725–1765* (Oxford: Clarendon Press, 1995), 184–5, and M. Walsh, *Shakespeare, Milton and Eighteenth-Century Literary Editing: The Beginnings of Interpretative Scholarship* (Cambridge: Cambridge University Press, 1997), 182–4.

[42] De Grazia notes Malone's efforts to go back to the original in commissioning the Royal Academy miniaturist Ozias Humphry to copy the Chandos portrait for his 1786 edition, and in substituting Shakespeare's likeness from the Chandos portrait in reproducing the Stratford monument; *Shakespeare Verbatim*, 83–5.

[43] Steevens, 'Advertisement', *The plays of William Shakspeare*, vol. I, iii–iv.

deceptions inherent to referential anchoring, showing that the author's portrait is a changing cultural composite.

Steevens's critique of portraiture is driven home with a brilliant attack on Houbraken's monumental series of illustrious men:[44] 'Among the heads of illustrious persons engraved by Houbraiken [*sic.*], are several imaginary ones.' Drawing on an anecdote gathered from the auctioneer Abraham Langford, Steevens points out that 'the grandfather of Cock the auctioneer had the honour to personate the great and amiable Thurloe, secretary of state to Oliver Cromwell'.[45] Such imaginary impersonations become an opportunity for Steevens to bring into the paratext the portraits of Houbraken, Langford and Cock from a detail in a print of Hogarth's *Beggars' Opera*, and Johannes Thurloe taken 'From a medal in the possession of Dr Mead', instead of Houbraken's series. The substitution points to Steevens's desire to establish his superiority to Houbraken in identifying documentary evidence.

The accumulation of portraits evokes the Shakespeare collection of *Bibliotheca Steevensiana* and it brings into the body of the book the antiquarian's work of collecting and evaluating specimens—the work of Vertue, Reynolds and Steevens. Giving a face to those who participated in the effort to establish the eighteenth-century Shakespeare archive and representing the visual corpus that the text challenges, Steevens proves his point that the portraits 'are all unlike each other, and convey no distinct resemblance of the poor remains of their avowed original'.[46] As it interrupts the act of reading, extra-illustration breaks up the unities of the book. In the transition between two pages of letterpress, the volume opens up a space where specimens from all editions can be brought together into one meta-edition.[47] Much as the variorum footnotes illuminate the text with observations attributed to a variety of editors and other authors, the apparatus of extra-illustrations tests Jacques Derrida's notion that nothing is outside the text.[48] In this expanded 'hors-texte', the extra-illustrated book brings all books within the bindings and support of one book, showing the intersections between the orders of the book and the library and the dynamic collection that can open up in the space between words and pages.

How extra-illustration can host one book within another varies depending on the number, frequency and intervals that mark the inscription and dissemi-

---

[44] See Thomas Birch, *Heads of Illustrious Persons of Great Britain, engraven by Mr. Houbraken, and Mr. Vertue, With their lives and characters* (London: J. and P. Knapton, 1743).

[45] Jacobus Houbraken after Samuel Cooper, *John Thurloe*, line engraving, published 1738, NPG D28918.

[46] Steevens, 'Advertisement', *The plays of William Shakspeare*, vol. I, i.

[47] On the variorum and Samuel Johnson's sense of the 'syncretic character' of textual criticism, 'to be assembled by collecting the efforts of the many', see Jarvis, *Scholars and Gentlemen*, 162–5.

[48] J. Derrida, *Of Grammatology*, corrected edition, trans. G. C. Spivak (Baltimore: Johns Hopkins Press, 1997), 158; the bibliographical imagination in Derrida's sentence is theorized in P. McDonald, 'Ideas of the Book and Histories of Literature: After Theory?', *PMLA* (January 2006), 214–28, on 222–3.

nation of its plates, whether the book is alluded to by the systematic adoption of a series of plates or only represented by way of its frontispiece, or occasional plates; whether insertions are prompted by a local reference or a regular attempt to document a historical setting. Manuscript captions mark the regular inscription of plates from Joseph Strutt's *Regal and Ecclesiastical Antiquities* (1773). Strutt addressed the curious and the artist: 'those who have occasion to represent scenes from English history, may find the dress and character of the ancient times'.[49] The connection between dress and history, and the methodological practice of the antiquarian engraver, are spelt out in the work's subtitle: 'the Figures are principally introduced in Antient Delineations of the most remarkable Passages of History; and are correctly copied from the Originals ... The whole carefully collected from Antient Illuminated Manuscripts'. Drawn from specimens in the Royal Collection at the British Museum, the Bodleian Library and the Corpus Christi Library in Cambridge, Strutt's etchings provide a uniform idiom that subsumes differences in genre, from charters and articles of the peace between Edward III and David King of Scotland to the Pseudo-Bonaventure's life of Christ. His illustrations include the horizontal composition adopted to depict the presentation of books to kings with figures taken from capital initial letters. The unifying agency of mechanical reproduction abstracts the portraits and manners of an earlier period and translates them into the coherent visual template of Strutt's publication. Yet Strutt's visual paradigm is disrupted in the visual economy of Steevens's extra-illustrated Shakespeare. When plates are disseminated across volumes, the attempt to translate the world of the illuminated manuscript is interrupted by the letterpress, by prints produced in different periods in a miscellany of styles and techniques, and by heterogeneous series of illustrious men, Oxford and Cambridge colleges, and landscapes. For instance, a footnote in *The Merchant of Venice* refers to deaths that occurred because of the bitter cold during Edward III's siege of Paris on the day after Easter as the source for the expression 'Black-Monday'.[50] This reference prompts the insertion of a portrait of Edward III in an oval frame decorated with foliage engraved by Vertue to illustrate Paul Rapin de Thoyras and Nicolas Tindal's *History of England*,[51] which is in stark stylistic contrast to the subsequent illustration, 'Edward III, giving to his son (Edward the black Prince) the conquered Provinces of France', reproduced from an illuminated initial letter in a charter by Strutt.[52] Both register the diversionary possibilities

---

[49] J. Strutt, *The Regal and Ecclesiastical Antiquities of England: containing ... representations of all the English Monarchs from Edward the Confessor to Henry the eigthth. Together with many of the great persons eminent under their reigns* (London, 1773), I; listed as item 1734 in *Bibliotheca Steevensiana*, 112.

[50] Steevens, *The plays of William Shakspeare*, Spencer 22347, vol. XIII, 442.

[51] Vertue, 'K. Edward III', in *The History of England. Written in French by Mr. Rapin de Thoyras. Translated into English, with Additional Notes, by N. Tindal*, 3rd edn, 4 vols (London: Knapton, 1743–1745), vol. IV, 190. See also Vertue's *The Heads of the Kings of England, proper for Mr Rapin's History* (London: Knapton, 1736).

[52] Strutt, *Regal and Ecclesiastical Antiquities*, 12.

of footnotes, which, in illuminating the historical substrate of Shakespeare's language, shift the attention from Shakespeare's play to the literary genres and visual formats of historical narrative.

Strutt's plates are more frequently inserted to illustrate the historical plays. Five feature in *King John*, where a hunting scene, which Strutt reproduced from a Forest Charter, is extra-illustrated as a frontispiece for the play. Its strong paratextual position mediates access to the text, anchoring it to Strutt's historical iconography.[53] However, this early manuscript aesthetic is soon subverted when 'bastard' Philip Falconbridge suggests wearing a rose in the ear. His choice prompts an iconographical footnote in which Steevens reminisces about Van Dyck's pictures in the Queensbury's collection at Ambrosbury and about a portrait of Elizabeth at Kirtling. This train of associations sets off an alternative visual order: to illustrate these references Steevens inserts a view of Ambrosbury, five portraits of Van Dyck, a print after one of his portraits and a 1791 view of Kirtling. This sequence is followed by Strutt's depiction of Henry II. This abrupt return to Strutt's manuscript aesthetic coincides with the transition to the next page of Shakespeare's play, where Henry II is invoked in a footnote to explain the line 'Arise Sir Richard, and Plantagenet': 'the surname of the royal house of England, from the time of King Henry II'.[54] The genealogical line is marked out by recourse to Strutt's manuscript aesthetic. The juxtaposition of different styles from different sources and periods emphasizes the miscellaneous, distracting and competing kinds of investigation explored in the footnotes. In the last two plates from Strutt's series inserted in *King John*, which represent the King receiving a cup of poison and Henry III's coronation,[55] the transition from the death of one king to the coronation of another is first sutured by the juxtaposition of two images taken from Strutt. However, the attempt to assert the continuity of the body politic is disrupted by a reminder of the mortality of the king's natural body on turning the page. The next print inserted in the play comes from a different time, a different medium and iconography: an aquatint captioned 'The body of King John, as it appeared on opening his tomb in Worcester cathedral, Monday July 17 1797'. In this case, extra-illustration exhibits the narrative potential of visual juxtapositions. The 1797 print supplements Steevens's edition of 1793 by updating the historical record; yet in doing so the aquatint not only disrupts the period setting, proposing an alternative to Strutt's style, it also subverts the continuity of kingship interrupted by the death of King John. The dead king's body brings into focus his questionable death and questions left unresolved centuries after

---

[53] Steevens, *The plays of William Shakspeare*, Spencer 22347, vol. VIII, 5; Strutt, *Regal and Ecclesiastical Antiquities*, 36.

[54] Steevens, *The plays of William Shakspeare*, Spencer 22347, vol. VIII, 16.

[55] Ibid., 174; Strutt, *Regal and Ecclesiastical Antiquities*, 10.

his decease.[56] These disjunctions show the contemporaneity of uncontemporaneous visual forms and historical codes in eighteenth-century visual culture.

While Strutt simulates the world of fifteenth-century manuscripts to establish the historical mise en scène of Shakespeare's plays, other books are represented in Steevens's extra-illustrated book by their frontispieces. Extra-illustrated frontispieces bring a potential library within the boundaries of the book. Yet this act of supplementation may distract from reading the text. Unlike illustrations, frontispieces are less adapted to be repurposed as separate plates to a new text. Instead of mediating the entrance to the text, marking its boundaries, guiding the reader into its fictional world and distinguishing the reading experience from its outside, extra-illustrated frontispieces are disturbed from their position at the threshold of the text for which they were intended. Inserted into the middle of the new book, they interrupt the textual continuum, disrupt the relationship between the new paratext and text, and guide the reader out of the reading experience. Their insertion also disrupts the hierarchy of the book at the level of the page. When they anchor a footnote to its referent, extra-illustrations emphasize how Shakespeare is read through a body of modern writing, spelling out his place in the expanded field of English writing. Wenceslaus Hollar's 1660 frontispiece for the posthumous edition of Richard Lovelace's *Lucasta Posthume Poems of R.L.*, followed by two portraits of the author, illustrate a footnote that identifies in a passage in *Coriolanus* the source of two lines from 'To Althea from Prison', a poem not included in Lovelace's posthumous collection.[57] The frontispiece to the last edition of Samuel Daniel's *The Civile Wares betweene the Howses of Lancaster and Yorke corrected and continued* (1609), first published in 1595 and discussed as a source for the historical plays, especially *Richard II*, is inserted instead in *Cymbeline,* chosen for its portrait of the author to illustrate a footnote reference to other works by Daniel, *Cleopatra* (1599) and *Hymen's Triumph a Masque* (1623).[58] Thomas Blount's *The Academy of Eloquence* (1654) puts Shakespeare's *Pericles* in the context of the art of rhetoric.[59] A series of compliments in *King John*, explained in footnote in relation to an essay by Sir William Cornwallis that 'ridicules

---

[56] The contemporaneity of the question of the body of the king is noted in handwriting in Edmond Malone's copy of Steevens's 1793 edition in the margin of the passage extra-illustrated by Steevens in Spencer 22347: see *The plays of William Shakspeare*, vol. VIII, 185, University of Oxford, Bodleian Library, Mal. C.186: '[*At Worcester must his body be interr'd*] A stone coffin, containing the Body of King John, was discovered in the Cathedral Church of Worcester, July 1. 1797. STEEVENS'.

[57] Steevens, *The plays of William Shakspeare*, Spencer 22347, vol. XII, 63.

[58] Ibid., vol. XIII, between 16 and 17, illustrating footnote on 17.

[59] Ibid., notice of *Pericles. The Academie of Eloquence. Containing a Compleat English Rhetorique, Exemplified, with Common-Places, and Formes, digested into an easie and Methodical way to speak and write fluently, according to the mode of the present times* (London: Moseley, 1654). The frontispiece includes oval portraits of Demosthenes, Cicero, Bacon and Sir Philip Sidney; the only direct connection can be drawn from 'The Epistle Dedicatory': 'Pericles (the orator) was no less Tyrant in Athens then Pysistratus; without acknowledging other difference, then that this exercis'd his Empire armed, the other without armes, by the sole terror of his speech.'

the extravagance of compliment in our poet's days', prompts the insertion of the title page of Cornwallis's *Essays* (1632).[60] A long footnote in *Pericles* on 'hatch'd' doors in brothels prompts the facsimile of the frontispiece of *Essayes and Characters of a Prison and Prisoners* (1638), a work that Steevens owned.[61] Leonard Mascall's *The Government of Cattle* (1662) enters the world of *Hamlet* through a footnote detailing the debate on how to spell the word 'plurisy', including an observation attributed to Tollet: 'this passage is fully explained by one in Mascal's treatise on cattle, 1662, p. 187'.[62] Steevens's range exhibits the supplementary relationship between footnotes and extra-illustrated frontispieces. In disrupting the continuity of the work with attempts to stand for books within the book, frontispieces emphasize the work's reference to other books, its dynamic shape in the fantastic hybrid permutations of the library.

The tension between restoring the meaning of the author's words and dissolving them in the medium of the English language was captured by Capell when he opted for a clean page aesthetic, isolated Shakespeare's text, and thus attempted to avoid what he called the 'paginary intermixture of text and comment' by moving the critical apparatus to a different volume.[63] Against Capell's separation of text and commentary, Steevens's variorum edition and his practice of extra-illustration exhibit the work's syncretic and dialogical materiality. In its encyclopedic reaches, Steevens's assemblage incorporates portraits of kings, authors, religious reformers, artists and other figures mentioned in the text. In addition to more predictable sets of Shakespeare illustrations and plates from John Thane's *British Authography* (1788–93) that reproduced portraits with facsimiles of handwriting, Steevens also disseminated across his Shakespeare volumes sets such as the highly decorated portraits of Sultans from Theodore de Bry's *Vitae et Icones Sultanorum Turcicorum* (1596). Steevens's extra-illustrated Shakespeare is established as unique not for its integrity as a material object, nor for the uniqueness of what he chose to extra-illustrate in his volume, but as a composite form, a collection of curious specimens from a variety of periods, styles and sources.

The other extra-illustrated Shakespeare in the Althorp collection was assembled between 1790 and 1806 by Margaret Bingham, Lady Lucan, with the help of her daughter Lavinia, Countess Spencer, aristocratic amateur artists who had gained a reputation for their practice of copying, which Kim Sloan argues was the key medium for women's connoisseurship.[64] Lady Lucan's progress in miniature was celebrated by Horace Walpole in *Anecdotes of Painting in England*: 'she has transferred the vigour of Raphael to her copies in water-colour'.[65] Her

---

[60] Steevens, *The plays of William Shakspeare*, Spencer 22347, vol. VIII, 22.

[61] Ibid., vol. XIII, 533–55; see *Bibliotheca Steevensiana*, 66, no. 1108.

[62] Steevens, *The plays of William Shakspeare*, Spencer 22347, vol. XV, 289.

[63] Quoted in Walsh, *Shakespeare, Milton, and Eighteenth-Century Literary Editing*, 183.

[64] Kim Sloan, *A Noble Art: Amateur Artists and Drawing Masters c. 1600–1800* (London: British Museum, 2000), 213.

[65] Walpole, 'Advertisement', *Anecdotes of Painting in England* (1771), vol. IV, viii; mother and daughter are listed under 'Works of Genius at Strawberry Hill by Persons of rank & Gentlemen not

attitude as a connoisseur is captured in a portrait by Angelica Kauffmann in the pose of a Michelangelesque sibyl while leafing through a book of engravings.[66] Walpole's correspondence documents mother and daughter copying in the Uffizi Gallery, loaning pictures to copy, and finally the daughter's marriage to John George Earl Spencer in 1780.[67]

Lady Lucan's extra-illustrations are inlaid in an edition published in numbers between 1791 and 1800 by William Bulmer at the Shakespeare Press to accompany the engravings from the Boydell Shakespeare Gallery. From the Boydell edition they take the elegant letterpress set by Bulmer using Caslon types, but discard the body of illustrations, reclaiming Shakespeare from the bourgeois aesthetic of the portable gallery of prints:

> These magnificent volumes ... are at once beautified and secured by green velvet binding, with embossed clasps and corners of solid silver, washed with gold. Each volume is preserved in a silken cover—and the whole is kept inviolate from the impurities of bibliomaniacal miasmata, in a sarcophagus-shaped piece of furniture of cedar and mahogany.[68]

Dibdin's account is borne out by bills copied in handwriting on the first page of the Lucan Spencer Shakespeare, which describe the binding by Charles Hering, who bound Spencer's prized copy of the *Odyssey* published by Aldus Manutius in 1504, as well as three Caxtons. Although Lady Lucan's Shakespeare was stored separately in a bespoke cabinet made by Hugh Dalrymple, its bindings spell out physical properties shared with the most valuable treasures in the collection.[69] The bill bound in the first volume details the purchase of 'very richly chased Gothic corners for the binding of Shakespear's works with the cognizances of the different Kings on each in silver-gilt, & 10 very richly chased Gothic clasps'. While Boydell's Shakespeare celebrated the patronage of the people against the monopoly of

---

Artists'.

[66] See mezzotint by James Watson, 1 April 1776, and in a later stipple engraving by Samuel Freeman, published by Dibdin after Robert William Satchwell, after Angelica Kauffmann (both National Portrait Gallery).

[67] Horace Mann to Horace Walpole, 27 October 1778, *The Yale Edition of Horace Walpole's Correspondence*, ed. W. S. Lewis (New Haven, CT: Yale University Press, 1937–83), vol. 24, 417; Walpole to Mann, 9 May 1779, vol. 24, 475; Walpole to Mann, 12 December 1780, vol. 25, 104.

[68] Dibdin, *Bibliomania*, 667. A few years later the cabinet was held responsible for the 'muriatic leprosy' that had, in so few years, spotted the volumes, and was disposed of in favour of one entirely in mahogany; see *Bibliographical Decameron*, vol. II, 340n, quoted in Judith Goldstein Marks, 'Bookbinding practices of the Hering Family, 1794–1844', *British Library Journal* (1980), 44–60, on 47.

[69] Marks, 'Bookbinding practices of the Hering Family, 1794-1844', 46–7; see Dibdin, *Bibliotheca Spenceriana*, vol. II, 520, and 525 on Charles Hering as 'rather sound and substantial, than elegant and classical'; vol. II, 349 on a Hering binding in the Aldine Cabinet; see also vol. III, 29, 357.

Royal painters, the Lucan Spencer Shakespeare inscribes the bard in a royal and aristocratic lineage.

The customized volumes' structure of address is expressed in the new paratext. New title pages for each play customize the edition as 'The Historical Plays written by William Shakespeare and Illuminated for George John Earl Spencer by Margaret Lady Lucan'. In a letter accompanying the last parcel completing her Shakespeare, dated October 1806, Lady Lucan presents the book to Lord Spenser: 'if ye performance was equal to my love of you it wou'd be a nonpareille of a book indeed'.[70] The family gift articulates a relationship marked by the desire to acknowledge and elevate the visual heritage that the Lucans have joined in their match with the Spencers. Alongside her recognized ability to reproduce the aesthetic of seventeenth-century miniature portraits, Lady Lucan's economy of emulation is expressed in her practice of copying the Old Masters and Modern paintings in the Althorp collection and then presenting her miniatures as gifts. Her extra-illustrations of Shakespeare similarly attempt to recreate and inhabit an anachronistic past with which to overwrite eighteenth-century print culture. Watercolour illuminations delicately inlaid in precious golden frames evoke an aesthetic of manuscript illumination, which is at its most evident in its references to the Bedford Book of Hours and the visual culture of the Duc de Berri in the illustrations to *Henry V*.[71]

The portrait of John Plantagenet, Duke of Bedford and Regent of France, offers a point of comparison between Lady Lucan's and Steevens's extra-illustrations. Both extra-illustrate *Henry V* with a portrait of the Duke drawn from the Bedford Book of Hours. In the illuminated manuscript the owner is represented in a kneeling position in the act of praying to St George.[72] The portrait had been copied by Vertue, who abstracted this detail from its original composition and its medium, added a decorative frame in the mode of the heads of illustrious men, and engraved it as part of his collection of heads of the Kings and Queens of England to be inserted in Rapin's *History of England*. While Steevens inserts Vertue's engraved portrait with its original caption, which mentions its illuminated manuscript source,[73] Lady Lucan's watercolour emulates the original manuscript illumination and discards the portrait's afterlife as an engraving.[74]

---

[70] Margaret Bingham, Lady Lucan to John George Earl Spencer, October 1806, British Library, Althorp Papers G.210, Add. 75982.

[71] The Bedford Book of Hours was in the sale catalogue of the Duchess of Portland's Museum (1786) and George III aimed to buy it for Eton College, but was outbid by the bookseller James Edwards. It was discussed in R. Gough, *An Account of the Rich Illuminated Missal Executed for John Duke of Bedford* (London, 1794), then appeared in the sale catalogue of Edwards' library in 1815; see A.N.L. Munby, *Connoisseurs and Medieval Miniatures* (Oxford: 1972), 3–8.

[72] British Library, Add. MS 18850, f. 256v, reproduced online at http://www.bl.uk/onlinegallery/sacredtexts/bedford_lg.html, accessed 9 January 2015.

[73] 'From a curious Limning in a (MS) rich Prayerbook presented by himself to K. Hen 6 now in the possession of the Earl of Oxford.'

[74] Dibdin, *Bibliotheca Spenceriana*, vol. III, after p. 58; Dibdin, *Aedes Althorpianae*, 202.

Lady Lucan's ambivalent relationship with the world of collecting and extra-illustration comes through Dibdin's suggestion that it requires a sarcophagus-shaped cabinet and a binding protected by silver gilt clasps to keep the volumes safe from what he calls 'bibliomaniacal miasmata'. The analogy between opening the volumes and a corpse that should not be disinterred rearticulates a recurrent metaphoric of illness also used to describe 'the poisonous miasmata floating in the auction-room' and the 'the miasmata of the BOOK-PLAGUE'.[75] Dibdin's medical metaphoric suggests the need for special binding and storage arrangements to protect and preserve Lady Lucan's Shakespeare abstracted from the circuits of commodity exchange and inscribed in aristocratic orders of books. In his expanded description of the edition in *Aedes Althorpianae*, Dibdin praised Lady Lucan's choice of the historical plays, 'because the characters introduced, the events in which they were engaged, and the places which were the most remarkable scenes of their transactions, were capable of being judiciously represented by means of portraits, or of local transcripts'.[76] Turning Shakespeare's text into a series of antiquarian subjects and operations, Dibdin raises the expectation of a grangerite work. The antiquarian trail and copying practice of extra-illustrators certainly informs Lady Lucan's choice of subjects. Scenes are often decorated with watercolour head vignettes that visualize and caption the site where the action takes place, as well as portraits, cognizances of the aristocratic figures involved and maps of battles. Lady Lucan's reliance on a shared body of print culture comes across in her letter to Lord Spencer, in which she declares the extra-illustration project 'I believe finish'd but if you find any thing more I can very easily add it, I have used every thing I cou'd find'.[77] However, the aristocratic focus and the uniform medium of execution differentiate her work from the prints of the same subject in other extra-illustrated editions of the plays. Unlike the miscellaneous world of grangerite collections, the Lucan Spencer illuminations remediate an earlier aesthetic practice.

Against the impression that the present is being erased and the text restored to the visual aesthetic of the times in which the action takes place, the work's eighteenth-century inflections are spelt out in the title pages, which often allude to the eighteenth-century canonizations and memorializations of Shakespeare. Each volume includes two plays and therefore two iterations of the title page, each with a different illumination. In Volume I, the second title page, which precedes *Richard II*, inscribes epigraphs going from Milton's sonnet on Shakespeare, published in the second folio in 1632, to lines from *L'Allegro* ('Sweetest Shakespeare, Fancy's child, / warbles his native woodnotes wild'), but also from Dryden, Akenside, Ben Jonson, Otway, Dr Johnson, Gray, Thomson, Churchill and Hayley, most of which could be read in the Prolegomena of Steevens's

[75] Dibdin, *Bibliomania*, 405, 543; see also 458, 554.
[76] Dibdin, *Aedes Althorpianae*, 200–1.
[77] Margaret Bingham, Lady Lucan to John George Earl Spencer, October 1806, British Library, Althorp Papers G.210, Add. 75982.

1793 edition.[78] The title page opening Volume III is inscribed with a depiction of the Temple erected by David Garrick in honour of Shakespeare;[79] the second title page in the volume features a sculpture of Shakespeare, inscribed again with Milton's epigraph. The second title page for Volume III, introducing *Henry VI Part I*, reproduces Thomas Banks's alto relievo sculpture of Shakespeare touching the shoulder of genius while the dramatic muse reaches up to crown him with laurel, which was placed above the entrance to the Shakespeare Gallery in Pall Mall, and reproduced as a frontispiece to its 1803 collection of prints. The title page for Volume IV, introducing *Henry VI Part II*, features a sketch of the funerary monument to Shakespeare in Holy Trinity Church, Stratford-upon-Avon, easily available in Harding's collection of prints for extra-illustrators, among others. The play concludes with the vignette of a naval scene inscribed 'Battle of ye Nile on yr 1st and 2d of Aug 1798'. Similarly, the end vignette of *Henry VI Part III* is inscribed with 'The success | of Patriotic Labour' and features a pedestal with a crown of leaves, in each of which is inscribed the name of a battle. Combined with the flag and the Magna Carta on the title page of Volume I, these inscriptions inflect Shakespeare in the present tense as a homage to Spencer as Lord of the Admiralty.

Like the theatre, which is being stretched so that it may hold the fields of France in the First Chorus of Shakespeare's *Henry V*, extra-illustration extends the book to hold a portable library of excerpts within its bindings. However, while the battle of Agincourt can only fit in the 'wooden O' by a stretch of the imagination, at the cost of dematerializing the walls of the theatre, extra-illustration materializes the words on the page. Against the editor's task to establish the letter of the text, the referential impulse of extra-illustration brings into view the digressive possibilities of words, their paradigmatic flight into series and catalogues. 'The imaginary ... grows among signs, from book to book, in the interstice of repetitions and commentaries. It is born and takes the shape in the interval between books. It is a phenomenon of the library,' argued Foucault. Extra-illustration exhibits its materiality. Dispersed in the cornucopian forms of the extra-illustrated book, the multiplication of referents, documents, prints and copies inlaid again and again from one extra-illustrator to another shows the non-identity of multiples in the varying anchorings, combinations and rhythms of each collector's act of reading.

---

[78] Steevens, *Shakespeare*, vol. II, 507 ff.

[79] On Garrick's monument and the Shakespeare Jubilee, see M. Dobson, *The Making of the National Poet: Shakespeare, Adaptation, and Authorship, 1660–1769* (Oxford: Clarendon Press, 1992), 134–84, 214–22.

CHAPTER 30

Paperslips

Leanna McLaughlin

In 1728, William Moore's infant great nephew and nieces brought a chancery lawsuit against Martha Daniel, housekeeper, accusing her of forging his will, diminishing the value of the estate, lying, embezzling, and conspiracy to defraud. In the investigation that legally (if not morally) exonerated her, a bundle of manuscript poems from the Revolution of 1688 was found among the estate papers. These verses were handwritten by multiple people, but not produced by a scriptorium; they were loosely kept together, but not preserved in a commonplace book. Today, these slips of paper are lying in a box at the National Archives, bound in linen tape, begging the question: why did the third Earl of Drogheda's brother keep them?

All of the poems sympathized with the Whig position at the Revolution.

"Four Toms and Nat" accused the royal family of conspiring to foist a changeling child onto the nation to promote Catholicism's grasp on the country; "The Fable of the Pot and the Kettle" warned Whigs against believing James II's conciliatory gestures towards dissenters. One poet expressed anger "on the Lord Chancellor's restoring the citty charter":

A thief that gravely beares away the prize

Proclaimes his valour in the enterprise

But hee who basely steales & brings it home

L. McLaughlin (✉)
Department of History, University of California, Riverside, CA, USA
e-mail: leanna.mclaughlin@email.ucr.edu

© The Author(s) 2016
A. Craciun, S. Schaffer (eds.), *The Material Cultures of Enlightenment Arts and Sciences*, Palgrave Studies in the Enlightenment, Romanticism and the Cultures of Print, DOI 10.1057/978-1-137-44379-3_30

Fig. 30.1   Satirical Verses in Moore v. Daniel (c.1688), C110/80, Permission to publish granted by The National Archives of the United Kingdom

Let Herr van Brugh or Tyburne be his doome

X Dutch for the Mobile[1]

The threat of a Dutch invasion was looming. James's attempt to win London's loyalty by restoring the corporation charter in October 1688 was too little, too late. Popular support was for the Dutch invasion, and the Dutch, in turn, would support the mobile army. For the Moores, however, the poems represented their family's personal involvement in the "Glorious" Revolution. In 1689, the Irish Parliament attainted Drogheda for his absence, and the next year he earned notoriety fighting against James II at the Battle of the Boyne. These poems reflected, and arguably confirmed, Drogheda's political actions.

Revolutionary poetry was a culmination of the explosion of political verse throughout the 1680s. Different from treatises, pamphlets, or sermons, in both length and rhetorical style, verses were the early modern version of the Internet meme. Utilizing cultural and political concepts familiar to its audience, poetry became a meeting ground for rhetorical warfare, provoking retaliations and parodies, and evolving to meet emerging interpretations and circumstances. Verses were as ephemeral as political consciousness. Initially, much of this critical verse originated in the quarrels of court factions. As national anxiety regarding Catholicism heightened, Whig and Tory partisans used the poetry to garner popular support for parliamentary agendas. By leaking court criticism into the city of London on paperslips, poems undermined the authority of the government by fostering doubt in the minds of the populace. Distinctively, poetry

---

[1] National Archives, "Four Toms and Nat," "The Fable of the Pot and Kettle," and "On the Lord Chancellor's Restoring the Citty Charter," C110/80.

popped up everywhere. Verse were found tacked over chamber and church doors, on statues, over privy stairs, left on tabletops of parlors, coffeehouses, or pubs, and pinned onto gates. Shortly after James II's accession, John Newman "saw a paper stuck about four foot high upon the gate … fastened only with four small pins."[2] This alarming paperslip accused James II of planning 'Prodistant' massacres reminiscent of Queen Mary's reign.[3] Reactions to the message, however, depended entirely on the reader.

To an anxious population, verses exposed secrets. To astute partisans, they provided justification for political change. In 1688, "most [were] of opinion" that "the prince of wale [*sic.*] /…When he come out / A double clout / Will cover his dominion."[4] Anti-Catholic partisans seized the opportunity afforded by a Dutch invasion to overthrow their existing government. In short, poetry had a political life and paperslip verse was a revolutionary political tool.

[2] BL Add. MSS 41803, f. 164.

[3] Ibid., f. 163. NB: This document does have what appears to be a pinhole in the upper left-hand corner.

[4] National Archives, "Four Toms and Nat," C110/80.

CHAPTER 31

Advertising and Print Culture in the Eighteenth Century

Philippa Hubbard

Following the death of her husband in 1749, Elizabeth Griffin became proprietor of a print shop on Fleet Street[1] and updated the business's shop bill to include her name.[2] In contrast to text-dominated newspaper advertisements and handbills, Griffin's elaborate trade card did not merely disseminate information on the store's new owner, location and stock. It offered a visual display designed to instruct and entertain while shaping ideas about consumption and graphic print in the eighteenth century.

Trade cards were engraved and printed in the same workshops as other prints and shared a graphic vocabulary with images offering visual commentaries on everything from modern manners to scientific progress.[3] Griffin's engraved 'medley' print invited readers to decode its maze of competing images.[4] This visual cornucopia, arranged around a calligraphic trade card, promoted

---

[1] Sheila O'Connell (ed.), *London 1753* (London: The British Museum Press, 2003), 65.

[2] The contemporary terms 'shop bill' or 'shopkeepers' bill' were used to describe the graphic notices that tradespeople employed to promote their businesses. Malachy Postlethwayt's dictionary defines 'bill' as 'an account of merchandises or goods delivered to a person, or of work done for one' and a 'written and printed' statement 'handed about'. See Postlethwayt, *The Universal Dictionary of Trade and Commerce* ..., 3rd edn. vol. I. (London, 1766). Today these notices are commonly referred to as trade cards, a term coined by nineteenth-century collectors.

[3] Maxine Berg and Helen Clifford, 'Selling Consumption in the Eighteenth Century: Advertising and the Trade Card in Britain and France', *Cultural and Social History*, 4:2 (2007), 145–170, on 149.

[4] For an in-depth study on medley prints, see Mark Hallett, 'The Medley Print in Early Eighteenth-Century London', *Art History*, 20:2 (1997), 214–237, and Hallett, *The Spectacle of Difference: Graphic Satire in the Age of Hogarth* (New Haven and London: Yale University Press, 1999).

P. Hubbard (✉)
Independent Scholar, Institute of Advanced Study, University of Warwick,
Coventry, UK
e-mail: philippahubbard@gmail.com

© The Author(s) 2016   259
A. Craciun, S. Schaffer (eds.), *The Material Cultures of Enlightenment Arts and Sciences*, Palgrave Studies in the Enlightenment, Romanticism and the Cultures of Print, DOI 10.1057/978-1-137-44379-3_31

Fig. 31.1 Trade card of Elizabeth Griffin, printseller (*c.* 1749). City of London, London Metropolitan Archives

Griffin's more traditional stock in trade—maps and mezzotints—alongside a plate from Matthias Lock's *A Book of Ornaments*, a watch paper, a drawing study and satirical prints. Collectively these disparate engravings celebrated the rise of an English print market offering a wider range of consumers a greater variety of images,[5] the appeal of which was grounded in the novel, didactic and subversive, qualities embodied by Griffin's own trade card.

As small engravings selectively distributed to shoppers, trade cards played a role as commercial gifts in credit relations.[6] Tradespeople frequently adapted their shop bills to record invoices, issuing customers with a polite reminder of their status as both privileged consumer and debtor. These finely engraved

---

[5] Timothy Clayton, *The English Print, 1688–1802* (New Haven and London: Yale University Press, 1997).

[6] For more on this theme see Philippa Hubbard, 'Trade Cards in 18th-Century Consumer Culture: Movement, Circulation and Exchange in Commercial and Collecting Spaces', *Material Culture Review*, 74–75 (Spring 2012), 30–46.

prints endorsed with personal information became private gifts of thanks and a form of contract between shopkeepers and customers.

The material character of Griffin's trade card indicates its transition from commercial notice to personal possession. This damaged and incomplete example includes annotations suggestive of an attempt to link its visual detail to topical events. 'Eliz'h Canning', written above the face of a screaming woman, refers to the servant at the centre of a scandal in 1753. Griffin's card is also lacking its original text, representing the practice by collectors of occasionally removing textual elements from trade cards. The mounted image conceals any potential evidence of its former use as an invoice or receipt, further indicating the motivations of a collector who retained the object for its visual appeal rather than its value as trade literature.

Griffin's advertisement inserts the trade card into the wider narrative of print culture in the mid-eighteenth century. It celebrates the expanding market for graphic images at that time and the trade card as an established print genre. Visually sophisticated trade cards like Griffin's embodied the commercial potential for English print, helping shape a flourishing market for printed commodities. As engravings and business notices, trade cards challenge perceptions of what constituted collectable graphic art in the past.

CHAPTER 32

Kitty Fisher: The Commodification of Celebrity

Faramerz Dabhoiwala

In the spring of 1759, Kitty Fisher was the most famous sexual celebrity in the English-speaking world. She was only 17, and fresh on the scene as a leading courtesan. Yet already she was so well known as to be regularly and casually referred to by poets, journalists and writers of all kinds. The public appetite for news about her seems to have been huge.[1]

So feverish was this media interest and exploitation that even the tiniest incident could get blown up into a major media affair. When, one day in March 1759, she fell off her horse during a regular ride in St James's Park, this split-second incident inspired literally *months* of public comment, songs, verses, pictures and pamphlets—entire books were written about it.

Kitty Fisher was of course a fallen woman, so her actually falling off a horse was, to eighteenth-century sensibilities, just too perfectly symbolic. However, this extraordinary episode also marked an important turning point. In response to it, Kitty Fisher did two completely unprecedented things.

First, she took out a prominent newspaper advertisement, deploring the constant exploitation of her persona by mercenary 'little Scribblers' and print sellers, who foisted spurious writings and images of her on the public. 'She hopes to prevent the success of their Endeavours', it concluded confidently, 'by thus publickly declaring that nothing of that Sort has the slightest Foundation

---

[1] <Footnote ID="Fn1"><Para ID="Par4">Faramerz Dabhoiwala, *<Emphasis aid:cstyle="Italic" Type="Italic">The Origins of Sex: A History of the First Sexual Revolution</Emphasis>* (London, 2012), chapter 6.</Para></Footnote>

F. Dabhoiwala (✉)
Faculty of History, University of Oxford, Oxford, UK
e-mail: faramerz.dabhoiwala@exeter.ox.ac.uk

© The Author(s) 2016
A. Craciun, S. Schaffer (eds.), *The Material Cultures of Enlightenment Arts and Sciences*, Palgrave Studies in the Enlightenment, Romanticism and the Cultures of Print, DOI 10.1057/978-1-137-44379-3_32

Fig. 32.1   Nathaniel Hone, *Kitty Fisher* (1765), oil on canvas, 749×622 mm. ©
National Portrait Gallery, London

in Truth'.[2] Then, just a few days later, with equal assurance, she walked into the
studio of Joshua Reynolds, the greatest image maker of the day.

Together, over the years that followed, the two of them took control of Kitty
Fisher's public image. From the spring of 1759 onwards, Reynolds painted a
series of exquisite portraits, showing her as she wanted to be seen—as a stun-

[2] <Footnote ID="Fn2"><Para ID="Par8"><*Emphasis aid:cstyle="Italic" Type="Italic">The
Public Advertiser</Emphasis*> (24 and 29 March 1759).</Para></Footnote>

ning, self-possessed woman; as a flirtatious lover; as a great beauty of antiquity. Most importantly, these authorized, self-promoting images were made immediately available to a mass audience, as cheap prints in all shapes and sizes. In the space of just five or six years, perhaps as many as a dozen different prints of Kitty Fisher were published. There were even tiny circular ones for insertion into one's pocket watch, so that her admirers could walk around all day with a private picture of her close to their heart.[3]

This was the moment at which the commodification of sexual celebrity really took off. Henceforth, Reynolds and other society portraitists regularly exhibited (and then published as prints) portraits of leading *demi-mondaines*—boosting their own public profile, and fuelling the celebrity of their sitters, to their mutual benefit. By 1765, it was noted that prints of celebrated ladies of pleasure were both extraordinarily cheap ('a few guineas will buy a whole seraglio') and issued in huge editions, of 3000–4000 at a time.[4] Even after Kitty Fisher's death in 1767, Reynolds continued to paint new versions of her.

No engraving is known of the 1765 portrait by Nathaniel Hone illustrated here, but it nonetheless illustrates Fisher's mastery of visual self-presentation. Notice how alluringly she gazes out at us. Notice the prominent visual pun on her name. But notice above all the tiny reflection of the window of the room in which she is sitting. Just visible there is a crowd of people, pressed up against the panes, trying to catch a glimpse of the woman they adore. It is a brilliant visual epitome of the nature of modern celebrity, and of Kitty Fisher's witty, self-conscious manipulation of it.

[3] <Footnote ID="Fn3"><Para ID="Par10">Marcia Pointon, 'The Lives of Kitty Fisher', <Emphasis aid:cstyle="Italic" Type="Italic">Journal for Eighteenth-Century Studies</Emphasis> 27 (2004), 77–97; 'Catherine Maria Fischer', <Emphasis aid:cstyle="Italic" Type="Italic">Oxford Dictionary of National Biography</Emphasis> (Oxford, 2004).</Para></Footnote>

[4] <Footnote ID="Fn4"><Para ID="Par12">[Ange Goudar], <Emphasis aid:cstyle="Italic" Type="Italic">The Chinese Spy</Emphasis>, 6 vols (London, 1765), vol. 6, 208.</Para></Footnote>

CHAPTER 33

An Admirable Typology

Billie Lythberg, Maia Nuku, and Amiria Salmond

In the British Museum stores there is a broken bone needle attached to an old, curled label by a fine cord. Its faded copperplate inscription reads 'No. 65 Cloth from New Zeland'.

A number, a type of thing, a place; yet only the place name is immediately comprehensible. 'No. 65' and 'Cloth' depend on other elements for elucidation. The 'cloth' (since found and reunited with its label) is a finely woven Maori cloak of a kind that some call *kaitaka paepaeroa*. The significance of 'No. 65' is more mysterious.

A letter found in Cambridge offers a clue. In 1988 Peter Gathercole, former Curator of the University's Museum of Archaeology and Anthropology, wrote to the British Museum to propose a means of identifying items in the national collection acquired during Captain Cook's first Pacific voyage.[1] Gathercole was working with the largest group of artifacts known to have been collected on that voyage, belonging to Trinity College, Cambridge. Donated by the 4th Earl of Sandwich, it arrived in Cambridge in 1771 with a delivery note entitled 'An Inventory of Weapons, Utensils and Manufactures of various kinds collected by Capn. Cook of

---

[1] MAA archives (Box 252, folder OA4/1/6).

B. Lythberg (✉)
Mira Szászy Research Centre, University of Auckland, Auckland, NZ

Cambridge University Museum of Archaeology and Anthropology, UK
e-mail: b.lythberg@auckland.ac.nz

M. Nuku
Metropolitan Museum of Art, New York, US

A. Salmond
Anthropology Department, University of Auckland, Auckland, NZ

267

A. Craciun, S. Schaffer (eds.), *The Material Cultures of Enlightenment Arts and Sciences*, Palgrave Studies in the Enlightenment, Romanticism and the Cultures of Print, DOI 10.1057/978-1-137-44379-3_33

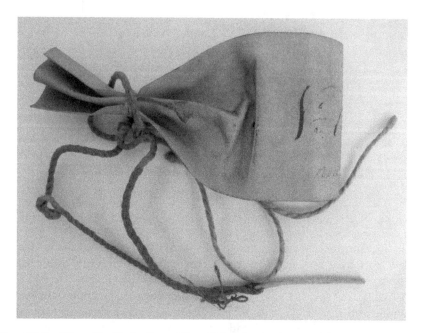

Fig. 33.1 'No. 65 Cloth from New Zeland'. Parchment label and bone pin. Photograph by Billie Lythberg (2011). © British Museum

His Maj. Ship the Endeavour in the years 1768, 1769, 1770 and 1771 in the new discovered South Sea Islands'. It listed the objects despatched from the Earl's seat at Hinchingbrooke according to numbered categories, including 'No. 1 Pad[d]les from New Ze[a]land', 'No. 49 Belts from Otaheite', 'No. 62 Dog Skin Dresses, from New Ze[a]land' and 'No. 73 Hemp from New Ze[a]land'. The list shows that a typology encompassing the many kinds of objects acquired on Cook's first voyage was drawn up either on board ship or at the Admiralty prior to the distribution of selected items to a number of recipients; gaps indicate that it had not been possible to provide representative examples of every type to every collector.

In his letter, Gathercole speculated that the types established in this initial sorting process might be related to numbers still attached to objects in the British Museum,[2] thus allowing them to be identified with the 'curious collection of weapons, utensils and manufactures of various sorts, sent from the Hota Hita and other newly discovered islands in the South Sea, and from New Zealand made by Captain Cook', received by the institution from the Admiralty in October 1771 (the same month that Sandwich's collection arrived in

---

[2] Gathercole mentions the survival of these numbers in catalogue entries in Adrienne Kaeppler's *"Artificial Curiosities" An Exposition of Native Manufactures Collected on the Three Pacific Voyages of Captain James Cook, R. N.* (Honolulu: Bishop Museum, 1978).

Cambridge).[3] Yet it was not until June 2011 that this connection was established, when the bone 'needle'—a cloak-fastening pin—drew attention to the label and its concise description, which matched the corresponding type number on the Sandwich inventory.[4]

In all, five objects in the British Museum stores were found to have labels corresponding to the Sandwich typology, and registration slips reveal at least a further two similarly categorized according to these types. Gathercole's suspicions confirmed by the finding of a 'needle', the reinstatement of their first-voyage provenance reconnected these objects with some of the earliest attempts to classify, categorize, understand, compare and contrast objects newly encountered, made and used by people in places long imagined but only recently 'discovered' by Europeans.

[3] *British and Medieval Antiquities Register* of the British Museum (1757–1878).

[4] Discoveries made by the authors during the AHRC- and ESRC-funded Artefacts of Encounter project at Cambridge University Museum of Archaeology and Anthropology, working alongside Jill Hasell of the British Museum in June 2011.

CHAPTER 34

Connoisseurship and the Communication of Anatomical Knowledge: The Case of William Cheselden's *Osteographia* (1733)

Alexander Wragge-Morley

It has often been claimed that eighteenth-century Britain witnessed a growing separation of artistic and scientific concerns. As the philosopher Jerome Stolnitz and many others have shown, the first half of the century witnessed the emergence of an autonomous aesthetic discourse, accompanying the emergence of a viable art market and of artistic institutions. Articulated by thinkers such as Joseph Addison, Anthony Ashley Cooper, 3rd Earl of Shaftesbury, and the moral philosopher Frances Hutcheson, this discourse idealized artistic appreciation as a disinterested pursuit of beauty, unburdened by material or financial considerations.[1] Such claims about the growing autonomy of the arts dovetail neatly with the equally widespread suggestion that, at exactly the same time, natural philosophers (the closest thing in the eighteenth century to scientists) were starting to see powerful affective experiences as having no place in scientific work. Lorraine Daston and Katharine Park have, for example, shown that many natural philosophers working in the eighteenth century came to see such experiences as prejudicial to calm, rational and useful scientific inquiry.[2] Arguments for the growing autonomy of the arts and sciences in the early eighteenth century have therefore been founded on the emergence of aesthetics as an intellectual discipline, paradoxically linked to the emergence of artistic

---

[1] J. Stolnitz, 'On the Origins of "Aesthetic Disinterestedness"', *The Journal of Aesthetics and Art Criticism* 20:2 (1961), 131–143, on 131–2.

[2] L. Daston and K. Park, *Wonders and the Order of Nature, 1150–1750* (New York: Zone Books, 2001), 355.

A. Wragge-Morley (✉)
Department of History, University College London, UK
e-mail: alexander.wragge-morley@ucl.ac.uk

A. Craciun, S. Schaffer (eds.), *The Material Cultures of Enlightenment Arts and Sciences*, Palgrave Studies in the Enlightenment, Romanticism and the Cultures of Print, DOI 10.1057/978-1-137-44379-3_34

commerce and institutions, and the apparent simultaneous hollowing out of the aesthetic content of the sciences.

Notwithstanding the continued influence of these broad claims, it is in fact well known that there were deep and persistent connections between the arts and sciences in the eighteenth century, connections that found intellectual, technical and social expressions.[3] In this essay I reconsider a body of evidence that has long proved difficult to incorporate into narratives of the emergence of the arts and sciences in their modern, autonomous forms—the mixture of aesthetic and scientific concerns that characterized the lives and works of Britain's elite medics in the eighteenth century. Many of the most successful medics of eighteenth-century Britain, including the physicians Richard Mead (1673–1754) and John Woodward (1665/67–1728), along with the surgeon William Cheselden (1688–1752), were committed to collecting and discussing material things of perceived value: paintings, drawings, prints, books and antiquities. They were important connoisseurs of the arts in their own right, and they backed up their commitment with considerable financial and social capital.[4]

While scholars have paid attention to the fact that eighteenth-century medics invested time, effort and money in the connoisseurship of art, antiquities and books, they have not generally appreciated the extent to which these activities informed the communication of medical knowledge itself. The best-known work on this subject is an essay by Ludmilla Jordanova concerning the choices in portraiture by the wealthy collector-physician Richard Mead. Over the course of his life, Mead gathered an enormous collection of paintings, drawings, prints, books, busts, medals and gems. Jordanova shows that Mead used his collection to draw attention to aspects of his identity as a medical practitioner in highly specific ways.[5] He used ancient coins apparently bearing representations of physicians, for example, to argue that medics of his own day ought to be

---

[3] E. Spary, 'Scientific Symmetries', *History of Science* 42 (2004), 1–46; J. Riskin, *Science in the Age of Sensibility: the Sentimental Empiricists of the French Enlightenment* (Chicago: University of Chicago Press, 2002); C.A. Hanson, *The English Virtuoso: Art, Medicine, and Antiquarianism in the Age of Empiricism* (Chicago: University of Chicago Press, 2009).

[4] In using the term 'connoisseurship', I simply wish to note that a great part of their activity consisted not only in aesthetic criticism, but in appraising the authenticity and value of artistic and antiquarian objects. I am therefore indebted to the large number of works on the history of connoisseurship in the eighteenth century, especially the ways in which connoisseurship was contested among the partisans of different artistic styles. A recent and instructive example is H. Mount, 'The Monkey with the Magnifying Glass: Constructions of the Connoisseur in Eighteenth-Century Britain', *Oxford Art Journal* 29 (2006), 167–184.

[5] As Jordanova shows, the size and scope of Mead's collection can be gathered from the auction catalogues printed in advance of its sale. His paintings, prints, drawings, sculptures, medals and coins were divided into three main sales, detailed in *A catalogue of the genuine and capital collection of pictures [...] of that late great and learned physician, Doctor Richard Mead* (London, 1754); *A catalogue of the genuine, entire and curious collection of prints and drawings [...] of the late Doctor Mead* (London, 1755); and *A catalogue of the genuine and entire collection of valuable gems, bronzes, marble and others busts and antiquities, of the late Doctor Mead* (London, 1755). His library was also sold off and catalogued in *Bibliotheca Meadiana, sive Catalogus Librorum Richardi Mead* (London, 1754).

accorded greater esteem by society. Mead employed his collection of coins and medals, so to speak, as an instrument for defining his own social standing and that of physicians in general. By surveying patterns in Mead's acquisition and display of portraits, Jordanova shows that eighteenth-century medics used connoisseurship to shape their social standing and thus their authority as medical practitioners.[6]

Here I will push questions about the interconnections between connoisseurship and medical knowledge in a different direction. While acknowledging the tremendous value of Jordanova's demonstrations of the imbrication of connoisseurship with the social and cultural world of elite medics, I suggest that the links she has identified ran even deeper. I do this by discussing in detail a beautiful and expensive anatomical atlas produced by the surgeon William Cheselden, *Osteographia, or the Anatomy of the Bones*, published in 1733. Cheselden advertised it for subscription in 1727, alerting potential subscribers that his proposed book would be as much a beautiful and expensive art object as a source of authoritative osteological knowledge.[7] I do not intend to restate the familiar, and entirely valid, argument that Cheselden, in common with other surgeons of his time, sought to raise the status of his discipline by associating it with the world of luxurious books, prints and works of art.[8] Instead, through a close engagement with the materiality of the *Osteographia*, I will uncover some of the connections that Cheselden and his readers made between the performance of connoisseurship, and the communication of useful anatomical knowledge.

One demonstration of these connections will be sought in Cheselden's own discussion of his book, in which, promiscuously mixing claims to ingenuity in connoisseurship and anatomy alike, he urged his readers to interpret the beauty and cost of the *Osteographia* as a sign of his own abilities as a philosopher of nature. I will also turn, however, to the only extended response to the book that has come down to us—one that has received virtually no scholarly attention. This is a pamphlet entitled *Animadversions on a Late Pompous Book, Intituled, Osteographia: or, The Anatomy of the Bones* (1735), by the surgeon John Douglas (d. 1743).[9] Sharply satirical in tone, this little pamphlet bursts the bubble of Cheselden's book through an assay of its entire materiality: from the text, to the absence of page numbers, to every single one of its many illustrations. Douglas used his observations on the *Osteographia* to demonstrate

---

[6] L. Jordanova, 'Portraits, People and Things: Richard Mead and Medical Identity', *History of Science* 41 (2003), 293–313, on 307. Jordanova derives this from the biographical account of Mead offered in W. MacMichael, *The Gold-headed Cane*, 2nd edn (London, 1828), 109.

[7] Cheselden advertised the work for potential subscribers in the London *Daily Journal* on each day that it came out from 18 April–1 May 1727.

[8] See for example M. Terrall, 'Natural Philosophy for Fashionable Readers,' in *Books and the Sciences in History*, ed. M. Frasca-Spada and N. Jardine (Cambridge: Cambridge University Press, 2000), 239–254.

[9] John Douglas, *Animadversions on a Late Pompous Book, Intituled, Osteographia: or, The Anatomy of the Bones* (London, 1735).

that Cheselden had defrauded the book's purchasers by attempting to pass off as beautiful and useful something that was, in reality, ugly and useless. Indeed, the qualities that Douglas identified in the book's prints—ugliness, inutility and excessive luxury—stood as powerful arguments against Cheselden's ability to make a range of judgements, including those concerning surgery and anatomy. Thus Douglas employed acts of connoisseurship to cast doubt on Cheselden's authority as a surgeon and anatomist, and vice versa.

CHESELDEN AND HIS OSTEOGRAPHIA

William Cheselden's fame has endured to our own times because of his contribution to eighteenth-century debates about vision and cognition. His report of what happened when, in 1728, he restored sight to a boy who had been blind since birth had immense significance for subsequent philosophical discussions concerning the interplay between sensation, cognition and the emotions, along with aesthetic theory.[10] In his own time, however, Cheselden was famous mainly as a surgeon, largely on account of his improvements to, and skills in, the surgical procedure for removing bladder stones—lithotomy. In 1723 Cheselden reported on his successes in using a method of lithotomy devised by John Douglas in a short book, *A Treatise on the High Operation for the Stone* (1723).[11] Although Cheselden acknowledged his debt to Douglas's work, Douglas nevertheless took umbrage at what he saw as the appropriation of his priority. This is indicated by the appearance in the same year of a short pamphlet by Robert Houston with the title *Lithotomus castratus; or, Mr. Cheselden's treatise on the high operation for the stone, throughly examin'd, and plainly found to be Lithotomia Douglassiana* (1723). Dedicated to the physician and satirist John Arbuthnot (bap. 1667–1735), this pamphlet sets out to show that Cheselden had falsely claimed Douglas's procedure as his own.[12] By 1725, Cheselden had in fact altered Douglas's procedure significantly (and for the better), as was advertised in pamphlets written by Cheselden's partisan James Douglas, the brother (confusingly) of John Douglas.[13]

---

[10] W. Cheselden, 'An Account of Some Observations Made by a Young Gentleman, Who Was Born Blind, or Lost His Sight so Early, That He Had no Remembrance of Ever Having Seen, and Was Couch d between 13 and 14 Years of Age', *Philosophical Transactions* 35 (1727–1728), 447–450. The best account of Cheselden's account and its role in the works of Condillac is J. Riskin, *Science in the Age of Sensibility: the Sentimental Empiricists of the French Enlightenment* (Chicago: University of Chicago Press, 2002), 19–67. On Edmund Burke's use of a racially charged moment in this account in his aesthetic theory, see M. Armstrong, '"The Effects of Blackness": Gender, Race, and the Sublime in Aesthetic Theories of Burke and Kant', *The Journal of Aesthetics and Art Criticism* 54 (1996), 213–36, on 219–20.

[11] W. Cheselden, *A treatise on the high operation for the stone* (London, 1723).

[12] R. Houstoun, *Lithotomus Castratus; or, Mr Cheselden's Treatise on the High Operation for the Stone, thoroughly examin'd, and plainly found to be Lithotomia Douglassiana [...]*. (London, 1723).

[13] James Douglas, *The History of the Lateral Operation: or, an account of the method of extracting a stone by making a wound near the great protuberance of the Os Ischium* (London, 1726) and

The attacks that John Douglas and his supporters made did little to sully Cheselden's reputation. His second published work, *The Anatomy of the Humane Body* (1713), was republished continually during the eighteenth century, serving effectively as the standard Anglophone anatomical textbook.[14] In common with many other successful medics of eighteenth-century London (such as his close friend Richard Mead), Cheselden maintained interests in art and connoisseurship that transgress modern disciplinary boundaries. It is clear that he had much more than a passing interest in fine art and that he had at least some mastery of its discourses and practices. Moreover, there is quite a lot of evidence to suggest that Cheselden's contemporaries saw him as a man of good judgement in architecture, art and *belles lettres*. From 1720 to 1724 Cheselden made a study of drawing, attending classes at the academy of art run by the painter Louis Chéron and the portraitist John Vanderbank. Ilaria Bignamini and Martin Postle have suggested that the Huguenot painter Chéron modified his approach to anatomical studies as a result of his interactions with Cheselden.[15] Cheselden also counted some of the leading artists of the day, including William Hogarth and Jonathan Richardson, as friends.[16]

From almost the beginning of his career in the publication of anatomical books, Cheselden chose to address anatomical knowledge, in the form of books and lectures, squarely to genteel, non-specialist listeners and readers (although he also continued to publish cheap books for medical students).[17] In doing so, he was emulating what many of his contemporaries were undertaking to win prestige in the fiercely competitive London medical scene. Richard Mead, for example, arranged the publication of a second edition of William Cowper's *Myotomia Reformata* (1724), a work that had been issued as a plain and instructive octavo volume in 1694. The second edition, by contrast, is a lavish folio featuring large numbers of finely executed prints by the fashionable engraver Michael Vandergucht.[18] Subsequently, in making the *Osteographia*,

Douglas, *An appendix to the history of the lateral operation for the stone. Containing Mr Cheselden's present method* (London, 1731).

[14] By 1792, 13 editions of the work had been printed.

[15] I. Bignamini and M. Postle, *The Artist's Model: Its Role in British Art from Lely to Etty* (Nottingham: Nottingham University Art Gallery, 1991), 10.

[16] Bignamini and Postle, *The Artist's Model*, 12–13, 86; J. Kirkup, "Cheselden, William (1688–1752)," in Oxford Dictionary of National Biography, ed. H. C. G. Matthew and Brian Harrison (Oxford: OUP, 2004); online ed., ed. Lawrence Goldman, October 2006, http://www.oxforddnb.com/view/article/5226 (accessed July 15, 2013).

[17] In the first edition of his *Anatomy of the Humane Body*, Cheselden explained that he intended his book to be read by those who 'study Anatomy for their Entertainment'. See W. Cheselden, *The Anatomy of the Humane Body* (London, 1713), vii. In a number of his other published works, and in advertisements for public lectures, Cheselden made similar statements, explaining that his audiences would not be troubled by anything displeasing or tedious. See for example an advertisement placed in the *Daily Courant* No. 6057, 21 March 1721; W. Cheselden, *The Anatomy of the Human Body*, 5th edn (London, 1740), preface (unpaginated); W. Cheselden, *Osteographia, or The Anatomy of the Bones* (London, 1733), epistle to the reader (unpaginated).

[18] W. Cowper, *Myotomia Reformata, or an Anatomical Treatise on the Muscles of the Human Body* 2nd edn (London, 1724). See C. A. Hanson, 'Anatomy, Newtonian Physiology and Learned

Cheselden and his engraver, Michael's son Gerard, drew heavily on the layout of historiated initials, head- and tailpieces established in the *Myotomia Reformata*.

The *Osteographia* was an expensive book, both for its maker and its purchasers. When Cheselden advertised it for subscription in 1727, he offered copies of the book for four guineas each. To indicate that the book would always remain a valuable object, he promised to print no more than 300 copies.[19] By 1740 Cheselden was poised to guarantee the value of the book for ever by making certain that no more could be printed. He promised, in an advertisement affixed to the fifth edition of the *Anatomy of the Humane Body*, that he would 'break all the plates [of the *Osteographia*], which will sufficiently secure my promise to the subscribers'.[20] In the advertisement of 1727, Cheselden also saw fit to inform the public that the plates for the *Osteographia* had cost a great deal of money: 600 guineas in all.[21] By 1740 he had sold only 97 of the books to subscribers.[22] If the plates really had cost 600 guineas to make, then he must have made a substantial loss. At the original price of four guineas per book, he would have lost at least 212 guineas on the cost of the plates alone. By 1740 Cheselden had started cutting up the books and selling the plates as separate sets, perhaps to be used as 'proper ornaments for a surgery'.[23]

The sumptuousness promised by the price of the book and the alleged cost of the plates is carried through in its material execution. The unnumbered pages are of very thick paper, folded to folio size, and there are 225 of them in all. The 56 plates showing the human bones are repeated in their entirety, to give 112 of these plates in total. The plates are presented once without any type of explanation, and a second time with key letters referring to brief explanations or names on the left-hand facing page (Fig. 34.1). Of the remaining 113 pages, 13 more are full-page engravings. The first of these is a frontispiece depicting the Roman physician Galen chancing on the skeleton of a dead thief (Fig. 34.2). The figure of Galen is modelled after a figure in an etching by the Italian painter Salvator Rosa (1615–73), depicting the Greek cynic Diogenes of Sinope casting away his bowl after happening on someone who was able to drink using only his hands.[24] Others include a fron-

Culture: The *Myotomia Reformata* and its Context within Georgian Scholarship', in *Anatomy and the Organization of Knowledge, 1500–1850*, ed. M. Landers and B. Muñoz (London: Pickering & Chatto, 2012).

[19] W. Cheselden, advertisements placed in the London *Daily Journal* on each day that it came out from 18 April–1 May 1727.

[20] Cheselden, *Anatomy*, 5th edn (London, 1740), 'Advertisement' (unpaginated).

[21] Cheselden, advertisements in the London *Daily Journal*, 18 April–1 May 1727.

[22] Cheselden, *Anatomy*, 5th edn (London, 1740), 'Advertisement' (unpaginated), 'There were two hundred and three remaining after the subscribers had their books, four score and three of which I have cut to pieces.'

[23] Ibid., 'Advertisement' (unpaginated).

[24] J. Belchier, 'An Account of a Book: Osteographia, or, the Anatomy of the Bones by William Cheselden', *Philosophical Transactions*, 38 (1733–1734), 194–98, on 195. Belchier was Cheselden's

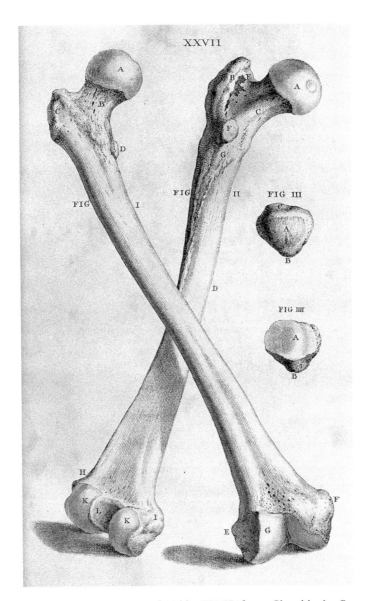

Fig. 34.1 The lettered version of Table XXVII from Cheselden's *Osteographia*, depicting the femur and patella from the front and rear. © Wellcome Library, London

Fig. 34.2 Frontispiece to the *Osteographia* depicting Galen happening on a skeleton. © Wellcome Library, London

tispiece to the dedication with the queen's arms and a plate that does homage to Vesalius's *De Humani Corporis Fabrica* (1543). Moreover, there are frontispieces for the epistle to the reader and the introduction, as well as for each of the eight chapters. All of these latter frontispieces depict animal skeletons or parts of them. In addition to the full-page prints, each chapter is adorned with an engraved head- and tailpiece, as well as a copperplate historiated initial (an example of one of the headpieces may be found in Fig. 34.3).[25] In sum, the *Osteographia* contains 225 pages, of which 125 are full-page plates. There are 100 pages of text, of which 56 are descriptions of the representations in the plates. Only 44 pages are given over to the chapters themselves; that is, to sustained descriptions of the bones or discussions of their workings. Moreover, many of these pages are also adorned with engravings of animal bones and skeletons.

CHAPTER VIII.

COMPARATIVE SCELETONS &c

Fig. 34.3 Headpiece depicting the skeletons of a weasel and a rat, from Chapter VIII of the *Osteographia*. © Wellcome Library, London

apprentice. Although Belchier does not explain exactly which of Salvator Rosa's prints the figure in the frontispiece was based on, it is clearly derived from 'Diogenes Casting Away his Bowl', Salvator Rosa, Rome, 1661–62, which may be found in the Victoria and Albert Museum, London (Museum number 24448).

[25] The *Osteographia*'s initials, along with its head- and tailpieces, are stylistically similar to those in Cowper's *Myotomia Reformata*, 2nd edn (London, 1724). On Cowper's initials, see M. A. Sanders, 'William Cowper and his Decorated Copperplate Initials', *The Anatomical Record Part B: The New Anatomist*, 282:1 (2005), 5–12.

To draw all of the bones and to make prints from the resulting drafts, Cheselden employed Gerard Vandergucht, the most fashionable and capable artist-engraver then working in London, along with Jacobus Schijnvoet, about whom very little is now known. Although Cheselden gave some indication that he esteemed Vandergucht and Schijnvoet as skilful practitioners of their art, he was at pains to demonstrate that the accuracy of the plates flowed from his own role in the project. Indeed, Cheselden praised the artists for understanding that, unaided, their skills were inadequate to the task of anatomical representation: 'my engravers, Mr. Vandergucht and Mr. Shinevoet not less skilled in drawing than in their own proper art [engraving], knew too well the difficulties of representing irregular lines, perspective, and proportion, to despise such assistance'.[26] Cheselden's philosophical authority guaranteed the accuracy of the plates:

> The actions of all the skeletons both human and comparative, as well as the attitudes of every bone, were my own choice: and where particular parts needed to be more distinctly expressed on account of the anatomy, there I always directed; sometimes in the drawings with the pencil, and often with the needle upon the copper plate, and where the anatomist does not take this care, he will scarce have his work well performed.[27]

Many statements like this can be found in seventeenth- and eighteenth-century illustrated scientific books. Such claims were conventional and sought to help readers to view representations of anatomical and philosophical subjects as epistemologically useful, in spite of the role played by non-anatomists and non-philosophers in their production.[28]

Even when he came to discuss the work of etching and engraving the philosophically accurate images onto copper plates, something that might be considered the proper province of Vandergucht and Schijnvoet, Cheselden broadcast his own involvement. Consider, for example, his discussion in the epistle to the reader of the style of Vandergucht's etching and engraving. It begins with praise: 'how great an artist he is, the open and free stile in which these plates are etched and engraved, and the inimitable manner of expressing the different textures of the parts sufficiently shew'.[29] Largely through his adeptness in etching, which permits a far greater tonal range than is afforded by engraving straight onto copper plates, Vandergucht had managed to produce a very fine impression of the different textures of the bones. Not much

---

[26] Cheselden, *Osteographia*, Epistle to the Reader (unpaginated).

[27] Ibid.

[28] Consider for example this disclaimer in Nehemiah Grew's *The Anatomy of Plants. With an Idea of a Philosophical History of Plants, And several other Lectures, Read before the Royal Society* (London, 1682), Preface (unpaginated), 'Some of the *Plates*, especially those which I did not draw to the *Engravers* hand, are a little hard and stiff: but they are all well enough done, to represent what they intend.'

[29] Cheselden, *Osteographia*, Epistle to the Reader (unpaginated).

further on, however, Cheselden asserted that he himself had had a hand in ensuring that the representation of the textures and surfaces of the bones was as vivid as possible. He took credit, rather dubiously, for the idea of better representing the smoothness of the ends of the bones (those parts that fit into the sockets of joints) by means of strokes engraved into the copper plates with a burin, while etching all the rest.[30]

The technique is readily apparent in the depiction of the ends of the bones in Table XXVII (Fig. 34.4). The forceful, thick and regular impressions left by the burin (with characteristic tapering towards the ends of the strokes) give the ends of the bones a texture that is distinct from all the other parts. These are represented with the lighter, thinner and less regular impressions that characterize Vandergucht's etching. We should not, I think, see this as yet another guarantee that the representations were the product of Cheselden's mind, and thus philosophically sound. Cheselden here identified himself as someone who was involved in the stylistic and technical work of image making and

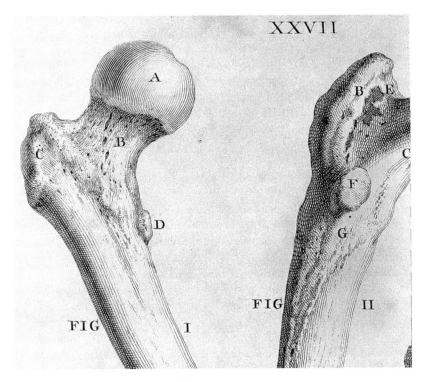

Fig. 34.4 Detail of the lettered version of Table XXVII from Cheselden's *Osteographia*. The rounded end of the femur labelled 'A' has been engraved with a burin, while the rest of the image is etched. © Wellcome Library, London

[30] Ibid.

reproduction. In fact, he took credit for creating a better effect of smoothness than might otherwise have been adequately achieved, not for having improved the accuracy of the representations.

Thus the whole tenor of the *Osteographia*, and of Cheselden's account of his involvement in its production, is that of useful instruction carried out in a sumptuous, pleasurable and expensive medium. Even its most obviously decorative components, the frontispieces, head- and tailpieces depicting animal bones were to be understood as simultaneously ornamental and usefully instructive. Since the *Osteographia* has no contents page, the reader is surprised to discover that the eighth chapter, 'Chapter VIII. Comparative Sceletons etc.', contains an account of all of the things that the decorative plates depict. Positioning the frontispieces, head- and tailpieces as a kind of supplementary course in comparative anatomy, the chapter includes some details about the functioning of the bones and skeletons displayed.[31] The review of the *Osteographia* in the Royal Society's *Philosophical Transactions*, written by Cheselden's apprentice John Belchier, unsurprisingly concurs with this assessment of the plates.[32] So we can see that Cheselden's engagement with the materiality of his book, expressed largely in his advertisements and in his discussions of the work's plates, reflected his concern to give the book epistemological, aesthetic and moral credibility in his chosen social setting. By describing the cost of the plates, the techniques of their production and his final responsibility for these, Cheselden hoped to establish them as tasteful objects for consumption that nevertheless provided useful knowledge.

JOHN DOUGLAS'S *ANIMADVERSIONS*

John Douglas's *Animadversions on a Late Pompous Book, Intituled, Osteographia: or, The Anatomy of the Bones*, in spite of its bias, contains a range of important critical responses to almost every intellectual and material aspect of the *Osteographia*. While Douglas drew negative conclusions, he accepted the premises and terms of Cheselden's positioning of the *Osteographia* almost entirely. He agreed that a work of osteology for non-specialist readers should be a beautiful and desirable object, basing his attack to a large extent on what he took to be Cheselden's failure in making such an object. Using terms drawn from connoisseurship, he concluded that the *Osteographia* was not fit for consumption by a genteel audience, and that its maker—Cheselden—possessed poor judgement in the arts and, crucially, in anatomy and surgery too. With an advertisement placed at the end of his pamphlet, Douglas proposed the publication of a new book to replace the *Osteographia*. It was to be an expensive consumer good that pleased as much as it instructed, as Douglas promised, 'a Really

---

[31] Cheselden, *Osteographia*, 'Chapter VIII. Comparative Sceletons etc.' (unpaginated).
[32] J. Belchier, 'An Account of a Book', 197.

useful, as well as a beautiful work'.[33] It would have been more modest than the *Osteographia* since it was to be printed in quarto, but it would nevertheless have been expensive, costing two guineas, and it would have contained a large number of high-quality engravings. Douglas promised, moreover, that the plates would be produced using the same techniques that Cheselden had employed. That is, they were to be for the most part etched, and then touched up with line engraving to make them vivid and expressive.[34] Douglas, then, embraced and sought to emulate, the luxurious and beautiful form of the *Osteographia*.

Rather than dismiss Cheselden's project, Douglas thus proceeded by attempting to demonstrate that Cheselden had failed to make a book as beautiful and useful as was suggested by its high price. His commentary on the book's plates, which takes up the final quarter of the *Animadversions*, shows in particularly sharp relief how he marshalled the materiality of the *Osteographia* against the moral and intellectual credibility of its author. By showing that the work's plates were in many respects deficient—neither beautiful nor especially useful—and by showing them to be emanations of Cheselden's own mind, he could trace a direct link from the former to the latter. Indeed, Douglas did his utmost to paint Cheselden as a man who had acted out of pride and vanity, and with conspicuous laziness; the sorts of moral characteristic that were likely to corrupt his judgement. Strikingly, he sought evidence for Cheselden's vanity in the cost and sumptuousness of the *Osteographia*'s plates, as well as in the poorly judged account of his own role in their design and production. The *Osteographia* was, Douglas asserted, excessively costly, its price bumped up by the repetition of the entire set of 56 anatomical plates for no considerable purpose.[35] Moreover, Cheselden could only have gone to such a great expense, and tolerated such severe losses, because his motivation in publishing the *Osteographia* was an excessive pride and regard for his own hypotheses: 'I cannot imagine what would move a man to set out with a view of being 400 guineas out of pocket! except innate -----y [vanity], and ----e [pride].'[36] This is representative of the procedure that Douglas deployed throughout the *Animadversions*. He used a critical discussion of some aspect of the *Osteographia* to make insinuations about Cheselden's character. On account of these, he argued, Cheselden was unfit to make the sorts of judgements, either in anatomy or in matters of taste, necessary for an anatomical work to be truly beautiful and useful.

Douglas also attacked Cheselden's account of his involvement in the production of the plates and of his relationship to his artist-engravers, Vandergucht and Schijnvoet. Cheselden's account of his working relationship with Vandergucht and Schijnvoet was, Douglas explained, nothing more than

[33] J. Douglas, 'Proposals for Printing (in Quarto) by Subscription, *Osteographia Anatomico-Practica*', attached at the very end of the *Animadversions*, 28.

[34] Ibid.

[35] Ibid., 30.

[36] Ibid., 28.

'a sneer on the Painters and Engravers, and an *Encomium* on himself, as being their Director'.[37] There was nothing exceptional about the commissioner of an artwork or illustration giving directions as to what he wanted to be drawn and engraved, and pointing out those features deserving of particular attention:

> don't every one who employs a Painter, tell him whether he would have him paint a Busto, a half length, or a whole length, or in what posture he would choose to be drawn? does not every man, who has a Sign to be painted, do the same? ... What an harangue is here, as if he had done something extraordinary, which never was done before! there I always directed! i.e. when he set the scull down before the *Painter*, he took his probe, and pointed out the Sutura Transversalis, Os Unguis, Septum Nasi, &c. and said, be sure, Sir, to delineate these little parts fairly, &c. ... Have not all the Anatomists upon earth done so?[38]

Douglas did not dispute the extent of Cheselden's participation in the intellectual and material realization of the *Osteographia* or argue that the division of labour that he described was inappropriate. Instead, he explained that such practices as choosing the parts to be represented and specifying the exact manner of their depiction were the regular and normal practices of the connoisseur and the anatomist. It followed, therefore, that Cheselden had made excessive claims for his own involvement because of his vanity. Once again, Douglas claimed to have exposed the true motivation for Cheselden's behaviour. He had made a pompous book with too many engravings, trumpeted his role in their production immodestly, and shouldered an enormous financial loss, all because he was vain.[39]

Douglas thus mobilized the ideals and practices of connoisseurship to demonstrate that Cheselden was a man of poor character, and that his *Osteographia* was a bad book. In a series of very detailed, and often penetrating, critical discussions of every single plate and paragraph, he drew links between Cheselden's capacities as a connoisseur and his ability to make sound judgements of medical and anatomical matters. Douglas proceeded with two distinct forms of criticism. The first was designed to expose Cheselden's failures in strict matters of anatomical judgement. It consisted mainly in arguing that he had chosen to

---

[37] Ibid., 25–6.

[38] Ibid., 26.

[39] It is interesting to note that the engraver George Vertue, one of Gerard Vandergucht's immediate contemporaries, found Cheselden's remarks to be quite proper. As he put it, 'I think the characters (Mr. Chiselden in his preface to his most excellent book of Osteology or discription of bones) of the Engravers who perform that work very skilfully are truly what they well deserve, and G. Vander Gucht has shown all the Art that possibly can be performed in such a work not excelld, or to be out done in yt part by the famousst Engravers abroad ... Shinvot has also well succeed in his part, this I mention in respect to a branch of Art I am best able to Judge of, that it will be a lasting monument to their honour, and this Nation. For perfection of Art in any part of the World is very rare.' See G. Vertue, *Note Books*, ed. K.A. Esdaile, H.M. Hake, G.S.H. Fox-Strangeways, 6 vols (Oxford: Walpole Society, 1930–55), vol. 3 (printed as the 22nd volume of the Walpole Society), 77.

represent things that were not valuable, all the while neglecting those things that could have contributed usefully to the work. Importantly, Douglas applied these criticisms both to the anatomical plates themselves and to the book's decorative elements. He asked, for example, why Cheselden had used the frontispieces, head- and tailpieces to represent animal skeletons. For Douglas, these plates contributed little to the work, since they did nothing to explicate the human bones represented at large in the book. They would have been even more beautiful and instructive if they had represented the parts of the human body dependent on the skeleton for their functioning:

> if he had been as solicitous about making his work useful as pompous, i.e. all of a piece, both in contrivance and goodness of work, he might for the same expence, have filled the places of these useless monsters, with other parts of the human body, which would have been more beautiful, and very instructive[40]

Douglas fashioned his comments on the anatomical plates and their labelling after the same pattern. Everywhere, he identified images in the plates that ought never to have been included—'good for nothing, but to fill up gaps'—and others that either did not include subjects of importance or included them without sufficient explanation to make their importance apparent. Cheselden's plates were the work of confused judgement. He had failed to distinguish between those anatomical subjects that might have given edification and those that had no place in a work of osteology.[41]

The second set of criticisms concerned Cheselden's taste, and again Douglas applied these criticisms equally to the anatomical plates and the decorative elements. Moreover, he called Cheselden's judgements of taste into question in much the same manner as he had his anatomical choices—by trying to show that he had chosen to represent things that were not beautiful, while rejecting those things that might have beautified the book. Commenting on the anatomical plates, Douglas argued that those which he had dismissed as contributing little to osteological knowledge also detracted from the book because of their ugliness. He rejected a series of plates depicting diseased bones as 'a parcel of rotten bones, and all incurable cases, not worth delineating'.[42] Similarly, he cast many of the decorative plates as not only useless, but inelegantly so. Consider, for example, his treatment of the frontispiece and headpiece adorning the letter to the reader. The frontispiece depicts a male deer stopping and turning, while the headpiece represents a sleeping dog. Although Douglas had already registered his fundamental disagreement with the choice of animal skeletons for these plates, he nevertheless judged the plates on their individual qualities. He found the frontispiece, depicting 'the sceleton of a young buck, stopping suddenly and turning', 'not only well contrived, but also very well

---

[40] Ibid., 30.
[41] Ibid., 28–38. The quotation is on 32.
[42] Ibid., 38.

executed'. Yet he objected in strong terms to the headpiece, which displays a dog lying asleep. The buck at least made an agreeable sight for the book's purchasers. But what of the sleeping dog?

> Pray, is there no posture of a Dog more graceful, than when he is asleep? Would not the figure of a fine Greyhound bounding over the field, when eagerly expecting his game, have made a more agreeable print, than a Cur-Dog asleep ...?[43]

Douglas therefore argued that the purposelessness that he had identified in the decorative plates was matched by the poor taste in which they had been chosen. The majority, he declared, hardly presented a fit sight for the purchasers of such an expensive book.

To understand Douglas's response to Cheselden's book, we must recognize that Douglas chose, at least in the *Animadversions*, to agree that osteological knowledge should be presented in a beautiful, expensive form. The way to discredit Cheselden, then, was to show that the *Osteographia* was not truly as valuable as had been advertised. This was to be achieved by inverting the values that Cheselden assigned to the formal, material and intellectual aspects of the book. Cheselden had used his own intellectual involvement, the book's cost and the techniques of its production to show that it had aesthetic, epistemological and pecuniary value. As I have argued, Douglas's criticisms of Cheselden were motivated in part by an attempt to portray Cheselden as a disingenuous sort of person. He represented the *Osteographia* as a grand piece of misrepresentation, as if it had been designed (albeit without success) to distract the public from an appreciation of his real capacity for aesthetic, anatomical and medical judgements alike.

CONNOISSEURSHIP AND THE COMMUNICATION OF ANATOMICAL KNOWLEDGE

Cheselden's presentation of the materiality of the *Osteographia*, and Douglas's detailed engagement with that materiality, show us that eighteenth-century discourses and practices that may usefully be grouped under the heading 'connoisseurship' could animate the production and consumption of an anatomical book in a consequential fashion. The fact that medics like Cheselden preoccupied themselves with both medical matters and connoisseurship is less significant than the fact that he and his contemporaries, including a vengeful antagonist, felt that the values of connoisseurship could usefully be applied to the making and consuming of certain forms of anatomical and medical knowledge.

The status of books like the *Osteographia* as beautiful, expensive consumer goods was of consequence to their valuation as useful or not so useful sources

---

[43] Cheselden, *Osteographia*, 'Chapter VIII. Comparative Sceletons etc.' (unpaginated); Douglas, *Animadversions*, 29.

of knowledge. This is demonstrated by the range of associations that both Cheselden and Douglas gave to the *Osteographia* in its totality, from the size of its pages and the expense lavished on its prints, to the exact representational choices made in the plates and descriptions. The manner in which Cheselden and Douglas swiftly linked the materiality of the *Osteographia* to the moral status of the person responsible for its form is important to our understanding of the interplay between connoisseurship and anatomical/medical knowledge. They used the evidence of a range of good or bad judgements, whether pertaining to anatomy proper or to matters of taste, to make more general suggestions about the capacity of the *Osteographia*'s maker to serve as the guarantor of real anatomical knowledge. In other words, Cheselden's ability to judge properly of the tastefulness of his decorative head- and tailpieces could usefully serve as evidence for his anatomical judgement, and vice versa. Additionally, Douglas tried to argue that there was a gap between the claims that Cheselden made for the beauty and utility of his book, and the book's real qualities. This failure of connoisseurship made Cheselden into a sort of impostor, someone who claimed to possess qualities that in reality he lacked.

This brings us back full circle to the surgical priority dispute that had first so inflamed Douglas's hatred for Cheselden. Little is known about Robert Houston, the author of *Lithotomus castratus*, except that he was a medical doctor who supported Douglas's claim. It is worth paying close attention, however, to the manner in which he tried to demonstrate that Cheselden had merely copied Douglas's lithotomy procedure. Surgery hardly figured at all in Houston's polemic. Instead, he chose to treat the accounts of the procedure offered by Cheselden and by Douglas as artifacts with which the moral status of their makers might be found out. By comparing Cheselden's description of the surgery with that offered by Douglas, Houston tried to show that the former was simply a copy of the latter. This made Douglas a virtuous discoverer and sharer of knowledge and made Cheselden a prideful fraud: 'it [Cheselden's account] looks at best, like a poor and ill-design'd endeavour of one artful and crafty man, to pass for what he is not'.[44] Even in the surgical priority dispute that led Douglas to engage in his aggressive criticism of the plates of the *Osteographia*, practices closely resembling those of connoisseurship had an important role to play in helping readers to form an opinion about the true origins of the procedure and the true nature of those who purported to have invented it.

I would like to end this essay by suggesting that by paying closer attention to eighteenth-century worries about the use of the senses, we might be able to understand better why connoisseurship and medical knowledge were so closely connected. As is well known, the turn of the eighteenth century marked a decisive shift in the emergence of a consumer culture, especially in centres of commerce such as London. It is equally well known that this proliferation of consumer goods provoked worry among members of the cultural and intel-

---

[44] Houston, *Lithotomus Castratus*, 5.

lectual elite. As Preben Mortensen has noted, there were those in eighteenth-century England who aired the concern that the sensory pleasures provoked by luxurious things would lead people to use their senses in the pursuit of gratifications that would ruin their morals. Such was the dim view of these things taken by many members of the Society for the Reformation of Manners, a group that sought to curb immorality in London around the turn of the eighteenth century. Even more unsettlingly for the upholders of conventional morality, the philosopher Bernard Mandeville argued in his *The Fable of the Bees* (1714) that the consumption of luxuries was motivated by private vices, but that these vices taken together produced the public benefit of ever greater prosperity.[45] Surely Cheselden and Douglas could not have agreed with Mandeville's pessimistic assessment. Had they agreed wholeheartedly with the moral of *The Fable of the Bees*, they would have had to accept that their readers likely had sinful motives for buying luxurious books like the *Osteographia*.

In the face of such worries, theorists of art and philosophers alike tried to show that it was not only possible to reconcile sensory gratification with the pursuit of virtue, but that the cultivation of good taste in the arts, antiquities and books could help people further along the path of virtue. Cheselden's friend Jonathan Richardson (1676–1745), the painter and art theorist, argued that the formation of good taste in paintings was consequential far beyond its immediate sphere of application. In his *Essay on the Whole Art of Criticism as it relates to Painting* (1719), he took time in several places to distinguish the morally improving edification to be gained by looking on tasteful paintings from the 'Impertinent, or Criminal Amusements' to be had by receiving sense impressions from the wrong things.[46] This was a theme that the philosopher Francis Hutcheson picked up in his *An Inquiry into the Original of our Ideas of Beauty and Virtue* (1725). In that work and others he argued that those who could make proper judgements about beauty must also be capable of good moral judgements and that, conversely, those who could not rightly perceive beauty were also very unlikely to be able to make good moral judgements.[47] Richardson too, albeit without resorting to a radically new aesthetic theory as had Hutcheson, argued that the ability to make good judgements about art betokened an ability to make a range of other judgements, including being able to tell the difference between those pleasures corresponding to virtue and those corresponding to bad behaviour. Indeed, Richardson argued (after the fashion of John Locke) that the exercise of judgement, regardless of its subject, consisted in the distinction of ideas one from another. Therefore, this was 'as necessary to a *Connoisseur* as

[45] P. Mortensen, 'Francis Hutcheson and the Problem of Conspicuous Consumption', *The Journal of Aesthetics and Art Criticism*, 53:2 (1995), 155–65, on 156–7; B. Mandeville, *The Fable of the Bees: or, Private vices publick benefits* (London, 1714).

[46] J. Richardson, *Two Discourses. I. Essay On the whole Art of Criticism as it relates to Painting [...]. II. An argument in behalf of the science of a connoisseur* (London, 1719), 5.

[47] Mortensen, 'Hutcheson and Conspicuous Consumption', 162; F. Hutcheson, *An Inquiry into the Original of our Ideas of Beauty and Virtue* (London, 1725).

to a Philosopher, or Divine to be a good Logician; The Same Faculties are employ'd, and in the Same manner, the difference [was] only in the Subject.'[48]

In response to concerns, which they often expressed themselves, about the possibility that the new world of luxury goods could lead people away from the path of virtue, Richardson and Hutcheson tried to show that what connoisseurs did when they judged that things were beautiful and valuable made them more virtuous. However, this also led them to argue that failures of connoisseurship were not necessarily simple errors, but perhaps indicative of much broader failures of judgement. Richardson, as we have seen, claimed that connoisseurs made use of just the same faculties and procedures for thinking about paintings as they might employ in matters of philosophy and logic. Hutcheson even claimed that the capacity to recognize beauty was inherently related to the capacity to make moral judgements. In this essay I have shown that, in his criticism of the *Osteographia*, Douglas drew similar links between Cheselden's capacities as a connoisseur and his moral state. Perhaps this was because he also believed, or chose to appear to believe, that failures to judge well in matters of taste betokened deeper intellectual and moral failings. This could help to explain why Cheselden, Douglas and their contemporaries in the world of medicine attached so much consequence to acts of connoisseurship. Much could be inferred about the intellectual and moral state of those who offered public judgements about the qualities of luxurious things.

Acknowledgements I am very grateful for the opportunity afforded to me by the organizers of the 'Material Cultures of the Long Eighteenth Century' workshop at the Huntington Library (April 2012), Adriana Craciun and Simon Schaffer, to present my work at that event, and for the subsequent opportunity to publish it in this volume. I am also very grateful for the helpful comments on this work from Rebecca Addicks, Rebecca Bowd, Sarah Easterby-Smith, Craig Ashley Hanson, Simon Schaffer and Anna-Marie Roos. I am as ever extremely happy to acknowledge the help and support of Cécile Bishop.

---

[48] Richardson, *Essay On the whole Art of Criticism*, 203.

BIBLIOGRAPHY

F. Accum, *Culinary Chemistry* (Ackermann, London, 1821)

G. Adams, *Micrographia Illustrata* (For the Author, London, 1746)

M. Adams, N. Thomas, *Cook's Sites: Revisiting History* (Otago University Press, Dunedin, 1999)

T. Adorno, *Minima Moralia: Reflections on a Damaged Life* (New Left Books, London, 1974)

M. Akenside, *The Pleasures of the Imagination. A Poem in Three Books* (R. Dodsley, London, 1744)

S.J.M.M. Alberti, *Morbid Curiosities: Medical Museums in Nineteenth-Century Britain* (Oxford University Press, Oxford, 2011)

G. Alm (ed.), *Kina Slott* (Byggförlaget, Stockholm, 2002)

R. Altick, *The Shows of London* (Belknap Press of Harvard University Press, Cambridge, MA/London, 1978)

Anon., *A New and Exact Map of Toryland, with the Dangerous Rocks and Shoals of All the Jacobite Islands Lying in the Same Parallel with ye Red Sea Whose Latitude is 1688, and Longitude 1714* (no publisher given, London, 1729)

Anon., *Catalogue raisonné des minéraux, coquilles, et autres curiosités naturelles contenues dans le cabinet de feu M. Geoffroy de l'Académie royale des sciences* (Paris, Guerin and Delatour, 1753)

Anon., *Bibliotheca Meadiana, Sive Catalogus Librorum Richardi Mead* (Baker, London, 1754a)

Anon., *A Catalogue of the Genuine and Capital Collection of Pictures [...] of that Late Great and Learned Physician, Doctor Richard Mead* (Langford, London, 1754b)

Anon., *A Catalogue of the Genuine and Entire Collection of Valuable Gems, Bronzes, Marble and Others Busts and Antiquities, of the Late Doctor Mead* (Langford, London, 1755a)

Anon., *A Catalogue of the Genuine, Entire and Curious Collection of Prints and Drawings [...] of the Late Doctor Mead* (Langford, London, 1755b)

Anon., *Catalogue systématique et raisonné des curiosités de la nature et de l'art, qui composent le cabinet de M. Davila*, 2 vols. (Briasson, Paris, 1767)

© The Author(s) 2016

A. Craciun, S. Schaffer (eds.), *The Material Cultures of Enlightenment Arts and Sciences*, Palgrave Studies in the Enlightenment, Romanticism and the Cultures of Print, DOI 10.1057/978-1-137-44379-3

Anon., *The Life of La Pérouse, the Celebrated and Unfortunate French Navigator*, 3rd edn. (A. Neil, Somers Town, 1801)

Anon., *An Address to the Officers of His Majesty's Navy, by an Old Naval Surgeon* (Hatchard and Son, London, 1824)

Anon., 'Vestiges of La Pérouse'. *The Asiatic Journal and Monthly Miscellany* **26**, 381 (1828a)

Anon., 'Peter Dillon's report on La Pérouse'. *Asiatic Journal and Monthly Miscellany* **26**, 443–452 (1828b)

Anon., 'Captain Dillon's voyage'. *Oriental Herald* **19**, 145–153 (1828c)

Anon., 'Museé de la Marine'. *Le Magasin Pittoresque* **6**, 272 (1838)

Anon., 'A sketch of the life, and some account of the works, of the late Dr James Johnson'. *Medico-Chirurgical Review and Journal of Practical Medicine* **48**, 1–48 (1846)

Anon., 'Relics and memorials'. *The Ladies' Cabinet* 197–200 (1855)

Anon., 'The Royal United Services Institution'. *The Leisure Hour* **435**, 260 (1860)

A. Appadurai (ed.), *The Social Life of Things: Commodities in Cultural Perspective* (Cambridge University Press, Cambridge, 1986)

Aristotle, *The Politics*, trans. by T.A. Sinclair (Penguin, London, 1992)

D.N. Armintor, 'The sexual politics of Brobdingnag'. *Studies in English Literature* **47**, 619–640 (2007)

J. Armstrong, *The Women's Guide to Virtue, Economy, and Happiness*, 6th edn. (MacKenzie and Dent, Newcastle upon Tyne, 1817)

M. Armstrong, 'The effects of blackness': Gender, race, and the sublime in aesthetic theories of Burke and Kant'. *The Journal of Aesthetics and Art Criticism* **54**, 213–236 (1996)

L.D. Arnault de Nobleville, F. Salerne, *Suite de la matière medicale de M. Geoffroy*, 7 vols. (Desaint et Saillant, Paris, 1757)

D. Arnold, *Science, Technology and Medicine in Colonial India* (Cambridge University Press, Cambridge, 2000)

Association Salomon, *Le mystère La Pérouse, ou le rêve inachevé d'un roi* (Editions de Conti, Paris, 2008)

J. Aubrey, *Brief Lives*, ed. by R. Barber (Boydell, Woodbridge, 1998)

A. Babadzan, *Les dépouilles des dieux: essai sur la réligion tahitienne à l'époque de la découverte* (Maison des Sciences de l'Homme, Paris, 1993)

G.H. Baillie, *Watchmakers and Clockmakers of the World* (NAG Press, London, 1969)

J. Banks, *Banks' Florilegium: A Publication in Thirty-Four Parts of Seven Hundred and Thirty- Eight Copperplate Engravings of Plants Collected on Captain James Cook's First Voyage Round the World in H.M.S. Endeavour, 1768–1771* (Alecto Historical Editions in association with the British Museum, London, 1981–1988)

Baptist Missionary Society, *Periodical Accounts Relative to the Baptist Missionary Society*, vol. 1 (John Morris, Clipstone, 1800)

E.J. Barillet, *Sur le Mannequin* (Au Bureau des Annales du Musée, Paris, 1809)

J.E. Barnard, Barnard, John, the younger (1704/5–1784), in *Oxford Dictionary of National Biography* (Oxford University Press, Oxford, 2004), http://www.oxforddnb.com/view/article/64847

J. Basford, *'A Commodity of Good Names': The Branding of Products, c.1650–1900* (Ph.D. thesis, University of York, 2012)

E. Bassani, *African Art and Artefacts in European Collections 1400–1800* (British Museum Press, London, 2000)

J.C. Beaglehole (ed.), *The Endeavour Journal of Joseph Banks 1768–1771*, 2 vols. (Angus and Robertson, Sydney, 1962)

J.C. Beaglehole, *The Life of Captain James Cook* (Stanford University Press, Palo Alto, 1974)

G. Bearce, *British Attitudes Towards India, 1784–1858* (Oxford University Press, Oxford, 1961)

J. Belchier, 'An account of a book: Osteographia, or, the anatomy of the bones by William Cheselden'. *Philosophical Transactions of the Royal Society* **38**, 194–198 (1733–1734)

F. Bellec, *Les Esprits de Vanikoro* (Gallimard, Paris, 2005)

B. Benedict, 'Encounters with the object: Advertisements, time and literary discourse in the early eighteenth century thing-poem'. *Eighteenth-Century Studies* **40**, 193–207 (2007)

J.A. Bennett, 'The English quadrant in Europe—Instruments and the growth of consensus in practical astronomy'. *Journal for the History of Astronomy* **23**, 1–14 (1992)

J.A. Bennett, Shopping for instruments in Paris and London, in *Merchants and Marvels: Commerce, Science, and Art in Early Modern Europe*, ed. by P.H. Smith, P. Findlen (Routledge, New York/London, 2002), pp. 370–395

B. Bennett, 'Naturalising Australian trees in South Africa: Climate, exotics and experimentation'. *Journal of Southern African Studies* **37**, 265–280 (2011)

M. Berg, 'From imitation to invention: Creating commodities in eighteenth-century Britain'. *Economic History Review* **55**, 1–30 (2002)

M. Berg, 'In pursuit of luxury: Global history and British consumer goods in the eighteenth century'. *Past Present* **182**, 85–142 (2004)

M. Berg, *Luxury and Pleasure in Eighteenth-Century Britain* (Oxford University Press, Oxford, 2005)

M. Berg, H. Clifford, 'Selling consumption in the eighteenth century: Advertising and the trade card in Britain and France'. *Cultural and Social History* **4**, 145–170 (2007)

N.Z. Berliner, *The Emperor's Private Paradise: Treasures from the Forbidden City* (Peabody Essex Museum in Association with Yale University Press, New Haven, 2010)

A. Bewell, 'Traveling natures'. *Nineteenth-Century Contexts* **29**(2–3), 89–110 (2007)

I. Bignamini, M. Postle, *The Artist's Model: Its Role in British Art from Lely to Etty* (Nottingham University Art Gallery, Nottingham, 1991)

T. Birch, *Heads of Illustrious Persons of Great Britain, Engraven by Mr. Houbraken, and Mr. Vertue, with Their Lives and Characters* (J. and P. Knapton, London, 1743)

J. Bird, *The Method of Dividing Astronomical Instruments* (Commissioners of Longitude, London, 1767)

B. Black [John Banville], *The White Swan* (Pan Macmillan, London, 2007)

W. Blackstone, *Commentaries on the Laws of England*, 4 vols. (Clarendon Press, Oxford, 1773)

M. Blackwell, The it-narrative and eighteenth-century thing theory, in *The Secret Life of Things: Animals, Objects and It-Narratives in Eighteenth-Century England*, ed. by M. Blackwell (Associated University Presses, Cranbury, 2007), pp. 9–18

D. Bleichmar, 'Learning to look: Visual expertise across art and science in eighteenth-century France'. *Eighteenth-Century Studies* **46**, 85–111 (2012)

E. Blunden, *Undertones of War* (Doubleday, New York, 1929)

P. Boomgaard, Dutch medicine in Asia, 1600–1900, in *Warm Climates and Western Medicine: The Emergence of Tropical Medicine, 1500–1900*, ed. by D. Arnold (Rodopi, Atlanta, 1996)

J. Bradley, 'A letter to the Rt. Hon. George, Earl of Macclesfield, concerning an apparent motion in some of the fixed stars'. *Philosophical Transactions* **45**, 1–43 (1748)

B. Bramsen, *Sophienberg, Bygning og Beboere gennem 250 år* (Gymnasieskolernes Lærerforening, Copenhagen, 1994)

M. Bravo, Ethnographic navigation and the geographical gift, in *Geography and Enlightenment*, ed. by C. Withers, D. Livingstone (Chicago University Press, Chicago, 1999), pp. 199–235

T.H. Breen, *The Marketplace of Revolution: How Consumer Politics Shaped American Independence* (Oxford University Press, Oxford, 2004)

M. Bressani, M. Grignon, 'Henry Labrouste and the lure of the real'. *Art History* **28**(5), 712–751 (2005)

D. Brewster (ed.), *The Edinburgh Encyclopedia*, 18 vols. (Printed for William Blackwood and others, Edinburgh, 1808–1830)

J. Brewer, 'The most polite age and the most vicious': Attitudes towards culture as a commodity, 1660–1800, in *The Consumption of Culture 1600–1800: Image, Object, Text*, ed. by A. Bermingham, J. Brewer (Routledge, London, 1995), pp. 341–360

J. Brewer, *The Pleasures of the Imagination: English Culture in the Eighteenth Century* (Harper Collins, London, 1997)

J. Brewer, R. Porter (eds.), *Consumption and the World of Goods* (Routledge, London, 1993)

H. Brougham, *An Inquiry into the Colonial Policy of the European Powers* (Balfour, Manners & Miller; and Constable, Edinburgh, 1803)

B. Brown, 'Thing theory'. *Critical Inquiry* **28**, 1–22 (2001)

C.L. Brown, *Moral Capital: Foundations of British Abolitionism* (University of North Carolina for the Omohundro Institute, Chapel Hill, 2006)

R.N. Buckley, *The British Army in the West Indies: Society and the Military in the Revolutionary Age* (University Press of Florida, Gainesville, 1998)

J.M. Bulloch, *The Art of Extra-illustration* (Treherne, London, 1903)

J.H. Bunn, 'The aesthetics of British mercantilism'. *New Literary History* **11**, 303–321 (1980)

R. Butler, Les Sauvages de la Mer Pacifique: In England, America and Australia, in *Les Sauvages de la Mer Pacifique* (Art Gallery of New South Wales, Sydney, 2000), pp. 15–20

L. Calè, A. Craciun, 'The disorder of things'. *Eighteenth-century Studies* **45**, 1–13 (2011)

R. Campbell, *The London Tradesman* (T. Gardner, London, 1747)

E. Capon, Foreword, in *Les Sauvages de la Mer Pacifique* (Art Gallery of New South Wales, Sydney, 2000), p. 4

C. Caraccioli, *The Life of Robert Lord Clive, Baron Plassey*, 4 vols. (T. Bell, London, 1775–1777)

P. Carson, *The East India Company and Religion, 1698–1858* (Boydell and Brewer, Woodbridge, 2012)

T. Castle, *The Female Thermometer: Eighteenth-Century Culture and the Invention of the Uncanny* (Oxford University Press, New York, 1995)

W. Chambers, *Designs of Chinese Buildings, Furniture, Dresses, Machines, and Utensils* (Published for the Author, London, 1757)

W. Chambers, *A Dissertation on Oriental Gardening* (W. Griffin, London, 1772)

N. Chambers, *Joseph Banks and the British Museum: The World of Collecting, 1770–1830* (Pickering & Chatto, London, 2007)

S.D.J. Chaplin, *John Hunter and the 'Museum Oeconomy', 1750–1800* (Ph.D. thesis, King's College London, 2009)

A. Chapman, 'The accuracy of angular measuring instruments used in astronomy between 1500 and 1850'. *Journal of the History of Astronomy* **14**, 133–137 (1983)

A. Chapman, *Dividing the Circle. The Development of Critical Angular Measurement in Astronomy 1500–1850* (Ellis Horwood, Chichester, 1990)

V.-E. Charles, *Nouvelles Annales des Voyages*, vol. 13 (Librairie de Gils Fils, Paris, 1829)

R. Chartier, *Cultural History: Between Practices and Representation* (Cornell University Press, Ithaca, 1989)

R. Chartier, *The Order of Books: Readers, Authors, and Libraries in Europe Between the Fourteenth and the Eighteenth Centuries*, trans. by L.G. Cochrane (Stanford University Press, Stanford, 1994)

A. Chatelle, *Le Musée de la Marine* (Editions de L'Institut Maritime et Colonial, Paris, 1943)

B. Chatwin, *Utz* (Viking Penguin, New York, 1988)

W.E. Cheong, *The Hong Merchants of Canton: Chinese Merchants in Sino-Western Trade* (Richmond, Curzon, 1997)

W. Cheselden, *The Anatomy of the Humane Body* (N. Cliff and D. Jackson, and W. Innys, London, 1713)

W. Cheselden, *A Treatise on the High Operation for the Stone* (John Osborn, London, 1723)

W. Cheselden, 'An account of some observations made by a young gentleman, who was born blind, or lost his sight so early, that he had no remembrance of ever having seen, and was couch'd between 13 and 14 years of age'. *Philosophical Transactions* **35**, 447–450 (1727–1728)

W. Cheselden, *Osteographia, or the Anatomy of the Bones* (William Bowyer, London, 1733)

W. Cheselden, *The Anatomy of the Human Body*, 5th edn. (William Bowyer, London, 1740)

G. Clark, 'Indigenous transfer of La Pérouse artefacts in the southeast Solomon Islands'. *Australian Archaeology* **57**, 103–111 (2003)

R. Clay (ed.), *Matthew Boulton and the Art of Making Money* (Brewin, Studley, 2009)

T. Clayton, *The English Print, 1688–1802* (Yale University Press, New Haven/London, 1997)

T. Clemmensen, M.B. Mackeprag, *Kina og Danmark 1600–1950: Kinafart og Kinamode* (Nationalmuseet, Copenhagen, 1980)

J. Clubbe, *Physiognomy; Being a Sketch Only of a Larger Work upon the Same Plan: Wherein the Different Tempers, Passions, and Manners of Men, Will Be Particularly Considered* (R. and J. Dodsley, London, 1763)

C. Clunas, *Superfluous Things: Material Culture and Social Status in Early Modern China* (Polity, Cambridge, 1991)

J. Cohen, *Human Robots in Myth and Science* (Allen & Unwin, London, 1966)

D. Coleman, *Romantic Colonization and British Anti-slavery* (Cambridge University Press, Cambridge, 2005)

L. Colley, The reach of the state, the appeal of the nation: Mass arming and political culture in the Napoleonic wars, in *An Imperial State at War*, ed. by L. Stone (Routledge, London, 1994), pp. 165–184

Condorcet, Eloge de M. Guettard. Histoire de l'Académie Royale des Sciences 47–62 (1786)

H.J. Cook, Time's bodies: Crafting the preparation and preservation of naturalia, in *Merchants and Marvels: Commerce, Science and Art in Early Modern Europe*, ed. by P.H. Smith, P. Findlen (Routledge, London, 2002), pp. 223–247

R.G.S. Cooper, *The Anglo-Maratha Campaigns and the Contest for India: The Struggle for the Control of the South Asian Military Economy* (Cambridge University Press, Cambridge, 2003)

T. Cooper, *Searching for Shakespeare* (National Portrait Gallery, London, 2006)

J. Cordiner, *A Voyage to India* (Brown and Co./Longman, Aberdeen/London, 1820)

B.G. Corney (ed.), *The Quest and Occupation of Tahiti by Emissaries of Spain During the Years 1772–6*, 3 vols. (Cambridge University Press, Cambridge, 1919)

W. Cowper, *Myotomia Reformata, or an Anatomical Treatise on the Muscles of the Human Body*, 2nd edn. (Jacob Tonson, London, 1724)

A. Craciun, 'What is an explorer?' *Eighteenth-Century Studies* **45**, 29–51 (2011)

A. Craciun, 'The Franklin mystery'. *Literary Review of Canada* 3–5 (May 2012)

A. Craciun, 'The Franklin relics in the Arctic archive'. *Victorian Literature and Culture* **42**, 1–30 (2014)

J.L. Cranmer-Byng, T.H. Levere, 'A case study in cultural collision: Scientific apparatus in the Macartney embassy to China, 1793'. *Annals of Science* **38**, 503–525 (1981)

D.G. Crawford, *A History of the Indian Medical Service, 1600–1913* (W. Thacker, London, 1914)

J. Cruikshank, *Do Glaciers Listen? Local Knowledge, Colonial Encounters and Social Imagination* (University of British Columbia Press, Vancouver, 2005)

C. Curtis, *An Account of the Diseases in India, as They Appeared in the English Fleet, and in the Naval Hospital at Madras, in 1782 and 1783, with Observations on Ulcers and the Hospital Sores of that Country* (W. Laing, Edinburgh, 1807)

A.D. D'Argenville, *Histoire naturelle éclaircie dans deux de ses parties principales, la lithologie et la conchyliologie* (Quillau, Paris, 1742)

F. Dabhoiwala, *The Origins of Sex: A History of the First Sexual Revolution* (Oxford University Press, New York/London, 2012)

B. Dam-Mikkelsen, T. Lundbæk, *Etnografiske Genstande i det Kongelige Danske Kunstkammer 1650–1800/Ethnographic Objects in the Royal Danish Kunstkammer 1650–1800* (Danish National Museum, Copenhagen, 1980)

J.E. Dandy, *The Sloane Herbarium: An Annotated List of the Horti Sicci Composing It; with Biographical Accounts of the Principal Contributors* (The British Museum, London, 1957)

L. Daston, 'Type specimens and scientific memory'. *Critical Inquiry* **31**, 153–182 (2004)

L. Daston, P. Galison, *Objectivity* (Zone Books, New York, 2007)

L. Daston, K. Park, *Wonders and the Order of Nature, 1150–1750* (Zone Books, New York, 2001)

J. Davidson, *Peter Dillon of Vanikoro: Chevalier of the South Seas* (Oxford University Press, Oxford, 1975)

J. Davies, *A Tahitian and English Dictionary, with Introductory Remarks on the Polynesian Language and a Short Grammar of the Tahitian Dialect* (LMS Press, Tahiti, 1851)

M. de Certeau, *Heterologies: Discourse on the Other*, trans. by B. Massumi (Minnesota University Press, Minneapolis, 1986)

G. de Fouchy, Eloge de M. Geoffroy. Histoire de l'Académie Royale des Sciences 153–164 (1752)

M. de Grazia, *Shakespeare Verbatim: The Reproduction of Authenticity and the 1790 Apparatus* (Clarendon, Oxford, 1991)

G. de Jode, *Thesaurus Sacrarum Historiarum Veteris Testamenti* (Sumptibus atque expensis Gerardi de Iode, Antwerp, 1585)

J.-J. de la Billardière, *Voyage in Search of La Pérouse*, 2 vols. (Stockdale, London, 1800)

J.-F. de G. de La Pérouse, *Voyage de La Pérouse autour du monde*, ed. by L.A. Milet-Mureau, 4 vols. (de l'Imprimerie de la République, Paris, 1797)

J.-F. de G. de La Pérouse, *A Voyage Round the World, Performed in the Years 1785, 1786, 1787, and 1788*, 3rd edn., 3 vols. (Printed for Lackington, Allen, and Co., London, 1807)

J.-F. de G. de La Pérouse, *Journal of Jean-François de Galaup de La Pérouse*, trans. and ed. by J. Dunmore, 2 vols. (Hakluyt Society, London, 1994–1995)

G. de Maupassant, Who knows?, in *A Parisian Affair and Other Stories*, trans. by S. Miles (Penguin, London, 2004)

P. de Maupertuis, *The Figure of the Earth* (Printed for T. Cox and others, London, 1738)

A. de Montaiglon, J. Guiffrey (eds.), *Correspondance des directeurs de l'Académie de France à Rome avec les surintendants des bâtiments*, 18 vols. (Charavay, Paris, 1887–1908)

R.A.F. de Réaumur, 'Moyens d'empêcher l'évaporation des liquides spiritueuses, dans lesquelles on veut conserver des productions de la nature de différens genres'. *Mémoires de l'Académie Royale des Sciences* 483–538 (1746)

E. de Waal, *The Hare with the Amber Eyes: A Hidden Inheritance* (Vintage Books/ Farrar, Strauss, Giroux, London/New York, 2010)

D. Defoe, *The Life and Surprizing Adventures of Robinson Crusoe*, ed. by J.R. Crowley (Oxford University Press, Oxford, 1983)

F. Delamarre, B. Guineau, La boîte de couleurs dite 'de Fragonard': Analyse du contenu des flacons, in *Jean-Honoré Fragonard, peintre de Grasse* (Villa-Musée Fragonard, Grasse, 2006), pp. 25–31

M.G. Delaney, *Autobiography and Correspondence*, ed. by L. Llanover, 6 vols. (Bentley, London, 1861–1862)

J. Derrida, *Of Grammatology*, corrected edition, trans. by G.C. Spivak (Johns Hopkins Press, Baltimore, 1997)

R. Dias, *John Boydell's Shakespeare Gallery* (Ph.D. thesis, University of York, 2003)

R. Dias, *Exhibiting Englishness: John Boydell's Shakespeare Gallery and the Formation of a National Aesthetic* (Yale University Press, New Haven/London, 2013)

T.F. Dibdin, *Bibliomania; or, Book Madness: A Bibliographical Romance, in Six Parts. Illustrated with Cuts* (Printed for the Author, by J. McCrerry, London, 1811)

T.F. Dibdin, *Bibliotheca Spenceriana; or A Descriptive Catalogue of the Books Printed in the Fifteenth Century, and of Many Valuable First Editions, in the Library of George John Earl Spencer*, 4 vols. (Bulmer, London, 1814)

T.F. Dibdin, *Aedes Althorpianae; or an Account of the Mansion, Books, and Pictures, at Althorp: The Residence of George John Earl Spencer* (Nicol, London, 1822)

C. Dickens, *Sketches by Boz* (Odhams, London, 1930)

C. Dickens, *Oliver Twist* (Odhams, London, 1934)

C. Dickens, *Great Expectations*, ed. by M. Cardwell (Oxford University Press, Oxford, 2008)

D. Diderot, J. le Rond d'Alembert (eds.), *Encyclopédie, ou dictionnaire raisonné des sciences, des arts, et des metiers*, ed. by R. Morrissey (University of Chicago: ARTFL Encyclopédie Project, 2011), online at http://encyclopedie.uchicago.edu

B. Dietz, 'Mobile objects: The space of shells in eighteenth-century France'. *Journal for the History of Science* 39, 363–382 (2006)

P. Dillon, Letter to the editor, *The Morning Chronicle* (21 January 1829), 3.

P. Dillon, *Narrative and Successful Result of a Voyage in the South Seas*, 2 vols. (Hurst, Chance, & Co., London, 1829)

M. Dobson, *The Making of the National Poet: Shakespeare, Adaptation, and Authorship, 1660–1769* (Clarendon Press, Oxford, 1992)

J. Douglas, *The History of the Lateral Operation: or, an Account of the Method of Extracting a Stone by Making a Wound Near the Great Protuberance of the Os Ischium* (Strahan, London, 1726)

J. Douglas, *An Appendix to the History of the Lateral Operation for the Stone: Containing Mr Cheselden's Present Method* (Strahan, London, 1731)

J. Douglas, *Animadversions on a Late Pompous Book, Intituled, Osteographia: or, the Anatomy of the Bones* (For the Author, London, 1735)

F. Driver, *Geography Militant: Cultures of Exploration and Empire* (Blackwell, Oxford, 2001)

F. Driver, L. Jones, *Hidden Histories of Exploration* (Royal Holloway, University of London in Association with the RGS-IBG, London, 2010)

C.J. Duffin, 'Porcupine stones'. *Pharmaceutical Historian* **43**, 13–22 (2013)

M. Duffy, *Soldiers, Sugar, and Seapower: The British Expeditions to the West Indies and the War Against Revolutionary France* (Oxford University Press, New York, 1987)

J. Dumont D'Urville, *Voyage de la corvette* L'Astrolabe. *Histoire du voyage*, 5 vols. (J. Tastu, Paris, 1833)

R. Dunn, *The Telescope: A Short History* (National Maritime Museum, London, 2009)

R. Dunn, R. Higgitt, *Finding Longitude* (Harper Collins, London, 2014)

C. Eagleton, 'Collecting African money in Georgian London: Sarah Sophia Banks and her collection of coins'. *Museum History Journal* **6**, 23–38 (2013)

E. Edwards, *Memoirs of Libraries* (Trübner, London, 1859)

W. Ellis, *Polynesian Researches*, 4 vols. (Tuttle, Rutland, 1831)

R. Etlin, *Symbolic Space: French Enlightenment Architecture and Its Legacy* (University of Chicago Press, Chicago, 1996)

J.L. Evans, Graham, George (*c.*1673–1751), in *Oxford Dictionary of National Biography* (Oxford University Press, Oxford, 2004), online edition, http://www.oxforddnb.com/view/article/11190

C. Evans, A. Withey, 'An enlightenment in steel? Innovation in the steel trades of eighteenth-century Britain'. *Technology and Culture* **53**, 2–29 (2012)

J. Evelyn, *The Diary of John Evelyn*, ed. by W. Bray, 2 vols. (M. Walter Dunne, New York/London, 1901)

A. Falconbridge, *Narrative of Two Voyages to the River Sierra Leone During the Years 1791-1792-1793*, ed. by C. Fyfe (Liverpool University Press, Liverpool, 2000)

P. Fara, 'A treasure of hidden vertues': The attraction of magnetic marketing'. *British Journal for the History of Science* **28**, 5–35 (1995)

P. Fara, *Sex, Botany and Empire: The Story of Carl Linnaeus and Joseph Banks* (Columbia University Press, New York, 2004)

J. Farington, *Memoirs of the Life of Sir Joshua Reynolds* (Cadell and W. Davies, London, 1819)

E. Fay, *Original Letters from India (1817)* (Harcourt, Brace & Co., New York, 1925)

J. Fennell, 'Napoleon's Tomb and its willows'. *Mirror of Literature* **28**, 362–366 (1836)

P. Findlen, *Possessing Nature: Museums, Collecting, and Scientific Culture in Early Modern Italy* (Univ. of California Press, Berkeley, 1994)

R. Finlay, *The Pilgrim Art: Cultures of Porcelain in World History* (University of California Press, Berkeley, 2010)

R. Firth, *Tikopia Songs* (Cambridge University Press, Cambridge, 1990)

H. Flachenecker, Automaten und lebende Bilder in der höfischen Kultur des Spätmittelalters, in *Automaten in Kunst und Literatur des Mittelalters und der frühen Neuzeit*, ed. by K. Grubmüller, M. Stock (Harrassowitz in Kommission, Wiesbaden, 2003), pp. 172–195

J. Flavel, *Navigation spiritualiz'd: Or, A New Compass for Seamen* (M. Fabian, London, 1698)

M. Flinders, *A Voyage to Terra Australis*, 2 vols. (Nicol, London, 1814)

E.G. Forbes, *Tobias Mayer (1723–62) Pioneer of Enlightened Science in Germany* (Vandenhoeck und Ruprecht, Göttingen, 1980)

M. Foucault, *Language, Counter-Memory, Practice*, ed. and trans. by D. Bouchard (Cornell University Press, Ithaca, 1977a)

M. Foucault, The fantasia of the library, in *Language, Counter-Memory, Practice*, ed. and trans. by D. Bouchard (Cornell University Press, Ithaca, 1977b)

M. Foucault, *Discipline and Punish* (Vintage Books, New York, 1979)

C. Fox, *The Arts of Industry in the Age of Enlightenment* (Yale University Press, New Haven/London, 2009)

W.T. Franklin (ed.), *Memoirs of the Life and Writings of Benjamin Franklin*, 3 vols. (H. Colburn, London, 1818)

T. Fulford, D. Lee, 'Mental traveler: Joseph Banks, Mungo Park, and the romantic imagination'. *Nineteenth-Century Contexts* **24**, 117–137 (2002)

M. Garthshore, 'A case of difficult deglutition ocasioned by an ulcer in the oesophagus, with an account of the appearances on dissection'. *Medical Communications* **1**, 242–255 (1784)

J. Gascoigne, *Science in the Service of Empire: Joseph Banks, the British State and the Uses of Science in the Age of Revolution* (Cambridge University Press, Cambridge, 1998)

B. Gee, A. McConnell, A.D. Morrison-Low, *Francis Watkins and the Dollond Patent Controversy* (Ashgate, Farnham, 2014)

A. Gell, The technology of enchantment and the enchantment of technology, in *Anthropology, Art and Aesthetics*, ed. by J. Coote, A. Shelton (Oxford University Press, Oxford, 1992), pp. 40–63

A. Gell, *Art and Agency: An Anthropological Theory* (Clarendon Press, Oxford, 1998)

C.-J. Geoffroy, 'Observations sur le bezoard, et sur les autres matières qui en approchent'. *Mémoires de l'Académie Royale des Sciences* 235–242 (1710)

C.-J. Geoffroy, 'Suite des observations sur les bezoards'. *Mémoires de l'Académie Royale des Sciences* 199–208 (1712)

C.-J. Geoffroy, 'Différens moyens d'enflammer, non-seulement les huiles essentielles, mais même les baumes naturels, par les esprits acides'. *Mémoires de l'Académie Royale des Sciences* 95–105 (1726)

C. Georgel, The museum as metaphor in nineteenth-century France, in *Museum Culture*, ed. by D. Sherman, I. Rogoff (University of Minnesota Press, Minneapolis, 1994), pp. 113–122

E. Gersaint, *Catalogue raisonné de coquilles, insectes, plantes marines, et autres curiosités naturelles* (Flahault and Perrault, Paris, 1736)

M. Gibbs, *Tales of Snugglepot and Cuddlepie* (Angus & Robertson, Sydney, 1918)

J.B. Gilchrist, *The General East India Guide and Vade Mecum: For the Public Functionary, Government Officer, Private Agent, Trader or Foreign Sojourner, in British India* (Kingsbury, Parbury, & Allen, London, 1825)

C. Gildon, *The Golden Spy* (J. Woodward, London, 1709)

O. Goldsmith, *The Citizen of the World, or Letters from a Chinese Philosopher to His Friends in the East*, 2 vols. (J. Newbery, London, 1762)

A. Goudar, *The Chinese Spy*, 6 vols. (Bladon, London, 1765)

R. Gough, *An Account of the Rich Illuminated Missal Executed for John Duke of Bedford* (Nichols, London, 1794)

N. Grew, *The Anatomy of Plants. With an Idea of a Philosophical History of Plants, and Several Other Lectures, Read Before the Royal Society* (W. Rawlins for the Author, London, 1682)

H. Grosser, *Historische Gegenstände an der Universitäts-Sternwarte Göttingen* (Akademie der Wissenschaften zu Göttingen, Göttingen, 1998)

X. Guan, Chinese timepieces, in *Timepieces in the Imperial Palace*, ed. by The Palace Museum (The Imperial Palace Museum: The Forbidden City Publishing House, Beijing, 2007)

J.E. Guettard, 'Mémoire sur plusieurs morceaux d'histoire naturelle, tirés du cabinet de S.A.S. M. le duc d'Orléans'. *Mémoires de l'Académie Royale des Sciences* 369–400 (1753)

J.E. Guettard, Mémoire sur les nids des oiseaux, in *Nouvelle collection de mémoires sur différentes parties intéressantes des sciences et arts*, vol. 1, 3 vols. (Lamy, Paris, 1786), pp. 324–418

B. Gundestrup, *Det Kongelige Danske kunstkammer 1737/The Royal Danish Kunstkammer 1737* (Nyt Nordisk Forlag Arnold Busck: Nationalmuseet, Copenhagen, 1991)

M. Hallett, 'The medley print in early eighteenth-century London'. *Art History* 20, 214–237 (1997)

M. Hallett, *The Spectacle of Difference: Graphic Satire in the Age of Hogarth* (Yale University Press, New Haven, 1999)

T. Hamling, *Decorating the Godly Household: Religious Art in Post-Reformation Britain* (Yale University Press, New Haven, 2010)

C. Hankamer, M. Maunders, The role of botanic gardens in conservation of Europe's overseas territories. *Botanic Gardens Conservation News* 3 (1998)

C.A. Hanson, *The English Virtuoso: Art, Medicine, and Antiquarianism in the Age of Empiricism* (University of Chicago Press, Chicago, 2009)

C.A. Hanson, Anatomy, Newtonian physiology and learned culture: The *Myotomia Reformata* and its context within Georgian scholarship, in *Anatomy and the Organization of Knowledge, 1500–1850*, ed. by M. Landers, B. Muñoz (Pickering & Chatto, London, 2012), pp. 157–170

S. Harcourt-Smith, *A Catalogue of Various Clocks, Watches, Automata: And Other Miscellaneous Objects of European Workmanship Dating from the XVIIIth and the Early XIXth Centuries, in the Palace Museum and the Wu ying tien* (Palace Museum, Beijing, 1933)

J. Harriot, *Struggles Through Life, Exemplified in the Various Travels and Adventures in Europe, Asia, Africa, & America, of Lieut. John Harriott* (Inskeep and Bradford, New York, 1809)

W. Harrison, *The Description of England* (1587), ed. by G. Edelen (Dover, New York, 1994)

M. Harrison, "The tender frame of man': Disease, climate, and racial difference in India and the West Indies, 1760–1860'. *Bulletin of the History of Medicine* 70, 68–93 (1996)

M. Harrison, *Climates and Constitutions: Health, Race, Environment and British Imperialism in India, 1600–1850* (Oxford University Press, New York, 1999)

M. Harrison, *Medicine in an Age of Commerce and Empire* (Oxford University Press, New York, 2010)

E. Hawker, *The Navy: A Letter to His Grace the Duke of Wellington, K.G., upon the Actual Crisis of the Country in Respect to the State of the Navy* (A. Spottiswoode, London, 1838)

R. Hayden, *Mrs Delany and Her Flower Collages*, 2nd edn. (British Museum, London, 1992)

J. Hein, *The Treasure Collection at Rosenborg Castle, the Inventories of 1696 and 1718, Royal Heritage and Collecting in Denmark-Norway 1500–1900* (Museum Tusculanum Press, Copenhagen, 2009)

T. Henry, *Ancient Tahiti*. Bishop Museum Bulletin 48 (University of Hawaii, Honolulu, 1928)

T. Henry, *Mythes Tahitiens*, ed. by A. Babadzan (Éditions Gallimard, Paris, 1993)

R. Higgitt (ed.), *Maskelyne: Astronomer Royal* (Robert Hale, London, 2014)

M. Hillier, *Automata and Mechanical Toys: An Illustrated History* (Jupiter, London, 1976)

T. Hobbes, *Leviathan*, ed. by R. Tuck (Cambridge University Press, Cambridge, 2004)

M. Honig, R. Cowling, D. Richardson, 'The invasive potential of Australian Banksias in South African fynbos'. *Australian Journal of Ecology* **17**, 305–312 (1992)

T. Hood, Ode to Mr Graham, the aeronaut, in *Odes and Addresses to Great People*, 2nd edn. (Printed for Baldwin, Cradock, and Joy, London, 1825), pp. 1–13

S. Hooper, Embodying divinity: The life of A'a, in *Polynesian Art: Histories and Meanings in Cultural Contexts*, ed. by S. Hooper. *Journal of the Polynesian Society* (Special issue) **116**, 131–179 (2007a)

S. Hooper (ed.), *Polynesian Art: Histories and Meanings in Cultural Contexts. Journal of the Polynesian Society* (Special issue) **116** (2007b)

P.G. Horman, B. Hudson, R.C. Rowe, *Popular Medicines: An Illustrated History* (Pharmaceutical Press, London, 2008)

R. House, *Family Cookery, Combining Elegance and Economy: With Various Receipts for Making Gravies, Soups, Sauces, and Made Dishes, Directions for Roasting and Boiling Game, Poultry, Meat, Fish, &c* (J. Bailey, London, 1810)

R. Houstoun, *Lithotomus Castratus; or, Mr Cheselden's Treatise on the High Operation for the Stone, Thoroughly Examin'd, and Plainly Found to Be Lithotomia Douglassiana* (T. Payne, London, 1723)

D. Howse, 'Britain's Board of Longitude: The finances, 1714–1828'. *The Mariner's Mirror* **84**, 400–417 (1998)

D. Howse, Sisson, Jeremiah (bap. 1720, d. 1783/4), in *Oxford Dictionary of National Biography* (Oxford University Press, Oxford, 2004), online edition, http://www.oxforddnb.com/view/article/37969

P. Hubbard, 'Trade cards in 18th-Century consumer culture: Movement, circulation and exchange in commercial and collecting spaces'. *Material Culture Review* **74–75**, 30–46 (Spring 2012)

D. Hume, *Essays and Treatises on Several Subjects*, 2nd edn., 4 vols. (Kincaid and Donaldson, Edinburgh, 1753)

D. Hume, *Treatise of Human Nature*, ed. by L.A. Selby-Bigge, P.H. Nidditch (Clarendon Press, Oxford, 1978)

J. Hunter, *Observations on the Diseases of the Army in Jamaica; and on the Best Means of Preserving the Health of Europeans in that Climate* (G. Nicol, London, 1788)

F. Hutcheson, *An Inquiry into the Original of Our Ideas of Beauty and Virtue* (W. and J. Smith, London, 1725)

W.B. Hyman, *The Automaton in English Renaissance Literature* (Ashgate, Farnham, 2011)

E. Ives, *A Voyage from England to India, in the Year MDCCLIV. And an Historical Narrative of the Operations of the Squadron and Army in India* (Edward and Charles Dilly, London, 1773)

S. Jarvis, *Scholars and Gentlemen: Shakespearean Textual Criticism and Representations of Scholarly Labour, 1725–1765* (Clarendon Press, Oxford, 1995)

M. Jasanoff, *Edge of Empire: Conquest and Collecting in the East, 1750–1850* (Fourth Estate, London, 2005)

M. Jessop [Nuku], *Unwrapping Gods: Encounters with Gods and Missionaries in Tahiti and the Austral Islands, 1797–1830* (Ph.D. thesis, Sainsbury Research Unit, University of East Anglia, 2007)

A. Johns, *Piracy: the Intellectual Property Wars from Gutenberg to Gates* (University of Chicago Press, Chicago, 2009)

J. Johnson, *The Oriental Voyager; or, Descriptive Sketches and Cursory Remarks, on a Voyage to India and China* (James Asperne, London, 1807)

J. Johnson, *The Influence of Tropical Climates on European Constitutions: Being a Treatise on the Principal Diseases Incidental to Europeans in the East and West Indies, Mediterranean, and Coast of Africa*, 3rd edn. (Dobson, Philadelphia, 1821)

C. Jones, 'The great chain of buying: Medical advertisement, the bourgeois public sphere and the origins of the french revolution'. *American Historical Review* **101**, 13–40 (1996)

L. Jordanova, 'Portraits, people and things: Richard Mead and medical identity'. *History of Science* **41**, 293–313 (2003)

E. Jørgensen, J. Skovgaard, *Danske Dronninger, Fortællinger og Karakteristikker* (H. Hagerup, Copenhagen, 1910)

A. Kaeppler, *'Artificial Curiosities': An Exposition of Native Manufactures Collected on the Three Pacific Voyages of Captain James Cook, R. N* (Bishop Museum, Honolulu, 1978)

A. Kaeppler, Containers of divinity, in *Polynesian Art: Histories and Meanings in Cultural Contexts*, ed. by S. Hooper. J. Polyn. Soc. (Special Issue) **116**, 97–130 (2007)

M. Kang, *Sublime Dreams of Living Machines: The Automaton in the European Imagination* (Harvard University Press, Cambridge, MA, 2011)

I. Kant, Conjectures on the beginning of human history, in *Kant: Political Writings*, ed. by H. Reiss (Cambridge University Press, Cambridge, 1991[1786])

B. Kennedy, Foreword, in *Les Sauvages de la Mer Pacifique* (Art Gallery of New South Wales, Sydney, 2000), p. 4

N.E. Kindersley, *Letters from the Island of Teneriffe, Brazil, the Cape of Good Hope, and the East Indies* (J. Nourse, London, 1777)

G.A. King, First Fleet Relics. *Sydney Morning Herald* (24 January 1931), 9.

M. Kirby Talley Jr., 'All good pictures crack': Sir Joshua Reynolds's practice and studio, in *Reynolds*, ed. by N. Penny (Royal Academy of Arts/Weidenfeld and Nicolson, London, 1986), pp. 55–70

J. Kirkup, Cheselden, William (1688–1752), in *Oxford Dictionary of National Biography* (OUP, Oxford, 2004), online edition, http://www.oxforddnb.com/view/article/5226

B. Kirschenblatt-Gimblett, *Destination Culture: Tourism, Museums, and Heritage* (University of California Press, Berkeley/Los Angeles, 1998)

J. Klancher, Wild bibliography: The rise and fall of book history in nineteenth century Britain, in *Bookish Histories*, ed. by I. Ferris, P. Keen (Palgrave, Basingstoke/New York, 2009), pp. 19–41

J. Klancher, *Transfiguring the Arts and Sciences: Knowledge and Cultural Institutions in the Romantic Age* (Cambridge University Press, Cambridge, 2013)

U. Klein, W. Lefèvre, *Materials in Eighteenth-Century Science* (MIT Press, Cambridge, MA, 2007)

V. Knox, *Winter Evenings; or, Lucubrations on Life and Letters*, 3 vols. (Richardson, London, 1788)

C.J. Koepp, The alphabetical order: Work in Diderot's Encyclopédie, in *Work in France: Representations, Meaning, Organization and Practice*, ed. by S.L. Kaplan, C.J. Koepp (Cornell University Press, Ithaca, 1986), pp. 229–257

L. Koerner (ed.), *Linnaeus: Nature and Nation* (Harvard University Press, Cambridge, MA, 1999)

D. Kopf, *British Orientalism and the Bengal Renaissance: The Dynamics of Indian Modernization, 1773–1835* (University of California Press, Berkeley, 1969)

A.P. Kup, 'John Clarkson and the Sierra Leone Company'. *International Journal of African Historical Studies* 5, 203–229 (1972)

M. Kwass, 'Ordering the world of goods: Consumer revolution and the classification of objects in eighteenth-century France'. *Representations* 82, 87–116 (2003)

M. Laird, A. Weisberg-Roberts (eds.), *Mrs Delany & Her Circle* (Yale Center for British Art/Sir John Soane's Museum, New Haven/London, 2009)

J. Lamb, *The Things Things Say* (Princeton University Press, Princeton, 2011)

D.S. Landes, *Revolution in Time: Clocks and the Making of the Modern World* (Belknap Press of Harvard University Press, Cambridge, MA, 1983)

M. Larkin, 'Tales and textiles from Cook's Pacific voyages'. *Bulletin of the Bibliographical Society of Australia and New Zealand* 28, 20–33 (2004)

E.C.P. Lascelles, *Granville Sharp and the Freedom of Slaves in England* (Oxford University Press, Oxford, 1928)

B. Latour, *Science in Action* (Harvard University Press, Cambridge, MA, 1987)

B. Latour, On the partial existence of existing and nonexisting objects, in *Biographies of Scientific Objects*, ed. by L. Daston (University of Chicago Press, Chicago, 2000a), pp. 247–269

B. Latour, 'When things strike back'. *British Journal of Sociology* 51, 107–123 (2000b)

J.K. Laughton, Blackwood, Sir Henry, first baronet (1770–1832), rev. Andrew Lambert, *Oxford Dictionary of National Biography* (Oxford University Press, Oxford, 2004a), online edition, www.oxforddnb.com/view/article/2548

J.K. Laughton, Ommanney, Sir John Acworth (1773–1855), rev. Andrew Lambert, *Oxford Dictionary of National Biography* (Oxford University Press, Oxford, 2004b), online edition, http://www.oxforddnb.com/view/article/20757

C. Le Guen, La Pérouse: Les graines de banksia n'ont pas parlé. *Le Telegramme* (5 July 2012)

B. Lemire, *Fashion's Favourite: The Cotton Trade and the Consumer in Britain, 1660–1800* (Oxford University Press, Oxford, 1991)

W. Lempriere, *Practical Observations on the Diseases of the Army in Jamaica, as They Occurred Between the Years 1792 and 1797* (T. N. Longman and O. Rees, London, 1799)

E. Leong, 'Making medicines in the early modern household'. *Bulletin of the History of Medicine* **82**, 145–168 (2008)

J. Lind, *An Essay on Diseases Incidental to Europeans in Hot Climates* (T. Becket and P. A. de Hondt, London, 1768)

J. Linnekin, 'Ignoble savages and other European visions'. *Journal of Pacific History* **26**, 3–26 (1991)

J. Locke, *Two Treatises of Government*, ed. by Peter Laslett (New American Library, New York, 1963)

J. Locke, *An Essay Concerning Human Understanding*, ed. by P.H. Nidditch (Clarendon Press, Oxford, 1975)

J. Lovell, *The Opium War: Drugs, Dreams and the Making of China* (Picador, London, 2011)

S. Lowengard, *The Creation of Color in Eighteenth-Century Europe* (Columbia University Press, New York, 2006)

D. Lynch, Personal effects and sentimental fictions, in *The Secret Life of Things*, ed. by M. Blackwell (Bucknell University Press, Lewisburg, 2007), pp. 265–291

D. MacDonald, *The New London Family Cook: Or, Town and Country Housekeeper's Guide* (J. Cundee, London, 1808)

N. MacGregor, *The History of the World in 100 Objects* (Penguin, London, 2012)

W. MacMichael, *The Gold-Headed Cane*, 2nd edn. (John Murray, London, 1828)

P.-J. Macquer, *Elements of the Theory and Practice of Chymistry*, 2 vols. (Nourse and Millar, London, 1758)

N. Mander, The painted cloths at Owlpen Manor, Gloucestershire, in *Setting the Scene: European Painted Cloths from the Fourteenth to the Twenty-First Century*, ed. by N. Costaras, C. Young (Archetype Publications, London, 2013), pp. 24–32

B. Mandeville, *The Fable of the Bees: or, Private Vices, Publick Benefits* (J. Roberts, London, 1714)

G. Marcel, Les navigations des Français dans la mer du sud au xviiie siècle. La Géographie: Bulletin de la Société de géographie (1900), pp. 490–492

D. Margocsy, *Commercial Visions: Science, Trade and Visual Culture in the Dutch Golden Age* (University of Chicago Press, Chicago, 2014)

G. Markham, *Hunger's Prevention or the Whole Art of Fowling* (A[ugustine] Math[ewes] for Anne Helme and Thomas Langley, London, 1621)

G. Markham, *The Whole Duty of a Woman* (J. Gwillim, London, 1696)

J.G. Marks, 'Bookbinding practices of the Hering Family, 1794–1844'. *British Library Journal* 44–60 (1980)

E. Marquard, *Kongelige Kammerregnskaber fra Frederik III.s og Christian V.s tid* (G. E. C. Gad, Copenhagen, 1918)

A. Marr, 'Understanding automata in the late Renaissance'. *Journal de la Renaissance* **2**, 205–222 (2004)

A. Marr, Gentille curiosité: Wonder-working and the culture of automata in the late renaissance, in *Curiosity and Wonder from the Renaissance to the Enlightenment*, ed. by R.J.W. Evans, A. Marr (Ashgate, Aldershot, 2006), pp. 149–170

F. Marryat, *The Naval Officer; or, Scenes and Adventures in the Life of Frank Mildmay*, 3 vols. (Henry Colburn, London, 1829)

P. Marshall, 'The whites of British India, 1780–1830: A failed colonial society?' *International History Review* **12**, 26–44 (1990)

P.J. Marshall, The great map of mankind, in *Pacific Empires: Essays in Honour of Glyndwr Williams*, ed. by A. Frost, J. Samson (University of British Columbia Press, Vancouver, 1999), pp. 237–250

A. Martin, 'Introduction: Surfing the revolution: The fatal impact of the Pacific on Europe'. *Eighteenth-Century Studies* **41**, 141–147 (2008)

K. Marx, *Capital*, trans. by S. Moore, E. Aveling, ed. by F. Engels (Lawrence and Wishart, London, 1954)

N. Maskelyne, 'A letter from the Rev. Nevil Maskelyne, M.A. F.R.S. to the Rev. Thomas Birch, D.D. Secretary to the Royal Society: Containing the results of observations of the distance of the moon from the sun and fixed stars, made in a voyage from England to the island of St. Helena'. *Philosophical Transactions* **52**, 558–577 (1761–1762)

N. Maskelyne, 'Astronomical observations made at the Island of Barbados'. *Philosophical Transactions* **54**, 389–392 (1764)

N. Maskelyne, Preface, in *The Method of Dividing Astronomical Instruments*, ed. by J. Bird (Commissioners of Longitude, London, 1767), pp. iii–iv

T. Mayer, *Tabulae Motuum Solis et Lunae* (W. & J. Richardson, London, 1770)

J. McAleer, Displaying its wares: Material culture, the East India Company and British encounters with India in the long eighteenth century, in *Global Connections: India and Europe in the Long Eighteenth Century*, ed. by G. Sánchez Espinosa, D. Roberts, S. Davies (Voltaire Foundation, Oxford, 2014), pp. 199–221

F. McClintock, *Voyage of the 'Fox' in the Arctic Seas* (John Murray, London, 1859)

A. McConnell, 'From craft workshop to big business—The London scientific instrument trade's response to increasing demand, 1750–1820'. *The London Journal* **19**, 36–53 (1994)

A. McConnell, Bird, John (1709–1776), in *Oxford Dictionary of National Biography* (Oxford University Press, Oxford, 2004), online edition, www.oxforddnb.com/view/article/2448

A. McConnell, *Jesse Ramsden (1735–1800). London's Leading Scientific Instrument Maker* (Ashgate, Aldershot, 2007)

C. McCreery, Catherine Maria Fischer, in *Oxford Dictionary of National Biography* (Oxford University Press, Oxford, 2004), online edition, www.oxforddnb.com/view/article/9489

P. McDonald, 'Ideas of the book and histories of literature: After theory?' *PMLA* **121**, 214–228 (2006)

N. McKendrick, J. Brewer, J.H. Plumb, *The Birth of a Consumer Society* (Hutchinson, London, 1983)

H. McLean, *An Enquiry into the Nature, and Causes of the Great Mortality Among the Troops at St. Domingo: With Practical Remarks on the Fever of that Island* (T. Cadell and W. Davies, London, 1797)

H. Melville, *Moby-Dick; or, The Whale*, ed. by H. Beaver (Penguin, Harmondsworth, 1978)

J.R. Millburn, *Adams of Fleet Street, Instrument Makers to King George III* (Ashgate, Aldershot, 2000)

J. Montgomery, *Journals of Voyages and Travels by Revd. Daniel Tyerman and George Bennet* (F. Westley and A. H. Davis, London, 1831)

R.O. Morris, Cust, Sir Herbert Edward Purey- (1857–1938), in *Oxford Dictionary of National Biography* (Oxford University Press, Oxford, 2004), online edition, http://www.oxforddnb.com/view/article/41230

I. Morrison, 'The cloth, the catalogue, and the collectors'. *Bulletin of the Bibliographical Society of Australia and New Zealand* **27**, 48–59 (2003)

P. Mortensen, 'Francis Hutcheson and the problem of conspicuous consumption'. *Journal of Aesthetics and Art Criticism* **53**, 155–165 (1995)

W.F.J. Mörzer Bruyns, *Sextants at Greenwich* (Oxford University Press, Oxford, 2012)

H. Mount, 'The monkey with the magnifying glass: Constructions of the connoisseur in eighteenth-century Britain'. *Oxford Art Journal* **29**, 167–183 (2006)

H.H. Mulliner, *The Decorative Arts in England, 1660–1780* (B. T. Batsford, London, 1924)

A.N.L. Munby, *Connoisseurs and Medieval Miniatures* (Oxford University Press, Oxford, 1972)

P. Mundy, *The Travels of Peter Mundy in Europe and Asia, 1608–1667*, ed. by R.C. Temple, L.M. Anstey, 5 vols. (Hakluyt Society, London, 1919)

S. Muthu, *Enlightenment Against Empire* (Princeton University Press, Princeton, 2003)

L. Namier, J. Brooke, *House of Commons 1754–1790*, 3 vols. (Secker, London, 1964)

T. Nechtman, *Nabobs: Empire and Identity in Eighteenth-Century Britain* (Cambridge University Press, New York, 2010)

J. Needham, *Clerks and Craftsmen in China and the West: Lectures and Addresses on the History of Science and Technology* (Cambridge University Press, Cambridge, 1970)

J. Needham, *Science and Civilization in China, vol. 2, History of Scientific Thought* (Cambridge University Press, Cambridge, 1986)

J. Needham, W. Ling, D.J. de Solla Price, *Heavenly Clockwork: The Great Astronomical Clocks of Medieval China* (University Press, Cambridge, 1960)

C. Newbury (ed.), *The History of the Tahitian Mission 1799–1830, Written by John Davies … with Supplementary Papers from the Correspondence of the Missionaries* (Cambridge University Press and Hakluyt Society, Cambridge, 1961)

J. Newell, Irresistible objects: Collecting in the Pacific and Australia in the reign of George III, in *Enlightenment: Discovering the World in the Eighteenth Century*, ed. by K. Sloan (British Museum Press, London, 2003), pp. 246–257

H.M. Nixon, English Bookbindings X. *Book Collector* **3** (Summer 1954)

G. Obeyesekere, Narratives of the self: Chevalier Peter Dillon's Fijian cannibal adventures, in *Body Trade: Captivity, Cannibalism and Colonialism in the Pacific*, ed. by B. Creed, J. Hoorn (Routledge, London), pp. 69–111 (2001)

S. O'Connell (ed.), *London 1753* (The British Museum Press, London, 2003)

L. Olschki, *Guillaume Boucher: A French Artist at the Court of the Khans* (The Johns Hopkins Press, Baltimore, 1946)

C. Orliac, *Fare et habitat à Tahiti* (Éditions Parenthèses, Marseille, 2000)

C. Pagani, 'Clockmaking in China under the Kangxi and Qianlong emperors'. *Arts Asiatiques* **50**, 76–84 (1995)

C. Pagani, *Eastern Magnificence and European Ingenuity: Clocks of Late Imperial China* (The University of Michigan Press, Ann Arbor, 2001)

F. Parkes, *Wanderings of a Pilgrim in Search of the Picturesque* (Oxford University Press, London, 1975)

R. Paulson, *Hogarth's Graphic Works* (Print Room, London, 1989)

W. Pearson, Circle, in *Cyclopaedia*, vol. 8, 39 vols., ed. by A. Rees (Printed for Longman, Hurst, Rees, Orme, & Brown and others, London, 1802–1819)

L. Peltz, 'Engraved portrait heads and the rise of extra-illustration: The Eton correspondence of the Reverend James Granger and Richard Bull, 1769–1774'. *Walpole Society* **66**, 1–161 (2004)

L. Peltz, Facing the text: The amateur and commercial histories of extra-illustration, c. 1770–1840, in *Owners, Annotators, and the Signs of Reading*, ed. by R. Myers, M. Harris, G. Mandelbrote (Oak Knoll Press and The British Library, New Castle/London, 2005), pp. 91–135

L. Peltz, 'A friendly gathering: The social politics of presentation books and their extra-illustration in Horace Walpole's circle'. *Journal of the History of Collections* **19**, 33–49 (2007)

J. Petiver, *Musei Petiveriani* (S. Smith & B. Walford, London, 1699)

W. Phillips, *Catalogue of the Missionary Museum* (London Missionary Society, London, 1826)

E. Phillips, *Making Time Fit: Astronomers, Artisans and the State, 1770–1820* (Ph.D. thesis, University of Cambridge, 2014)

A. Picon, Gestes Ouvriers, Opérations et Processus Techniques: La Vision du Travail des Encyclopédistes. *Recherches sur Diderot et l'Encyclopédie* **13**, 131–147 (1992)

J. Pimentel, Across nations and ages: The Creole collector and the many lives of the Megatherium, in *The Brokered World: Go-Betweens and Global Intelligence, 1770–1820*, ed. by S. Schaffer et al. (Science History Publications, Sagamore Beach, 2009), pp. 321–354

L. Plukenet, *Amaltheum Botanicum* (For the author, London, 1705)

J.G.A. Pocock, *Virtue, Commerce, and History* (Cambridge University Press, Cambridge, 1985)

J.G.A. Pocock, 'Enthusiasm: The antiself of enlightenment'. *Huntington Library Quarterly* **60**, 7–28 (1997)

J.G.A. Pocock, *Barbarism and Religion, Vol. I: The Enlightenments of Edward Gibbon* (Cambridge University Press, Cambridge, 1999)

M. Pointon, 'The lives of Kitty Fisher'. *Journal for Eighteenth-Century Studies* **27**, 77–97 (2004)

K. Pomian, *Collectors and Curiosities: Paris and Venice 1500–1800* (Polity, Cambridge, 1990)

R. Porter, 'The patient's view: Doing medical history from below'. *Theory and Society* **14**, 175–198 (1985)

R. Porter, S. Schaffer, J. Bennett, O. Brown, *Science and Profit in 18th-Century London* (Whipple Museum of the History of Science, Cambridge, 1985)

M. Postle (ed.), *Joshua Reynolds: The Creation of Celebrity* (Tate, London, 2005)

M. Postlethwayt, *The Universal Dictionary of Trade and Commerce*, 3rd edn., 2 vols. (Woodfall and Others, London, 1766)

L.W. Proger, *Descriptive Catalogue of the Pathological Series in the Hunterian Museum of the Royal College of Surgeons of England*, 2 vols. (Livingstone, Edinburgh, 1966–1972)

S. Pufendorf, *Of the Law of Nature and Nations*, 2 vols., trans. by B. Kennett (J. Walthoe and Others, London, 1729)

C. Ramsden, *London Book-Binders 1780–1840* (Batsford, London, 1956)

J. Raven, *Judging New Wealth: Popular Publishing and Responses to Commerce in England, 1750–1800* (Clarendon Press, Oxford, 1992)

W. Reddy, Structure of a cultural crisis: Thinking about cloth before and after the French revolution, in *The Social Life of Things: Commodities in Cultural Perspective*, ed. by A. Appadurai (Cambridge University Press, Cambridge, 1986), pp. 261–284

M. Rediker, *The Slave Ship: A Human History* (John Murray, London, 2008)

A.A. Renouard, *Annales de l'imprimerie des Alde, ou Histoire des trois Manuce et de leurs Éditions*, 2 vols. (Renouard, Paris, 1803)

H. Richard, *Le Voyage d'Entrecasteaux* (Comité des travaux historiques et scientifiques, Paris, 1986)

J. Richardson, *Two Discourses. I. Essay on the Whole Art of Criticism as It Relates to Painting [...]. II. An Argument in Behalf of the Science of a Connoisseur* (W. Churchill, London, 1719)

G. Riello, 'Strategies and boundaries: Subcontracting and the London trades in the long eighteenth century'. *Enterprise and Society* **9**, 243–280 (2008)

N. Rigby, The politics and pragmatics of seaborne plant transportation 1769–1805, in *Science and Exploration in the Pacific*, ed. by M. Lincoln (Boydell Press and NMM, London, 1998), pp. 81–100

J. Riskin, *Science in the Age of Sensibility: The Sentimental Empiricists of the French Enlightenment* (University of Chicago Press, Chicago, 2002)

J. Riskin (ed.), *Genesis Redux: Essays in the History and Philosophy of Artificial Life* (University of Chicago Press, Chicago, 2007)

J.-B.-L. Romé de Lisle, *Catalogue systématique et raisonné des curiosités de la nature et de l'art, qui composent le cabinet de M. Davila*, 3 vols. (Briasson, Paris, 1767)

H. Rosenau, Engravings of the *Grands Prix* of the French academy of architecture, in *Architectural History*, vol. 3 (Society of Architectural Historians of Great Britain, London, 1960), pp. 15–180

P. Rosenberg, *Fragonard* (Metropolitan Museum of Art, New York, 1987)

P. Rudd, Les Sauvages de la Mer Pacifique: Tableau pour décoration en papier peint, in *Les Sauvages de la Mer Pacifique* (Art Gallery of New South Wales, Sydney, 2000), pp. 32–40

A. Salmond, *The Trial of the Cannibal Dog. Captain Cook in the South Seas* (Penguin, London, 2003)

M.A. Sanders, 'William Cowper and his decorated copperplate initials'. *New Anatomist* **282**, 5–12 (2005)

J. Savary des Bruslons, P.-L. Savary, *Dictionnaire universel de commerce, d'histoire naturelle, et des arts et métiers*, 3 vols. (Cramer, Geneva, 1742)

S. Schaffer, Visions of empire: Afterword, in *Visions of Empire: Voyages, Botany, and Representations of Nature*, ed. by D.P. Miller, P.H. Reill (Cambridge University Press, Cambridge, 1996), pp. 335–352

S. Schaffer, Enlightened automata, in *The Sciences in Enlightened Europe*, ed. by W. Clark, J. Golinski, S. Schaffer (University of Chicago Press, Chicago, 1999), pp. 126–165

S. Schaffer, 'Instruments as cargo in the China trade'. *History of Science* **44**, 217–246 (2006)

S. Schaffer, "On seeing me write': Inscription devices in the south seas'. *Representations* **97**, 90–122 (Winter 2007)

L. Schiebinger, *Plants and Empire* (Harvard University Press, Cambridge, MA, 2007)

Scottish Missionary Society, *Letter of Instructions from the Directors of the Scottish Missionary Society to Their Missionaries Among the Heathen* (Scottish Missionary Society, Edinburgh, 1828)

A. Seaton, 'War and thanatourism: Waterloo 1815–1914'. *Annals of Tourism Research* **26**, 130–158 (1999)

G. Seddon, *The Old Country: Australian Landscapes, Plants and People* (Cambridge University Press, Port Melbourne/New York, 2005)

G. Selgin, *Good Money: Birmingham Button Makers, the Royal Mint, and the Beginnings of Modern Coinage, 1775–1821* (University of Michigan Press, Ann Arbor/Oakland, 2008)

S. Semmel, 'Reading the tangible past: British tourism, collecting, and memory after Waterloo'. *Representations* **69**, 9–37 (2000)

S. Sillars, *Painting Shakespeare: The Artist as Critic* (Cambridge University Press, Cambridge, 2006)

S. Sillars, The extra-illustrated edition, in *The Illustrated Shakespeare, 1709–1875* (Cambridge University Press, Cambridge, 2008)

S. Sillars, 'Reading illustrated editions: Methodology and the limits of interpretation'. *Shakespeare Survey* **62**, 162–181 (2009)

J. Simon, Taste, order, and aesthetics in eighteenth-century mineral collections, in *From Public to Private: Natural Collections and Museums*, ed. by M. Beretta (Science History Publications, Sagamore Beach, 2005), pp. 97–112

S. Sivasundaram, *Nature and the Godly Empire: Science and Evangelical Mission in the Pacific, 1795–1850* (Cambridge University Press, Cambridge, 2005)

K. Sloan, *A Noble Art: Amateur Artists and Drawing Masters c. 1600–1800* (British Museum, London, 2000)

H. Sloane, 'A letter from Sir Hans Sloane ... containing accounts of the pretended serpent-stone ... and the Rhinoceros Bezoar, together with the figure of a Rhinoceros with a double horn'. *Philosophical Transactions* **46**, 118–125 (1749–1750)

B. Smith, *European Vision and the South Pacific* (Yale University Press, New Haven, 1989), p. 104

R. Smith, 'James Cox (c. 1723–1800): A revised biography'. *Burlington Magazine* **142**, 353–361 (2000)

V. Smith, N. Thomas (eds.), *Mutiny and Aftermath: James Morrison's Account of the Mutiny on the Bounty and the Island of Tahiti* (University of Hawaii, Honolulu, 2013)

R. Sorrenson, 'George Graham, visible technician'. *British Journal for the History of Science* **32**, 203–221 (1999)

R. Southey, *Letters from England*, 2nd edn., 2 vols. (Longworth, New York, 1808)

E.C. Spary, 'Scientific symmetries'. *History of Science* **42**, 1–46 (2004)

E.C. Spary, Pierre Pomet's Parisian cabinet: Revisiting the invisible and the visible in early modern collections, in *From Public to Private: Natural Collections and Museums*, ed. by M. Beretta (Science History Publications, Sagamore Beach, 2005), pp. 59–80

F.D. Stanhope, *Genuine Memoirs of Asiaticus, in a Series of Letters to a Friend, During Five Years' Residence in Different Parts of India* (G. Kearsley, London, 1784)

W. Staughton, *The Baptist Mission in India: Containing a Narrative of Its Rise, Progress, and Present Condition, a Statement of the Physical and Moral Character of the Hindoos, Their Cruelties, Tortures and Burnings, with a Very Interesting Description of Bengal, Intended to Animate to Missionary Co-operation* (Hellings and Aitken, Philadelphia, 1811)

G. Steevens, *The Plays of William Shakspeare. With the Corrections and Illustrations of Various Commentators. To Which Are Added, Notes by Samuel Johnson and George Steevens. The Fourth Edition; Revised and Augmented (with a Glossarial Index) by the Editor of Dodsley's Collection of Old Plays*, 15 vols. (Longman, London, 1793)

S. Stewart, *On Longing: Narratives of the Miniature, the Gigantic, the Souvenir, the Collection* (Duke University Press, Durham, 1993)

J. Stolnitz, 'On the origins of 'aesthetic disinterestedness''. *Journal of Aesthetics and Art Criticism* **20**, 131–143 (1961)

J. Strutt, *The Regal and Ecclesiastical Antiquities of England: Containing ... Representations of All the English Monarchs from Edward the Confessor to Henry the Eighth. Together with Many of the Great Persons Eminent Under Their Reigns* (Shropshire, London, 1773)

D. Sturdy, *Science and Social Status: The Members of the Académie des Sciences, 1666–1750* (Boydell Press, Woodbridge, 1995)

J. Styles, 'Product innovation in early modern London'. *Past Present* **168**, 124–169 (2000)

P. Symes, *The Colonial Paper Money of Sierra Leone*, online at http://www.pjsymes.com.au/articles/SierraLeone.htm

J. Swift, *Travels into Several Remote Parts of the World by Lemuel Gulliver*, 2 vols. (Benjamin Motte, London, 1726)

L. Taub, 'On scientific instruments'. *Studies in History and Philosophy of Science* **40**, 337–343 (2009)

B. Taylor, A day at St Helena, in *The Atlantic Souvenir for 1859* (Derby and Jackson, New York, 1859), pp. 75–85

S. Tcherkézoff, L'humain et le divin: quand les Polynésiens ont découvert les explorateurs européens au XVIIIe siècle. *Éthnologies Comparées* **5** (Autumn 2002), online at http://alor.univ-montp3.fr/cerce/r5/s.t.htm

M. Terrall, 'Heroic narratives of quest and discovery'. *Configurations* **6**, 223–242 (1998)

M. Terrall, Natural philosophy for fashionable readers, in *Books and the Sciences in History*, ed. by M. Frasca-Spada, N. Jardine (Cambridge University Press, Cambridge, 2000), pp. 239–254

M. Terrall, *Catching Nature in the Act: Réaumur and the Practice of Natural History in the Eighteenth Century* (University of Chicago Press, Chicago, 2014)

M. Terrall, Masculine knowledge, the public good, and the scientific household of Réaumur. *Osiris* **30**, 182–201 (2015)

N. Thomas, *Entangled Objects: Exchange, Material Culture and Colonialism in the Pacific* (Harvard University Press, Cambridge, MA, 1991)

N. Thomas, *Islanders: The Pacific in the Age of Empire* (Yale University Press, New Haven, 2010)

N. Thomas, *In Oceania* (Thames and Hudson, London, 2012)

B. Tomlinson, 'The explorers of the north-west passage: Claims and commemoration'. *Church Monuments* **22**, 111–132 (2007)

T. Trautmann, *Aryans and British India* (University of California Press, Berkeley, 1997)

R. Travers, 'Death and the nabob: Imperialism and commemoration in eighteenth-century India'. *Past Present* **196**, 83–124 (2007)

T. Trotter, *Medicina Nautica* (Longman, Hurst, Rees, and Orme, London, 1804)

G.L.'.E. Turner, 'Decorative tooling on 17th and 18th century microscopes and telescopes'. *Physis* **8**, 99–128 (1966)

G.L.'.E. Turner, 'The London trade in scientific instrument-making in the eighteenth century'. *Vistas in Astronomy* **20**, 1–21 (1976)

G. Vertue, *The Heads of the Kings of England, Proper for Mr Rapin's History* (Knapton, London, 1736)

G. Vertue, *Note Books*, ed. by K.A. Esdaile, H.M. Hake, G.S.H. Fox-Strangeways, 6 vols. (Walpole Society, Oxford, 1930–1955)

D. Vice, *Coinage of British West Africa and St Helena, 1684–1958* (P. Ireland, Birmingham, 1983)

A. Voskuhl, *Androids in the Enlightenment: Mechanics, Artisans, and Cultures of the Self* (University of Chicago Press, Chicago, 2013)

H. Walpole, *Correspondence*, ed. by W.S. Lewis, 48 vols. (Yale University Press, New Haven, 1937–1983)

M. Walsh, *Shakespeare, Milton and Eighteenth-Century Literary Editing: The Beginnings of Interpretative Scholarship* (Cambridge University Press, Cambridge, 1997)

W. Ward, *View of the History, Literature, and Mythology of the Hindoos: Including a Minute Description of Their Manners and Customs, and Translations from Their Principal Works* (Kennikat Press, Port Washington, 1970)

D. Warner, 'What is a scientific instrument, when did it become one, and why?' *British Journal for the History of Science* **23**, 83–93 (1990)

V. Webb, Voyages, in *Les Sauvages de la Mer Pacifique* (Art Gallery of New South Wales, Sydney, 2000), pp. 7–14

L. Whaley, *Women and the Practice of Medical Care in Early Modern Europe, 1400–1800* (Palgrave, London, 2011)

J.G. Wille, *Mémoires et journal de J. -G. Wille*, ed. by G. Duplessis (Veuve Jules Renouard, Paris, 1857)

H. Willemsen, *Norske reise anno 1733: beskrivelse af kong Christian 6. og dronning Sophie Magdalenes rejse til Norge 12. maj-23. september: faksimileudgave af håndskrift i Hendes Majestæt Dronningens håndbibliotek*, ed. by K. Herning, K. Kjølsen (Hendes Majestæt Dronningens håndbibliotek, Copenhagen, 1992)

J. Williams, *A Narrative of Missionary Enterprises in the South Seas; with Remarks upon the Natural History of the Islands Origin, Languages, Traditions, and Usages of the Inhabitants* (J. Snow, London, 1841)

R. Williams, *Keywords* (Flamingo, London, 1983)

T. Williamson, *East India Vade-Mecum; or Complete Guide to Gentlemen Intended for the Civil, Military, or Naval Service of the Hon. East India Company* (Black, Parry, and Kingsbury for the Honorable East India Company, London, 1810)

J. Wilson, *A Missionary Voyage to the Southern Pacific Ocean in the Years 1796,1797 and 1798, in the Ship 'Duff', Commanded by Captain James Wilson* (T. Chapman, London, 1799)

A. Winter, *Mesmerized: Powers of Mind in Victorian Britain* (University of Chicago, Chicago, 2000)

A.S. Wood, *Thomas Haweis 1734–1820* (SPCK Church Historical Society, London, 1957)

O. Worm, *Museum Wormianum, seu, Historia rerum rariorum: tam naturalium, quam artificialium, tam domesticarum, quam exoticarum, quae Hafniae Danorum in aedibus authoris servantur* (John Elsevir, Leiden, 1655)

B. Wright, *Painting and History During the French Restoration: Abandoned by the Past* (Cambridge University Press, Cambridge/New York, 1996)

H. Young (ed.), *The Genius of Wedgwood* (Victoria and Albert Museum, London, 1995)

Y. Zheng, *China on the Sea: How the Maritime World Shaped Modern China* (Brill, Leiden/Boston, 2012)

INDEX

© The Author(s) 2016
A. Craciun, S. Schaffer (eds.), *The Material Cultures of Enlightenment
Arts and Sciences*, Palgrave Studies in the Enlightenment, Romanticism
and the Cultures of Print, DOI 10.1057/978-1-137-44379-3